Folklore, Culture, and Aging

Folklore, Culture, and Aging

A Research Guide

DAVID P. SHULDINER

Bibliographies and Indexes in Gerontology, Number 34

GREENWOOD PRESS
Westport, Connecticut • London

Library of Congress Cataloging-in-Publication Data

Shuldiner, David Philip.
    Folklore, culture, and aging : a research guide / David P.
Shuldiner.
        p.   cm.—(Bibliographies and indexes in gerontology, ISSN
0743–7560 ; no. 34)
    Includes bibliographical references and indexes.
    ISBN 0–313–29897–1 (alk. paper)
    1. Aging—Folklore.   2. Aged—Folklore.   3. Aging—Research.
I. Title. II. Series.
GR452.S58   1997
016.30526—dc21   96–52497

British Library Cataloguing in Publication Data is available.

Library of Congress Catalog Card Number: 96–52497
ISBN: 0–313–29897–1
ISSN: 0743–7560

First published in 1997

Greenwood Press, 88 Post Road West, Westport, CT 06881
An imprint of Greenwood Publishing Group, Inc.

Printed in the United States of America

The paper used in this book complies with the
Permanent Paper Standard issued by the National
Information Standards Organization (Z39.48–1984).

10 9 8 7 6 5 4 3 2 1

This work is dedicated to the memory of Max Shuldiner (1918-1996), my father, mentor, and favorite elder, and to Kenneth Goldstein (1927-1995), intellectual and spiritual elder for generations of folklorists still committed to humanistic methods and outlooks.

Contents

Acknowledgements

Thanks to all of the people, too numerous to mention, who offered citations, sent me booklets and film catalogues, and otherwise encouraged the growth and development of this project; a special debt of gratitude is owed to Lynn Sweet and Robert Vrecenak, as well as Judith DeLottie and Lana Babij, interlibrary loan staff at the University of Connecticut, who labored to bring tons of material from far-flung lending institutions before my eyes; to Laurel Horton and Sarah Howard of *Uncoverings* for steering back issues of that journal my way, Mike Jones for sharing his annotated filmography; Steve Zeitlin for sending me a copy of City Lore's *Nourishing the Heart* (see **G.47**); and Marie Guman, colleague from the Connecticut aging network, for doing an eleventh-hour search for me; thanks to Nita Romer, Liz Leiba, and Jane Lerner, my editors at Greenwood, for shepherding me through the publishing process; gratefulness to my beloved life partner Anne for proofreading the manuscript and weathering the moods of book writing; finally, a warm appreciation to the members of an informal "advisory board" of respected colleagues that I recruited for their sage counsel, and who are now duly assured that I assume sole responsibility for any errors and omissions. They are:

Simon J. Bronner
American Studies
Pennsylvania State University, Harrisburg

Patrick B. Mullen
Program Center for Folklore Studies
Ohio State University

Mary Hufford
American FolklifeProgram
Library of Congress

Michael Owen Jones
Folklore & MythologyProgram
University of California, LosAngeles

Marjorie Hunt
Center for Folklife Programs and
  Cultural Studies
Smithsonian Institution

Janet Theophano
Department of Folklore
University of Pennsylvania

Royalties from the sale of this book will be donated to Elders Share the Arts (ESTA), a community organization based in Brooklyn, New York, that uses oral history and creative arts "to honor diverse traditions, connect generations and cultures and to validate the worth of lifetime experience" (from *Generating Community* [see **G.123**]).

Introduction

BACKGROUND

This book is the outcome of years of work developing community-based educational programs for older adults. My initial training was in anthropology and folklore; interested in everything from ballads to ethnic and occupational folklore, as well as the lore of social movements, I ventured, as a doctoral candidate in Folklore & Mythology at UCLA in the early 1980s, into oral history. As the child of Jewish radical activists, it was natural that I would interview elderly Jewish immigrants who participated in the ethnic left subculture known as the Jewish Labor Movement. Serendipity guided me in 1984 to a "post-doc" job in Connecticut as a "scholar-in-residence" with the State Department on Aging, funded by a grant from the Connecticut Humanities Council.

Assigned the mission of developing models and a resource inventory for on-site educational programs in senior centers, nursing homes, elder housing projects and the like, I collected cultural and historical materials, and recorded personal narratives, which were woven into a variety of educational projects, a number of them reflecting the content, methods and outlook of the folklorist (see **G.56**).

Having come into the field of aging through the "back door," I eventually made my way to the front by earning a certificate in Gerontology from the School of Family Studies at the University of Connecticut. Over a decade later, I continue, under the aegis of the Department of Social Services (into which the Department on Aging merged a few years back) to offer community-based educational programs for elders, and take on occasional college/university teaching assignments in gerontology and folklore.

PURPOSE

All of this is by way of at least partially explaining the purpose and scope of the present work. Reflecting both scholarly and community-action approaches, it is designed to serve those engaged in researching or preparing to teach about folklore, culture, and aging, and is also addressed to the specialist and nonspecialist alike working with the elderly who seek information on the value of folklore in providing culturally sensitive care, services and advocacy. In order to meet these different but often related needs, this work is organized, though not consistently, by ethnicity, region, gender and folklore genre, as well as by social practice, with a chapter on applied folklore listing citations that specifically address the application of folklore methods, concepts and materials to social interventions of various kinds, from health care to education.

SCOPE

This book is a guide to methods and resources for researching folklore of and about aging and the aged in its broadest sense, encompassing the exploration of beliefs and customs related to elders and the aging process, as well as the expressive behavior of older adults engaged in creative activities within and around the boundaries of traditions and cultures. Most of these citations are scholarly works, but many of them are included not so much for the factual material they present but for other insights they may consciously or inadvertently reveal about cultural attitudes or perspectives of the authors related to folklore, culture and aging.

Some of these entries "push the envelope"–in fact just enough of the entries stray into broader popular culture areas to cause some potential discomfort for those plagued by issues of definition and scope (boundaries), hence the insertion of the appellation "culture" between "folklore" and "aging." This is one way of indicating that the present work does not restrict itself to textbook examples of expressive behavior and aging. Rather, it paints from a broader palette in order to enable the reader not only to discover scholarly analyses of folklore and aging, but also to see the ways in which aging and the aged are presented and represented within the kinds of cultural contexts that folklorists have worked, driven by motivations that may include the literary, journalistic, or other practical concerns (such as health care delivery or other culturally sensitive social interventions). All of these concerns have, of course, also inspired folkloristic endeavors. Hopefully, readers, rather than being disconcerted, will take advantage of the possibilities for further exploration posed by the interdisciplinary, expansive (and occasionally whimsical) nature of the materials cited in this work.

Having addressed the broad scope of these listings, I must now address their limitations. First, I have concentrated on those readings and films published or released from the 1970s to the present, with a fair–but less comprehensive–sample from the 1960s, and a few items (very few) predating this period. Second, in order to expose the user of this volume to as broad a range of materials as desirable, I have ended up with a listing that is a good representative sample of what is available, without, however, being by any means an exhaustive catalogue of all material on the subject (particularly as broadly defined). Therefore, while including many examples, this work does not cite all known published personal narratives of older adults in which references to traditional beliefs, customs or expressive behavior are made; it does not include references to all stories told by or about the aging; it does not list all works dealing with life review, reminiscence, oral history and the like; it does not cite all works describing the role of folk beliefs, traditional health care practices, or the use of folk songs, dances and other traditional expressive forms in social programs for the elderly.

Other limitations imposed are those of language and geographical scope. This work is restricted to English-language works, which is reflected in the proportions of entries for the regions and peoples cited. The most comprehensive listings are for materials related to the peoples and cultures of North America, with some references to other English-speaking countries, and a sample of published works on elders of other world cultures. Based on the availability of published works, some groups of elders may be more heavily repre-sented than others; for example, by far the largest listing in Chapter D ("Narratives") is that for Native American Indians, owing at least in part to the great popularity of personal narratives of Native Americans and the efforts of many Native peoples to publish oral accounts of their elders.

While these materials represent a variety of published sources, there are others that may be, for some, conspicuous by their absence. While articles from many folklore journals are cited, there are few citations from the dozens of newsletters and magazines published by folklore societies, universities, ethnic organizations and other public and private institutions and special-interest groups that may include references to older adults. To include citations from all of them would have made the preparation of this work an endless task. However, Chapter A ("Research Methods") lists resource guides that will help to locate other periodicals and features a selected list of them (see also **B.14-B.18**).

What I have endeavored to do, in the time and space allotted for the preparation of this work, is to present as broad a listing as possible of English language works (some of them bilingual) exploring the full range of concepts, materials and approaches related to expressive behavior of and about elders. Hopefully, this will serve as a point of departure for those investigating the lore of aging and the aged.

THE AGE OF LORE

Folklorists, anthropologists and other fieldworkers have long recognized the aging as sources of cultural knowledge and wisdom and have sought them out as cultural informants. But it is another matter to consider the relevance of age to the cultural data that is tapped from the aging, or to consider the role that age and the aging play within cultural contexts. One of the uses to which this research guide might be put is to explore the ways in which the perspective of old age may or may not be reflected in the expressive behavior of elders, whether in specific rituals, or implicit in their narratives, be they personal experience, collective history or myth (the boundaries between these genres are often blurred).

What is it then, that constitutes an operating definition of aging and the aged? The works cited here cover just about every kind of response to that question. What gerontologists and folklorists have come to acknowledge (though by no means universally) is the fact that elders may have special qualities, but they are not a distinct species. We all continue to be essentially who we have been all along as we age (only more so, some would add!). We may undergo dramatic personal, political and cultural transformations, but most of us age more or less ontologically intact. We look at the present with the eyes of age, but we may also look at the past with the eyes of our age in that past.

Another way of looking at aging is to acknowledge that the aging process is something that begins at birth and continues throughout the lifespan, and that late life is simply the final stage of a journey along the path of human development. This path has often been characterized as one that begins with growth (childhood and youth) and ends with degeneration (old age). An alternate view that has gained currency posits these two aspects as a pair whose dialectical tension defines the entire experience of living. From this perspective, one might, for instance, embrace the idea that even while a person's physical functions may slow down in late life ("degeneration"), she or he may continue to accumulate knowledge, gain new insights, and engage in creative pursuits (growth).

Acknowledging the perspective of lifespan studies of aging, for present purposes, the focus of many of the readings and films cited in this research guide on folklore, culture and aging will be on the experiences of a lifetime as viewed from the vantage point of old age. This is particularly the case for many of the works cited in Chapter D, "Narratives," and a number in Chapter E, "Traditional Arts," where reference to the remembered past of elders is embodied in stories or folk art reflecting upon earlier events in their personal lives and upon collective experiences within the communities of which they have been a part.

As to the age of elders cited in this research guide, the assignation of a fixed year marking the commencement of old age is unavoidably arbitrary. The designation of "elder" is made in relation to a person's relative position in the lifecourse; at least one important factor conditioning the actual age at which such a position or status is realized is the average life expectancy for a given group of people. As an instance, in a traditional society where the average life expectancy is 50, an elder may be someone in his or her mid to late 40s, and whose status may be reflected by a position of authority usually reserved for elders, such as spiritual leader, shaman, and/or head of a household that may well include grandchildren and even great-grandchildren. All things considered, however, the elders to whom attention is drawn in the readings and films cited in this book are almost all 60 years of age and older, with a small number in their fifties. (A few citations deal with traditions related to developmental processess that presage old age, such as menopause; a book on the symbolism of age 40 as a common cultural marker of the beginning of old age is cited; and a collection of fairy tales on the theme of midlife is noted for its insights on narratives depicting the gateway to late life; but these, and a few others, are exceptions.)

THE LORE OF AGE

The common denominator of aging may be the inevitable chronological process of growing older (if not wiser), but the world experienced by an elder is a world seen through the eyes of a person whose core identity may have been formed early on, changing little, or may have transformed dramatically. Understanding the words of elders may involve ascertaining the identity and sensibilities that an older person brings to that moment or moments when his/her narrative is recorded, or when s/he commits their life story to paper. Since we are focusing for the moment on one form of expressive behavior–the life story–it will be useful to keep in mind the fact that the published narratives cited in this work may or may not refer specifically to age or aging (many, in fact, focus predominantly on earlier life experiences).

To say that the window through which the past is viewed is the window of age is not to mean that an elder's narrative is necessarily dominated by the perspective of late life. A person born in 1900 may be 90 years old in 1990, but in the act of recalling the past may also become the 20-year-old she or he was in 1920. Some elders maintain a distance between past and present, temporarily suspended in moments of remembrance. Others–perhaps those whose subsequent experiences have not met their expec-tations–become lost in memories of early life, retreating into a childhood from which they never fully separated. For many elders, though, the past is viewed through the lens of the present, refracted by the prism of old age.

The folklore of aging, therefore, is not restricted to views of old age and the elderly, nor age-specific forms of expressive behavior, but may comprise aspects of culture generated, articulated and preserved (or transformed) within the context of personal development, historical events, or other changes that have been incorporated into the experiential gestalt embodied and performed by older adults in a variety of forms of expressive behavior, only some of them overtly relating to chronological age. The citations in this research guide are not limited to considerations of aging itself, but also identify works that present the words and deeds of elders whose creativity, reflected in life stories, tales, folk art, and other forms, has no explicit age referents. In some of these latter works, those creative outputs are analyzed; in others, it is left to the reader to integrate the "age of lore" with the "lore of age."

The lore of age is, in fact, both age-bound and age-less. It may reflect the fact of chronological age ("older and wiser") or it may reflect a personal/social experience shared by members of the same generation (the "cohort effect"). What folklorists often tap in interviewing the elderly is both an individual embodiment of a remembered past and also the product of a collective memory–a shared experience of the particular historical eras through which they have lived and the cultural group(s) within which they were socialized. As such it may be the recreation of a frozen cultural moment. But the truth of the matter is probably more fuzzy (Shuldiner's model of the "ontological blur"). All of us, including those of us who are elders, live in the moment, though that moment may be occupied with images past and present. Time is simply one of the settings within which the play of life is enacted.

Folklorists and other cultural workers have become increasingly aware of just how integral a role they play in setting the stage upon which the elders with whom they interact present themselves. If it has become cliché to suggest that the cultural past experienced by many elders is a "vanished world," it is certainly the case that the cultural contexts within which elders have had well-defined roles have changed dramatically, often leaving elders isolated from families and communities within whose embrace they might be valued as sages, teachers and healers. Many a folklorist has become, through the artifice of field recording, a surrogate member of a community from which an elder may have become socially, temporally, or geographically removed, enabling him–at least momentarily–to have an audience for the performance of expressive behavior. This may constitute an enactment, albeit within an artificial context, of cultural roles they might have assumed in communities with which they are no longer in touch (or which are no longer intact). Or it might be the case that the particular individual with whom a fieldworker makes contact may be enabled to perform a role she has never played before, for whatever reasons: perhaps she was shy, and always being upstaged by more gregarious community members; or she may have been a social misfit, whose only audience ever would have been an "outsider" (the anthropologist's perennial dilemma: is this the narrative of a fantastic informant, or the fanciful story of "the odd person out"?).

This is all by way of saying that the aging, and the lore embodied in their remembered past, are as varied and variable as for community members of any age. What is important, as in all matters cultural, is the setting within which the lore of age, the lore of aging, and the lore of the aged are presented. Whether conducting research in print, film or "in the field" it is important, when coming across lore about elders, or witnessing elders creating and recreating the cultural present or past, to consider the context in which it is generated–be it the physical space (home, church, community center, factory or farm), social setting (family members in the kitchen swapping stories; women [and occasionally men] at a quilting bee; elders at a senior center; an interviewer and interviewee interacting) or historical events (the Depression, WW II, other events global and local). This is just another way of saying that in viewing the works cited below, keep in mind the larger stage, sometimes revealed, often hidden, upon which each aspect of expressive behavior and material culture (narrative, song, dance, craft, belief, custom, etc.) is presented in tales, oral histories, straight descriptions, analyses and fanciful speculations, from those who have studied elders, and from the words and deeds of elders themselves.

A

Research Tools

The listings here may be said to provide a framework for inquiry and point to sources beyond the scope of the bibliography/filmography to follow. Below are lists of directories for research in traditional cultures, selected periodicals whose contents, for the most part, are not cited in the present work, but might have useful material on traditional elders, and suggested readings on the conduct of fieldwork in general, and oral history in particular.

FOLKLORE/FOLKLIFE REFERENCE WORKS

A.1. *Folklife Sourcebook: A Directory of Folklife Resources in the United States.* 2nd ed. Prepared by Peter T. Bartis and Hillary Glatt. Washington, D.C.: Library of Congress, 1994.

> This is one of the best "one-stop" sources of information for folklore research in general. It includes listings of federal agencies that support the conservation and study of traditional culture; public agencies and organizations in the U. S. (and some in Canada and Mexico) that engage in folklife programming; archives of special collections of folklore, folklife and ethnomusicology; higher education programs in folklife and folklore; state, local and regional societies that support folklife studies, cultural conservation and the like; a list of serial publications, including newsletters, journals and magazines; publishers of books and monographs on folklore, ethnomusicology and folk music; and a list of directories of general and specific resources in the field of folklore/folklife.

Among the many directories cited in the *Folklife Sourcebook* are:

Directory of Historical Societies and Agencies in the United States

Directory of Oral History Collections

Encyclopedic Directory of Ethnic Newspapers and Periodicals in the United States

Ethnic Information Sources of the United States

Guide to Ethnic Museums, Libraries and Archives in the United States

The *Folklife Sourcebook* is available directly from the American Folklife Center, Library of Congress, Washington, D.C .20540-8100.

[Note: While the *Folklife Sourcebook* lists organizations that engage in public folklore programs, the *Public Programs Newsletter,* issued by the Public Sector Section of the American Folklore Society (AFS), features an updated directory, as well as news of ongoing projects, exhibits, publications, and the like–many of them featuring elders–as reported by these organizations. It is distributed to AFS members who belong to the Section, but you may contact the AFS office (4350 N. Fairfax, Arlington, VA 22203 703/528-1902) to inquire about individual copies of the newsletter.]

A.2. *Pickaxe and Pencil: References for the Study of the WPA.* Compiled by Marguerite D. Bloxom. Washington, D.C.: Library of Congress, 1982.

Among the many activities of the monumental Works Progress Administration of the late 1930s and early 1940s in the United States was the Federal Writers Project. WPA writers in every state collected local folklore, anecdotes and tales, recorded life histories of longtime residents, took surveys of ethnic and occupational groups, and interviewed former slaves. Much of the material has been published, but much still sits in archives of state libraries, museums and other institutions. *Pickaxe and Pencil* lists published and archival sources for these materials, among which are many personal narratives and other lore of elders (some collections of WPA narratives are listed in chapter E: "Narratives").

A.3. Bataille, Gretchen M., Miguel Carranza and Laurie Lisa. *Ethnic Studies in the United States: A Guide to Research.* New York: Garland, 1996.

The authors provide descriptions of over 800 ethnic studies programs or departments in U. S. colleges and universities, including African-American, Asian-American, Chicano/Latino, Native American, Puerto Rican, Portuguese, Jewish and others; features includes a bibliography of additional resources and a listing of journals with an ethnic-studies focus.

A.4. Brunvand, Jan Harold, ed. *American Folklore: An Encyclopedia.* New York: Garland, 1996.

This is a comprehesive general reference work on subjects related to North American folklore," including Canadian, but excluding, except for a few general topics, the folklore of Native American Indians, which will be covered in its own encyclopedia" [the *Encyclopedia of Native American Folklore,* edited by Andrew Wiget, is scheduled for publication by Garland sometime in 1997]; there is an entry by Mary Hufford on "Folklore and Aging" (see **B.75.**), and references to elders and aging appear in other entries.

A.5. Buttlar, Lois J., and Lubomyr R. Wynar, comp. *Guide to Information Resources in Ethnic Museum, Library and Archival Collections in the United States.* Westport, Connecticut: Greenwood, 1996.

This guide cites 786 cultural institutions–representing over 70 ethnic groups–that have resources available for teaching, providing information to ethnic communities, and conducting research, and describes not only the collections they house, but also the sponsoring organizations' publications and other special services they may offer.

A.5.a. Dorson, Richard M., and Inta Gale Carpenter, eds., *Handbook of American Folklore*. Bloomington: Indiana University Press, 1983.

Featuring the work of 60 scholars and practitioners, this work presents a broad array of approaches to the study of folklore, and is divided into sections on topics, interpretation, methods and presentation of research.

A.6. Klein, Barry T., ed. *Reference Encyclopedia of the American Indian*. 7th ed. Nyack, New York: Todd Publications, 1995.

This comprehensive guide lists thousands of Native American associations, organizations, centers, reservations, tribal councils, museums, monuments, libraries, books, magazines, newsletters, films and video-cassettes and a "who's who" featuring short biographies of notable Native Americans and non-natives active in Indian affairs. Among the books and films listed are numerous portraits of elders, many–but by no means all–of which are cited in the book you have in hand, and many of the newsletters and magazines listed regularly feature Native elders.

A.7. Steinhurst, Susan. *Folklore and Folklife: A Guide to English-Language Reference Sources*. New York: Garland, 1992.

This two-volume work, aimed at nonspecialists, is an annotated bibiliography of references works available in American university library collections, indicating the range of folklore scholarship over the past 100 years, and arranged (following the Modern Language Association's annual bibliography of folklore publications) in sections on: Introduction to folklore and folklife; History and study of folklore; Folk literature, Ethnomusicology, Folk belief systems; Folk rituals; and Material culture.

A.8. Wilson, Charles Reagan, William Ferris, Ann J. Abadie and Mary L. Hart, eds. *Encyclopedia of Southern Culture*. Chapel Hill: University of North Carolina Press, 1989.

Among the many sections into which this comprehensive volume is divided are "Black Life," "Ethnic Life," "Folklife," "History and Manners," "Music," "Mythic South," "Recreation" and "Women's Life," each with entries that may contain useful information and references on traditional culture and elders. [Note: inspired by its southern cousin, the *Encyclopedia of New England Culture*, edited by Burt Feintuch and David Watters, is scheduled for publication by Yale University Press in 1997.]

PERIODICALS WITH OCCASIONAL REFERENCES TO FOLKLORE & AGING

There are dozens of journals and newsletters whose contents, for the most part, are not cited in *Folklore, Culture, and Aging* but that feature, with varying frequency, short (auto)biographies, sketches, or other bits of news and information about traditional elders. To list all of these items would be beyond the scope of this work. However, the following is a sample of the kinds of periodicals, ranging from scholarly to popular, that may offer occasional articles and other feature presentations on traditional elders. These include the periodicals of specific ethnic groups or regions, magazines devoted to various traditional arts, and the newsletters of local, state, regional and federal folklife programs, community organizations, folklore societies (some that also publish scholarly journals) or academic folklore departments (for more comprehensive lists, see the reference works cited above).

AAGE Newsletter [Association for Anthropology and Gerontology]
Department of Anthropology
The Ohio State University
Columbus, OH 43210-1364

Akwesasne Notes: A Journal of Native and Natural Peoples
Mohawk Nation Territory
P.O. Box 196
Rooseveltown, NY 13683

Cape Breton's Magazine (see **D.104.**)
Ronald Caplan, Editor
Wreck Cove, Cape Breton
Nova Scotia B0C 1H0

City Lore
72 East 1st Street
New York, NY 10003

Common Ground: A Journal Where Grassroots Women Speak From the Heart
P. O. Box 64717
Baton Rouge, LA 70896

Crone Chronicles: A Journal of Conscious Aging.
P.O. Box 81
Kelly, WY 83011

Ethnic Folk Arts Center Newsletter
Ethnic Folk Arts Center
131 Varick Street, Room 907
New York, NY 10013

Folk Art (formerly *The Clarion*)
Museum of American Folk Art
61 West 62nd Street
New York, NY 10023-7015

Folklife Center News
American Folklife Center
Library of Congress
Washington, D.C. 20540-8100

Foxfire News (see **B.2-B.13.**)
Rabun Gap, GA 30568

Journal of Alaska Native Arts
Institute of Alaska Native Arts
P.O. Box 80583
Fairbanks, AK 99708

Living Blues
Center for the Study of Southern Culture
The University of Mississippi
University, MS 38677

Michigan Folklife News
Michigan Traditional Arts Program
Michigan State University Museum
East Lansing, MI 48824-1045

The Milkweed; The New England Folklife Center Newsletter [formerly *Folklines*]
New England Folklife Center
400 Foot of John Street
Lowell, MA 01852

Mississippi Folklife (formerly *Mississippi Folklore Register*)
Center for the Study of Southern Culture
University of Mississippi
University, MS 38677

New York Folklore Newsletter
New York Folklore Society
P.O. Box 130
Newfield, NY 14867

News from Native California
P. O. Box 9145
Berkeley, CA 94709

Nations: The Native American Magazine
P.O. Box 30510
Seattle, WA 98103

Parabola: The Magazine of Myth and Tradition (see **B.17.**)
P.O. Box 3000
Denville, NJ 07834

Precious Memories
Route 1, Box 1876
Young Harris, GA 30582

Salt (see **B.13.a, B.13.b.**)
P.O. Box 4077
Portland, ME 04101

Shaman's Drum: A Journal of Experiential Shamanism
Cross-Cultural Shamanism Network
290 North Main Street
Ashland, OR 97520

Sing Out!: The Folk Song Magazine
P.O. Box 5253
Bethlehem, PA 18015-0235

Smithsonian Talk Story
Center for Folklife Programs and Cultural Studies
955 L'Enfant Plaza, SW, Suite 2600
Washington, D.C. 20560

Southern Exposure (see **B.18.**)
P.O. Box 531
Durham, NC 27702

Visit'n: Conversations with Vermonters
Vermont Folklife Center
Painter House, Box 422
Middlebury, VT 05753

Works in Progress
Philadelphia Folklore Project
719 Catherine Street
Philadelphia, PA 19147

CONDUCTING FIELDWORK

This book does not offer a guide to conducting fieldwork; however, the following works are useful references for the study of concepts, methods and materials in folklore field research. While there are a few guides specifically focused upon field research with the elderly, the techniques outlined in the works below are based on the authors' experience conducting research with subjects of all ages, but elders in particular, since among the first community members sought in field studies are those with the most extensive knowledge and experience, based on longstanding participation in community life. (Several works devoted specifically to interview techniques with the eldery are listed in the section on "Oral History" below).

A.9. Bartis, Peter. *Folklife and Fieldwork: A Layman's Introduction to Field Techniques.* Washington, D. C.: American Folklife Center, Library of Congress, 1979.

This is a short, basic guide, providing a broad overview of such subjects as how to choose informants, ideas for collecting lore, how to interview and what to do with field data.

A.10. Bauman, Richard, ed. *Folklore, Cultural Performances and Popular Entertainments: A Communications-Centered Handbook.* New York: Oxford University Press, 1992.

Drawn from Oxford's *International Encyclopedia of Communications*, this is a collection of short articles on concepts, genres and forms of performance in traditional and popular culture; while not a fieldwork guide, it is a good summary for the nonspecialist (as well as a useful review for the folklorist) of the basic terms and ideas used by those researching and studying expressive behavior and material culture.

A.11. Georges, Robert A., and Michael O. Jones. *People Studying People: The Human Element in Fieldwork.* Berkeley: University of California Press, 1980.

This book provides insights on fieldwork by way of selected accounts of fieldworkers' experiences, with an underlying plea for keeping in mind the human element, not only when conducting field research, but also when analyzing and presenting the collected data.

A.12. Goldstein, Kenneth S. *A Guide for Fieldworkers in Folklore.* Hatboro, Pennsylvania: Folklore Associates, 1964.

A pioneering work, this book offers practical advice on preparing for fieldwork, establishing rapport with interview subjects, conducting an interview, and developing methods of observation; Goldstein introduced the idea of creating a "natural context" for field interviews.

A.13. Jackson, Bruce. *Fieldwork.* Urbana: University of Illinois Press, 1987.

Jackson's book deals with the practical (planning and conducting fieldwork, including interviewing), mechanical (basic technical advice on audio and film recording), ethical and theoretical aspects of collecting data, illustrated with anecdotes from his field experiences and those of others.

A.14. Schoemaker, George. *The Emergence of Folklore in Everyday Life: A Fieldguide and Sourcebook.* Bloomington, Indiana: Trickster Press, 1990.

Designed for beginning students of folklore, it is a good work for nonspecialists, introducing them to the "lingua franca" of folklore, with chapters sampling the varieties of forms of expressive behavior and material culture, and ways to document and analyze them.

A.15. Wax, R. H. "Gender and Age in Fieldwork and Fieldwork Education: No Good Thing Is Done by Any Man Alone." *Social Problems* 26:5 (1979), 509-523.

Wax addresses the effects of age and gender on the way field research is conducted, citing as an example the experiences of a young couple doing fieldwork among the Sioux, noting taboos against men socializing with females, restricting them to research among men, and the difficulty young women may experience establishing relationships with female age-mates; asserting that female elders are feared and respected among the Sioux, the author opines that older women may have an advantage in fieldwork under these conditions.

A.16. Yocum, Margaret Rose. "Fieldwork in Family Folklore and Oral History: A Study in Methodology." Doctoral dissertation, University of Massachusetts, 1980.

"This study proposes a methodology for fieldworkers, especially those in folklore and oral history, who want to research the cultural and historical traditions of their own families"; it is based on observation, interviews and photographs of members of the author's Pennsylvania German family from 1975 to 1979, as well as a review of the literature on folklore, oral history and family research, and correspondence and interviews with others conducting personal-family research.

ORAL HISTORY/LIFE STORIES

The books on fieldwork listed above generally include guides to interviewing; however, the works in this section are focused primarily on theorectical and practical issues in the recording and presentation of life stories, some of which address aging in particular. Chapter B ("General Works") has sections on "Life Review/Life Course Studies" and "Oral History," listing case-studies and cross-cultural anthologies; another good place to look for works on recording life stories among the aging and across generations is Chapter G ("Applied Folklore")–some of the works listed there describing community projects also offer practical advice on life history recording techniques (see, for example, **G.47** and **G.123**). And, of course, Chapter D ("Narratives") contains an extensive listing of life stories, most of which are based on oral history interviews, and many of which contain analytical sections.

Bibliographies/Anthologies

A.17. Dunaway, David K., and Willa K. Baum, eds. *Oral History: An Interdisciplinary Anthology.* Nashville, Tennessee: American Association for State and Local History, 1984.

This collection of 37 articles includes contributions by many of the "movers and shapers" of the field of oral history, and represents such subjects and disciplines as folklore, anthropology, gerontology, and local, family, ethnic and women's history, as well as oral history in the classroom.

A.18. Havlice, Patricia Pate. *Oral History: A Reference Guide and Annotated Bibliography.* Jefferson, North Carolina: McFarland and Co., 1985.

> This book lists over 770 books, journal articles and dissertations which have appeared in print from the 1950s to late 1983; among the subject headings into which this book is organized are cultural journalism, genealogy, classroom, and development (the history of the field since World War II); citations are limited largely to the United States.

A.19. Perks, Robert. *Oral History: An Annotated Bibliography.* London: British Library National Sound Archive, 1990.

> This is a listing of over 2100 published works and sound recordings based on or using oral history, with coverage of related topics, covering history, sociology, social work, gerontology and anthropology; it is comprehensive for Great Britain, with strong representation from North America and Australasia, and selective entries for the rest of the world; of particular interest is his inclusion of dozens of citations of booklets of oral histories of elders produced by local aging agencies, community groups, homes for the elderly, and the like, throughout the United Kingdom.

(Re)Presenting Lives: How-To

A.20. Birren, James E., and Donna E. Deutchman. *Guiding Autobiography Groups for Older Adults: Exploring the Fabric of Life.* Baltimore: Johns Hopkins University Press, 1991.

> While this book was designed primarily to provide theoretical and practical guidelines for professionals who conduct activity programs for older people, with an emphasis on written autobiographies, chapters on leading group discussions, organizing life stories around themes, and methods of stimulating recall offer useful ideas that may be applied to research projects among the aging.

A.21. Dixon, Janice T., and Dora D. Flack. *Preserving Your Past: A Painless Guide to Writing Your Autobiography and Family History.* Garden City, New York: Doubleday, 1977.

> While aimed at a popular audience, this is a comprehensive approach to writing one's own life story, within the context of family history and culture, including methods of archival research, techniques of interviewing relatives and the particular value of collecting family tales and anecdotes.

A.22. Fletcher, William P. *Recording Your Family History: A Guide to Preserving Oral History With Videotape, Audiotape, Suggested Topics and Questions, Interview Techniques.* Berkeley, California: Ten Speed Press, 1989. [Previously published as *Talking Your Roots* (Washington, D.C.: Belmont Estates Press, 1983)]

> This guide to recording life stories of elders focuses on three general areas: individual and family life cycle, the personal experience of historical events, and personal values; included in the section of suggested topics and questions are special sets for Jewish, African-American and Hispanic interview subjects.

A.23. Humphries, Stephen. *The Handbook of Oral History: Recording Life Stories.* London: Inter-Action Imprint, 1984.

> This publication offers practical advice on oral history projects, with chapters on family history, schools, and the role of oral history in literacy programs and work

among unemployed youth; the implied interview subjects are primarily elders (the back cover boldly states that "oral history is compiled from the living memories of older people"); a chapter on "Old People" offers advice on "self-directed groups," as well as "reminiscence socials" to generate interest in oral history among elders.

A.24. Hunt, Marjorie, with Mary Hufford and Steven Zeitlin. *The Grand Generation: Interviewing Guide and Questionnaire.* Washington, D. C.: Smithsonian Institution Traveling Exhibition Service (SITES), 1987.

This guide accompanied the SITES exhibition *The Grand Generation: Memory, Mastery, Legacy.*, featuring the traditional arts of elders (see **E.1**); categories of suggested questions include origins, family folklore, social history and local history.

A.25. Ives, Edward D. *The Tape-Recorded Interview: A Manual for Fieldworkers in Folklore and Oral History.* 2nd. ed. Knoxville: University of Tennessee Press, 1995 [1974].

While taking the reader through the steps of the field collecting process, Ives focuses upon the tape-recorded interview, including procedures for processing and archiving data, as well as such topics as recording music, handling group interviews, and using photographs and other visual media during interviews (see also **H.136**).

A.26. Jenkins, Sara. *Past Present: Recording the Life Stories of Older People.* Washington, D. C.: St. Alban's Parish, 1978.

One of two major sections of this book is devoted to "Conducting a Listening Project," which offers practical advice on the interview process, the training of interviewers, and the administration of an oral history project; this is preceded by a section entitled "Here I Am," with a description, and selected examples from, an oral history project sponsored by St. Alban's Parish, in Mount St. Alban, Washington, D. C.

A.27. Kaminsky, Marc, ed. *The Uses Of Reminiscence: New Ways of Working With Older Adults.* New York: Haworth Press, 1984. (Also published as a special issue of *Journal of Gerontological Social Work* 7:1-2 [1984]).

This groundbreaking work on life review among elders features fifteen articles on concepts and practices from the perspectives of drama, art, poetry, literature, and working class and ethnic history.

A.28. Lichtman, Allan J. *Your Family History.* New York: Vintage, 1978.

This is a comprehensive guide for conducting family history research, including sections on oral history interviewing, photographs, and searching archival records; includes a bibliography.

A.29. Oblinger, Carl. *Interviewing the People of Pennsylvania: A Conceptual Guide to Oral History.* Harrisburg: Pennsylvania Historical and Museum Commission, 1981.

This guide is noteworthy for its inclusion of a "senior citizens questionnaire,"and its focus on elders as resources of community memory; the categories it considers important in conducting oral histories are ethnicity, work, community and family.

A.30. Ritchie, Donald A. *Doing Oral History.* New York: Twayne Publishers, 1995.

This recent entry into the ranks of oral history manuals is also one of the most comprehensive in scope, covering such topics as starting an oral history project, conducting interviews, videotaping life stories, the use of oral history in research and writing, archiving, teaching oral history, and forms of presentation (such as community and family history projects, exhibits, radio, theater productions, and therapeutic settings).

A.31. Sitton, Thad, George L. Mehaffy and O. L. Davis, Jr. *Oral History: A Guide for Teachers (and Others).* Austin: University of Texas Press, 1983.

Designed for classroom teachers, this book was inspired by the Foxfire model, where students were sent out into the local community to interview elders about traditional customs, beliefs and material culture (see **B.2-B.13**).

A.32. Thompson, Paul. *The Voice of the Past: Oral History.* 2nd ed. Oxford: Oxford University Press, 1988 [1978].

This is the classic British oral history handbook, containing information on methods and uses of oral history, and offering practical advice on interviewing, archiving and community projects.

A.33. Yow, Valerie Raleigh. *Recording Oral History: A Practical Guide for Social Scientists.* Thousand Oaks, California: Sage Publications, 1994.

In addition to chapters on preparation for interview projects, interview techniques, interpersonal relations in the interview, and legal and ethical issues, there are also chapters on varieties of oral history projects: community studies, biography and family research; appendices include sample interview questions and an oral history evaluation guide.

(Re)Presenting Lives: Analysis

A.34. Bertaux, Daniel, ed. *Biography and Society: The Life History Approach in the Social Sciences.* Beverly Hills, California: Sage Publications, 1981.

The title of this work notwithstanding, Bertaux notes that most of the contributors to this anthology, aimed at sociologists, deal exclusively with "life stories," or oral histories, which he distinguishes from "life histories," which supplement the narratives of one individual with biographical data collected from other sources; one author presents an argument to sociologists that life stories are better than survey data at uncovering the nature of social relationships.

A.34.a. Bornat, Johanna. "Oral History as a Social Movement: Reminiscence and Older People." *Oral History* 17:2 (1989), 16-24.

Bornat notes that reminiscence is something that people do throughout their lives, but has a more developed role and more significant outcomes in old age; it is also an activity that not only links past and present but transcends individual memory; she describes the work of *Recall,* a tape/slide program that became a model for oral history projects among elders in homes and centers in the British Isles.

A.35. Burgos, Martine. "Life Stories, Narrativity and the Search for the Self." *Life Stories/Récits de vie* 5 (1989), 29-37.

Burgos argues that life stories are the best research material for studies on the ways in which individuals construct their social self-image through the lifecourse.

A.36. Coleman, Peter. "The Past in the Present–A Study of Elderly People's Attitudes to Reminiscence." *Oral History* 14:1 (1986), 50-59.

Coleman examines the relation between past and present as reflected in the attitudes of the elderly, many of whom harbor both accepting and critical views of the past; Coleman cautions oral historians to be sensitive to the attitudes of elders toward the past when encouraging them to review their life experiences.

A.37. Comwell, Joyce, and Brian Gearing. "Biographical Interviews With Older People." *Oral History* 17:1 (1989), 36-43.

The authors, who have interviewed elders for a study of health beliefs in old age for London's Open University, note the context-dependent nature of people's stories, and the ways in which narratives are driven by the tension between the agendas of interviewer and narrator.

A.38. Gluck, Sherna, and Daphne Patai, eds. *Women's Words: The Feminist Practice of Oral History.* New York: Routledge, 1991.

This is a collection of essays exploring the theoretical, methodological, and practical issues arising from the use of oral history by feminist scholars, with contributions from the perspectives of anthropology, history, folklore, literature, psychology, sociology, linguistics and speech communications (see also **B.94** and **B.95**).

A.39. Langness, L. L., and Gelya Frank. *Lives: An Anthropological Approach to Biography.* Novato, California: Chandler & Sharp, 1981.

This is a classic work on the anthropological approach to life history research, addressing such issues as the use of biography in the social sciences, methods, the structure of autobiographical accounts, and ethical and moral concerns.

A.40. Luborsky, Mark R. "Alchemists' Visions: Cultural Norms in Eliciting and Analyzing Life History Narratives." *Journal of Aging Studies* 4:1 (1990), 17-29.

Based on a study of 37 tape recorded life histories of Irish, Italian and Jewish men widowed 2-8 years, Luborsky notes cultural differences in narratives styles, identifying three dimensions: unilineal (straight chronological presentation), recursive (addressing themes from cultural life or personal experience) and aggregate (no apparent sequential or thematic links).

A.41. McMahan, Eva M., and Kim Lacy Rogers, eds. *Interactive Oral History Interviewing.* Hillsdale, New Jersey: Lawrence Erlbaum Associates, 1994.

This collection of essays is based on the premise that "oral history interviews [are] subjective, social constructed, and emergent events" in which the "understanding, interpretation, and meaning of lived experiences are interactively constructed" in the interview process, and considers such subjects as power relations, intersubjectivity, gender, ethnicity, and the use of photographs in interviewing.

A.42. Oakley, Judith, and Helen Callaway, eds. *Anthropology and Autobiography.* London: Routledge, 1992.

This work presents several perspectives on current concerns among anthropologists about reflexivity and political responsibility; essays discuss how ethnicity, nationality, gender, age and the personal history of fieldworkers affect both the process of collecting life stories and the nature of the texts that they eventually publish.

A.43. Robinson, John A. "Personal Narratives Reconsidered." *Journal of American Folklore* 94:371 (1981), 58-85.

Robinson argues that personal narratives do not necessarily involve the relating of unusual events or the making of a specific point; they are situated communications that reflect the centrality of storytelling in everyday life.

A.44. Shenk, Dena, and Don McTavish. "Aging Women in Minnesota: Rural–Non-Rural Differences in Life-History Text." *Journal of Rural Studies* 4:2 (1988), 133-140.

Based on a content analysis of the personal narratives of 30 women aged 60 to 93 living in farms, villages and small towns in central Minnesota, the authors examine the extent to which themes and expressions in life histories reflect their rural/non-rural background.

A.45. Titon, Jeff Todd. "The Life Story." *Journal of American Folklore* 93 (1980), 276-292.

In the author's words, "my intention is to define and develop an approach to the life story as a self-contained fiction"; he distinguishes between oral history (personal narrative as an historical document) and life story (personal narrative viewed not as a "factual" account but as a window into the world of the teller).

A.46. Tonkin, Elizabeth. *Narrating Our Pasts: The Social Construction of Oral History.* Cambridge: Cambridge University Press, 1992.

Anthropologist Tonkin examines the nature of memory, ethnohistory and orality, and draws attention to oral accounts of the past as social activities in which tellers claim authority to speak to particular audiences; she draws from a range of examples, and also devotes one chapter to oral histories from the Jlao Kru of Liberia, with a special focus on the narratives of Sieh Jeto (1899-1975), whom she interviewed in 1972.

A.47. Wallace, J. Brandon. "Reconsidering the Life Review: The Social Construction of Talk About the Past." *The Gerontologist* 32:1 (1992), 120-125.

What is fascinating about this article from a folkloristic perspective is the "discovery" by a gerontologist of the importance of context in storytelling events; Wallace observes that life review is not, as some gerontologists see it, a "natural" activity in old age, but rather a social construction prompted and shaped by the demands of specific social situations.

A.48. Watson, Lawrence C., and Maria-Barbara Watson-Franke. *Interpreting Life Histories: An Anthropological Inquiry.* New Brunswick, New Jersey: Rutgers University Press, 1985.

The authors present, through a review of past practices, and analyses of case studies, an argument for ethnographic studies that life histories be approached with a view to the individuality and subjectivity of personally recounted lives, and not simply as data for testing cultural theories or methodologies.

A.49. Wrye, Harriet, and Jacqueline Churilla. "Looking Inward, Looking Backward: Reminiscence and the Life Review." *Frontiers* 2:2 (1977), 98-105.

Part of a special issue on women's oral history (see **B.94**), this essay discusses life review with the aged, life history in gerontological research, and the role of life review in intergenerational communication.

DOCUMENTING AND PRESENTING FOLKLIFE

Several of the fieldwork and oral history manuals cited above have chapters on documentation and presentation of field data; however, there are also guides focusing on folklife in a particular region or community. The list below is a very brief sample of these kinds of works, as well as works focusing on specific artifacts or media for documentation and presentation. Many cultural organizations, especially local, state and regional folklife programs, have guides for documenting and presenting the folklife in their region (see *Folklife Sourcebook* [**A.1**] and issues of the *Public Programs Newsletter* [cited above] for complete lists of such organizations).

A.50. _____*The Arts of Black Folk*. New York: Schomberg Center for Research in Black Culture, New York Public Library, 1988.

This is a collection of papers presented at the Arts of Black Folk Conference for Community Organizations on African-American Folk Arts, organized by the Schomberg Center, held in 1988; it includes papers on revitalizing Black folk arts, documenting and presenting African-American culture, funding African-American folk arts and others.

A.51. Allen, Barbara. "Family Albums, Family Images." In *Folklife Annual 1990*. Washington, D. C.: American Folklife Center, Library of Congress, 1991, 70-81.

Allen discusses family photographs not only as static records of a shared past but as material objects, images that may be manipulated to express a sense of self, and to convey meaning through content and through their arrangement and use.

A.52. Baker, Holly Cutting, Amy Kotkin and Margaret Yocum. *Family Folklore: Interviewing Guide and Questionnaire*. Washington, D. C.: Smithsonian Institution Traveling Exhibition Service (SITES),1975.

This is a short, straightforward introduction, written for the nonspecialist, and includes various interviewing techniques, suggestions for presenting materials, and some examples of family folklore projects.

A.53. Brecher, Jeremy. *History From Below: How to Uncover and Tell the Story of Your Community, Association or Union*. 2nd. ed. New Haven, Connectictut: Common-works/Advocate Press, 1996 [1986].

Written for the nonspecialist, it is a "primer, enabling 'ordinary' people to recover their own personal and community's past"; while designed for history projects, its lessons are applicable to folklife programs as well: it includes sections on planning a project, gathering and using documents, oral history techniques, using visual materials, and ideas for presentation, such as photo exhibits, public events, publications and media productions (self-distributed, it is available from Commonworks, Box 151, West Cornwall, CT 06796).

A.54. Gammerdinger, Harry Albert, Jr. "The Use of Film and Videotape to Document and Present Folklore." Doctoral dissertation, Indiana University, 1988.

In addition to anaylzing the use of film and videotape by folklorists, and the presentation of folklore to general audiences, appendices list two archival collections of folklore films in Indiana, and the work contains not only a bibliography but also an annotated 65-page "Filmography of American Folklore Films and Videotape."

A.55. Lux, Karen. *Folk Arts Programming in New York State: A Handbook and Resource Guide.* Syracuse, New York: Regional Council of Historic Agencies, 1990.

This work includes chapters on fieldwork and documentation, exhibition, performance and demonstration, apprenticeship, publication, recording, media production, fundraising and marketing.

B

General Works

The works in this section cover many bases: anthropology, history, literature, and mythology. They are listed here either because they cover more than one subject area within the field of folklore (belief, custom, oral history, folk medicine, etc.) or because their focus is not on folklore per se, but may contain material of folkloristic interest–or because I didn't know where else to put them! (Selected essays from some of the collections cited below are listed in other relevant sections of this book.)

One work in particular must be mentioned first off:

B.1. Schweitzer, Marjorie M. *Anthropology of Aging: A Partially Annotated Bibliography.* New York: Greenwood Press, 1991.

> This is an impressive listing of over 2,000 titles covering a wide range of subjects within the field, including demography, biology, medicine, social structure, modernization, community organization, women, death and dying, and large sections devoted to nonindustrialized societies, national cultures and ethnic and rural aging in the United States. I view *Anthropology of Aging* as a companion work, since many of the titles listed may provide insights or lead to information on the cultural contexts of expressive behavior relating to age and the aged. For convenience, selected titles from that bibliography that contain material of folkloristic interest are annotated in the present work (largely in this chapter); the reader is encouraged to consult the latter work for a broader topical range of ethnographic titles.

****

Another work, or rather series of works, bears mentioning at the head of this list:

Wigginton, Eliot, et al., eds. *Foxfire.* Vol 1-10. New York: Doubleday, 1972-1993.

> Back in the 1960s, Wigginton, a high school English teacher in Rabun Gap-Nacoochie School, in the Appalachian hills of northeastern Georgia, started up the *Foxfire* magazine (see the periodicals list in Chapter A) as a way of reviving his interest in teaching and his students' interest in learning; he sent them out into the hills to collect the lore of mountain people, mostly elders; the stories and lore they gathered filled the pages of their journal and over the years, have been reprinted in the *Foxfire* book series; a few offshoots that have been published are also noted below; for convenience, the full series titles are listed, though they could by rights fit into any of

the categories of this bibliography, since the subjects covered include personal narratives, folk histories, crafts, foodways, plant lore, vernacular architecture, healing and countless other "affairs of plain living." (*Foxfire* is not without flaws; for critiques, see **D.200**, **D.239**.)

B.2. *The Foxfire Book: Hog dressing, log cabin building, mountain crafts and foods, planting by the signs, snake lore, hunting tales, faith healing, moonshining and other affairs of daily living* (Wigginton, ed.). 1972.

B.3. *Foxfire 2: Ghost stories, spring wild plant foods, spinning and weaving, midwifing, burial customs, corn shuckin's, wagon making and more affairs of plain living* (Wigginton, ed.). 1973.

B.4. *Foxfire 3: Animal care, banjos and dulcimers, hide tanning, summer and fall wild plant foods, butter churns, ginseng, and still more affairs of plain living* (Wigginton, ed.). 1975.

B.5. *Foxfire 4: Fiddle making, springhouses, horse trading, sassafras tea, berry buckets, gardening, and further affairs of plain living* (Wigginton, ed.). 1977.

B.6. *Foxfire 5: Ironmaking, blacksmithing, flintlock rifles, bear hunting, and other affairs of plain living* (Wigginton, ed.). 1979.

B.7. *Foxfire 6: Shoemaking, 100 toys and games, gourd banjos and song bows, wooden locks, a water-powered sawmill, and other affairs of just plain living* (Wigginton, ed.). 1980.

B.8. *Foxfire 7: Ministers, church members, revivals, baptisms, shaped-note and gospel singing, faith healing, camp meetings, footwashing, snake handling, and other traditions of mountain religious heritage* (Paul Gillespie, ed.). 1982.

B.9. *Foxfire 8: Southern folk pottery from pug mills, ash glazes, and groundhog kilns to face jugs, churns and roosters; mule swapping and chicken fighting* (Wigginton and Margie Bennett, eds.). 1984.

B.10. *Foxfire 9: General stores, the Jud Nelson wagon, a praying rock, a Catawban Indian potter—and haint tales, quilting, home cures, and the log cabin revisited* (Wigginton and Margie Bennett, eds.). 1985.

B.11. *Foxfire 10: Railroad lore, boardinghouses, Depression-era Appalachia, chairmaking, whirligigs,, snake canes, and gourd art* (George P. Reynolds, Susan Walker, and Rabun County High School Students, eds. [With the assistance of Wigginton]). 1993.

B.12. *"I Wish I Could Give My Son a Wild Raccoon."* (Wigginton, ed.). New York: Anchor/Doubleday, 1976.

As a project for the U. S. Bicentennial, Wigginton got hundreds of students from across the country to interview elders in their own communities; among the personal narratives selected for this volume were those of "a Cajun trapper from Louisiana, an Eskimo teacher from Alaska, a banjo maker from North Carolina, a fireman from Illinois, and those of over thirty-five others."

B.13. *Sometimes a Shining Moment: The Foxfire Experience.* (Wigginton). Garden City, New York: Anchor Press/Doubleday, 1985.

Wigginton describes the background to the Foxfire project he developed some 20 years earlier, in which his English and journalism students recorded the life and traditions of mostly older Appalachians; he addresses issues it has raised, and reviews several "lesson plans" that illustrate the workings of the Foxfire program.

I cite the following two works here because they are spiritual kin with *Foxfire*:

B.13.a. Wood, Pamela, ed. *The Salt Book: Lobstering, Sea Moss Pudding, Stone Walls, Rum Running, Maple Syrup, Snowshoes, and Other Yankee Doings*. Garden City, New York: Anchor/Doubleday, 1977.

This book presents portraits, drawing from oral history interviews, of Maine residents, many of them elders, involved in such activities as lobstering, sea moss harvesting, and keeping watch in lighthouses, who discuss their lives "down East" and how things have changed over the years; like its *Foxfire* cousins, this is an anthology, drawn from the magazine *Salt* (see the periodicals list in Chapter A).

B.13.b. Wood, Pamela, ed. *Salt 2: Boatbuilding, Sailmaking, Island People, River Driving, Bean Hole Beans, Wooden Paddles, and More Yankee Doings*. Garden City, New York: Anchor/Doubleday, 1980.

This sequel to *The Salt Book* covers a number of subjects relating to country life, handicrafts, and social customs of Maine residents.

SPECIAL ISSUES OF JOURNALS

B.14. "The Aging Society." *Daedalus* 115:1 (1986), 1-399. [Also published as *Our Aging Society*, edited by Alan Pifer and Lydia Bronte (New York: W. W. Norton, 1986)].

The point of departure for the essays in this issue is the demographics of aging; with authors addressing aging in early U. S. history, changing meanings of age, sex and gender, family and intergenerational relations, health care, work and retirement, and articles focusing on Black and Hispanic elderly respectively.

B.15. "Crones, Sages and Elders." *Circle Network News: Nature Spirituality Quarterly* 17:3 (1995), 1-32.

This is an eclectic mix of short articles from traditional and New Age perspectives on issues of spirituality and aging.

B.16. "Nurturing the Creative Spirit: Drawing on Life." *Aging* 366 (1994)1-88. [Published by the Administration on Aging, U. S. Dept. of Health and Human Services.]

This issue is devoted to arts and aging, with descriptions of a number of older folk artists and selected projects and programs with the elderly throughout the U. S. that draw on themes of traditional arts, family folklore and the like.

B.17. "The Old Ones." *Parabola: Myth and the Quest for Meaning* 5:1 (1980), 1-128.

This journal, blends literary, scholarly and traditional cultural perspectives; each issue is devoted to a theme; while the focus of this issue is on elders, views by and about elders and aging appear in other issues of this journal (see the periodicals list in Chapter A).

B.18. "Older, Wiser, Stronger: Southern Elders." *Southern Exposure* 13:2-3 (1985), 1-152. Mary Eldridge, Special Editor.

Southern Exposure (see the periodicals list in Chapter A) is devoted to "working for progressive change in the region"; this issue features older activists, and elders living active lives, with concerns ranging from the preservation of traditional culture to facing the challenges of aging and social injustice.

LIFE REVIEW/ LIFE COURSE STUDIES

B.19. Bornat, Joanne, ed. *Reminiscence Reviewed: Perspectives, Evaluations, Achievements.* Buckingham, England: Open University Press, 1994.

Contributors to this volume–including psychologists, gerontoglogists, social workers, nurses and community workers with firsthand experience in reminiscence work–describe their work in hospitals, schools and community settings, and take a critical look at the field, reflecting on theory and practice.

B.20. Erikson, Erik H., Joan M. Erikson and Helen Q. Kivnick. *Vital Involvement in Old Age.* New York: Norton, 1986.

This "portrait of the experience of old age in our time" is based on interviews with 29 octogenerians, among the participants in the Guidance Study of the Institute of Human Development of the University of California at Berkeley, which followed the lives of individuals born in 1928 and 1929, and from whom life history data had been collected for more than 50 years.

B.21. Haight, Barbara K., and Jeffrey D. Webster, eds. *The Art and Science of Reminiscence: Theory, Research, Methods, and Applications.* Washington, D.C.: Taylor & Francis, 1995.

"This work was written to provide a definitive resource for teachers, students, clinicians and researchers who work in the field of reminiscing"; articles examine such issues as the social construction of memories, the life history as a formative experience for the aging, and methods of encouraging reminiscence.

B.22. Kaminsky, Marc, ed. *The Uses of Reminiscence: New Ways of Working With Older Adults.* New York: Haworth Press, 1984.

This collection of articles presents the perspectives of artists, service providers, and scholars who discuss life review in clinical research and literature and describe a variety of projects involving reminiscence, ranging from oral history interviews to plays and poetry workshops.

B.23. Matthews, Sarah H. *Friendships Through the Life Course: Oral Biographies in Old Age.* Beverly Hills, California: Sage Publications, 1986.

Matthews examines the quality of friendships throughout the lifespan, with an emphasis on the comparative quality of relationships with old and more recently acquired friends among elders, based on an analysis of personal narratives collected fom 63 women and men, whose stories are generously excerpted throughout the text.

B.24. Sherman, Edmund. *Reminiscence and the Self in Old Age.* New York: Springer, 1991.

Sherman reviews the imagery and language of reminiscence, the role of memorabilia and cherished possessions, the expression of life themes in personal narratives, and the creative and aesthetic elements of reminiscence, as expressed both in oral and written forms.

B.25. Unruh, David R., and Gail S. Livings, eds. *Personal History Through the Life Course.* [*Personal Perspectives on Aging and the Life Cycle: A Research Annual, Volume 3*] Greenwich, Connecticut: JAI Press, 1989.

This collection of essays is devoted to theoretical and methodological concerns in the study of "self-narratives," including the perspectives of gerontology, folklore, anthropology, psychology, and sociology.

ORAL HISTORY

B.26. Benmayor, Rina, and Andor Skotnes, eds. *Migration and Identity* [*International Yearbook of Oral History and Life Stories, Vol. III*]. Oxford: Oxford University Press, 1994 .

The essays in this anthology explore the ways in which the identities of migrants are shaped not only by gender, class and ethnicity, but also by the experience of migration (see, e.g., **D.294**).

B.27. Bertaux, Daniel, and Paul Thompson, eds. *Between Generations: Family Models, Myths, and Memories* [*International Yearbook of Oral History and Life Stories, Vol. II*]. Oxford: Oxford University Press, 1993.

This collection of essays is a response to the question: "what is it that parents pass down to their children?"; each contribution addresses the application of a life-story approach to the dynamics of the family and social change (see, e.g., **D.78**).

B.28. Grele, Ronald J. *Envelopes of Sound: The Art of Oral History*. 2nd ed. New York: Praeger, 1991.

This collection of essays presented by Grele explores the nature of oral history, and includes conversations with, and contributions from, such notable practitioners as Studs Terkel, Jan Vansina, Dennis Tedlock, Saul Benson and Alice Kessler Harris; in one chapter, "Listen to Their Voices," Grele compares narrative style and content in two oral histories of elderly Jews, Mel Dubin, born in 1894 in New York's Lower East Side, and Bella Pincus, born between 1893 and 1895 in Russian Poland, and who arrived in the U. S. in 1911.

B.29. Grele, Ronald J. *Subjectivity and Multiculturalism in Oral History*. International Annual of Oral History, 1990. Westport, Connecticut: Greenwood Press, 1992.

The essays in this collection examine the trend within oral history wherein researchers explore ways in which the "object of investigation," the interviewee, may become the subject, generating narratives based on his or her own personal and cultural identity, and prompted by their own questions and ideas (see, e.g., **D.132**).

B.30. Portelli, Alessandro. *The Death of Luigi Trastulli and Other Stories: Form and Meaning in Oral History*. Albany: State University of New York Press, 1991.

Portelli, a professor of American Literature at the University of Rome, in examining cultural conflict and communication between social groups and classes, addresses concerns of particular interest to folklorists, as well as gerontologists, such as the ways in which individuals (re)construct memories in order to make sense of their lives, the nature of the storytelling experience, and the impact of the fieldwork encounter on the researcher.

ANTHROPOLOGY/SOCIOLOGY/ETHNIC STUDIES

B.31. Albert, Steven M., and Maria G. Cattell. *Old Age in Global Perspective: Cross-Cultural and Cross-National Views*. New York: G. K. Hall, 1994.

Among the subjects of potential folkloristic interest covered in this broad overview are "Culture and the Lifecourse," "Family Relationships of the Elderly," "The Aged and Intergenerational Relationships," and "Succession to Seniority."

B.32. Amoss, Pamela T., and Stevan Harrell. *Other Ways of Growing Old: Anthropological Perspectives.* Stanford, California: Stanford University Press, 1981.

The essays in this collection include social structural studies from nine cultures, and a chapter each on physical anthropology and primatology.

B.33. de Beauvoir, Simone. *The Coming of Age.* New York: G. P. Putnam's Sons, 1972 [1970].

The renowned existential philosopher, feminist and writer takes the reader on a journey across time and cultures in her exploration of the ambiguous and often contradictory attitudes toward, and treatment of, elders; she investigates the ethnological data, old age in historical and present-day societies, and old age as experienced in everyday life.

B.34. Brandes, Stanley. *Forty: The Age and the Symbol.* Knoxville: University of Tennessee Press, 1985.

It is useful to consider this work in light of Brandes' treatment, from the perspective of symbolic anthropology, of the meaning of 40, commonly conceptualized as the gateway to late life.

B.35. Cowgill, Donald O., and Lowell D. Holmes, eds. *Aging and Modernization.* New York: Appleton-Century-Crofts, 1972.

This collection of essays is based on a symposium on "the role of the aged in various primitive and peasant societies" in which a group of anthropologists was invited "to reexamine their field notes and abstract from them relevent material on aging"; featured are cross-cultural analyses, as well articles on specific traditional communities in Africa, Asia, the Pacific Islands, Europe, and the Middle East.

B.36. Cowgill, Donald O. *Aging Around the World.* Belmont, California: Wadsworth, 1986.

This cross-cultural study presents overviews of demography, value systems, kinship systems and family, economic, political, religious and educational roles of the aged, as well as a discussion of theories of aging and types of societies.

B.37. Foner, Nancy. *Ages in Conflict: A Cross-Cultural Perspective on Inequality Between Old and Young.* New York: Columbia University Press, 1984.

Drawing on ethnographic studies of nonindustrialized societies, Foner examines age as a basis for structured inequality, and looks at various aspects of the resultant tension; of particular folkloristic interest is the chapter on "The Old Person as Witch" (see **C.115**).

B.38. Fry, Christine L., ed. *Aging in Culture and Society.* South Hadley, Massachusetts: Bergin & Garvey, 1980.

This collection of essays is divided into sections on "Biology and Aging"; "Culture and Aging: Classification, Life Cycles and Appropriate Behavior"; Cultures and Communities: Alternate Roles and Resources for Older Adults"; and "Coping With Aging: Problems and Strategies."

B.39. Fry, Christine L., ed. *Dimensions: Aging, Culture and Health.* New York: J. F. Bergin, 1981.

The articles in this cross-cultural anthology include perspectives from gerontology and anthropology on social support systems for elders in rural and urban, and industrial and non-industrial societies, as well as health care and the role of biomedicine among the aging in community and institutional settings.

B.40. Fry, Christine L., and Jennie Keith, eds. *New Methods for Old Age Research.* South Hadley, Massachusetts: Bergin & Garvey, 1986.

The contributors to this work offer strategies for culturally sensitive collection of qualitative and comparative data about aging, with reference to ethnic communities in the U. S. and other countries.

B.41. Gelfand, Donald E., and Charles M. Barresi, eds. *Ethnic Dimensions of Aging.* New York: Springer, 1987.

The essays in this collection address issues of theory, research, practice and policy, and cover such topics as ethnic identity, retirement, social support networks and organizational activities among the aging in ethnic communities in the U. S.

B.42. Guttmann, David. *Jewish Elderly in the English-Speaking Countries.* New York: Greenwood Press, 1989.

This is an annotated bibliography of nearly 300 journal articles published in the 1970s and 80s; among the subjects addressed are customs and traditions, as well as cultural attitudes toward aging and the aged.

B.43. Hazan, Haim. *Old Age: Constructions and Deconstructions.* Cambridge: Cambridge University Press, 1994.

Drawing from a variety of ethnographic accounts, Hazan presents a social constructivist perspective on the realities of old age as it is experienced by elders, in contrast to views held by "outsiders" about the world of the aging.

B.44. Holmes, Ellen Rhoads, and Lowell D. Holmes, eds. *Other Cultures, Elder Years.* 2nd ed. Thousand Oaks, California: Sage, 1995.

A survey work on the anthropology of aging, it presents summaries of comparative studies worldwide, and discusses such issues as family relations, beliefs and practices related to the life cycle, and the effects of modernization.

B.45. Keith, Jennie. *The Ethnography of Old Age.* Special Issue of *Anthropological Quarterly* 52 (1979), 1-73.

The papers in this issue were presented in a symposium on "Old Age and Community Creation" at the 75th annual meeting of the American Anthropological Association, and the authors are all anthropologists who have conducted ethnographic fieldwork in residential settings for elders in the U. S.

B.46. Kertzer, David I., and Jennie Keith, eds. *Age and Anthropological Theory.* Ithaca, New York: Cornell University Press, 1984.

"This book represents the first attempt to develop a systematic framework for the anthropological study of age, calling for a convergence of anthropological concerns with recent developments in other social sciences," and addresses anthropological perspectives on social structure, the life course and culture.

B.46.a. Laslett, Peter. *A Fresh Map of Life: The Emergence of the Third Age.* Cambridge: Harvard University Press, 1991 [1989].

The 74-year-old British sociologist notes the ways in which the recent growth of the aging population has changed the nature of the social landscape; with a focus on Great Britain, Laslett reviews such subjects as demography, family relations, retirement and beliefs and attitudes regarding the aging; in one chapter he addresses "The Responsibilities of Older British People" where, among other observations, he speculates that it may "become the long-term duty of those in the Third Age to assume responsibility for the maintenance of the tradition of craftsmanship in our country and its role in our cultural life."

B.47. Myerhoff, Barbara and Andrei Simic, eds. *Life's Career–Aging: Cultural Variations on Growing Old.* Beverly Hills, California: Sage Publications, 1978.

This volume presents the research of five anthropologists who investigate common themes as well as variations on old age in Tanzania, Yugoslavia, Mexico, and in Jewish and Hispanic communties in the U. S.

B.48. Pickard, Susan. *Living on the Front Line: A Social Anthropological Study of Old Age and Ageing.* Aldershot, England: Avebury, 1995.

This work, based on over 60 interviews conducted with elders in South Wales, is an analysis, with illustrative oral narrative excerpts, of the experience of old age, a discussion of continutiy and change over the lifespan, and an examination of the extent to which old age is "a disjunction, a time apart, from the life stages that have preceded it."

B.49. Rubinstein, Robert L., ed., with Jennie Keith, Dena Shenk and Darryl Wieland. *Anthropology and Aging: Comprehensive Reviews.* Dordrecht, The Netherlands: Kluwer, 1990.

This cross-cultural collection of essays is divided into sections on "Biological and Health Issues," "Cultural Issues," and "Areal Studies," and addresses such varied topics such as nursing and aging, the relations of nature, culture, gender and age, the life course, and aging in Japan and China.

B.50. Simmons, Leo W. *The Role of the Aged in Primitive Society.* New Haven: Yale University Press, 1945. [reprinted by Archon Books, Hamden, CT, 1970]

This is a pioneering ethnographic study on the status and treatment of elders in traditional societies worldwide; among the cultural traits surveyed are beliefs and practices relating to the aging, and the ritual authority of elders in different cultures.

B.51. Sokolovsky, Jay, ed. *The Cultural Context of Aging: Worldwide Perspectives.* New York: Bergin & Garvey, 1990.

The essays in this anthology are organized into sections on "Culture, Aging and Context"; "The Cultural Construction of Intergenerational Ties"; "Aging, Modernization and Societal Change"; "The Ethnic Dimension in Aging"; "Community, Environment and Aging" and "Culture, Health and Aging."

B.52. Sokolovsky, Jay, ed. *Growing Old in Different Societies: Cross-Cultural Perspectives.* Acton, Massachusetts: Copley, 1987 [originally published by Wadsworth Press in 1983].

The essays in this anthology, more than half of which were prepared especially for this work, address such varied issues as the experience of growing old, aging women, intergenerational relations, aging and social change, ethnic identity and aging, social networks and community creation among elders.

B.53. Sokolovsky, Jay, and Joan Sokolovsky, eds. *Aging and the Aged in the Third World, Part II: Regional and Ethnographic Perspectives* [Publication 23 in the series *Studies in Third World Societies*]. Williamsburg, Virginia: Department of Anthropology, William and Mary College, 1982.

The essays in this volume address aging and the aged through ethnographic case studies of small-scale communities in Papua New Guinea, China, India, the Sudan and Mexico.

B.54. Spencer, Paul, ed. *Anthropology and the Riddle of the Sphinx: Paradoxes of Change in the Life Course.* London: Routledge, 1990.

This is a collection of papers presented at the 1988 Conference of the Association of Social Anthropologists, whose theme was "The Social Construction of Youth, Maturation and Ageing"; they offer "a holistic approach to the life course," with cross-cultural topics covering aging (including "coming of age") from a lifespan developmental perspective.

B.55. Stearns, Peter N., ed. *Old Age in Preindustrial Society.* New York: Holmes & Meier, 1982.

This collection of essays offers both cross-cultural and historical perspectives on the position of elders in communities in Kenya, Tibet, India, Renaissance Italy, 17th century England, 18th century France, and 19th century Russia, with a chapter on old age and witchcraft in early modern Europe.

B.56. Strange, Heather, and Michele Teitelbaum, eds. *Aging and Cultural Diversity: New Directions and Annotated Bibliography.* South Hadley, Massachusetts: Bergin & Garvey, 1987.

Essays in this collection cover Malaysia, Liberia, and Newfoundland, as well as African-Americans, Puerto Ricans and Kalmuk Mongols in the U. S.; the bibliography is divided into sections on social roles, American culture, ethnic, regional and national surveys in the U. S. and other countries, and comparative and cross-cultural studies.

Surveys of Ethnicity and Aging in the U. S.

B.57. Harel, Zev; Edward A. McKinney and Michael Williams, eds. *Black Aged: Understanding Diversity and Service Needs.* Newbury Park, California: Sage Publications, 1990.

Among the data provided on the collective historical experiences, cultural values and social status of contemporary African-American elders are oral history narratives describing the experiences of migrants from the southern U. S. to a midwestern urban community.

B.58. Lichtman, Allan J., and Joan R. Challinor, eds. *Kin and Communities: Families in America.* Washington, D. C.: Smithsonian Institution Press, 1979.

Essays on role of ethnicity, community, place, personal and social history, the state and generational relations in family life in the U. S. are followed by the transcripts of workshops and colloquia from a Smithsonian symposium held in 1977, addressing issues in family history research such as family photo interpretation, collecting oral history, and the use of family documents.

B.59. Manuel, Ron C., ed. *Minority Aging: Sociological and Social Psychological Issues.* Westport, Connecticut: Greenwood Press, 1982.

Contributors to this volume address economic and health issues, familial and social support, retirement, death and dying, public policies and social services, and theory and methodology for the study of the minority aging.

B.60. Markides, Kyriakos S., and Charles H. Mindel. *Aging and Ethnicity.* Newbury Park, California: Sage Publications, 1987.

The authors discuss theoretical and methodological issues, demographic and socioeconomic factors, mortality and health, family structure and relations, mental health, death and dying, work and retirement, and social problems and policies.

Ethnographies of Aging Subcultures (Retirement Communities, Elderly Housing Facilities, Nursing Homes, etc.)

B.60.a. Cohen, Carl I., and Jay Sokolovsky. *Old Men of the Bowery: Strategies for Survival Among the Homeless.* New York: The Guilford Press, 1989.

The authors look at the intersection of biography and society in this study of the social world of older homeless men, beginning with profiles of three individuals identified as Uncle Ed, Miles (the Fry Cook), and Roland (the Super-Runner); excerpts of interviews with them appear throughout the text.

B.61. Francis, Doris. *Will You Still Need Me, Will You Still Feed Me, When I'm 84?* Bloomington: Indiana University Press, 1984.

Comparisons and contrasts are drawn in the ways in which two groups of elderly Jews–in Cleveland, Ohio, and Leeds, England–cope with old age; featured are descriptions of daily life and ritual activities, and excerpts of oral history interviews.

B.62. Gubrium, Jaber F. *Speaking of Life: Horizons of Meaning for Nursing Home Residents.* New York: Aldine De Gruyter, 1993.

Gubrium explores the issue of quality of life in long-term care facilities through an analysis of personal narratives of nursing home residents; features generous excerpts of these interviews.

B.63 Hochschild, Arlie R. *Unexpected Community: Portrait of an Old Age Subculture.* Berkeley, California: University of California Press, 1978.

Hochschild studied the residents of a small apartment building in San Francisco, most of them widows in their late 60s and migrants from the rural Midwest and Southwest; she looks at the customs, gossip, humor and other forms of expressive behavior generated within the subculture of the housing project.

B.64. Jacobs. Jerry. *Fun City: An Ethnographic Study of a Retirement Community.* New York: Holt, Rinehart and Winston, 1974.

This is a study of a self-contained retirement community in Arizona.

B.65. Johnson, Sheila K. *Idle Haven: Community Building Among the Working-Class Retired.* Berkeley: University of California Press, 1971.

This ethnographic study describes a community of retired white working-class individuals who live in an age-homogeneous mobile-home park, addressing relationships with friends, neighbors and their children and grandchildren, the social structure of the park, and informal patterns of mutual assistance.

B.66. Keith, Jennie. *Old People, New Lives: Community Creation in a Retirement Residence.* Chicago: University of Chicago Press, 1982 [1977].

This is a study of the residents of an apartment for elders on the outskirts of Paris; Keith discusses social relationships within the residence, including how those relationships are defined in large part by residents' prior membership or non-membership in the French Communist Party.

B.67. Kinoshita, Yasuhito, and Christine W. Kiefer. *Refuge of the Honored: Social Organization in a Japanese Retirement Community.* Berkeley: University of California Press, 1992.

This study describes the process of community creation by aged residents in a type of setting that is relatively new in Japanese culture; includes descriptions of patterns of social interaction, such as the exchange of traditional forms of respect.

B.68. Krell, Roberta. *Folklore and the Elderly: Aging, Creativity and Community.* Doctoral dissertation, University of California, Los Angeles, 1986.

This study of residents of a retirement community, and a day care center for frail elderly, both in southern California, explores the influence of social and physical environment on community identity and expressive behavior.

B.69. Legesse, A. "Age Sets and Retirement Communities: Comparison and Comment." *Anthropological Quarterly* 52:1 (1979), 61-69.

Legesse looks at the process of "resocialization" that elders undergo when joining a retirement community, and notes the resemblance of this process to tribal entry rituals studied by anthropologists.

B.70. Rubinstein, Robert L. *Singular Paths: Old Men Living Alone*. New York: Columbia University Press, 1986.

This is a study, based to a large extent on life history interviews conducted by the author and others at the Philadelphia Geriatric Center, examining the lifestyles, worldview, and personal experiences of older men living alone, and features generous interview excerpts.

B.71. Shield, Renee Rose. *Uneasy Endings: Daily Life in an American Nursing Home*. Ithaca, New York: Cornell University Press, 1988.

This is an ethnographic study of a 200-bed nonprofit Jewish nursing home in the Northeastern United States, and an observation on the effects of the absence of community support and ritual in a "total institution"; features excerpts of personal experience narratives of residents and staff.

B.72. Smithers, Janice A. *Determined Survivors: Community Life Among the Urban Elderly*. New Brunswick, New Jersey: Rutgers University Press, 1985.

Smithers presents a study of a public housing project for elders in downtown Los Angeles, looks at the elders' struggle to maintain independence, and offers anecdotes about their daily life, in particular the residence's lobby, the center of community life.

B.73. Van Willigen, John. *Gettin' Some Age on Me: Social Organization of Older People in a Rural American Community*. Lexington: University of Kentucky Press, 1989.

Van Willigen looks at the social life and formal and informal support networks among elders in rural Kentucky.

B.74. Vesperi, Maria D. *City of Green Benches: Growing Old in a New Downtown*. Ithaca, New York: Cornell University Press, 1985.

Vesperi presents a portrait of the elderly in St. Petersburg, Florida, looking at their social conditions, their interactions with the city around them, and the contradiction between how they see themselves and how they are viewed by the community at large.

FOLKLORE AND MYTHOLOGY

B.75. Hufford, Mary. "Folklore and Aging." In Jan Harold Brunvand, ed. *American Folklore: An Encyclopedia*. New York: Garland Publishing, 1996, 12-14.

Hufford offers a broad overview of the "traditional expressive culture created around the experience of growing old," divided into sections on "The Social and Cultural Organization of Aging," and "The Elderly as Culture Makers."

B.76. de Luce, Judith. "Mythology." In James E. Birren, ed. *Encyclopedia of Gerontology, Volume 2*. San Diego, California: Academic Press, 1996, 187-196.

This is a broad cross-cultural overview of images of aging as reflected in the mythological narratives of the world.

B.77. McClerran, Jennifer, and Patrick McKee. *Old Age in Myth and Symbol: A Cultural Dictionary.* New York: Greenwood Press, 1991.

This is a survey, in dictionary format, of several hundred terms and phrases that bear some symbolic or mythological associations with age; sources cited range from art, literature and classical mythology to worldwide traditional folktales, legends and myths.

B.78. Shuldiner, David. "Folklore." In James E. Birren, ed. *Encyclopedia of Gerontology, Volume 1.* San Diego, California: Academic Press, 1996, 531-540.

A broad overview of folklore by and about the aging, and a discussion of the application of concepts, methodology and content of folklore studies to social interventions in care and service providing for elders.

HUMANITIES

B.79. Bagnell, Prisca von Dorotka, and Patricia Spencer Soper, eds. *Perceptions of Aging in Literature: A Cross-Cultural Study.* Westport, Connecticut: Greenwood Press, 1989.

This is a collection of essays surveying aging as depicted in classical Greek and Roman, British and American, French, German and Austrian, Hispanic American, Arabic, Japanese and Chinese literature, with an introductory essay on interpreting historical and cross-cultural literature on aging.

B.80. Bailey, William G. *Human Longevity from Antiquity to the Modern Lab: A Selected, Annotated Bibliography.* New York: Greenwood Press, 1987.

This work, containing 1300 English-language references relating to human longevity, includes a section on alchemy, quackery and folk beliefs.

B.81. Cole, Thomas R. *The Journey of Life: A Cultural History of Aging in America.* Cambridge: Cambridge University Press, 1992.

This survey of changing public attitudes about aging and the aged looks at representative texts and images of Northern European middle-class, and later American culture, and the transformations in popular views of the "journey of life" from imported Victorian notions up to "postmodern" views positing a renewed awareness of spirituality and the potential for growth in late life.

B.82. Cole, Thomas R., and Sally Gadow, eds. *What Does it Mean to Grow Old?: Reflections from the Humanities.* Durham, North Carolina: Duke University Press, 1986.

This is quite useful as a summary of perspectives from scholars representing the disciplines of gerontology, social medicine, politics, health, anthropology and ethics, and addressing personal, cultural, spiritual and historical issues; a "select bibliography" is divided into sections on history, philosophy, religion, psychology, sociology and anthropology, gerontology, and art and literature.

B.83. Cole, Thomas R., David D. Van Tassel and Robert Kastenbaum, eds. *Handbook of the Humanities and Aging.* New York: Springer, 1992.

With essays in the arts, philosophy, literature, religion and history, there are contributions on views of aging in ancient Greece and Rome; aging in Eastern cultures; perspectives from Christianity, Judaism and Hinduism; and an essay by Allan Chinen on "Fairy Tales and Spiritual Development."

B.84. Cole, Thomas R., and Mary G. Winkler, eds. *The Oxford Book of Aging: Reflections on the Journey of Life.* Oxford: Oxford University Press, 1994.

In addition to fiction, poetry, memoirs, essays and children's stories, *The Oxford Book of Aging* features folktales and legends from different cultures, and well as selections from the Koran and the Bible.

B.85. Porter, Laurel, and Laurence M. Porter, eds. *Aging in Literature.* East Lansing, Michigan: Michigan State University, 1984.

The contributors to this anthology, described as a collection of essays in "humanistic gerontology," address such topics as "Sex and Senescence in Medieval Literature"; "Celestina: The Aging Prostitute as Witch"; "*King Lear* and the Crisis of Retirement"; "Balzac's Myth of Rejuvenation"; and "Farce and Idealization: Dostoevsky's Ambivalence Toward Aging."

B.86. Spicker, Stuart F., Kathleen M. Woodward and David D. Van Tassel, eds. *Aging and the Elderly: Humanistic Perspectives in Gerontology.* Atlantic Highlands, New Jersey: Humanities Press, 1978.

Scattered throughout these essays on aging, as viewed from the perspectives of history, art, literature, philosophy, religion, law and political science, are insights from folklore and mythology, including beliefs of the ancient Hebrews and Greeks.

B.87. Van Tassel, David, ed. *Aging, Death and the Completion of Being.* Philadelphia: University of Pennsylvania Press, 1979.

Originally presented at a conference on "Human Values and Aging: New Challenges to Research in the Humanities" at Case Western University in 1975, these essays offer insights on the origins of contemporary attitudes on aging and death, as revealed in historical records, literature, folklore, mythology and art.

B.88. Yahnke, Robert A., and Richard M. Eastman, eds. *Literature and Gerontology: A Research Guide.* Westport, Connecticut: Greenwood Press, 1995.

"This is a book for gerontologists, about the ways in which literary works–autobiographical works, novels, plays, poems and stories–can illuminate the problems and potentials of older persons"; it is also a good source for investigating popular culture images of aging.

RELIGION/SPIRITUALITY

B.89. Koenig, Harold George, Monao Smiley, and Jo Ann Ploch Gonzales. *Religion, Health and Aging: A Review and Theoretical Integration.* New York: Greenwood Press, 1988.

Among the topics addressed in this book is the way in which religious beliefs, attitudes and rituals condition the experience of physical and mental health, as well as provide ways of coping with stress and illness.

B.90. LeFevre, Carol, and Perry LeFevre, eds. *Aging and the Human Spirit: A Reader in Religion and Gerontology.* Chicago: Exploration Press, 1981.

This is a collection of articles by theologians, researchers, practitioners and activists, organized into sections on "Aging in the Western Religious Tradition"; "Theology of Aging"; "Facts and Myths of Aging"; "Social Science Research"; "Policy and Program"; and "Ministry to the Aging."

B.91. Thomas, L. Eugene, and Susan Eisenhandler, eds. *Aging and the Religious Dimension.* Westport, Connecticut: Auburn House, 1994.

Among the subjects addressed in this collection are the beliefs of religious renunciates, personal narratives of spiritual journeys, fairy tales about aging and the aged, biblical images of aging, and aging women in Jewish tradition.

EDUCATION

B.92. Francis, Doris, Dena Shenk and Jay Sokolovsky, eds. *Teaching About Aging: Interdisciplinary and Cross-Cultural Perspectives.* Gainesville, Florida: Association for Anthropology and Gerontology, 1990.

This guide features a broad range of syllabi, teaching resources and information about courses taught in universities in the U. S. and Canada; among the courses outlined are "The Anthropology of Aging," "Old Age in Cross-Cultural Perspective," "Aging, East and West," "Women and Aging," "Aging and Judaism," and "Death and Dying in Cross-Cultural Perspective."

B.93. Girton, Kathryn M. "Education as Expression: A Natural Expansion to a Theory of Geragogy." *Gerontology and Geriatriacs Education* 16:1 (1995), 53-69.

While adressed to educators who teach older adults ("geragogy" refers to a pedagogy, or instructional method, for old age), this article offers insights useful to those probing the memories of elders; in criticizing theories of geragogy that emphasize only past life, it suggests that meaning is actively created in the dialectic of ongoing life experiences [for folklorists, it confirms the observation that elders both create culture in the present and reflect on the cultural past through the lens of the present].

GENDER

B.94. _____ "Women's Oral History." Special issue of *Frontiers: A Journal of Women's Studies* 2:2 (1977). Guest edited by Sherna Gluck and Joan Jensen.

This special issue, presenting feminist perspectives on oral history, is a mix of "popular" and scholarly articles containing collaborative work, student-conducted interviews, and interdisciplinary research, with contributions by university and community women; several essays feature older women.

B.95. _____ "Women's Oral History Two." Special issue of *Frontiers: A Journal of Women's Studies* 7:1 (1988). Sue Armitage and Joan Jensen, special consulting editors.

This is the second issue of *Frontiers* devoted entirely to women's oral history, representing the "state of the art," reflecting refinements in methodology resulting from questions feminist historians have raised about the role of oral history interviews; again, several essays profile the lives of older women.

B.96. Allen, Katherine R. *Single Women/Family Ties: Life Histories of Older Women.* Newbury Park , California: Sage Publications, 1989.

Interviews were conducted with 30 older white women, 15 never-married women and 15 widows from the 1910 "birth cohort" to examine aspects of their life histories that contributed to their work in family-keeping activities; all of the women are described as having shared a common culture as daughters of working-class families, expected to work hard, value the autonomy of the family unit, and assume the responsibilities of caregivers.

B.97. Banner, Lois W. *In Full Flower: Aging Women, Power and Sexuality: A History.* New York: Vintage Books, 1993.

Banner offers a feminist analysis of the social and sexual status of aging women and the ways their position within patriarchal culture has conditioned their relationships with younger men; Banner examines images from myth, history, literature, and popular culture.

B.98. Borenstein, Audrey, ed. *Older Women in 20th-Century America: A Selected Bibliography.* New York: Garland, 1982.

Actually a bibliography on middle-aged (40+) and older women in 20th century North America, this work is divided into two major sections– humanities and social sciences, the former includes subjects such as autobiographies, personal documents of older women, and creativity; the latter includes cross-cultural as well as gerontological studies and others.

B.99. Coyle, Jean M., ed. *Women and Aging: A Selected, Annotated Bibliography.* Westport, Connecticut: Greenwood Press, 1989.

This work cites books, articles, films, government documents and dissertations, arranged in sections on roles and relationships, economics, employment, retirement, health, sexuality, religion, housing, racial and ethnic groups, policy issues, international concerns, and middle age.

B.99.a. Estés, Clarissa Pinkola. *The Dangerous Old Woman: Myths and Stories of the Wise Old Woman Archetype.* Toronto: A. A. Knopf Canada, 1996.

Estés surveys, from a Jungian perspective, popular images of older women in traditional narratives.

B.100. Grau, Lois, and Ida Susser, eds. *Women in the Later Years: Health, Social and Cultural Perspectives.* New York: Haworth Press, 1989. [Also published as a special issue of *Women and Health* 14:3-4 (1988)]

This series of articles addresses cross-cultural issues affecting the well-being of older women in industrialized western countries and developing nations, including social support networks, status and authority.

B.101. Kerns, Virginia, and Judith K. Brown, eds. *In Her Prime: New Views of Middle-Aged Women.* Urbana: University of Illinois Press, 1992.

This is a collection of ethnographic studies of middle-aged women in various cultures, ranging from small-scale traditional groups to industrial societies, addressing menopause, changing roles, status, authority and the relations between middle-aged women and their younger female kin.

B.102. Leydesdorff, Selma, Luisa Passerini and Paul Thompson, eds. *Gender and Memory* [*International Yearbook of Oral History and Life Stories, Vol. IV*]. Oxford: Oxford University Press, 1996.

> The contributors to this anthology address the shaping of memory by gender, and try to answer such questions as the differences in the ways women and men recall particular experiences, and the degree to which memory changes as gender roles evolve (see **D.50**, **D.79**, **D.97**, and **D.140**).

B.103. Lopata, Helena Znaniecka, ed. *Widows: Volume 1, Middle East, Asia and the Pacific.* Durham, North Carolina: Duke University Press, 1987.

> The articles in this collection focus on the social, community and personal support systems and resources available to widows; among the cross-cultural factors relating to widowhood considered in this work are family organization, formal and institutional supports, culturally assigned roles for widows, and religious beliefs and practices, including mourning rituals. [Volume 2 covers North America]

B.104. Matthews, Sarah H. *The Social World of Older Women: Management of Self-Identity.* Beverly Hills, California: Sage Publications, 1979.

> What is relevant about this book for folkloristics is that it describes the contexts within American society in which older widows grapple with their self-identity and role, including those situations in their lives in which they see themselves as conforming to stereotypical socio-cultural images of older women.

B.105. The Personal Narratives Group, ed. *Women's Lives: Feminist Theory and Personal Narratives.* Bloomington: Indiana University Press, 1989.

> This collection of essays "offers rich insights into the ways that women's voices and life stories can inform scholarly research and expand our understanding of both the shared experience of gender and the profound differences among women"; several essays discuss older women's narratives (see **D.16**, **D.25**, **D.29** and **D.81**).

B.106. Rossi, Alice S., ed. *Gender and the Life Course.* New York: Aldine, 1985.

> This is "an interdisciplinary collection of essays on the lives of women and men as they are affected by history, culture, demography, economic and political stratification, and the biopsychological processes that attend maturation and aging"; while these essays to do not examine personal narratives per se, they provide insights useful in the interpretation of life stories of older women and men.

B.107. Weigle, Martha. *Spiders and Spinsters: Women and Mythology.* Albuquerque: University of New Mexico Press, 1982.

> This book offers texts and graphic images about women as depicted in the mythologies of the Americas and "classical Judeo-Christian tradition"; among the archetypal figures represented in several sections is the "Wise Old Woman."

C

Beliefs and Customs

I have selected the works listed below either because they focus primarily on beliefs and customs related to aging, or because they contain, among other contents, enough relevant material on beliefs and customs of aging to warrant a citation. Occasionally, the decision to list a particular work here, rather than in another chapter, may seem arbitrary. In this respect, the list below may be viewed as part and parcel of the reader's initiation into the vagaries of classification, a companion to the perennial quandary about the boundaries of folklore, culture and aging (none of the latter terms being paragons of specificity). In any event, the reader is well-advised to search among the works listed in other chapters, particularly "Narratives," "Health and Healing," and "Applied Folklore," for further sources of information on customs and beliefs as recorded about, and recalled by, elders from various cultures and communities.

GENERAL/CROSS-CULTURAL WORKS

C.1. Albrecht, Ruth. "The Role of Older People in Family Rituals." In Clark Tibbitts and Wilma Donahue, eds. *Social and Psychological Aspects of Aging.* New York: Columbia University Press, 1962, 486-491.

> Albrecht summarizes the results of interviews with members of over 250 family groups, in which 600 rituals were described, over one third of which involved older members of the family, as the recipients of family visits and gifts, or as the hosts and/or organizers of ritual events, such as holiday gatherings.

C.2. Climo, Jacob J. "The Role of Anthropology in Gerontology: Theory." *Journal of Aging Studies* 6:1 (1992), 41-55.

> Among the suggested ways in which anthropological theory may contribute to social gerontology are the study of symbolism and rituals in life transitions among the aging, and culture-specific patterns, as well as cross-cultural comparisons of belief, behavior and treatment with regard to traditional elders.

C.3. Covey, Herbert C. "A Return to Infancy: Old Age and the Second Childhood in History." *International Journal of Aging And Human Development* 36:2 (1992-3), 81-90.

Covey reviews the popular belief of the "second childhood"–a reversion to childish behavior in old age–a cultural stereotype reflecting ambiguity in attitudes toward older persons in Western history.

C.4. Donow, Herbert. "Religion and Science: The Wandering Jew and Methuselah." *Journal of Aging Studies.* 3:1 (1989), 67-73.

Donow examines the views of Western science and religion on the issue of longevity; focusing upon a literary and religious theme, epitomized in the legend of the Wandering Jew, that longevity is a curse, he then looks at a contemporary science that seeks to extend life without a consideration of how a longer life might be spent.

C.5. Dulin, Rachel Z. *A Crown of Glory: A Biblical View of Aging.* New York: Paulist Press, 1988.

Dulin reviews the Hebrew Scriptures for characterizations of age and elders, attitudes toward the elderly in the family and society, and reflections on the meaning of old age.

C.6. Fischer, Kathleen. "Spirituality and the Aging Family: A Systems Perspective." *Journal of Religious Gerontology* 8:4 (1992), 1-15.

In an exploration of the spiritual dimension in the interaction of aging families, the author discusses the role of family rituals, such as baptisms, which strengthen intergenerational ties, and healing rituals that provide caregivers and other family members with spiritual support in dealing with the aging process and illness.

C.7. Gaylin, Ned L. "Intergenerational Perspective of Marriage: Love and Trust in Cultural Context." *Marriage and Family Review* 16:1-2 (1991), 143-159.

Gaylin looks at the changing nature of courtship and marriage across generations, with the emergence of new rituals, ceremonies and other traditions, and resultant sources of strain in marriage, particularly around gender roles.

C.8. Jeter, Kris. "Ancestor Worship as an Intergenerational Linkage in Perpetuity." *Marriage and Family Review* 16:1-2 (1991), 195-217.

Jeter describes patterns of ancestor worship among the Chinese, the Maring of New Guinea, and the Mexicans (specifically addressing the latters' "Day of the Dead" celebration), then takes a leap into the proposition that much of the practice of 20th century psychology is a thinly-disguised attempt to recreate ancestor worship through intergenerational connection.

C.9. Kalab, Milada. "Buddhism and Emotional Support for Elderly People." *Journal of Cross-Cultural Gerontology* 5:1 (1990), 7-19.

Based on fieldwork conducted in the mid-1980s among Cambodian refugees in Thailand, Australia, France, Germany and the United States, this article discusses the status and respect accorded elderly followers of Buddhism within traditional Cambodian culture and how the loss of an important role has been felt among older refugees.

C.10. McFadden, Susan H. "Attributes of Religious Maturity in Aging People." *Journal of Religion and Aging* 1:3 (1985), 39-48.

McFadden examines religious maturity among elders from the perspective of life review, in which memories of childhood religious objects are contrasted with a greater openness in late life to the transcendent spiritual meaning of the symbols, rituals and myths of their faith.

C.11. Seltzer, Mildred M. "Reunions: Windows to the Past and Present." *American Behavioral Scientist* 31:6 (1988), 644-653.

Among the perspectives explored in this essay is that of reunions as rituals that mark passages in the individual life cycle; it points to their particular significance in mid and late life as rituals of life review–meetings of past and present selves.

C.12. Silverman, P., and Robert J. Maxwell. "How Do I Respect Thee? Let Me Count the Ways: Deference Towards Elderly Men and Women." *Behavioral Science Research* 2 (1978), 91-108.

The authors review data from a random sample of 34 societies drawn from Murdock and White's Standard Cross-Cultural Sample of 186 "distinct world areas" for evidence of forms of expression of respect and appreciation for elders; among the categories of deference examined are spatial (e.g., special seats), victual (e.g., offering choice foods), linguistic (e.g., terms of respect), presentational (e.g. special postures assumed in their presence), prestative [authors' neologism for the giving of gifts], and celebrative (ceremonies conducted in their honor).

C.13. Sokolovsky, Jay. "Images of Aging: A Cross-Cultural Perspective." *Generations* 17:2 (1993), 51-54.

This article examines culturally constructed perceptions of age and the aged, including metaphors of aging reflected in folklore and mythology; research points to a connection between negative cultural images of elders and negative attitudes toward individual elders in a given society.

C.14. Stahmer, Harold M. "The Aged in Two Ancient Oral Cultures: The Ancient Hebrews and Homeric Greece." In Stuart F. Spicker, Kathleen M. Woodward and David D. Van Tassel, eds. *Aging and the Elderly: Humanistic Perspectives in Gerontology*. Atlantic Highlands, New Jersey: Humanities Press, 1978, 23-36.

This essay finds common attitudes about the elderly among ancient Jewish and Greek cultures, as reflected in oral traditions, in particular the ways in which legendary elders earned as much fear as they did respect.

C.15. Thomas, L. Eugene. "Metaphoric Analysis of Meaning in the Lives of Elderly Men: A Cross-Cultural Investigation." *Journal of Aging Studies* 4:1 (1990), 1-15.

Thomas examined the metaphors used by 100 older men from India and England, concluding that elders living in these two countries tended to occupy different psychological worlds; in particular, the Indian men expressed a belief in the cyclical nature of life and death, as contrasted with the linear view expressed by the English elders he interviewed.

C.16. Weisman, Celia B., and Paula Schwartz. "Spirituality: An Integral Part of Aging." *Journal of Aging and Judaism* 3:3 (1989), 110-115.

The authors examine three models of Jewish spiritual expression: behavioral, pietistic and intellectual; of relevance here is the behavioral model, in which elderly Jews compensate for diminished social roles by increased synagogue attendance and participation in rituals and other traditions.

WORKS LISTED BY COUNTRY OR REGION

Africa

C.17. Brain, James L. "Ancestors as Elders–Further Thoughts." *Africa* 43:2 (1973), 122-133.

Brain, responding to an essay by Igor Kopytoff (see **C.23**), argues that many, if not most, African societies make clear distinctions, both linguistically and conceptually, between "elders"–both living and dead–and "ancestral spirits."

C.18. Curley, Richard T. *Elders, Shades and Women: Ceremonial Change in Lango, Uganda.* Berkeley: University of California Press, 1973.

Among three ceremonial complexes described is a set of ceremonies by groups of Lango elders which represent several clans. These groups, called *etogo*, perform curing, funeral and rainmaking ceremonies as well as other rituals.

C.19. Diop, Amadou Moustapha. "The Place of the Elderly in African Society." *Impact of Science on Society* 39:1 (1989), 93-98.

Diop surveys the traditional roles of, and respect for, elders as figures of economic, religious and educational authority in many African societies, and the challenges to their traditional positions by the young, by the political leaders of new nation-states and by urbanization.

C.20. Griaule, Marcel. *Conversations With Ogotemmêli: An Introduction to Dogon Religious Ideas.* London: Oxford University Press, 1965 [1948].

This account of myth, religion and philosophy among the Dogon of Sudan, is based on conversations, recorded over 33 days by the author with Ogotemmêli, a Dogon elder whose narratives are generously excerpted throughout the text.

C.21. Hamer, John H. "Myth, Ritual and the Authority of Elders in an Ethiopian Society." *Africa* 46:4 (1976), 327-339.

Hamer discusses myths and rituals honoring dead elders among two descent segments of the Sadama of Southwest Ethiopia, and which involve ritual leaders and elders from the respective lineages.

C.22. Hammond, Tooke, and David William. "Who Worships Whom: Agnates and Ancestors Among Nguni." *African Studies* 44:1 (1985), 47-64.

The authors examine the office of *inkulu*, or ritual elder, among the Cape Nguni of Southern Africa, who is responsible for all sacrifices, and other rituals directed toward specific ancestors who make their wishes known through dreams or in illnesses diagnosed by diviners.

C.23. Kopytoff, Igor. "Ancestors as Elders in Africa." *Africa* 41:2 (1971), 129-141.

Kopytoff argues that the categories of "elder" and "ancestor" are both conceptually and terminologically united in many African cultures, citing activities and relationships among the Suku of southwestern Congo [present-day Zaire] (see **C.17**).

C.24. Missinie, Leo E. "Aging in a Bakongo Culture." *International Journal of Aging And Human Development* 11:4 (1980), 293-295.

Discusses the central role of the aging in this Central African culture, where a community ideal of respect belies conflicts between individual and group, youth and aging, from traditional and modern sources.

C.25. Rosenmayr, Leopold. "More than Wisdom: A Field Study of the Old in an African Village." *Journal of Cross-Cultural Gerontology* 3 (1988), 21-40.

Outlines the significance of the seniority principle in a Bambara village in Mali, as emphasized in myth, ritual, ancestor worship and socialization and discusses responses to the eroding position of the elderly in the African countryside.

C.26. Rosenmayr, Leopold. "The Position of the Old in Tribal Society: Report from a Field Study in West Africa." In M. Bergener, M. Ermini, and H. B. Stahelin, eds. *Challenges in Aging*. London: Academic Press, 1990, 25-51.

A study of the inhabitants of Sonongo, a Bambara village in the Sahel region of the Republic of Mali, in which childrearing practices, ancestor worship, and the body of myth and ritual tend to reinforce not so much old age itself as the principle of seniority, by virtue of which elders are seen as embodying the experience, knowledge and capability necessary to command ritual authority.

C.27. Sangree, Walter H. "Youth as Elders and Infants as Ancestors: The Complementarity of Alternate Generations, Both Living and Dead, in Tiriki, Kenya and Irigwe, Nigeria." In William H. Newell, ed. *Ancestors*. The Hague: Mouton, 1976, 297-304.

Sangree examines the conceptual congruences between the ways in which the relationship between living and dead elders is viewed, and the nature of intergenerational relationships in two African societies.

C.28. Teitelbaum, Michele. "Old Age, Midwifery and Good Talk: Paths to Power in a West African Gerontocracy." In Heather Strange and Michele Teitelbaum, eds. *Aging And Cultural Diversity: New Directions and Annotated Bibliography*. South Hadley, Massachusetts: Bergin & Garvey, 1987, 39-60.

The author reports on field research conducted in the mid 1970s among the Jokwele Kpelle in central Liberia; she notes that the *loi namu*, or owners of land, are elders who hold the highest ritual office, running the initiation or "bush" schools, whose rites are associated with continued fertility of the land and people, and who have earned a reputation as skilled orators and advisors.

C.29. Togunu-Bickersteth. "Perception of Old Age Among the Yoruba." *Journal of Comparative Family Studies* 1 (1988), 113-121.

Based on a study of Yoruba elders in Nigeria, this study stresses the importance of cultural context in assessing beliefs about aging, measures of life satisfaction, and appropriate government policies toward the elderly.

C.30. Traore, Gaoussou. "Profile of the Elderly in Mali." *African Gerontology* 3 (1985), 11-23.

Traore describes the ritual authority of Mali elders, who preside over the family's material and spiritual life, and are responsible for guiding community life through the Supreme Council of Elders, and through fetishes which guard the community and facilitate communication with the deities.

C.31. Udvardy, Monica, and Maria Cattell. "Gender, Aging and Power in Sub-Saharan Africa: Challenges and Puzzles." *Journal of Cross-Cultural Gerontology* 7:4 (1992), 275-288.

The authors provide an overview of articles in this special journal issue that look at life course events and experiences of old age in seven different ethnic groups in the sub-Saharan region, in particular, the disparity between cultural expectations and the actual experience of aging, and the need to use both traditional resources and new strategies for survival.

Asia/Pacific

C.32. Caffrey, Rosalie A. "Family Care of the Elderly in Northeast Thailand: Changing Patterns." *Journal of Cross-Cultural Gerontology.* 7:2 (1992), 105-116.

Caffrey discusses the status of rural Thai elders in terms of their ability to use their traditional ritual status to assure continued family care in old age; their role in traditional Buddhist rituals in a kin-based rural economy helped maintain their status, but with the change to a cash-based economy, this traditional role is losing its value as reciprocity for social support from their families.

C.33. Chin, Soo-Young. "Korean Birthday Rituals." *Journal of Cross-Cultural Gerontology* 6 (1991), 145-152.

Based on a study of late life rituals among Korean and Korean-Americans, this study focuses upon the *hwangap*, a sixtieth birthday ritual, as celebrated in Seoul, Korea, and within the Korean-American community in San Francisco.

C.34. Chit-Daw, Khin Myo. "Add Life to Years the Buddhist Way." *Journal of Religion and Aging* 4:3-4 (1988), 39-67.

The author discusses Burmese Buddhist traditions reflecting respect for the aged and the extended family system, such as *ka-daw*, the custom of the young bowing down at the feet of elders, and *dana*, contributions of alms, food, places to sleep, medicine and other needed things, considered part of the path to *nibbana*.

C.35. Crews, Douglas E. "Cultural Lags in Social Perceptions of the Aged." *Generations* 17:2 (1993), 29-33.

Crews addresses a lag existing between cultural definitions of old age and biomedical improvements in the condition of many elders, in a study of older Samoans, he attributes this lag in part to differences among generations in support for traditional perceptions of *masua*, or old age; he suggests that older and younger generations help each other bridge the cultural gap for mutual benefit.

C.36. Jernigan, Homer L., and Margaret B. Jernigan. *Aging in Chinese Society: A Holistic Approach to the Experience of Aging in Taiwan and Singapore.* New York: Haworth Pastoral Press, 1992 [also published as a special issue of *Journal of Religious Gerontology* 8:3 (1992) 1-116].

This study, conducted by a team of researchers interested in pastoral counselling and community health, looks at the experience of aging among a selected group of Chinese elders; included are excerpts of personal narratives, and a discussion of the impact of social change and industrialization on traditional Chinese family relationships.

C.37. Lesco, Phillip A. "Aging Through Buddhist Eyes." *Journal of Religion and Aging* 5:3 (1989), 59-66.

This article examines Buddhist teachings on aging by presenting depictions of aging primarily from Tibetan Buddhist literature.

C.38. Luhmann, Frederick J. "Respect for Older Persons: A Confucian Perspective." *Journal of Religion and Aging* 3:3-4 (1987), 83-90.

Luhmann reviews the Confucian tradition of filial piety in Korea and describes the diminishing influence of Confucianism since the Japanese invasion of Korea in 1910, and following western influences in the wake of WWII; rapid social change has been accompanied by conflicting views on the status of, and traditional respect for, the elderly.

C.39. Newman, Jacqueline M., and Elaine Kris Ludman. "Chinese Elderly: Food Habits and Beliefs." *Journal of Nutrition for the Elderly* 4:2 (1984), 3-13.

The authors compared foodways of 180 Chinese adults from the People's Republic of China and 157 Chinese-Americans from New York City, noting the preservation of cultural food habits (over half the respondents were over 40); almost 60 percent of those queried considered certain special foods as appropriate for the elderly; implications for dieticians, nutritionists and others serving the Chinese are discusssed.

C.40. Norbeck, Edward. "Age-Grading in Japan." *American Anthropologist* 55 (1953), 372-383.

In addressing age-grading throughout the life cycle, the author notes certain traditions relating to the aged, such as observances held at the end of the sixtieth year, customary clothing in old age, and religious rituals performed by elders.

C.41. O'Leary, James S. "A New Look at Japan's Honorable Elders." *Journal of Aging Studies* 7:1 (1993),1-24.

O'Leary evaluates recent literature in social gerontology on the effects on the status of elder of the changing structure of the Japanese family; he addresses such issues as ambiguity in Japanese attitudes towards the elderly, reflected in the concepts of *taemae* (outwardly culturally acceptable attitudes) and *hone* (actual widely accepted attitudes, such as the view of elders as slow-witted and a burden).

C.42. Palmore, Erdman. *The Honorable Elders: A Cross-Cultural Analysis of Aging in Japan.* Durham, North Carolina: Duke University Press, 1975.

In this pioneering study of Japanese elderly, Erdman looks at how traditions regarding elders in Japan have countered patterns of neglect found in other modern industrialized nations: rituals of respect tend to be preserved, but the decision-making authority of elders is restricted largely to traditional matters (see **C.43**).

C.43. Palmore, Erdman B., and Daisaku Maeda. *The Honorable Elders Revisited– Otoshiyori Saiko: A Revised Cross-Cultural Analysis of Aging in Japan.* Durham, North Carolina: Duke University Press, 1985.

This is a reexamination of the status and social integration of the aged in Japan, and a review of of the attitudes of elders in modern Japanese society; the authors look at the extent to which traditional respect persists, and conclude that while the status of Japanese elders has declined somewhat, it is still higher than those of elders in other industrialized nations (see **C.42**).

C.44. Shiang, Julia. "'Heart' and Self in Old Age: A Chinese Model." In Merry I. White and Susan Pollack, eds. *The Cultural Transition: Human Experience and Social Transformation in the Third World and Japan.* Boston: Routledge & Kegan Paul, 1986, 211-239.

In a study of Chinese families living in the United States, focusing on elderly parents and their adult children, the meaning of family interaction is discussed within the context of the Chinese concept of "heart."

C.45. van Arsdale, Peter W. "Disintegration of the Ritual Support Network Among Aged Asmat Hunter-Gatherers of New Guinea." In Christine L. Fry, ed. *Dimensions: Aging, Culture, and Health.* New York: Praeger, 1981, 33-45.

The author points out the ways in which elderly hunter-gatherers have lost ritual authority as their community has been absorbed into Indonesia's social and political system, inviting comparisons to those living in industrialized countries.

C.46. Yap, P. M. "Aging in Underdeveloped Asian Countries." In Clark Tibbitts and Wilma Donahue, eds. *Social and Psychological Aspects of Aging.* New York: Columbia University Press, 1962, 442-453.

While providing a brief overview of aging throughout Asia, much of the article focuses on traditional Chinese beliefs and customs, and notes such institutions as the *Chai T'ang,* or vegetarian halls, residential places of worship offered primarily to Buddhist elders pursuing self-cultivation in late life, and where inhabitants keep to a vegetarian diet and celibate lifestyle, in return for food and lodging (see also **C.105**).

C.47. Yee, Barbara W. K. "Elders in Southeast Asian Refugee Families." *Generations* 17:3 (1992), 24-27.

Yee looks at the problems faced by elders within Southeast Asian Refugee families for whom immigration has mean changes in the timing and definition of life stages, and conflicts between traditional roles of elders modeled on Confucian notions of filial piety and their diminishing credibility in the U. S.

South Asia

C.48. Goswami, M. C., and Ch. Budhi Singh. "Labour Organization of the Thanga Fishermen." *Eastern Anthropologist* 27:1 (1974), 35-43.

The authors examine *phoom* , a form of group fishing practiced among the Thanga, a peasant community in Manipur, India, in which ritual authority is vested in the *ahan*, or elders, who conduct preparatory ceremonies, and recite *hoi laoba*, a musical rhythm to strengthen group members for the intense physical labor required for *phoom* fishing.

C.49. Pal, Roma K., and Greesh C. Sharma. "Gerontology–Viewpoint of Hindu Psychology." *Indian Psychological Review* 28:1 (1985), 36-40.

The authors describe the Hindu perspective on aging, in which ideally elders are given prominence in the social hierarchy, forgo social and economic activities for a life of spiritual devotion, and are respected as teachers of the young; they also note the mental health benefits of belief in reincarnation: death lacks the sting it has for western peoples, for life and death are seen as part of a continuum.

C.50. Tilak, Shrinivas. *Religion and Aging in the Indian Tradition.* Albany: State University of New York Press, 1989.

Tilak looks at aging as a cultural construct within the Vedic religion, Buddhism and Hinduism, as revealed in religious doctrine and traditional narratives, including myths, tales and legends from classical religious texts.

Middle East/Central Asia

C.51. Ansari, Ghaus. "Modernization and the Old Age People: A Cultural Dilemma." *Bulletin–International Committee on Urgent Anthropological and Ethnological Research (Vienna)* 24 (1982), 11-16.

Ansari, a Kuwaiti anthropologist, notes the impact of modernization (represented in the Arabian Gulf by oil exploration) on the traditional roles of elders as symbols of family identity and cultural reference points; he argues that such "infrastructural changes" may make traditional people more conscious of their "cultural super-structure" (customs and beliefs) enabling older people to retain their roles.

C.52. Cibulski, Ora, and Simon Bergman. "Mutuality of Learning Between the Old and the Young: A Case Study in Israel." *Ageing and Society* 1:2 (1981), 247-262.

In a teaching/learning program exploring areas of knowledge exchanged by elders and schoolchildren in Jewish European, Yemenite Tunisian and Christian Arab communities in Israel, elders were most effective in their teaching of family traditions, cultural history, and as models for personal behavior.

C.53. Gutmann, David. "Alternatives to Disengagement: The Old Men of the Highland Druze." In Jaber F. Gubrium, ed. *Time, Roles and the Self in Old Age.* New York: Human Sciences Press, 1976, 88-108.

Research on middle-aged and older men of the highland Druze sect, residing in northern Israel and Syria; the "passive mastery" the author claims as a universal trait of aging, is transformed into ritual authority within Druze religious life.

C.54. Peters, Issa. "The Attitude Toward the Elderly as Reflected in Egyptian and Lebanese Proverbs." *The Muslim World* 76:1 (1986), 80-85.

The author's analysis of two major collections reveals that the body of both Egyptian and Lebanese proverbs about the aging are divided between positive and negative messages; the author speculates that this may reflect economic realities: elders are viewed as honorable if they continue to function well in society, but once they suffer physical or mental losses, they are viewed as burdens.

C.55. Raphael, Terrie G. "Learning to be Good Old Jewish Israelis: A Case Study in an Israeli Senior Center." *Journal of Aging and Judaism* 3:1-2 (1988), 41-57.

Raphael describes the ways in which the celebration of religious holidays at a multipurpose senior center in a town in northern Israel are used to create meaning in the lives of elderly Jews, and notes how special events, such as a Purim celebration, transmit not only cultural values but also positive images of old age.

C.56. Smirnova, Ia S. "Roles and Statuses of Old People in the Abkhazian Family." *Soviet Anthropology and Archeology* 24:1 (1985), 77-100.

Smirnova describes the roles of Abkhazian elders, including hospitality (the duty of the oldest male family member), organizing family activities, educating family members, and preserving religious rituals and other customs; it is argued that the active roles and high status of Abkhazian elders play a part in their longevity.

Europe

C.57. Bennett, Gillian. "Heavenly Protection and Family Unity: The Concept of the Revenant Among Elderly Urban Women." *Folklore* 96:1 (1985), 87-97.

Study, based on fieldwork conducted in 1981, of supernatural experiences among older residents of a middle-class suburb of Manchester, England; a sample of older women respond to questions about encounters with the dead.

C.58. d'Epinay, Christian Lalive, et. al. "Popular Culture, Religion and Everyday Life." *Social Compass* 18:4 (1981), 405-424.

This study compares the role of religion in everyday life among people aged 65 and older in two settings: the semi-rural, agricultural and largely Catholic town of Valais (representing "traditional popular culture") and Geneva, a largely Protestant city (representing "industrial urban society").

C.59. Heikkinen, Riitta Liisa. "Patterns of Experienced Aging With a Finnish Cohort." *International Journal of Aging and Human Development* 36:4 (1992-1993), 269-277.

Based on a study of almost 300 80-year-old residents of the town of Jyvaskyla in central Finland, 20 of whose life stories were recorded, the author concludes that these elders share ways of perceiving themselves as members of the same culture and age-cohort, but did not feel old, embracing a cultural view of the state of old age as one of failing memory and health, as well as social isolation.

C.60. Jerrome, Dorothy. *Good Company: An Anthropological Study of Old People in Groups.* Edinburgh, Scotland: Edinburgh University Press, 1992.

This is a study of the culture of old-age organizations, based on participant observation conducted among the retired population of a community in Great

Britain; Jerrome discusses the role of clubs and associations for retired people, and notes the predominance of women in the club culture.

C.61. Tobriner, Alice. "Old Age in Tudor-Stuart Broadside Ballads." *Folklore* 102:2 (1991), 149-174.

The social attitudes of sixteenth and seventeenth century English commoners are revealed in broadside ballads, "living history" in song, expressing the full range of emotions, from derision to acceptance of old age and the elderly.

C.62. Vincent, John, and Zeljka Mudrovic. "Lifestyles and Perceptions of Elderly People and Old Age in Bosnia and Hercegovina." In Sara Arber and Maria Evandrou. *Ageing, Independence, and the Life Course.* London: Jessica Kingsley Publishers, in association with the British Society of Gerontology, 1993, 91-103.

Among the results of life history interviews with women and men over 65 in Bosnia and Hercegovina, in addition to lifestyle observations, were statements that the elderly do not constitute a meaningful social category in Bosnia, and that passage through the life course was viewed as a progressive loss of *snaga*–life force, power, or strength; these results were contrasted with literature reports on social views of aging in Britain.

The Americas

C.63. Amoss, Pamela T. "Cultural Centrality and Prestige for the Elderly: The Coast Salish Case." In Christine L. Fry, ed. *Dimensions: Aging, Culture, and Health.* New York: Praeger, 1981.

Amoss discusses the erosion of ritual authority among Coast Salish elders in the Pacific Northwest–related to loss of traditional economic and social bases following European contact–which has been partially offset by a cultural revival during the 1960s.

C.64. Boatman, John F. *My Elders Taught Me: Aspects of Western Great Lakes American Indian Philosophy.* Lanham, Maryland: University Press of America, 1992.

The author relates stories, legends and other teachings collected from Ojibway elders who live on the islands between the Upper and Lower Peninsulas of Michigan, and from Menominee elders in Wisconsin.

C.65. Cole, Thomas R., and Terri Premo. "The Pilgrimage of Joel Andrews: Aging in the Autobiography of a Yankee Farmer." *International Journal of Aging And Human Development* 24:2 (1986-1987), 79-85.

Cole interprets the autobiographical writings of Joel Andrews of Bethany, Connecticut (1777-1865), in particular his musing on aging and health within the context of his culture, historical conditions and religious beliefs.

C.66. Davis, Donna Lee. "Belligerent Legends: Bickering and Feuding Among Outport Octogenarians." *Ageing and Society* 5-4 (1985), 431-448.

Davis observes that octogenarians in a Newfoundland fishing village are accorded a high status, giving them broader behavioral license, of which they may take advantage when engaging in disputes over past or present wrongs; a case study is presented of a feud between an elderly woman and man, in which community mores and traditional sex roles temper potentially disruptive behavior.

C.67. Doi, Mary L. "Ethnicity, Ritual and Aging Among Second Generation Japanese-Americans." Dissertation, University of California, San Francisco, 1990.

This thesis, based on fieldwork conducted in a Japanese-American community in San Francisco, focuses upon the *kanreki*–a traditional Japanese sixtieth birthday ritual–as adapted to an American setting.

C.68. Doi, Mary L. "A Transformation of Ritual: The Nisei 60th Birthday." *Journal of Cross-Cultural Gerontology* 6 (1991), 153-163.

A condensation of the author's doctoral dissertation, this essay describes rituals marking the sixtieth birthday of first-generation Japanese immigrants, as celebrated in the Japanese-American community in San Francisco.

C.69. Egbert-Edwards, Margie; Austin J. Lyman, and E. Daniel Edwards. "Living in Harmony With Navajo Indian Traditional Religious Beliefs: Honesty, Acceptance, and Understanding." *Journal of Religious Gerontology* 8:2 (1991), 41-61.

The authors recorded the religious beliefs and traditions of Navajo elders who participated in a poetry group as residents of a regional care center in Utah; among subjects addressed by the elders were the importance of medicine men, the loss of religious traditions among the young, and the difficulty of speaking of Navajo beliefs with non-Navajos; samples of poetry are presented.

C.70. Fowler, Loretta. "Colonial Context and Age Group Relations Among Plains Indians." *Journal of Cross-Cultural Gerontology* 5:2 (1990), 149-168.

Fowler compares the effects of federal policy on the status of Arapaho elders in Wyoming and Oklahoma, noting differences in the degree to which elders retained their influence in tribal affairs, linked in good measure to whether they held on to or lost their authority in matters of religious ritual.

C.71. Fowler, Loretta. "'Look at My Hair, It Is Gray': Age Grading, Ritual Authority, and Political Change Among the Northern Arapahos and Gros Ventres." *Smithsonian Contributions to Anthropology* 30 (1982), 73-93.

Research conducted in the 1960s and '70s show that differing ways in which the Gros Ventre of Montana and the Northern Arapahos of Wyoming reacted to political reorganization are reflected in varying ritual authority among the aging.

C.72. Johnson, Colleen Leahy. *Growing Up and Growing Old in Italian-American Families.* New Brunswick, New Jersey: Rutgers University Press, 1985.

As part of an overview of family life among Italian-Americans, Johnson addresses the traditional beliefs and practices of elders, within the context of family organization, rituals and intergenerational relationships.

C.73. Kotchek, Lydia. "'Of Course We Respect Our Old People, But...': Aging Among Samoan Migrants." *California Sociologist* 3:2 (1980), 178-212.

This is a discussion of the adaptation of older Samoan migrants who struggle to mediate between two forms of accommodation, *Fa' a Samoa* (Samoan customs of kinship and religion, oriented to the homeland) and "pan-Samoa" (unifying the Samoan-American community around ethnicity alone in order to make social gains), and its reflection in intergenerational relations with family households.

C.74. Lorenz, Carol Ann, and Christopher Vecsey. "Hopi Ritual Clowns and Values in the Hopi Life Span." In Lucille Nahemow, Kathleen A. McCluskey-Fawcett, and Paul E. McGhee, eds. *Humor and Aging*. Orlando, Florida: Academic Press, 1986, 199-220.

The authors describe the role of Hopi ritual clowns, or *chukuwimkiya*, as conservative forces, ridiculing those who do not conform to the model of an ideal Hopi person; healthy, productive elders are considered to be "ideal" Hopi, without regard to their age, but unhealthy old Hopis are not, and therefore become targets for the antics of the *chukuwimkiya*.

C.75. Lozier, John, and Ronald Althouse. "Retirement to the Porch in Appalachia." *International Journal of Aging and Human Development* 6:1 (1975), 7-15.

Transcending the stereotype of the aged mountaineer sitting endlessly on the front porch, the authors look at the porch, not as a site of aimless pastimes of old age, but rather as a nexus of social interaction for elders in rural Appalachia.

C.76. Marino, Cesare. "Honor the Elders: Symbolic Associations with Old Age in Traditional Eastern Cherokee Culture." *Journal of Cherokee Studies* 13 (1988), 3-18.

Marino explores such aspects of Cherokee culture as beliefs related to fire, corn and certain animals that reflect a positive valuation of aging; he also briefly addresses the problem of exposure to "white negative stereotypes" about aging and the impact of recent efforts at cultural revival on the role and status of Indian elders.

C.77. Maxwell, Robert J., and Eleanor Krassen Maxwell. "Cooperative Independence Among the Tlingit Elderly." *Human Organization* 42:2 (1983), 178-180.

Based on fieldwork conducted in southeast Alaska, this study describes the ways in which Tlingit elders share resources in ways that preserve traditional beliefs regarding reciprocal exchange, balancing cooperation and independence.

C.78. McCarl, Robert. "'You've Come a Long Way–And Now This is Your Retirement': An Analysis of Performance in Fire Fighting Culture." *Journal of American Folklore* 97:386 (1984), 393-422.

McCarl analyzes the retirement dinner at a suburban fire station outside the District of Columbia, in which friends recalls his exploits, and the retiree is collectively thanked by the group with a ritual meal followed by playful verbal abuse.

C.79. Moore, Michael Dane. "Resolving Conflict and Establishing Community: The Annual 'Old People's Day." In Michael Owen Jones, Michael Dane Moore, and Richard Christopher Snyder, eds. *Inside Organizations: Understanding the Human Dimension*. Newbury Park, CA: Sage, 261-269.

On the fourth Sunday of every June, in a hill community in northwestern Arkansas, former residents return home, and the entire community gathers for "Old People's Day," combining elements of church revivals and family reunions.

C.80. Nye, William. "Amazing Grace: Religion and Identity Among Elderly Black Individuals."*International Journal of Aging and Human Development* 36:2 (1992-93), 103-113.

Drawing from a sample of forty-three life stories recorded from elderly African-Americans living in southwestern Virginia, this study presents the perspective of Continuity Theory on the role of religion in the normal aging process; features excerpts of the personal narratives of four women and two men.

C.81. Rosenthal, Carolyn J., and Victor W. Marshall. "Generational Transmission of Family Ritual." *American Behavioral Scientist* 31:6 (1988), 669-684. In Lillian E. Troll, ed. "Rituals and Reunions." Special issue of *American Behavioral Scientist* 31:6 (1988), 669-684.

Looking at the transmission of rituals across three generations among North American families, this article focuses upon ceremonial occasions (e.g., holidays and birthdays) in terms of change and continuity over historical and family time.

C.82. Sánchez-Ayéndez, Melba. "Elderly Puerto Ricans in the United States." In Steven R. Applewhite, ed. *Hispanic Elderly in Transition: Theory, Research, Policy and Practice.* Westport, Connecticut: Greenwood Press, 1988, 17-31.

Among the topics addressed in this overview are family relations, sex roles—in which the daily activities of older Puerto Rican women are confined to the domestic realm, reflected in the term *ama de casa* ("governess of the house"), whereas for older men, their realm, reflecting the concept of *machismo*, is public, as reflected by their daily visits to the *bodega* (grocery store), a social center for elderly men—and the notion of *respecto*, referring both to age deference as well as recognition of the inherent value of elders (*dignidad*).

C.83. Schemper, Thomas Lee. "Aging, Religion and Mastery Style Among the Quechua of Pocona, Bolivia." Doctoral Dissertation, Northwestern University, 1987.

Schemper explores the psychology of religious experience among Quechuan elders, who worship both the Catholic patron saint Tata Consuelo and the Incan earth mother goddess Pachamam, describes folk beliefs, and addresses age differences in approaches to religious ritual.

C.84. Tijerina-Jim, Aleticia. "Three Native American Women Speak About the Significance of Ceremony." In Nancy D. Davis, Ellen Cole, and Esther D. Rothblum, eds. *Faces of Women and Aging.* New York: Haworth Press, 1993, 33-39.

Three Native women elders address such issues as the significance of ceremony in Hopi life, the Navajo view of death, the need to accept Native healers alongside physicians, and the role of ceremony in helping to accept the process of aging.

C.85. Weigle, Marta, and Thomoas R. Lyons. "Brothers and Neighbors: The Celebration of Community in Penitente Villages." In Victor Turner, ed. *Celebration: Studies in Festivity.* Washington, D. C.: Smithsonian Institution Press, 1982, 231-251.

This study of the Brothers of Our Father Jesus, also know as Penitentes, a group of mostly Hispanic men who live in rural communities of northern New Mexico, features the testimony of elder members who recall Penitente rituals.

C.86. Werner, D. "Gerontocracy Among the Mekranoti of Central Brazil." *Anthropological Quarterly* 54:1 (1981), 15-27.

In this study of the importance of social ties, personality and knowledge in accounting for leadership roles of the elderly, it is argued that knowledge of ceremonies—more than simply general knowledge—is a primary indicator of the influence wielded by Mekranoti elders, male and female.

GENDER

C.87. Allen, Paula Gunn. *Grandmothers of the Light: A Medicine Woman's Sourcebook.* Boston: Beacon Press, 1991.

Allen mines the mythology of Native American Indians for traditions relating to wise women, shamans and female spirit beings, among them the accounts of such elders as the Mayan goddess Xmucané ("Grandmother of the Sun") and Ts'its'nako ("Grandmother Spider"), a major deity of the Keres of New Mexico.

C.87.a. Allen, Paula Gunn. *The Sacred Hoop: Recovering the Feminine in American Indian Traditions.* Boston: Beacon Press, 1986.

As part of her treatment of the centrality of women in Native American Indian culture, Allen, a Laguna Pueblo/Souix, addresses the lives and roles of grandmothers, as well as the grandmother (and grandfather) figure in myths.

C.88. Arsenault, Sr. Lorraine. "The 'Jewish Mother' in a Nursing Home." In *The Older Woman.* West Hartford, Connecticut: University of Connecticut School of Social Work, 1980, 91-100.

The cultural stereotype of the "Jewish Mother," sometimes seen as negative in regard to parent-child relationships, is viewed here as a bundle of traits, several of which may facilitate positive adaptation to a nursing home setting.

C.89. Cattell, Maria G. "Nowadays It Isn't Easy to Advise the Young: Grandmothers and Granddaughters Among the Abaluyia Of Kenya." *Journal of Cross-Cultural Gerontology* 9:2 (1994), 157-178.

Based on field research conducted from 1982-1992 among Abaluyia people aged 50 and over, the author notes changes in grandmother-granddaughter relations over a decade; subjective aspects discussed include the role of grandmothers as teachers, mentors and sources of cultural knowledge.

C.90. Cattell, Maria G. "Praise the Lord and Say No to Men: Older Women Empowering Themselves in Samia, Kenya." *Journal of Cross-Cultural Gerontology* 7:4 1992), 307-330.

Older Samia women in rural western Kenya, asserting their personal autonomy and command of the domestic sphere following a spouse's death, use the traditional format of the funeral speech to publicly announce their resistance.

C.91. Dickerson-Putnam, Jeanette. "Old Women at the Top: An Exploration of Age Stratification Among Bena Women." *Journal of Cross-Cultural Gerontology* 9:2 (1994), 193-205.

This study of changes in the status of Bena women in the Eastern Highlands Province of Papua New Guinea notes that while older women continue to achieve respect, and have greater decision-making power in the domestic realm than in pre-contact society, their ritual authority over the education and behavior of young women has eroded.

C.92. Ellickson, Jean. "Never the Twain Shall Meet: Aging Men and Women in Bangladesh." *Journal of Cross-Cultural Gerontology* 3 (1988), 53-70.

Older Bangladeshi men benefit from lifelong preferential treatment, retaining familial and ritual authority; older women's ritual roles and authority are limited; "possession" by a *djin* (spirit) may be a disguised form of protest.

C.93. Johnson, Colleen Leahy. "A Cultural Analysis of the Grandmother." *Research on Aging* 5:4 (1983), 547-567.

As part of a larger project on American grandmothers' roles in the divorces of their children, parents and grandparents were asked to describe the role of grandmothers within the context of their cultural background; parents reported incongruity between an ideal of the grandmother as an old, traditional, domestic, nurturing woman, and their own self-image; grandparents reported a lack of acceptable traditional grandparenting role models in their own families.

C.94. Kenyan, Susan M. "Gender and Alliance in Central Sudan." *Journal of Cross-Cultural Gerontology* 9:2 (1994), 141-155.

Kenyan looks at changes in the mother-in-law/daughter-in-law relationship in the Sudan; in old age the former traditionally is referred to by the latter as "grandmother"; in urban settings, age-related relationships may be affected by new alliances, such as those based on economics, education, religion and ritual.

C.95. Kerns, Virginia, and Judith K. Brown, eds. *In Her Prime: New Views of Middle-Aged Women.* 2nd ed. Urbana: University of Illinois Press, 1992.

A central theme in this collection of articles about middle-aged women in different cultures throughout the world is that some women in traditional societies may actually experience greater opportunities and social recognition, including sexual freedom and ritual authority, as they age.

C.96. Kerns, Virginia. *Women and the Ancestors: Black Carib Kinship and Ritual.* Urbana: University of Ilinois Press, 1983.

"This is a book about how mature Black Carib women manage the ceremonial component of their culture so as to preserve much of its unique flavor in spite of massive out-migration by males and younger women."

C.97. Lebra, Takie Sugiyama. "The Dilemma and Strategies of Aging Among Contemporary Japanese Women." *Ethnology* 18:4 (1979), 337-353.

This article explores the ways in which middle-aged and older Japanese women seek mutual support and autonomy through social networks such as the *rojinkai* (old people's association), where members share friendship and knowledge, including traditional skills (e.g., weaving, calligraphy, flower arranging, etc.).

C.98. Lopata, Helena Znaniecki. "Role Changes in Widowhood: A World Perspective." In Cowgill, Donald O., and Lowell D. Holmes, eds. *Aging and Modernization.* New York: Appleton-Century-Crofts, 1972, 275-303.

Lopata examines widowhood in different societies; "focusing upon social roles and their interrelations rather than upon socio-psychological reactions to the death of a spouse," she addresses role shifts in the lives of widows.

C.99. Mantecon, Valerie H. "Where Are the Archetypes?: Searching for Symbols of Women's Midlife Passage." In Nancy D. Davis, Ellen Cole, and Esther D. Rothblum, eds. *Faces of Women and Aging.* New York: Haworth Press, 1993, 77-88.

A feminist "re-vision" of mythological portrayals of older women is offered, focusing on five archetypes representing the figure of the "Grandmother" or "Crone," that may be used to guide women through menopause into elderhood.

C.100. Niethammer, Carolyn. *Daughters of the Earth: The Lives and Legends of American Indian Women.* New York: Collier Books, 1977.

Drawing from interviews, early ethnographies and other sources, Niethammer has compiled descriptions of Native life, along with excerpts of personal experience and other traditional narratives, organized in sections on subjects such as childbirth, education, courtship, economic roles, crafts, healing, and religion; of particular relevance here is a chapter, "Completing the Cycle," on old women and death.

C.101. Paules, Greta Foff. *Dishing It Out: Power and Resistance Among Waitresses in a New Jersey Restaurant.* Philadelphia: Temple University Press, 1991.

Based on participant-observation and interviews conducted with women working at a family-style restaurant, ranging from teenagers to women in their 60s–some of whom had been waiting at tables for decades–Paules presents their strategies for challenging the restaurant's "symbolisms of servitude" and "countering the metaphors of waitress as servant"; especially telling are the narratives of the older "veteran" waitresses.

C.102. Poole, Fitz John Porter. "Transforming 'Natural Woman': Female Ritual Leaders and Gender Ideology Among Bimin-Kuskusmin." In Sherry B. Ortner and Harriet Whitehead, eds. *Sexual Meanings: The Cultural Construction of Gender and Sexuality.* Cambridge: Cambridge University Press, 1981.

This study focuses upon the androgynous role of the *waneng aiyem ser,* ("sacred woman") among the members of a Papua New Guinea community, a position held exclusively by post-menopausal women, ritual specialists who may perform rites of passage or healing invoking or counteracting male or female forces.

C.103. Rosenthal, Carolyn J. "Kinkeeping in the Familial Division of Labor." *Journal of Marriage and the Family* 47:4 (1985), 965-974.

Rosenthal discusses the nature of kinkeeping (efforts to keep family members in touch with each other) as a primarily female activity, passed down from older to younger family members, and emphasizing greater extended family interaction, particularly with regard to family rituals.

C.104. Rosenthal, Carolyn J., and Victor W. Marshall. "Generational Transmission of Family Ritual." *American Behavioral Scientist* 31-6 (1988), 669-684.

The authors report the results of the Generational Relations and Succession Project conducted in Hamilton, Ontario, Canada, among adults 40 and older, who were asked if family rituals conducted in their childhood had been passed on to their own children and in turn to the following generation; rituals described included holidays, birthdays, Sundays, family outings and vacations.

C.105. Sankar, Andrea. "The Conquest of Solitude: Singlehood and Old Age in Traditional Chinese Society." In Christine L. Fry, ed. *Dimensions: Aging, Culture, and Health.* New York: Praeger, 1981, 65-83.

This article describes "sisterhoods" of spinsters in China and Hong Kong who banded together in social networks or joined such religious sects as the Taoist *jaai tohng,* or "Great Way," organized around vegetarian residential halls that offer security, social contact and a compatible lifestyle for older celibate women (see also **C.46**).

C.106. Sered, Susan Starr. "The Liberation of Widowhood." *Journal of Cross-Cultural Gerontology* 2:2 (1987), 139-150.

The author describes the ways in which widowhood has had a liberating effect on a group of elderly Kurdish Jewish women in Jerusalem by providing opportunities to come out of their homes and participate in public religious rituals traditionally the exclusive domain of men.

C.107. Sered, Susan Starr. *Women as Ritual Experts: The Religious Lives of Elderly Jewish Women in Jerusalem.* New York: Oxford University Press, 1992.

In the mid 1980s, the author conducted fieldwork among elderly Jewish women who frequent a Senior Citizens Day Center in Jerusalem's Kurdish neighborhood, which serves as a focus for their religious lives, and provides them with a measure of autonomy from a traditional patriarchal culture.

C.108. Sered, Susan Starr. "Women, Religion and Modernization: Tradition and Transformation Among Elderly Jews in Israel." *American Anthropologist 92 (1990), 306-318.*

This article focuses on the effects of modernization on the religious choices of Oriental women in Israel within the context of a traditional male religion, and comparing their experiences with other women in male-dominated cultures.

C.109. Shomaker, Dianna. "Health Care, Cultural Expectations and Frail Elderly Navajo Grandmothers." *Journal of Cross-Cultural Gerontology* 5:1 (1990), 21-34.

Shomaker observes that the Navajo grandmother still retains significant power, including ritual authority, regardless of her health status; she notes the effects of cultural expectations of intergenerational reciprocity, including care of the elderly, taught by grandmothers to their grandchildren from infancy on.

C.110. Shenk, Dena. "Honor Thy Mother: Aging Women in the Jewish Tradition." In L. Eugene Thomas and Susan A. Eisenhandler, eds. *Aging and the Religious Dimension*. Westport, Connecticut: Auburn House, 1994, 115-129.

Explores the ways in which Jewish religious ethnicity provides a source of identity and continuity for elderly Jewish women in the United States, compensating in part for generational tensions, and historical and cultural changes.

C.111. Stephen, Lynn. *Zapotec Women.* Austin: University of Texas Press, 1991.

While not about aging per se, this study of the effects of commercial weaving on the lives of Zapotec women in several communities in and around Oaxaca, Mexico, does offer short life stories of two elders, and at several points addresses the relationship between age and authority in the course of examining the paradox of women holding positions of importance in ritual, weaving and local politics, while being subordinated in other areas of community life.

C.112. Udvardy, Monica. "Fertility of the Post-Fertile: Concepts of Gender, Aging and Reproductive Health Among the Giriama of Kenya." *Journal of Cross-Cultural Gerontology* 7:4 (1992), 289-306.

Udvardy describes the role of postmenopausal women among the Giriama of Kenya, who are considered to be the guardians of the ritual objects of a female society responsible for ensuring reproductive health.

Witchcraft

C.113. Barstow, Anne Llewellyn. *Witchcraze: A New History of the European Witch Hunts.* San Francisco: Pandora/Harper Collins, 1994.

Barstow reviews the history of 16th and 17th century witchcraft trials as one of violence against women; much attention is paid to the hostility directed towards older women, the majority of victims, who were paradoxically both sought after and reviled as folk healers and figures of wisdom and authority.

C.114. Bever, Edward. "Old Age and Witchcraft in Early Modern Europe." In Peter N. Stearns, ed. *Old Age in Preindustrial Society.* New York: Holmes & Meier, 1982, 150-190.

The author speculates on socio-political motives for the European witch trials, in which the elderly, most often women, were singled out for accusation, ostensibly for being "evil," but more likely for their role as vocal defenders of village custom and authority (in which they had a stake) against local magistrates.

C.115. Foner, Nancy. "The Old Person as Witch." In *Ages in Conflict: A Cross-Cultural Perspective on Inequality Between Old and Young.* New York: Columbia University Press, 1984, 157-191.

Foner presents case studies of witchcraft accusations in traditional societies, linking them to tensions generated by unequal distribution of powers by young and old; she divides these cases by gender, devoting a section each to instances of the "powerful old man" and the "dominating old woman" as targets of witchcraft accusations.

C.116. Horsley, Richard A. "Who Were the Witches? The Social Role of the Accused in the European Witch Trials." *Journal of Interdisciplinary History* 9:4 (1979), 689-715.

The author notes differing concepts of witchcraft during the 16th and 17th centuries between elites and peasants, as well as confusion over distinctions made by peasants among witches, sorcerers and "wise women"; what remains clear is that most of those accused during the witch trials were older women whose behavior was seen as disruptive to the patriarchal system.

C.117. Hufford, David J. "A New Approach to the 'Old Hag': The Nightmare Tradition Reexamined." In Wayland D. Hand, ed. *American Folk Medicine: A Symposium.* Berkeley: University of California Press, 1976.

While not about aging per se, this essay about Newfoundland beliefs regarding nocturnal visitations relates them to traditional notions attributing nightmares to witchcraft, embodied in the symbolic imagery of the elderly female "hag."

C.118. Sebald, Hans. "Justice by Magic: Witchcraft as Social Control Among Franconian Peasants." *Deviant Behavior* 7:3 (1986), 269-287.

Sebald addresses the belief, held among the peasants of Franconia, in central Germany, in witchcraft as an alternative to the official legal system, in particular, as a means for the poor, the destitute and the aged to exact retribution against those who mistreated them; at present this belief persists only among elders.

DEATH AND DYING

[NOTE: A chapter of *Anthropology of Aging: A Partially Annotated Bibliography* (see **B.1**) is devoted to this subject; the following list is largely complementary.]

C.119. Bryer, K. B. "The Amish Way of Death: A Study of Family Support Systems." *American Psychologist* 34:3 (1979), 255-261.

> Bryer emphasizes the importance of religious belief and community support during the period of dying and bereavement; he notes the high visibility of death (most Amish deaths take place in the home) and culturally sanctioned rituals of mourning that provide the Amish with ways of coping not available to many in modern societies.

C.120. Counts, David R., ed. *Coping With the Final Tragedy: Cultural Variation in Dying and Grieving.* Amityville, New York: Baywood, 1991.

> This work features essays, mostly by anthropologists, on customs and beliefs related to death and dying among the Huron of Ontario, the Maori of New Zealand, the Huicholes of western Mexico, the Burhanis (Sufi Muslim sect), traditional Russians, the Cree of Quebec, Tanacross Athabaskans of Alaska, the community of Kapiingmarang, Micronesia, the Lusi-Kalaili of Melanesia, rural Bretons in France, and Native Canadians in urban hospitals.

C.121. Counts, Dorothy Ayers, and David R. Counts, eds. *Aging and Its Transformations: Moving Toward Death in Pacific Societies* [*Association for Social Anthropology in Oceania (ASAO) Monograph No. 10*]. Lanham, Maryland: University Press of America, 1985.

> This series of articles looks at death in preindustrialized Pacific societies from the perspectives of culture, ideology and cosmology, and exploring such issues as gender roles, the negotiation of status, and involvement in community life.

C.122. Counts, Dorothy Ayers, and David R. Counts. "'I'm Not Dead Yet!' Aging and Death: Process and Experience in Kaliai." In Larry A. Platt and V. Richard Persico, Jr. *Grief in Cross-Cultural Perspective: A Casebook.* New York: Garland, 1992, 307-343.

> Among the Kaliai of Papua New Guinea, ritual authority and generational roles, more than chronological age or physical condition, determine the status of elders, and the categories of "old age" and "death" are not fixed.

C.123. Dickenson, Donna, and Malcolm Johnson, eds. *Death, Dying and Bereavement.* Newbury Park, California: Sage Publications, 1993.

> Published in association with the Open University of London, England, this is a broad, interdisciplinary work for those people providing support to the dying or bereaved; the first part addresses contemporary issues related to loss and dying, including ethnographic descriptions of beliefs, customs and rituals related to mortality among members of different societies and ethnic groups.

C.124. Harper, Bernice Catherine. "Some Snapshots of Death and Dying Among Ethnic Minorities." In Manuel, Ron C., ed. *Minority Aging: Sociological and Social Psychological Issues.* Westport, Connecticut: Greenwood Press, 1982, 131-134.

> In this brief overview, the author describes rituals and superstitions relating to death and dying among Native-Americans, African-Americans, Chinese-Americans and Puerto Ricans in the U. S., and conflicts that may arise because of the disparity between their customs and beliefs and those of the dominant culture.

C.125. Irish, Donald P., Kathleen F. Lundquist and Vivian Jenkins Nelson, eds. *Ethnic Variations in Dying, Death and Grief: Universality in Diversity.* Washington, D. C: Taylor & Francis, 1993.

This is a collection of articles, including sections on "Cross-Cultural and Personal Perspectives" and "Dying, Death and Grief Among Selected Ethnic Communities" (African-American, Mexican-American, Hmong, Native American, and the faiths of Judaism, Buddhism, Islam, and the Quakers and Unitarians).

C.126. Kagawa-Singer, Marjorie. "Diverse Cultural Beliefs and Practices About Death and Dying in the Elderly." *Gerontology and Geriatrics Education* 15:1 (1994), 101-116.

This article surveys cultural influences on the meaning of death for elders, and the ways in which cultural traditions provide predictabilty, stability and consolation; American rituals are contrasted with those of other cultures; health care professionals are advised to respect family and individual orientations to death and dying.

C.127. Kalish, Richard. "Contacting the Dead: Does Group Identification Matter?" In Robert Kastenbaum, ed. *Between Life and Death.* New York, Springer, 1979, 61-72.

Kalish examines the reports of over 400 adult residents of Los Angeles about contact with people they knew to be dead, through dreams, visitations, and the experience of feeling the presence of the departed; significant ethnic differences were found, both in type and likelihood of communication.

C.128. Kalish, Richard A. *Death, Grief, and Caring Relationships.* 2nd ed. Monterey, California: Brooks/Cole Publishing Co, 1985.

This is a work that addresses both personal concerns about death and dying, grief and caring relationships as well as academic and professional issues; among the subjects addressed are attitudes and beliefs about death, forms of expression of grief, and social roles and rituals related to mourning and bereavement.

C.129. Kalish, Richard A., and David K. Reynolds. *Death and Ethnicity: A Psychocultural Study.* Farmington, New York: Baywood, 1981.

Based on interviews with African-, Japanese-, Mexican- and Anglo-Americans, observation of settings such as funeral homes, coroners' facilities, and terminal wards, and analysis of ethnic newspapers, literature and other sources, Kalish discusses the effects of ethnicity on attitudes toward death and bereavement.

C.130. Kubler-Ross, Elizabeth, ed. *Death: The Final Stage of Life.* Englewood Cliffs, New Jersey: Prentice Hall, 1975.

Among the views on death of ministers, rabbis, doctors, nurses sociologists, and those near death are perspectives from various cultures, including papers on Alaskan Indians, Jews, Hindus and Buddhists.

C.131. Myerhoff, Barbara. "A Symbol Perfected in Death: Continuity and Ritual in the Life and Death of an Elderly Jew." In Barbara Myerhoff and Andrei Simic, eds. *Life's Career–Aging: Cultural Variations on Growing Old.* Beverly Hills, California: Sage Publications, 1978, 163-206.

Myerhoff describes the death of Jacob Kovitz in the midst of a celebration of his 95th birthday at a senior center in Venice, California, social epicenter of a beachfront community of Eastern European Jewish immigrants; she discusses the power of ritual in providing cultural, biological and spiritual continuity.

C.132. Rael, Roselyn, and Alvin O. Korte. "*El Ciclo de la Vida y Muerte*: An Analysis of Death and Dying in a Selected Hispanic Enclave." In Steven R. Applewhite, ed. *Hispanic Elderly in Transition: Theory, Research, Policy and Practice*. Westport, Connecticut: Greenwood Press, 1988, 189-202.

The authors describe customs and beliefs related to death and dying among Mexican-Americans in villages in northern New Mexico.

C.133. Rosenblatt, P., P. R. Walsh, and D. Jackson. *Grief and Mourning in Cross-Cultural Perspective*. New Haven, Connecticut: HRAF Press, 1976.

This work is a survey of customs related to grief and mourning drawn from the Human Relations Area File at Yale University.

C.134. Shine, Marsha, and Jean A. Steitz. "The Teachings of Judaism on Death: A Celebration of Life." *Journal of Aging and Judaism* 2:3 (1988), 191-195.

The authors describe Jewish beliefs and rituals surrounding death and mourning, and how they provide a framework within which a dying person may accept death with respect and serenity, and the bereaved may cope with loss through a culturally sanctioned set of burial and mourning rituals.

C.135. Sidell, Moyra. "Death, Dying and Bereavement." In John Bond, Peter Coleman and Sheila Peace. *Ageing in Society: An Introduction to Social Gerontology*. 2nd ed. London: Sage Publications Ltd., 1993, 151-179.

This chapter of a gerontology textbook widely used in the United Kingdom explores social and individual attitudes toward aging and dying, including the influences of different cultural and religious beliefs.

C.136. Smith, S. R. "Death, Dying and the Elderly in Seventeenth-Century England." In Spicker, Stuart F., Kathleen M. Woodward and David Van Tassel, eds. *Aging and the Elderly: Humanistic Perspectives in Gerontology*. Atlantic Highlands, New Jersey: Humanities Press, 1978, 205-219.

In this essay on the influence of religious beliefs on attitudes toward death in 17th century England, Smith examines the Christian notion of original sin, in which death is view as the end of suffering, and discusses astrological and folk beliefs related to death and dying, as well as deathbed rituals involving family members.

C.137. Stevens, Phillips, Jr. "Play and Liminality in Rites of Passage: From Elder to Ancestor in West Africa." *Play and Culture* 4:3 (1991), 237-257.

The author describes funeral ceremonies for elders among the Bachama of Nigeria, which provide the setting not only for rites of grieving and ceremonies for the transition of the soul of the departed to ancestral status, but also rituals of celebration, through the antics of clan joking partners.

C.138. White, Ken. "Living and Dying the Navajo Way." *Generations* 11:3 (1987), 44-47.

White profiles the life of Howard Taliwood, an 86-year-old Navajo man born in Piñon, Arizona, and discusses the illness and death of his wife, for whom Navajo funeral rites were conducted, including a burial ritual and an all-night ceremony in which her soul was sent to live with the Great Spirit.

C.139. Woodcock, Robert D. "Rituals Related to Death, Dying and Serious Infirmity: A Nursing Bibliography." In Thomas O. Blank, ed. *Topics in Gerontology*. Westport, Connecticut: Greenwood Press, 1993, 98-109.

Among the selections in this annotated bibliography are entries describing family interactions, topical literature (e.g., essays on rituals related to reminiscence and reconciliation, spirituality, loneliness and isolation), and transcultural essays.

C.140. Woodcock, Robert D. "Rituals Related to Death, Dying and Serious Infirmity: An Anthropological Bibliography." In Thomas O. Blank, ed. *Topics in Gerontology*. Westport, Connecticut: Greenwood Press, 1993, 98-109.

This annotated bibliography includes selections such as literature on death rituals conducted by members of different cultures; traditional healing rituals, involving residential and health care institutions, and theoretical literature (e.g., the relationship of aging and ritual, and the integrative functions of ritual).

D

Narratives

One of the difficulties of presenting a list of works on narrative is making choices about narrative categories. As students of storytelling are well aware, traditional narratives often defy the clear boundaries implied by such distinctions as "history" and "myth," "fact" and "fiction," and even personal and collective experience. As an example, an elder ostensibly recounting events in her life may submerge her own personal story into that of her community history and traditional narratives, making it more emblematic than distinct, and raising questions as to whether the narratives reflect the tellers' actual experiences. It is not the purpose of this section to address sticky issues of "truth," but rather to direct readers to works that present and examine narratives about and by aging and the aged, both imagined and experiential, as found in myths, tales, oral histories, anecdotes and other personal narratives.

For the convenience of researchers, I have divided this section along broad cultural lines. Within each group, publications cited may include:

1. Studies of storytelling by, and stories about, elders (focusing on tales and anecdotes rather than life histories).

2. Collections of short narratives (tales and anecdotes) by and about elders.

3) Studies of oral history/life story narratives.

4) Individual oral histories and collections of life stories. (This includes narratives ranging from transcriptions of oral history interviews to composed autobiographies to biographies incorporating oral and written material.)

NOTE: Narratives with major themes relating to other categories in this bibliography are cited under those respective categories. Thus, several life stories of traditional musicians, singers, craftspeople and folk artists are cited in Chapter E ("Traditional Arts"); similarly, there are narratives of shamans, herbalists and other healers in Chapter G ("Health and Healing").

GENERAL/CROSS-CULTURAL

D.1. Braid, Donald. "Personal Narrative and Experiential Meaning." *Journal of American Folklore* 109:431 (1996), 5-30.

> Braid examines the ways in which the experience of listening to narratives, including "following" one's own narrated memories, can generate meaning making; he demonstrates this by analyzing two short narratives of Beth, an 86-year-old resident of a retirement home in Seattle.

D.2. Chinen, Allan B. "Fairy Tales and Psychological Development in Late Life: A Cross-Cultural Hermeneutic Study." *Gerontologist* 27:3 (1987), 340-346.

> This authority on elder tales describes developmental issues raised by folk tales with older protagonists.

D.3. Chinen, Allan B. "Fairy Tales and the Spiritual Dimensions of Aging." In L. Eugene Thomas and Susan A. Eisenhandler, eds. *Aging and the Religious Dimension.* Westport, Connecticut: Auburn House, 1994.

> This study looks at a body of tales that, while set within a religious framework, address universal issues of transcendence and restore the spiritual role of elders in society.

D.4. Chinen, Allan B. "Fairy Tales and Transpersonal Development in Later Life." *Journal of Transpersonal Psychology* 17:2 (1985), 99-122.

> An earlier version of what was to become the author's book, *In the Ever After* (see **D.5**), it discusses "elder tales" within the framework of transpersonal psychology.

D.5. Chinen, Allan B. *In the Ever After: Fairy Tales and the Second Half of Life.* Wilmette, Illinois: Chiron Publications, 1989.

> A psychiatrist and Jungian analyst, Chinen addresses archetypal themes of psychosocial development and spirituality in a set of tales from around the world, retold by the author, which feature older protagonists.

D.6. Chinen, Allan B. *Once Upon a Midlife: Classic Stories and Mythic Tales to Illuminate the Middle Years.* New York: G. P. Putnam's Sons, 1992.

> Here Chinen has assembled and analyzed world tales that address such midlife themes as loss of ideals, lasting in careers and marriage, sex role differences, coping with crises, and facing aging and mortality.

D.7. Chinen, Allan B. "The Return of Wonder in Old Age." *Generations* 15:2 (1991), 45-48.

> In a brief overview, Chinen argues that "elder tales" convey a message that, despite losses, there is still great potential for psychological and spiritual renewal.

D.8. Degh, Linda. *Narratives in Society: A Performer-Centered Study of Narration.* Bloomington: Indiana University Press, 1995 [originally published as Folklore Fellows Communications No. 255].

> This is a collection of Degh's writings on folk narrative written over a thirty-year period; of particular interest for present purposes are "Two Old World Narrators on the Telephone," describing the telephone narrating sessions in the mid 1960s of two

immigrant women in their 70s and 80s living in the Hungarian ethnic colony of Gary, Indiana (see also **D.263**), and "The Legend Conduit" documenting the stories of older community storytellers in Kakasd, County Tolna, Hungary recorded in 1986 (see also **D.76.a**).

D.9. Ives, Edward D., Roger E. Mitchell, Jane C. Beck, Barry Lee Pearson, Jeff Todd Titon, Juha Yrjänä Pentikäinen, and Yvonne Hipakka Lockwood. "Symposium on the Life Story." In Alan Jabbour and James Hardin, eds. *Folklife Annual 86*. Washington, D.C.: Library of Congress, 1987, 154-173.

This collection of commentaries on the life story of Arvid Asplund (see **D.262**) touches on the differences between biography and autobiography; the life story as both historical document and fiction; the value of written versus oral life history; and the ethnic dimension of personal narrative.

D.10. Kaufman, Sharon R. *The Ageless Self: Sources of Meaning in Late Life*. Madison: University of Wisconsin Press, 1986.

Based on life history interviews with 60 white, middle-class women and men in California between 70 and 97, Kaufman examines the ways in which personal experience narratives reflect strategies for constructing a sense of continuity and meaning, including the creation of narrative themes.

D.11. Kirshenblatt-Gimblett, Barbara. "Authoring Lives." *Journal of Folklore Research* 26:2 (1989), 123-149.

While not exclusively devoted to the subject of aging, this essay offers folkloristic perspectives on life history and personal narratives, the importance of reminiscence as a developmental task, and indigenous forms of life review, in particular, the variety of ways that older people recall earlier experiences.

D.12. Myerhoff, Barbara. "Life History Among the Elderly: Performance, Visibility, and Re-Membering." In Jay Ruby, ed. *A Crack in the Mirror: Reflexive Perspectives in Anthropology*. Philadelphia: University of Pennsylvania Press, 1982, 99-117.

Myerhoff looks at strategies of self-presentation in the life stories of elderly Jews who are members of a secular Jewish senior center in Venice, California (see **D.13**, **D.307**).

D.13. Myerhoff, Barbara [Marc Kaminsky, ed.]. *Remembered Lives: The Work of Ritual, Storytelling and Growing Older*. Ann Arbor: University of Michigan Press, 1995.

This is a collection of most of the important essays of one of the leading figures in the ethnographic analysis of personal narratives and aging; it features an in-depth introduction by Kaminsky, Co-Director of the Myerhoff Center at the YIVO Institute for Jewish Research.

D.14. Myerhoff, Barbara. "Telling One's Story." *The Center Magazine* 13 (1980), 22-40.

This essay features a roundtable discussion on storytelling and aging with Myerhoff and a host of scholars, including folklorist Roger Abrahams, poet Jerome Rothenberg, and others.

D.15. Nussbaum, Jon F., and Lorraine M. Bettini. "Shared Stories of the Grandparent-Grandchild Relationship." *International Journal of Aging And Human Development* 39:1 (1994), 67-80.

> Audiotaped interactions between college students and their grandparents were examined for stories shared across generations that revealed something about the nature of their relationship.

D.16. Prell, Riv-Ellen. "The Double Frame of Life History in the Work of Barbara Myerhoff." In Personal Narratives Group, ed. *Interpreting Women's Lives: Feminist Theory and Personal Narratives.* Bloomington: Indiana University Press, 1989, 241-258.

> Prell examines the ways in which Myerhoff "transformed the subject-object relationship of the traditional life-history interview into a subject-subject relationship"; of particular interest is her discussion of Myerhoff's life history of Schmuel Goldman, one of the subjects of her study of elderly Jews at a senior center in Southern California (see **D.307** and **D.13**).

D.17. Wood, Juliette. "The Old Man of the Mountain in Medieval Folklore."*Folklore* 99:1 (1988), 78-87.

> The story of "The Old Man of the Mountain," legendary leader of a medieval sect called the Assassins, is compared with similar stories featuring a diabolic old man, found in Islamic, Jewish and Christian folklore.

D.18. Yocum, Margaret R. "Woman to Woman: Fieldwork and the Private Sphere." In Rosan A. Jordan and Susan J. Kalcik, eds. *Women's Folklore, Women's Culture.* Philadelphia: University of Pennsylvania Press, 1985, 45-53.

> In a discussion of gender differences in storytelling, the author recalls and compares the personal experience and family narratives of her paternal grandmother and maternal grandfather.

AFRICA

D.18.a. Barnes, Terri, and Everjoyce Win. *To Live a Better Life: An Oral History of Women in the City of Harare, 1930-70.* Harare, Zimbabwe: Baobab Books/Academic Books, 1992.

> This book presents transcripts of interviews conducted in the late 1980s by Barnes in English and Shona (through translator Win) of about 35 "ordinary" women (and four men), most of them in their 60s to 80s, who talk about life in the townships of Harare, Zimbabwe since the 1920s.

D.19. Bozzoli, Belinda (with Mmantho Nkotse). *Women of Phokeng: Consciousness, Life Strategy and Migrancy in South Africa, 1900-1983.* Portsmouth, New Hampshire: Heinemann, 1991.

> Bozzoli recounts, with generous interview excerpts, the lives of 22 black South African women, all born before 1915, from one small town in the Western Transvaal; included is a chapter on their experiences as "Grandmothers and Pensioners, 1980-1983."

D.20. Davison, Jean ("with the women of Mutira"). *Voices from Mutira: Lives of Rural Gikuyu Women*. Boulder, Colorado: Lynne Rienner Publishers, 1989.

Davison presents the recorded life stories of seven Gikuyu women from the Kirinyaga District in Kenya, five older and two younger, who reflect on the historical and cultural changes that have affected their lives.

D.21. Keegan, Tim. *Facing the Storm: Portraits of Black Lives in Rural South Africa*. London: Zed Books, 1988.

Based on oral history interviews conducted in 1984, Keegan presents life stories (in third person with interview excerpts) of four sharecroppers: Ndae Makume, born in 1903 in Viljoensdrif in South Africa's high veld region; Lucar Ngandela, born in 1898, from the township of Ledig; Barney Ngakane, born in 1902 in a post-Boer War refugee camp; and Petras Pooe, born on a farm in Orange Free State in 1902.

D.22. Kerner, Donna O. "Chaptering the Narrative: The Material of Memory in Kilimanjaro, Tanzania." In Marea C. Teski and Jacob J. Climo, eds. *The Labyrinth of Memory: Ethnographic Journeys*. Westport, Connecticut: Bergin & Garvey, 1995, 113-127.

Kerner describes the method of imparting traditional wisdom among the Chagga, who inhabit Mount Kilimanjaro in northeastern Tanzania; *mregho*, or inscribed sticks embodying historical memory and cultural knowledge, are carved by respected elders, or *meku*, who instruct initiates with the mregho and the recitation of traditional texts.

D.23. Laurentin, Anne. "Nzakara Women (Central African Republic)." In Denise Paulme, ed. [trans. from the French by H. M. Wright]. *Women of Tropical Africa*. Berkeley: University of California, 1963 [1960], 121-178.

Laurentin presents five life histories from among nearly 300 recorded from older and younger Nzakara women; one is the story of Natélégé (1860-1908), as recalled by older women with whom Laurentin spoke, another is Kafi, at age 72 "one of the very old women in the village," born into slavery in 1886, before the arrival of the Whites.

D.24. Mathabane, Mark. *African Women: Three Generations*. New York: HarperCollins, 1994.

Mathabane, the author of *Kaffir Boy*, a memoir of growing up in South Africa under apartheid, recorded the life stories of his grandmother, mother and sister; they are presented in alternating sections, chapters in the family saga in which each member details their experience as women in African traditional culture and as subjects of apartheid.

D.25. Mbilinyi, Marjorie. "'I'd Have Been a Man': Politics and the Labor Process in Producing Personal Narratives." In Personal Narratives Group, ed. *Interpreting Women's Lives: Feminist Theory and Personal Narratives*. Bloomington: Indiana University Press, 1989, 204-227.

Mbilinyi examines the construction of a life story from the author's interviews with Rebeka Kalindile, born in 1914 in colonial Tanganyika, now Tanzania; the author describes the nature and intensity of her working relationship with Kalindile, the ways in which she challenged Kalindile's memories and narratives to uncover the influences of class, gender, race and nationality.

D.26. Mirza, Sarah, and Margaret Strobel. *Three Swahili Women: Life Histories from Mombasa, Kenya.* Bloomington: Indiana University Press, 1989.

The authors present the recorded personal narratives of Bi Kaje, born in 1890, Mishi wa Abdala, born between 1900 and 1905, and Mwana Kutani, born in 1919, who talk about their lives in the midst of tremendous social changes in the Muslim Swahili community of Mombasa.

D.27. Romero, Patricia, ed. *Life Histories of African Women.* London: The Ashfield Press, 1988.

This is a collection of seven life histories of women, ranging in age from their 40s to their 70s, from traditional communities throughout sub-Saharan Africa, and ranging from autobiographical narratives to biographies with interview excerpts (with the exception of one historical reconstruction of the life of an Asante woman who, at age 60, was chief negotiator for the Anglo-Asante Treaty in 1831).

D.28. Shostak, Marjorie. *Nisa—The Life and Words of a !Kung Woman.* New York: Vintage, 1981.

Shostak recorded the life story of Nisa, a member of the !Kung tribe of southern Africa's Kalahari desert, an "elder" in her fifties, who describes her struggle to survive in the Bush through childhood, marriage, bearing children (none of whom survived), divorce, remarriage, widowhood and growing old.

D.29. Shostak, Marjorie. "'What the Wind Won't Take Away': The Genesis of *Nisa—The Life and Words of a !Kung Woman*" In Personal Narratives Group, ed. *Interpreting Women's Lives: Feminist Theory and Personal Narratives.* Bloomington: Indiana University Press, 1989, 228-240.

Shostak looks back on the nature of her relationship with a !Kung woman who became the subject of a published oral history (see **D.28**); she examines the differences in their backgrounds (Shostak was 24 and "a product of the American 1960s" and Nisa was 50 when they first met in 1969), the interview process, and the presentation of the narrative text incorporating three "voices"–Nisa's story, ethnographic analysis, and her own personal reflections.

D.30. Smith, Mary F. *Baba of Caro: A Woman of the Muslim Hausa.* New Haven: Yale University Press, 1981 [1964].

Smith presents the life story of Baba (1877-1951), a Hausa woman of Zaria Province, Northern Nigeria, recorded in handwritten field notes in Hausa "as far as possible *verbatim*" during conversations with her conducted during a six-week period from November 1949 to January 1950.

D.31. Strobel, Margaret. "Doing Oral History as an Outsider." *Frontiers* 2:2 (1977), 68-72.

Strobel describes the challenges of interviewing African women as a European, citing examples from her fieldwork in Mombasa, Kenya; she presents excerpts of her interviews with 80-year-old Bi Kaje (see **D.33**).

D.32. Strobel, Margaret. "The Life History of Misha wa Abdala, a Swahili Kungwi from Mobasa, Kenya." *The African Review* 11:1 (1984), 68-80.

Strobel presents a brief life history of a Muslim Swahili elder, based on field interviews conducted in Kenya in the 1970s (see **D.26**).

D.33. Strobel, Margaret. *Muslim Women in Mombasa, 1890-1975.* New Haven: Yale University Press, 1979.

Based on interviews conducted in Mombasa, Kenya, Strobel presents the life stories of several Swahili women who were born as early as 1890, and who describe life in Swahili society, including aspects of women's lives, and solidarity between slaves and freeborn women during the period up to 1907 when Mombasa was still a slave society.

D.34. Urdang, Stephanie. *And Still They Dance: Women, War and the Struggle for Change in Mozambique.* New York: Monthly Review Press, 1989.

Urdang describes the lives and activities of women since Mozambique won its independence, using traditional dance both literally and figuratively as a symbol of efforts to bridge the cultural past and the political present; as an example, she describes her encounter with Mama Leia, a women in her sixties, secretary of the women's organization in a newly-established communal village, who danced a greeting to her when she arrived for a visit, and danced her appreciation and farewell to her "granddaughter" when she left; later in the text she details Mama Leia's struggle to instill a cooperative spirit among village members.

D.35. van Onselen, Charles. "The Reconstruction of a Rural Life from Oral Testimony: Critical Notes on the Methodology Employed in the Study of a Black South African Sharecropper." *Journal of Peasant Studies* 20:3 (1993), 494-514.

Van Onselen discusses the challenges of interpreting the memories of 90-year-old Kas Maine, the patriarch of an immigrant BaSotho family of sharecroppers in South Africa's Transvaal region, including his recollections of cooperative sharecropping with poor white farmers (see **D.36**).

D.36. van Onselen, Charles. *The Seed Is Mine: The Life of Kas Maine, A South African Sharecropper 1894-1985.* New York: Hill and Wang, 1996.

While this is a biography, it is fashioned from years of interviews with Maine, his neighbors, employers, friends and family, as well as archival research; interview excerpts appear throughout the text (see **D.25**).

ASIA/PACIFIC

D.37. Barton, Roy F. *Autobiographies of Three Pagans in the Philippines.* New Hyde Park, New York: University Books, 1963 [1938].

Despite the unfortunate title (a product of its time), Barton's work is a good early example of oral history in the service of ethnography; he presents the life stories of three members of the Ifugao community, recorded in the late 1930s: Ngídulu, in his late 40s; Bugan Nak Manghe, in her mid-60s, and Kumíha, a 58 year old man.

D.38. Basgös, Ilhan. "Turkish *Hikaye*-Telling Tradition in Azerbaijan, Iran." *Journal of American Folklore* 83:330 (1970), 391-405.

Basgös, in his discussion of this folk narrative form resembling the *cante-fable*, describes the *ashiks*, or wandering minstrels, including the most renowned, Ashik Haj-Ali, in his 70s, who often addresses the subject of old age, and notes the role of elders, along with the well-known and well-to-do, in controlling the choice of *hikaye* in the coffeehouses where the *ashik* performs.

D.39. Coburn, Broughton. *Nepali Aama: Life Lessons of a Himalayan Woman.* New York: Anchor/Doubleday, 1995 [1982].

This book consists of recorded narratives of the life and teachings of Vishnu Maya Gurung, an elderly widow of the Gurung tribe of Central Nepal, known to fellow villagers as Aama, with whom Coburn came to live as a teacher with the Peace Corps in the 1970s; accompanying the text are photographs by Coburn.

D.40. Keesing, Roger M., ed. *'Elota's Story: The Life and Times of a Solomon Island Big Man.* Fort Worth, Texas: Holt, Rinehart and Winston, 1983 [1978].

Keesing recorded the life history of Kwaio elder 'Elota (1908-1973) in the 1960s, when the latter was in his late 50s and "growing old together" with his second wife, Tege; the narrative is presented in third person with interview excerpts; 'Elota philosophizes "in his latter years" to younger kin and fellow leaders about the lessons he has learned from experience.

D.41. Keesing, Roger M. "Kwaio Women Speak: The Micropolitics of Autobiography in a Solomon Island Society." *American Anthropologist* 87:1 (1988), 27-39.

Keesing presents an overview and analysis of the content and context of oral history interviews he conducted with 15 Kwaio women, from Malaita, Solomon Islands, ranging in age from a woman about 30 years old to a woman in her 80s.

D.42. Portnoy, Enid J. "Obasute Legend: Caregiving Insights in Literature." *Educational Gerontology* 16:6 (1990), 561-575.

The relevance of the theme of abandonment of the elderly Japanese folklore, as reflected in the legend of Obasute (in which an elderly parent is forced to leave a farming village to die on a nearby mountain, and a son is reluctant to let the parent go) is tested in interviews with Japanese and American college students.

D.43. Pruitt, Ida. *A Daughter of Han: The Autobiography of a Chinese Working Woman.* Stanford, California: Stanford University Press, 1967 [1945].

This is the life story of Ning Lao T'ai-t'ai, born in 1867, who grew up in the town of P'englai by the Yellow Sea in Shantung province, recorded by Pruitt when her subject was in her late sixties; Lao T'ai-t'ai describes Chinese customs, challenges of the Chinese family system, and her adjustment to personal and historical change.

D.44. Uysal, Ahmet Edip. "The Making of a Turkish Folk Narrator: Behçet Mahir of Erzurum." *International Folklore Review* 3 (1983), 26-35.

This is a brief description of the life, repertoire and performance style of Mahir, born in 1909 in Erzurum in eastern Turkey, and considered one of the country's greatest living storytellers.

AUSTRALIA/NEW ZEALAND

D.45. _____*In Those Days: A Study of Older Women in Wellington.* Wellington, New Zealand: Society for Research on Women in New Zealand, 1982.

This study of older women in New Zealand is based on the recorded life stories of 51 women aged 70 to 92.

D.46. Arden, Harvey. *Dreamkeepers: A Spirit-Journey Into Aboriginal Australia.* New York: HarperCollins, 1994.

Arden records meetings with a variety of Aboriginal women and men; an impressionistic travel narrative rather than an ethnography, it does contain generous excerpts of conversations with a number of elders, including spiritual leaders, artists, storytellers and healers.

D.47. Bell, Diane. *Daughters of the Dreaming.* 2nd. ed. Minneapolis: University of Minnesota Press, 1993 [1983].

Bell offers a personal account of her life among Aboriginal women in the late 1970s and mid-1980s; in addition to descriptions of the roles of older women, she presents excerpts of interviews, including the narratives of Nampijina–mother of 6, grandmother of 16 and great-grandmother of 7–in her late 50s, and Nungarrayi, in her 60s.

D.48. Busch, Glenn. *You Are My Darling Zita.* Philadelphia: Temple University Press, 1991.

Busch presents, with accompanying photographs, the narratives of six New Zealanders, all born around 1900, who reflect upon personal and historical events–two world wars, economic depression, immigration and emigration, economic and social change–and the experience and meaning of old age.

D.49. Cohen, Patsy, and Margaret Somerville. *Ingelba and the Five Black Matriarchs.* Sydney: Allen & Unwin, 1990.

This book was inspired by the Somerville's encounter with Cohen, a member of the Armidale Aboriginal community in Australia's Northern Territory, who sought to reconstruct the story of the community of Ingelba (80 km south of Armidale) through conversations with local elders (transcripts of which are presented in the text) who recall five 19th century matriarchs of Ingelba: "Grannies" Widders, Wright, Morris, Maria and Mackenzie.

D.50. Darian-Smith, Kate. "Remembrance, Romance, and Nation: Memories of Wartime Austrialia." In Leydesdorff, Selma, Luisa Passerini and Paul Thompson, eds. *Gender and Memory.* Oxford: Oxford University Press, 1996, 151-164.

Darian-Smith anaylizes interviews she conducted in the late 1980s with older women about their lives as civilians living in Melbourne during the Second World War, focusing on those who came of age during this period, and who recall the experience of personal transition at a time when traditional gender and generational roles were in flux.

D.51. Haviland, John B. "'That Was the Last Time I Seen Them, and No More': Voices Through Time in Australian Aboriginal Autobiography." *American Ethnologist* 18:2 (1991), 331-361.

Haviland presents and analyzes an "autobiographical fragment" transcribed from interviews with Roger Hart, one of the first to arrive, in the 1920s, at the Hopevale Community, a Lutheran Aboriginal mission near Cooktown, Queensland, on Australia's Cape York peninsula, recorded as part of a proposed book about his life and the demise of the Barrow Point tribe, of which he believed himself to be the last member.

D.52. Somerville, Margaret, with Marie Dundas, May Mead, Janet Robinson, and Maureen Sulter. *The Sun Dancin': People and Place in Coonabarabran.* Canberra: Aboriginal Studies Press, 1994.

> Four Aboriginal women in their 50s and 60s, from the land of Burrabeedee in New South Wales, Australia, tell the stories of their lives and those of the generations that preceded them, to ethnographer Somerville, who documents their interaction, as well as her own musings, weaving personal narratives with historical and cultural observations.

D.53. Stirling, Amiria, and Anne Salmond. *Amiria: The Life Story of a Maori Woman, Amiria Manutahi Stirling as Told to Anne Salmond.* Wellington, New Zealand: A. H. and A. W. Reed, 1976.

> This is the life story of a Maori woman born at the turn of the century as tape-recorded, transcribed and edited by Salmond.

D.54. Stirling, Eruera, and Anne Salmond. *Eruera: The Teachings of a Maori Elder, Eruera Stirling as Told to Anne Salmond.* Wellington, New Zealand: Oxford University Press, 1980.

> Salmond presents, from transcribed taped-recorded interviews, the oral biography of Stirling, an elder of the Whanau-a-Apanui tribe in Auckland, New Zealand, inspired by his desire to pass on traditional knowledge to a younger generation.

BRITISH ISLES/IRELAND

D.55. Andrews, Molly. *Lifetimes of Commitment: Aging, Politics, Psychology.* Cambridge: Cambridge University Press, 1991.

> Andrews presents excerpts of oral history interviews of 15 elder British socialist activists, each of whom have devoted at least 50 years of their lives to the struggle for social change, and discusses the importance of social identity for explaining the psychological makeup of these elderly lifetime activists.

D.56. Bennett, Gillian. "'Now All You Buggers With Clogs On': A Longnor Life." *Talking Folklore* 8 (1990), 3-12.

> Bennett presents an excerpt of her introduction to a work-in-progress based on oral history interviews with Arthur Mellor of Longnor, Staffordshire, England (1911-1989), who shared his memories of village life; she describes the nature and challenges of recording oral testimony.

D.57. Bennett, Gillian. "Tales My Mother Told Me: The Relevance of Oral History." In Theresa Buckland and Juliette Wood, eds. *Aspects of British Calendar Customs.* Sheffield, England: Sheffield Academic Press, 1993, 95-103.

> The author reviews his mother's recollections of childhood in Coreley, a village of scattered farms in south Shropshire, England, in the period "between the wars"; her account is dominated by two themes: the farming calendar and the church year.

D.58. Blythe, Ronald. *The View in Winter: Reflections on Old Age.* London: Allen Lane, 1979.

> Blythe presents a collection of narratives representing a cross-section of rural English elders who both discuss the remembered past and reflect upon the aging process.

D.59. Crook, Rosemary. "'Tidy Women': Women in the Rhondda Between the Wars." *Oral History* 10:2 (1982), 40-47.

Crook presents and analyzes excerpts of interviews with older women who recall life in a mining community in South Wales between the two world wars, who describe their daily lives, and the social network and moral values that held their community together in hard times.

D.60. Dhuibhne, Eilís Ní. "'The Old Woman as Hare': Structure and Meaning in an Irish Legend." *Folklore* 104 (1993), 77-85.

This essay describes an Irish form of the widespread legend of "The Witch That Was Hurt," in which an old woman transforms herself into a hare for the purpose of stealing milk or butter; among several common motifs is the depiction of intergenerational conflict.

D.61. Evans, George Ewart. *Ask the Fellows Who Cut the Hay*. 2nd. ed. London: Faber, 1965 [1956].

Evans, one of the pioneers of British oral history, recorded the recollections of older residents of the village of Blaxhall in East Suffolk, among the last to practice or recall hand-tool farming methods and domestic crafts.

D.62. Evans, George Ewart. *The Days That We Have Seen*. London: Faber, 1975.

A follow up to his oral history of East Suffolk (see **D.61**), he taps the memories of older Suffolk residents about country life prior to 1914; includes extensive recollection about fishing.

D.63. Evans, George Ewart. *Where Beards Wag All: The Relevance of Oral Tradition*. 2nd ed. London: Faber, 1977 (1970) [published in the U. S. As *Tools of Their Trades: An Oral History of Men at Work, c. 1900* (New York: Taplinger, 1970)].

Evans tapped the memories of the old women and men born in the village of East Anglia, between 1880 and 1895, to offer living history of the traditions of the British countryside at the turn of the century; chapters of the book are divided into sections on craftspeople, agriculture, village life, and migrant workers.

D.64. Featherstone, Simon. "Jack Hill's Horse: Narrative Form and Oral History." *Oral History Journal* 19:2 (1991), 59-62.

Featherstone reports on a study of the storytelling aspects of oral history, with reference to the narratives of Jack Hill, a retired miner from Ilkeston, Derbyshire, England, and examines the "ways which literary and historical analysis might find common ground."

D.65. Gmelch, Sharon. *Nan: The Life of an Irish Travelling Woman*. New York: W. W. Norton, 1986.

Gmelch, an anthropologist who has studied Ireland's indigenous gypsies or "tinkers," presents, with brief commentary, the oral history of Nan Donohoe, born in 1919, the daughter of an itinerant chimney sweep, who describes her harsh but eventful life among the Travelling People.

D.66. Hemmings, Susan. *A Wealth of Experience: The Lives of Older Women.* London: Pandora Press, 1985.

The oral histories of 18 British women, ranging in age from 40 to 80, transcend differences in age, culture and class, to reveal memories of personal experiences that reflect common roots in the culture of women in a patriarchal society.

D.67. Humphrey, Robin. "Social Participation and Older People: The Life Stories of Older Women in a Durham Ex-mining Town." In Peter Kaim-Caudle, Jane Keithley, and Audrey Mullender, eds. *Aspects of Ageing.* London: Whiting and Birch, 1993, 148-160.

Humphrey discusses the life story method of studying the social lives of older women in a former mining town in England, drawing from a sample of ten women aged 60-75, and ranging from socially involved to socially isolated.

D.68. John, Angela V. "Scratching the Surface: Women, Work and Coalmining History in England and Wales." *Oral History* 10:2 (1982), 13-27.

John reviews, with short excerpts, the results of interviews with 26 English and Welsh former "pit women"–most of them elders (10 born before 1900, and only three born after 1923)–who monitored, sorted and transported coal at the mine surface, and who recall work and family lives, as well as entertainment.

D.69. Jones, Rosamund. "Voices of Kentmere: A Lakeland Hill Farm Community." *Oral History Journal* 15:1 (1987), 35-41.

Jones summarizes, with interview excerpts, the memories of residents of the Lake District, in Cumbria, England (the oldest born in 1894, the youngest in 1932) about life in Cumbria from the 1890s to World War II.

D.70. Kightly, Charles. *Country Voices: Life and Lore in Farm and Village.* London: Thames and Hudson, 1984.

Kightly presents the personal narratives of people from seven different rural areas of England, all born around the turn of the century.

D.71. MacColl, Ewan, and Peggy Seeger. *Shellback Reminiscences of Ben Bright, Mariner.* London: History Workshop, n.d.

MacColl and Seeger present the narratives and songs of Bright, recalling his life as a seafarer, recorded over three visits in 1972.

D.72. MacColl, Ewan, and Peggy Seeger. *Till Doomsday in the Afternoon: The Folklore of a Family of Scots Travellers, the Stewarts of Blairgowrie.* Cambridge: Cambridge University Press, 1988.

This work is based on tape-recorded conversations with four generations of members of the Stewart family, conducted over a 20-year period.

D.72.a. MacDougall, Ian. *"Hard Work, Ye Ken": Midlothian Women Farm Workers.* Edinburgh: Canongate Academic, 1993.

MacDougall presents transcripts of oral history interviews with four rural women from the Midlothian District of southern Scotland, born between 1895 and 1923, in a text approximating the dialect and phrases characteristic of the region.

D.72.b. O'Neill, Gilda. *Pull No More Bines: An Oral History of East London Women Hop Pickers*. London: The Women's Press, 1990.

O'Neill, a hop picker herself as a girl, presents excerpts of interviews with women born between the turn of the century and the early 1950s (7 of the 10 women with whom O'Neill conducted extensive interviews were born between 1909 and 1926), and discusses the nature and role of memory and oral history.

D.73. Roper, Michael. "Fathers and Lovers: Images of the 'Older Man' in British Managers' Career Narratives." *Life Stories/Récits de vie* 4 (1988), 49-57.

In a study of the construction of managerial culture in British industry, Roper discusses the interweaving of managerial and mental structures in the personal narratives of middle/senior managers aged 55 to 65, focusing on depiction of the older manager.

D.74. Smith, Anne. *Women Remember: An Oral History*. London: Routledge, 1989.

A diverse group of 12 British women in their 80s recall the dramatic changes in lifestyles and values since their coming of age as members of the "unemancipated generation" born prior to the first World War.

D.74.a. Thistlethwaite, June. *Cumbrian Women Remember: Lake District Life in the Early 1900s*. Cumbria, England: Ellenbank Press, 1995.

Thistlethwaite presents transcripts of oral history interviews conducted with 16 women born in Cumbria between 1899 and 1922, who recall life in this rural district in northwestern England.

D.75. Thompson, Paul, Catherine Itzin and Michele Abenstern. *I Don't Feel Old: Understanding the Experience of Later Life*. Oxford: Oxford Univeristy Press, 1990.

This book features interviews with English women and men ranging in age from their 60s to their 80s, whose personal accounts reveal historical, cultural and generational differences in the experience of age, including the role of past memories in one's sense of identity in late life, and contrasts between the recalled traditions of the period of one's childhood and those of the present; also included are the remarks of children and grandchildren of elders on their perceptions of age, identity, traditions, and relationships.

EUROPE-MAINLAND

D.76. Cattani, Maurizio. "Social Life-History as Ritualized Exchange." In Bertaux, Daniel, ed. *Biography and Society: The Life History Approach in the Social Sciences*. Beverly Hills, California: Sage Publications, 1981, 212-222.

Cattani discusses his interviews with Aunt Suzanne, fomerly a milliner from the Meyenne, France, who has been married for 50 years to a Parisian watchmaker; the exchange between the two was mediated by remembered songs from Aunt Suzanne's youth, which she recited in a garden that served as a "ritual site" for the performance of her life story.

D.76.a. Degh, Linda. "The Legend Conduit." In Simon J. Bronner, ed. *Creativity and Tradition in Folklore: New Directions.* Logan: Utah State University Press, 1992, 105-126.

Degh describes a conversation that took place at the home of Mátyás Szentes, that served as a context for the exchange of legendary narratives with his wife Mári and three guests, all of them in their 60s and 70s (see also **D.8**).

D.76.b. Dolci, Danilo. *Sicilian Lives.* New York: Pantheon Books, 1981.

Dolci, who first arrived in the early 1950s in the village of Trappeto, in western Sicily as a peace worker, organizer and educator, presents excerpts of his coversations, written down over a period of several years, with residents ranging from children to elders in their 60s and 70s.

D.77. d'Epinay, Christian Lalive, and Jean Kellerhals. "The Old Speak Out: The Significance of Life Histories in a Study of Social Integration and Isolation of Old People." *Life Stories / Recits de vie* 1 (1985), 29-40.

The personal narratives of 150 residents of Geneva and the Valais region, Switzerland, aged 80 and older, were analyzed, using an approach in which these life stories are seen as revealing how culture is internalized in order to make meaning of everyday life and help one adjust to major life changes.

D.78. Inowlocki, Lena. "Grandmothers, Mothers and Daughters: Intergenerational Transmission in Three Jewish Families." In Daniel Bertaux and Paul Thompson, eds. *Between Generations: Family Models, Myths, and Memories [International Yearbook of Oral History and Life Stories, Vol. II].* Oxford: Oxford University Press, 1993, 139-153.

Inowlocki examines the ways in which the meaning of the past and traditionality are redefined in communication across generations in families in three Jewish communities in the Netherlands, addresssing such issues as negotiating changing views of traditionality and the difficulty of talking about the Nazi persecution.

D.79. Malysheva, Marina, and Daniel Bertaux. "The Social Experiences of a Countrywoman in Soviet Russia." In Leydesdorff, Selma, Luisa Passerini and Paul Thompson, eds. *Gender and Memory.* Oxford: Oxford University Press, 1996, 31-43.

The authors present and analyze the testimony of Maria Zolotareva, born in 1924 in a rural Russian village, whose narrative reflects the experience of many peasants whose lives, for better or worse, were transformed by the collectivization of agriculture in the 1930s, in a Soviet society that declared gender equality, but fell far short of its full achievement.

D.79.a. Milich, Zorka. *A Stranger's Supper: An Oral History of Centenarian Women in Montenegro.* New York: Twayne Publishers, 1995.

Milich, a descendant of the Montenegrins and fluent speaker of their Serbian language, presents the oral histories of 10 women over 100 years old, who recall life in the remote Balkan region they call *Crna Gora,* or Black Mountain.

D.80. Mintz, Jerome R. *The Anarchists of Casas Viejas.* Chicago: University of Chicago Press, 1982.

Anthropologist Mintz reconstructs the circumstances and events surrounding an anarchist uprising in the Spanish village of Casas Viejas in 1933, relying primarily on oral histories of eye witnesses and participants, recorded in the course of field research in 1965-66 and 1969-70; the text features excerpts of interview transcripts.

D.81. Passerini, Luisa. "Women's Personal Narratives: Myths, Experiences and Emotions." In Personal Narratives Group, ed. *Interpreting Women's Lives: Feminist Theory and Personal Narratives.* Bloomington: Indiana University Press, 1989, 189-203.

Oral testimonies from older working-class women of Turin, Italy, reveal the symbolic importance of images of rebelliousness in their personal narratives; cited is a traditional song whose imagery has been reinterpreted politically by two women who were long-time factory workers and former subjects of fascism.

D.82. Pentikäinen, Juha. *Oral Repertoire and World View: An Anthropological Study of Marina Takalo's Life History.* Helsinki: Academia Scientiarum Fennica, 1978. [Folklore Fellows Communications No. 219]

Based on extensive interviews conducted in 1962, Pentikäinen presents the life history of Takalo (1890-1970), a Karelian emigrant who moved from Russia to Finland in 1922, and discusses her vast knowledge of Karelian culture, and her world view as reflected in her repertoire of Karelian runes and folk tales.

D.83. Perks, Robert. "By Train to Samarkand: A View of Oral History in the Soviet Union." *Oral History Journal* 19:1 (1991), 64-67.

Perks took part in an expedition of the Oral History Centre of the Moscow State Institute of History and Archives in 1990, as part of an exchange with the British Library National Sound Archive, to interview Tatar elders who recalled Stalin's deportations from their homeland in Crimea to Uzbekistan; they recalled the transportatons, as well as the sense of loss of a displaced culture.

D.84. Shrover, Marilou. "Memory and Identity of Dutch Caravan Dwellers." *Oral History Journal* 18:1 (1990), 41-43.

Shrover interviewed 26 caravan dwellers in the Netherlands, mostly middle aged and elders, and found that their narratives seemed to combine their own remembered past with official accounts of their history.

LATIN AMERICA/ WEST INDIES

D.85. Beck, Jane C. *To Windward of the Land: The Occult World of Alexander Charles.* Bloomington: Indiana University Press, 1979.

This is an oral history of Charles (1901-1974), peasant fisherman, storyteller and "obeah man" (sorcerer), from the West Indian isle of St. Lucia.

D.86. Behar, Ruth. "A Life Story to Take Across the Border: Notes on an Exchange." In George C. Rosenwald and Richard L. Ochberg, eds. *Storied Lives: The Cultural Politics of Self-Understanding.* New Haven, Connecticut: Yale University Press, 1992, 108-123.

Behar discusses her efforts to record the life story of Esperanza Hernández, "a farmer, peddler and occasional domestic servant" in a rural Mexican town, whom she first met in 1982, gradually forming a relationship as *comadres* (co-mothers) over a period of several years; she reflects on the nature of this exchange "across the border"–not only political but also class and culture (see **D.87**).

D.87. Behar, Ruth. *Translated Woman: Crossing the Border With Esperanza's Story.* Boston: Beacon Press, 1993.

> Based on conversations, originally recorded in Spanish, with Esperanza Hernández, a 60-year-old street peddler living in Mexquitic in central Mexico, anthropologist Behar presents her life story and also discusses the challenges of this encounter across boundaries of culture and class, reflecting upon her own background as a Cuban emigré living in the United States .

D.88. Burns, Allan. "Spoken History in an Oral Community: Listening to Mayan Narratives." *International Journal of Oral History* 9:2 (1988), 99-113.

> Burns describes the recitation of historic texts among the Yucatec Mayan of southeastern Mexico, performed during sessions with many people interacting, citing examples of these "ancient conversations" as perfomed among the members of a separatist village, in which the interlocutor was a 90-year-old man who had founded the village at the turn of the century.

D.89. Craton, Michael. "Perceptions of Slavery: A Preliminary Excursion Into the Possibilities of Oral History in Jamaica." In Ann M. Pescatello, ed. *Old Roots in New Lands: Historical and Anthropological Perspectives on Black Experiences in the Americas.* Westport, Connecticut: Greenwood Press, 1977.

> This essay examines "the methodology and rationale" of 50 interviews concerning slavery that were conducted in 1973 among residents of Lluidas Vale in central Jamaica, between 53 and 100 years old; Craton discusses the nature of memory, its relation to tradition, and the importance of the age of those interviewed (for example, the richness of anecdotes about slavery recalled by some, but not all, elders who, as children, overheard their seniors exchanging stories).

D.90. Friedlander, Judith. "Pacts With the Devil: Stories Told by an Indian Woman From Mexico." *New York Folklore* 16:1-2 (1990), 25-42.

> Doña Zeferina Barreto, 85, who lives with her family in Hueyapan, a Mexican Indian village in the northeast corner of the state of Morelos, related both fairy tales, such as an encounter with the Devil, and narratives presented as true stories, to Friedlander, who presents several and discusses the storyteller and her stories.

D.91. Lewis, Oscar. *A Death in the Sanchez Family.* New York: Random House, 1969.

> In 1956, Lewis recorded the life stories of 50-year-old Jesús Sanchez and his family, Mexico City slum dwellers (published in *The Children of Sanchez* [NY: Random House, 1961]); in 1962 he returned to Mexico following the death of Guadalupe Sanchez, born in 1900, and the maternal aunt of the Sanchez children, three of whom he interviewed for what is essentially an oral history of her death, wake and burial at age 62.

D.92. Lewis, Oscar, Ruth M. Lewis and Susan M. Rigdon. *Four Men: Living the Revolution, An Oral History of Contemporary Cuba.* Urbana: University of Illinois Press, 1977.

> As if in answer to his critics, who chastized him for his notion that the poor lived in a self-perpetuating "culture of poverty," Lewis came to Cuba in 1969, at the invitation of Castro, who had read his works, to conduct life histories of people who had experienced the impact of the Cuban Revolution; of the four men whose narratives appear in this work, one is an elder: Lázaro Benedí Rodriguez, born in 1900 in a poor working-class neighborhood in Havana (see also **D.93**).

D.93. Lewis, Oscar, Ruth M. Lewis and Susan M. Rigdon. *Four Women: Living the Revolution, An Oral History of Contemporary Cuba.* Urbana: University of Illinois Press, 1977.

This is a companion volume to *Four Men* (**D.92**), and features, along with the the the oral histories of three women in their 20s, the personal narrative of Inocencia Acosta Felipe, a 54-year old former domestic servant.

D.94. Lewis, Oscar. *Pedro Martinez: A Mexican Peasant and His Family.* New York: Random House, 1964.

Lewis presents edited transcripts of the tape-recorded life histories of three members of a rural Mexican family: Pedro Martinez, the father, born in 1889, his wife Esperanza, and their eldest son Felipe.

D.95. Montejo, Esteban [Miguel Barnet, ed.; trans. by Jocasta Innes]. *The Autobiography of a Runaway Slave.* New York: Pantheon, 1968.

Barnet, Cuban poet and anthropologist, constructed the narrative of Montejo, born into slavery in Cuba in 1860, from two years of tape-recorded conversations and field notes; in the introduction to this book, he describes the process by which he shaped Montejo's "autobiography."

D.96. Muratorio, Blanca. *The Life and Times of Grandfather Alonso: Culture and History in the Upper Amazon.* New Brunswick, New Jersey: Rutgers University Press, 1991.

Ethnographer Muratorio recorded the life story of Rucuyaya Alonso, a Quichua elder from the upper Ecuadorian Amazon, as told to his eldest son in their home during 1982-1983; between chapters of Alonso's narrative Muratorio addresses the social and historical contexts, including cultural domination and resistance.

D.97. Piscitelli, Adriana. "Love and Ambition: Gender, Memory, and Stories from Brazilian Coffee Plantation Families." In Leydesdorff, Selma, Luisa Passerini and Paul Thompson, eds. *Gender and Memory.* Oxford: Oxford University Press, 1996, 89-103.

Piscitelli discusses interviews with members of three generations of men and women in Brazilian coffee plantation families, noting that older men and women, while addressing the same topics, introduced and shaped them differently in relating their life stories, reflecting historically and culturally conditioned gendered perspectives.

D.98. Sherzer, Joel. "Strategies in Text and Context: *Cuna kaa kwento.*" *Journal of American Folklore* 92:364 (1979), 145-163.

Sherzer describes *kaa kwento*, "The Story of the Hot Pepper," a tale told among the Cuna Indians of Panama about a *muu* (grandmother or old woman) who buries her grandson, as told by Mastayans, a *sakla* (chief or advisor) to an elderly *sakla* of another village.

CANADA

D.99. Aubé, Mary Elizabeth. "Oral History and the Remembered World: Cultural Determinants from French Canada." *International Journal of Oral History* 10:1 (1989), 31-49.

Aubé examines the oral history that she conducted with her paternal grandmother, Eva Labrecque Aubé, a French-speaking resident of Lewiston, Maine, who arrived there in 1919 from St. Justine, Quebec, where she was born in 1901; the narratives of the elder Aubé about her early years in St. Justine are not intended to evoke nostalgia or even a desire to relive the past; rather, "her stories are her claim to authority over her own life."

D.100. Billson, Janet Mancini. *Keepers of the Culture: The Power of Tradition in Women's Lives.* New York: Lexington Books, 1995.

Based on a combination of participant-observation and interviews, this study presents portraits and statements of women, many of them elders, from Native American, Mennonite, Jamaican, Chinese, Ukranian and other communities in Canada, who continue to preserve the positive elements of their heritage while also struggling to break with confining aspects of traditional culture.

D.101. Bowen, Lynne. *Boss Whistle: The Coalminers of Vancouver Island Remember.* Lantzville, British Columbia: Oolichan Books, 1982.

This is a collection of transcribed oral histories of retired coal miners from British Columbia's Vancouver Island, that began as a project conducted by local elders and others (see **D.102**).

D.102. Bowen, Lynne. "The Coalminers of Vanouver Island." *Canadian Oral History Association Journal* 6 (1983), 28-32.

Bowen relates the process of editing a collection of oral histories of retired Vancouver Island coal miners, initiated by a group of mostly elders under the direction of Myrtle Bergen, and seen through to publication by Bowen as *Boss Whistle* (see **D.101**); she also describes the responses of audiences at readings of the book.

D.102.a. Broadfoot, Barry, ed. *Ten Lost Years 1929-1939: Memories of Canadians Who Survived the Depression.* Don Mills, Ontario: Paperjacks/General Publishing, 1973.

Broadfoot, Canada's answer to Studs Terkel (see **D.155**), presents excerpts of oral history interviews with several dozen people, selected from the accounts of over 600 women and men from throughout Canada whose stories of life during the Depression he recorded in the early 1970s.

D.103. Butler, Victor (Wilfred W. Wareham, ed.) *The Little Nord Easter: Reminiscences of a Placentia Bayman* [*Canada's Atlantic Folklore and Folklife Series* 4]. St. John's, Newfoundland: Breakwater Books, 1975. [also published as *Memorial University of Newfoundland Folklore and Language Publications: Community Studies Series No. 1*].

This is an account by Butler, born in 1896, who, at the age of 74, began to write about life in his home community of Harbour Buffet, Placentia Bay, Newfoundland; Wareham, also born and raised in Harbour Buffet, and who returned there to do fieldwork, provides an introduction, notes, and photographs.

D.104. Caplan, Ronald, ed. *Down North: The Book of Cape Breton's Magazine.* Toronto: Doubleday Canada, 1980.

This collection is a sampling of stories recorded by Caplan, the editor and publisher of *Cape Breton's Magazine* (see periodicals list in Chapter A), most from older residents of this Nova Scotian island, "who share with you their work, their crafts, their stories and their reminiscences," some in French and Gaelic; with accompanying photographs.

D.105. Degh, Linda. *People in the Tobacco Belt: Four Lives* [*Canadian Centre for Folk Cultural Studies, Paper No. 13*]. Ottowa: National Museums of Canada, 1975.

Degh recorded these oral histories of four Hungarian immigrants to Canada, in their sixties to eighties, in and around Delhi in southwestern Ontario, a major tobacco farming district, "to show that immigrant life history is an important product of folklore creation."

D.106. Dossa, Parin A. "Critical Anthropology and Life Stories: Case Study of Elderly Ismaili Canadians." *Journal of Cross-Cultural Gerontology* 9:3 (1994), 335-354.

The author, an Ismaili-Canadian anthropologist, presents the personal narratives of Ismaili elders who describe their treatment in Canada, including emotional and spiritual suffering relating to the changing values of their adult children, and compare their situation with that of their parents' generation in East Africa.

D.107. MacNeil, Joe Neil (John Shaw, ed.). *Tales Until Dawn: The World of a Gaelic Story-Teller*. Kingston: McGill-Queen's University Press, 1987.

This work consists of the narratives of MacNeil, of Big Pond, Cape Breton County, Nova Scotia, assembled by Shaw–a specialist in Celtic folklore and fluent speaker of Gaelic–into a text in which the story of MacNeil's life is told as a series of encounters with other Gaelic storytellers, and the tales that he learned from them.

D.107.a. Makabe, Tomoko [trans. By Kathleen Chisato Merken]. *Picture Brides: Japanese Women in Canada*. North York, Ontario: University of Toronto Press, for the Multicultural History Society of Ontario, 1995 [based on a book published in Japanese (Tokyo: Mirai-sha, 1983)].

This book presents the life stories of five *issei* (first-generation immigrant) women, in their 80s and 90s when they were interviewed by Makabe in Toronto in the late 1970s and early 1980s; they recall their arrival in Canada in the 1920s as "picture brides" when they were about 20 years old, raising famlies and working as domestics and laborers on farms, in mines, and lumber and fishing camps.

D.108. Silverman, Eliane. "In Their Own Words: Mothers and Daughters on the Alberta Frontier, 1890-1929." *Frontiers* 2:2 (1977), 37-44.

Silverman, who interview 130 women from different class and ethnic backgrounds, including eastern and southern European, French Canadian, American, Anglo-Saxon, Indian and Metis, who arrived in Alberta before 1929, presents excerpts from edited transcripts that focus on daughters' perceptions of their mothers and grandmothers.

D.109. Sparks, Reg F. (Richard E. Buehler, ed.) *The Winds Softly Sigh.* [*Canada's Atlantic Folklore and Folklife Series 6*]. St. John's, Newfoundland: Breakwater Books, 1981 .

Sparks was born in 1906 in Jackson's Arm, White Bay, Newfoundland, in 1906; this book is his recollection of growing up in a small village; as the back-cover blurb states: "It is the story of childhood and poignant memories as told from the viewpoint of a mature man reflecting on his past."

D.109.a. Sugiman, Momoye. *Jin Guo: Voices of Chinese-Canadian Women*. Toronto: The Women's Book Committee, Chinese Canadian National Council, 1992.

This is a collection of excerpts of oral histories of about 30 Chinese-Canadian women, half of whom are elders (the oldest was born in China in 1902); the narratives are divided into two major sections, "Individual Stories" and "Themes."

D.110. Tallman, Richard S. "'You Can Almost Picture It': The Aesthetics of a Nova Scotia Storyteller." *Folklore Forum* 7:2 (1974), 121-130.

This is a portrait of Robert Coffil, 70, of Blomidon, Nova Scotia, who spent a life at sea freighting and fishing, has been a ship's pilot and captain, and learned a great deal of tall tales from his brother John, who inspired him to be a storyteller.

UNITED STATES

Topical, Regional and Cross-Cultural Collections

D.111. Adelman, Marcy, ed. *Long Time Passing: Lives of Older Lesbians.* Boston: Alyson Publications, 1986.

Adelman, a long time researcher in gay gerontology, solicited written personal narratives of lesbians over age 60, and presents over twenty of them, revealing a diversity of experiences within an underreported aging sub-culture.

D.112. Alexander, Maxine, ed. *Speaking for Ourselves: Women of the South.* New York: Pantheon, 1984.

This is a collection of essays, and a few short stories, by writers from throughout the Southern U. S., including short autobiographical pieces, as well as oral histories and characterizations of traditional elders; many of these have appeared in the magazine *Southern Exposure* (see **B.18**).

D.113. Arnold, Eleanor, ed. *Voices of American Homemakers.* Bloomington: Indiana University Press, 1985.

This book is the result of an oral history project directed by Arnold in conjunction with the 50th anniversary of the National Extension Homemakers Council, featuring selected excerpts from interviews by volunteers from 37 states with over 200 women (and one man) ranging in age from 27 to 100, the majority between 60 to 80; they reflect on their life and work, and talk about their involvement in homemaker clubs.

D.114. Banks, Ann, ed. *First Person America.* New York: Vintage/Random House, 1980.

This is one of several books featuring selected life history interviews of a variety of working-class people, old and young, collected for the WPA Federal Writers Project in the late 1930s and early 40s; to provide some background, Banks interviewed eleven former members of the FWP who were responsible for collecting half of the 80 life stories featured (see also **D.125**, **D.156**, and **D.174**).

D.115. Benson, Joan, Beverly Baca and Barbara Bolin. "Family History and Oral History." *Frontiers* 2:2 (1977), 93-97.

Benson, director of "The Working Lives of New Mexico Women," an oral history project at New Mexico State University, presents brief excerpts of family histories by two of her students: Baca, a Chicana, who interviewed her grandmother Isabel Roybal Sena, 87, of Albuquerque, and Bolin, an Anglo, who interviewed her great-grandmother Evelyn Edwards Fisher, whose family migrated from the midwest, eventually settling in Plain, New Mexico.

D.116. Berger, Raymond M. *Gay and Gray: The Older Homosexual Man.* 2nd. ed. New York: Haworth Press, 1996 [orig. pub. by University of Illinois Press, 1982].

As part of a study of gay aging and psychological adjustment that included a questionnaire sent to 112 gay men aged 41-77, and open-ended interviews with 10 of them, Berger presents the recorded personal narratives of six individuals who talk about their lives as gay men, their struggle for acceptance, and their generally positive adjustment to being gay and gray.

D.117. Brecher, Jeremy, Jerry Lombardi and Jan Stackhouse, eds. *Brass Valley: The Story of Working People's Lives and Struggles in an American Industrial Region.* Philadelphia: Temple University, 1982.

This is a collection of excerpts of oral history interviews with old and young women and men from diverse ethnic communities, all active or retired workers in Naugatuck Valley in central Connecticut, anchored by the town of Waterbury, and the one-time center of the U. S. brass industry; they reflect upon the work experience and their cultural and occupational heritage.

D.118. Burrison, John A. *Storytellers: Folktales and Legends from the South.* Athens: University of Georgia Press, 1989.

This is a collection of 260 tales recorded from 113 traditional narrators by folklore students at Georgia State University, and includes portraits of several individual storytellers–mostly elders–and storytelling communities; one chapter is devoted to "Two West Tennessee family legends across three generations."

D.119. Buss, Fran Leeper. *Dignity: Lower Income Women Tell of Their Lives and Struggles.* Ann Arbor: University of Michigan Press, 1985.

Buss presents the recorded oral history narratives of ten lower income women ranging in age from their 20s to their 70s, among them five elders, a Japanese-American, African-American, Yugoslav-American, Anglo-American, and a Menominee Indian.

D.120. Clayton, Robert Alan, and J. Bourge Hathaway. *Quiet Pride: Ageless Wisdom of the American West.* Hillsboro, Oregon: Beyond Words, 1992.

This is a collection of photographs (by Clayton) and life stories (text with interview excerpts by Hathaway) of older women and men "from the high plains of the Dakotas to the lush vineyards of northern California," who chose to live their lives in rural areas of western U. S., among them cowboys/girls and vacqueros, ranchers and farmers, a shepard, miner, logger, teacher, weaver, quilter, woodcarver, priest, and an Indian-rights activist.

D.121. Cohen, Cindy. *From Hearing My Mother Talk: Stories of Cambridge Women.* Cambridge, Massachusetts: Cambridge Council Fund, 1979.

This booklet was produced by the Oral History Center, then located at the Cambridge Town Hall (now with Boston University), dedicated to documenting community history and developing intergenerational projects with elders and local public schools; *From Hearing My Mother Talk* features narratives from a cross-section of Cambridge women young and old from local neighborhoods.

D.122. Cohen, David Steven, ed. *America, the Dream of My Life: Selections From the Federal Writers' Project's New Jersey Ethnic Survey.* New Brunswick, New Jersey: Rutgers University Press, 1990.

> Cohen presents edited selections from interviews with European immigrants conducted between 1939 to 1941 by fieldworkers for the WPA Federal Writers Project; the narratives, most of them by elders, are organized in sections by ethnic group: Irish, Italians, Poles, Lithuanians, Russians and Ukrainians, Dutch, and Jews.

D.123. Dorson, Richard M. *Land of the Millrats:* Cambridge: Harvard University Press, 1981.

> Among the many anecdotes and stories collected by Dorson and his graduate students at Indiana University in this survey of urban folklore in the Calumet region of northwest Indiana dominated by the steel industry, and including Gary, Whiting, East Chicago and Hammond, conducted, are several narratives of Anglo-, Serbian-, Greek-, Hispanic- and African-American elders.

D.124. Dyerly, Victoria. *Hard Times Cotton Mill Girls: Personal Histories of Womanhood and Poverty in the South.* Ithaca: IRL Press, New York State School of Industrial and Labor Relations, Cornell University, 1986.

> Dyerly, who grew up in a mill town herself, and briefly worked a mill, presents oral histories of 20 women, black and white, most of them over 60 (the oldest is 90), who tell about life and work on farms and in mill towns of North Carolina.

D.125. Federal Writers Project. *These Are Our Lives.* New York: W. W. Norton, 1975 [originally published by the University of North Carolina Press, Chapel Hill, 1939].

> This is a sample of 35 life histories from over 1000 collected for the WPA Federal Writers Project in the late 1930s, featuring portraits of old and young, black and white (see also **D.114, D.156**), part of a massive effort which included the recording of narratives of ex-slaves, most of them in their 80s (see **D.174**).

D.125.a. Ganzel, Bill. *Dust Bowl Descent.* Lincoln: University of Nebraska Press, 1984.

> Ganzel, a photographer and journalist from Lincoln, Nebraska, set out in 1974 to photograph the aftermath of the Depression in the "Dust Bowl" among farmers in midwestern U. S. and migrants to the west coast, carrying photographs taken for the Farm Security Adminstration in the 1930s; he found and took pictures of some of the same scenes and interviewed people depicted in the FSA photos 40 years earlier, and presents "then" and "now" photographs, along with interview excerpts.

D.126. Gluck, Sherna Berger. *Rosie the Riveter Revisited: Women, the War and Social Change.* New York: Meridian/New American Library, 1987.

> These oral histories of African-American, Mexican-American and Anglo-American women who became factory workers during World War II, recorded by Gluck, reveal the ways in which their experience doing "men's work" changed their orientation to traditional women's culture, including their views of themselves, how they raised their daughters, and their reception to feminism.

D.127. Greenberger, David, ed.. *Duplex Planet: Everybody's Asking Who I Was.* Boston: Faber and Faber, 1993.

> In 1979, Greenberger, an activities director at the Duplex, an all-male nursing home in Massachesetts, started interviewing the 45 residents for an eponymous magazine,

selections of which appear in this book; it is a quirky volume that pushes the folklore/aging envelope, for it consists of responses–from a single word to several paragraphs–to questions ranging from "What is the best thing that ever happened to you" and "Did you ever have a broken heart?" to "Where do manners come from?"; while by no means an ethnographic account, it is a revealing record of the expressive behavior of an aging male community (see **H.94**).

D.128. Hall, Jacquelyn Dowd, James Leloudis, Robert Korstad, Mary Murphy, LuAnn Jones, and Christopher B. Daly. *Like a Family: The Making of a Southern Cotton Mill World.* Chapel Hill: University of North Carolina Press, 1987.

The authors, in reconstructing family, work and community life around textile mills in the southern U. S.; draw upon interviews conducted in the late 1970s by the Southern Oral History Program at the University of North Carolina at Chapel Hill with former millhands who were born between 1891 and 1920; historical analysis is interwoven with interview excerpts: in the authors' words, "we committed ourselves to presenting the arguments in a storytelling style, by allowing millhands' voices to drive the narrative."

D.129. Hall, Jacquelyn D., and Della Pollock. "History, Story and Performance: The Making and Remaking of a Southern Cotton Mill World." In Gunter H. Lenz, Hartmut Keil, and Sabine Bröcke-Sallah, eds. *Reconstructing American Literary and Historical Studies.* New York: St. Martin's Press, 1990, 324-344.

Hall, a participant in an oral history project on Southern agriculture conducted through the University of North Carolina (see **D.128**), reflects on the people interviewed and the nature of their narratives, while Pollock describes a student production she developed and toured based on these narratives.

D.130. Hareven, Tamara K., and Randolph Langenbach. *Amoskeag: Life and Work in an American Factory-City.* New York: Pantheon, 1978.

This book presents excerpts of oral history interviews with 40 women and men in their 60s to their 80s, former workers at Amoskeag Mills, in Manchester, New Hampshire, and members of their families, who recall life, work, ethnic tensions, labor conflicts in a town founded by the Amoskeag Company in the 1830s, and which dominated town life until 1936 when the mills shut down.

D.131. Hareven, Tamara K. "Search for Generational Memory: Tribal Rites In Industrial Society." In Stephen R. Graubard, ed. *Generations.* New York: W. W. Norton and Co., 1979, 137-149.

Hareven takes a look at the search for roots in the U. S. in the wake of the Bicentennial and the publication of Alex Haley's book *Roots,* sparking great interest in genealogy and oral history; she looks at these attempts at the recovery of ethnic identity from the perspective of family history across generations.

D.132. Jones, LuAnn. "Voices of Southern Agricultural History." In Ronald J. Grele, ed. *International Annual of Oral History, 1990: Subjectivity and Multiculturalism in Oral History.* Westport, Connecticut: Greenwood Press, 1992.

Jones, of the National Museum of American History, Smithsonian Institution, describes a project initiated by the Museum in 1986 to document changes in farm life as experienced and recounted by older farmers in the South (see **D.128**).

D.133. Jones, Suzi, and Jarold Ramsey, eds. *The Stories We Tell: An Anthology of Oregon Folk Literature.* Corvallis: Oregon State University Press, 1994.

Among the varied materials compiled from a variety of archival and published sources for this collection are the traditional narratives of several elders, ranging from Native American storytellers to Irish rancoteurs to cowboy poets.

D.134. Kadlec, Robert F., ed. *They "Knew" Billy the Kid: Interviews with Old-Time New Mexicans.* Santa Fe: New Mexico: Ancient City Press, 1987.

This is a collection of interviews conducted in the late 1930s as part of the Federal Writers' Project among New Mexicans, most of them in their 60s to 90s, who recall stories about the famous bandit and his legendary exploits in the 1880s, and who, in a few instances, claim to be personal acquaintances of the Kid.

D.135. Kohl, Seena B. "Memories of Homesteading and the Process of Retrospection." *Oral History Review* 17:2 (1989), 25-45.

Kohl contrasts letters and diaries written by turn-of-the-century homesteaders on the North American plains with the retrospective accounts of elders, in which "time, intent, and audience affect subject matter, permitting narrators to transform and give new meanings to experience."

D.136. Krause, Corrine Azen. *Grandmothers, Mothers and Daughters: Oral Histories of Three Generations of Ethnic American Women.* Boston: Twayne, 1991.

Krause presents the edited transcripts, along with her interview questions, of oral histories conducted in the 1970s with 18 women representing three generations of Italian, Jewish and Slavic families living in Pittsburgh, Pennsylvania; the six grandmothers were born between 1887 and 1902; four of them emigrated to the U. S. in the early 1900s, while one was born in Vermont, and another in Pennsylvania.

D.137. Lauterer, Jock. *Wouldn't Take Nothin' for My Journey Now.* Chapel Hill: University of North Carolina Press, 1980.

Lauterer, cofounder/editor of a weekly newspaper in Rutherford County, North Carolina, conducted informal interviews and took photographs of a number of older craftspeople and others who recall life in rural Appalachia; essentially it is a series of verbal and visual portraits, with liberal quotes from interview subjects.

D.138. Livings, Gail S. "Discovering the World of Twentieth Century Trade Union Waitresses in the West: A Nascent Analysis of Working Class Women's Meanings of Self and Work." In Unruh, David R., and Gail S. Livings, eds. *Personal History Through the Life Course.* Greenwich, Connecticut: JAI Press, 1989, 141-173.

Livings looks at the social construction of meaning among a group of older women who recall, in personal narratives, the tension between their experiences as women in traditional households and their emerging trade union consciousness which transformed their lives and worldview.

D.139. Manning, Diane. *Hill Country Teacher: Oral Histories from the One-Room School and Beyond.* Boston: Twayne Publishers, 1990.

Manning presents the edited transcripts of interviews with eight retired teachers: six white women who began their teaching careers in one-room schools in rural Texas during the 1920s and 1930s and continued to teach after the desegregation of the public schools in the 1960s; and one married African-American couple who began teaching in rural Texas schools in 1931, and were responsible for the peaceful integration of the Kerrville public schools in the 1960s.

D.140. Modell, Judith, and John Hinshaw. "Male Work and Mill Work: Memory and Gender in Homestead, Pennsylvania." In Leydesdorff, Selma, Luisa Passerini and Paul Thompson, eds. *Gender and Memory.* Oxford: Oxford University Press, 1996, 133-149.

The authors examine the personal narratives of men, young and old, steelworkers–often the sons and fathers of steelworkers–in the late 1980s and early 1990s, in the wake of closing of USX Homestead Works in 1986, who recall the "old days" (for some a lifetime, for others a few years) of life and work in the social world shaped by the identification of the steel mills with male culture.

D.141. Montell, William Lynwood. *Don't Go Up Kettle Creek: Verbal Legacy of the Upper Cumberland.* Knoxville: University of Tennessee Press, 1983.

This account combines historical analysis with generous excerpts of interviews conducted with local residents born between 1874 to 1920, who recall life along the banks and tributaries of the Cumberland River that runs through Kentucky and Tennessee.

D.142. Mullen, Patrick. *Listening to Old Voices: Folklore, Life Stories and the Elderly.* Urbana: University of Illinois Press, 1992.

Based on his interviews with nine people in their seventies and eighties living in rural Virginia, North Carolina and southern Ohio, Mullen examines the ways in which the personal narratives of these elders not only present information on family history and folklife, but also reveal strategies used to pass on their wisdom.

D.142.a. Kathryn L. Nasstrom, ed. Women's Voices in the Southern Oral History Program Collection. Chapel Hill: University of North Carolina [Southern Oral History Program and Manuscripts Department], 1992.

This is a guide to oral histories of women, most of them elders, housed in the Southern Oral History Program Collection at the University of North Carolina at Chapel Hill; it is not a collection of transcripts, but rather a summary of the content of each of the interviews in the Collection.

D.143. Osterud, Nancy Grey, and Lu Ann Jones. "'If I must Say So Myself': Oral Histories of Rural Women." *Oral History Review* 17:2 (1989), 1-23.

This essay reviews a number of collections of oral histories conducted with rural women in the U. S., including Native American, African-American, Asian-American and Hispanic women (a number of the published oral histories noted by the authors are cited in this chapter).

D.144. Rothschild, Mary Logan, and Pamela Claire Hronek. *Doing What the Day Brought: An Oral History of Arizona Women.* Tucson: University of Arizona Press, 1992.

In the early 1980s, the authors interviewed a multicultural cross-section of "ordinary" women, born between 1890 and 1921, who recall their experiences in rural and urban communities throughout the state, in a project supported by the Arizona Humanities Council and the Women's Studies Program at Arizona State University.

D.145. Salber, Eva J. *"Don't Send Me Flowers When I'm Dead": Voices of Rural Elderly.* Durham, North Carolina: Duke University Press, 1983.

Salber presents excerpts of oral history interviews conducted with forty five elderly men and women, black and white, living alone in the rural communities of Ashton and Red Hill, in the Piedmont section of North Carolina; they describe their families, working lives, traditional values and faith.

D.146. Shuldiner, David, and Thomas Beardsley, eds. *Connecticut Speaks for Itself: Firsthand Accounts of People Who Have Lived in the Nutmeg State From Colonial Times to the Present Day.* Middletown: Connecticut Humanities Council, 1996.

This is a collection of extracts of diaries, journals, letters and oral histories, organized around three themes: "Immigrants, Migrants and Ethnics"; "Working Lives"; and "Women's Lives"; among the entries are the narratives of many elders, as varied as an 18th-century farm woman, a retired African-American woman who has worked in and organized shirt factories; an Italian immigrant, a retired teacher and a Mohegan elder–a leader and historian of her community.

D.147. Stafford, Kim R., ed. "Stories, Songs and Opinions of the Idaho Country." Special issue of *Rendezvous* 17:1-2 (1982), 1-154.

This is essentially a collection of three dozen transcriptions of stories, songs and oral history interviews, "forms of adaptation and continuity," recorded from Native American Indians, Mormons, farmers, housewives, musicians, shepherds and other residents of "Idaho Country," many if not most of them elders.

D.148. Stave, Bruce M. And John F. Sutherland, with Aldo Salerno. *From the Old Country: An Oral History of European Migration to America.* New York: Twayne, 1994.

Oral historians Stave and Sutherland, along with research assistant Salerno, present a compilation of their interviews and others conducted for the Works Progress Administration (WPA) in the late 1930s, covering several generations of immigrant experience, including the voices of Irish, Scandanavians, Italians, Jews, Poles, Slavs and others who arrived in the U. S. in the late 19th and early 20th centuries.

D.149. Strickland, Ron. *Alaskans.* Harrisburg, Pennsylvania: Stackpole Books, 1992.

Strickland presents excerpts of 60 oral history interviews with a broad cross-section of people who call Alaska home: "Natives and whites, whale hunters and schoolteachers, missionaries and mushers, artists and rescue workers, pilots and politicians," born between the 1880s and the 1950s.

D.150. Strickland, Ron. *River Pigs and Cayuses: Oral Histories from the Pacific Northwest.* New York: Paragon House, 1984.

Strickland presents edited transcripts of interviews conducted in the late 1970s with "rural old-timers" who talk about their experiences as log drive river runners (river pigs), wranglers of wild horses (cayuses), ranchers, prospectors, blacksmiths, fishermen, gamblers, cowboys and others (see also **D.153**).

D.151. Strickland, Ron. *Texans: Oral Histories from the Lone Star State.* New York: Paragon House, 1991.

Texans presents about four dozen short oral history interview excerpts with a cross-section of rural and urban residents of the Lone Star State, at least 30 of whom were born between 1892 and the mid-1920s, including ranchers, Gulf fishermen, a railroad worker, quilter, rodeo announcer, high school football coach, and others.

D.152. Strickland, Ron. *Vermonters: Oral Histories from Down Country to the Northeast Kingdom.* San Francisco: Chronicle Books, 1986.

This work presents oral histories and photographs of a broad cross-section of the Vermont population, most of them elders, including craftspeople, farmers, teachers, artists, public figures, and several people with professions peculiar to the region, such as an ice fisherman, a horse logger and a north country guide; features a glossary of local idioms.

D.153. Strickland, Ron. *Whistlepunks and Geoducks: Oral Histories from the Pacific Northwest.* New York: Paragon House, 1990.

Somewhat of a sequel to *River Pigs and Cayuses* (see **D.150**), *Whistlepunks* presents short excerpts of oral history interviews conducted in the 1980s with 50 rural residents of Washington State, born between the late 1800s and the 1940s, all but half a dozen born between 1879 and 1924.

D.154. Talarico, Ross. *Hearts and Times: The Literature of Memory.* Chicago: Kairos Press, 1992.

Talarico, who holds the unique position of "writer in residence" for the city of Rochester, New York, runs community-based creative writing programs; faced with a group of non-literate elders in a senior citizens group at a public housing facility, he conducted oral histories; in this book he has arranged transcribed excerpts as free verse poetry, preceded by a brief description of each narrator.

D.155. Terkel, Studs. *Coming of Age: The Story of Our Century By Those Who've Lived It.* New York: The New Press, 1995.

Terkel, perhaps the most well-known popularizer of oral history interviewing, offered this work the year he turned 83; it features excerpts of conversations with seventy North Americans, aged 70 to 99, and ranging from a Nebraska farmer to a retired bank president (other works of his with interviews of elders to be found amongst personal narratives of people of all ages and walks of life are: *Division Street, America; Hard Times: An Oral History of the Great Depression; Working; American Dreams, Lost and Found; The Good War: An Oral History of World War Two;* and *The Great Divide: Second Thoughts on the American Dream;* also of interest is his autobiography, *Talking to Myself*).

D.156. Terrill, Tom E., and Jerrold Hirsch, eds. *Such As Us: Southern Voices of the Thirties.* New York: W. W. Norton, 1978.

This is a collection of life stories of Southerners, black and white, from many walks of life, many of them elders, recorded in the late 1930s under the WPA Federal Writers Project; they talk about work on farms, in mills, oil fields, coal mines and "other people's houses," family life, religion, gender, poverty, and aging (see also **D.114, D.125,** and **D.174**).

D.157. Thomas, Sherry. "Digging Beneath the Surface: Oral History Techiniques." *Frontiers* 7:1 (1983), 50-55.

This is a transcript of a panel discussion in which Thomas describes the process of interviewing older farm women, and preparing their narratives for publication (see **D.158**); she discusses the problems of transcribing, the ethics of interviewing, and the nature of the testimony the women shared with her.

D.158. Thomas, Sherry. *We Didn't Have Much, But We Sure Had Plenty: Stories of Rural Women.* Garden City, New York: Anchor Books, 1981.

This is a collection of interviews with farm women from Kansas to Georgia to New Mexico to California, age 41-90 (most of them in their 60s-70s) recorded in the late 1970s by Thomas, a sheep rancher and editor of a magazine for country women.

D.159. Tucker, Susan. *Telling Memories Among Southern Women: Domestic Workers and Their Empoyers in the Segregated South.* Baton Rouge: Louisiana State University Press, 1988.

Tucker presents 42 edited oral history narratives, culled from 90 interviews conducted in Florida, Alabama and Louisiana, with African-American women born at the turn of the century, who were domestic workers, as well as their white employers, and other family members, in an "attempt to produce a collective memory of these women of the South."

D.160. Wolf, Mary Alice. "Call to Vocation: The Life Histories of Elderly Women Religious." *International Journal of Aging and Human Development* 31:3 (1990), 197-203.

Wolf presents the remembrances of three older women among 30 Catholic nuns she interviewed regarding the life events that led to their entering the convent as young girls; all three were the children of immigrants who found the religious life a way of getting an education and fulfilling expectations that at least one family member be a priest or nun.

African-American

D.161. Armitage, Sue, Theresa Banfield and Sarah Jacobus. "Black Women and Their Communities in Colorado." *Frontiers* 2:2 9 (1977), 45-51.

The authors present oral history excerpts about family life and social networks in several black communities in Colorado from interviews with six African-American women, at least three of whom were born before 1910.

D.162. Botkin, Benjamin A., ed. *Lay My Burden Down: A Folk History of Slavery.* Chicago: University of Chicago Press, 1945.

This was the first publication of excerpts of the Slave Narrative Collection, interviews of ex-slaves conducted under the aegis of the Federal Writers Project of the Works Progress Administration (WPA) during the 1930s; over 2,000 people were interviewed, most of them over 80 years old. Botkin arranged his selections in thematic order; one chapter, "Long Remembrance," focuses on the nature of memory, but all of the material begs analysis on the perspective of age in the recall of past events (see **D.174**).

D.163. Carlton-LaNey, Iris, ed. *Elderly Black Farm Women...as Keepers of the Community and the Culture.* n.p., North Carolina Humanities Council, 1989.

Cartlton-LaNey presents excerpts of interviews with ten elderly farm women in the Warsawa/Magnolia area of southeastern North Carolina, who continue to live and work on the land and who "contrary to commonly held beliefs, have been "a major force in shaping their communities."

D.164. Clayton, Ronnie W. *Mother Wit: The Ex-Slave Narratives of the Louisiana Writers' Project.* New York: Peter Lang, 1990.

These are selections of narratives of ex-slaves recorded under the WPA Federal Writers' Project; most of them were over eighty at the time the interviews were conducted during the late 1930s. (see **D.174**)

D.165. Delany, Sarah and A. Elizabeth Delany (with Amy Hill Hearth). *Having Our Say: The Delany Sisters' First 100 Years.* New York: Kodansha International, 1993.

This is a joint oral history, compiled from interviews conducted by Hearth from 1991-1993, of Sadie Delany, age 103, and her sister Bessie, age 101; their father was an ex-slave, their mother a "freeman" and child of a mixed-marriage; in alternating chapters they talk of growing up with eight siblings in North Carolina, confronting Jim Crow, migrating to Harlem in World War I, then to a still semi-rural Bronx, and finally a suburban community; they became professionals (Sadie became a teacher, Bessie a dentist), but never married, and remain independent.

D.166. Faulkner, Audrey Olsen, Marsel A. Heisel, Wendell Holbrook, and Shirley Geismar. *When I Was Comin' Up: An Oral History of Aged Blacks.* Hamden, Connecticut: Archon, 1982.

As part of a Rutgers University project conducted during the 1970s, older African-Americans in Newark, New Jersey, told interviewers stories of life in the South, their migration North, conditions in Newark when they first arrived in the 1920s, how things have changed, generational differences, and the effects of aging.

D.167. Fry, Gladys-Marie. *Night Riders in Black Folk History.* Knoxville: University of Tennessee Press, 1975.

While the main purpose of this book is to document supernatural beliefs of Southern blacks used by whites to intimidate them during the post-Civil War period, it is also serves as an exemplary study of the narratives of aged storytellers; Fry interviewed the descendants of slaves, ranging in age from their 60s to 103, in Washington, D. C., and elsewhere, many of them residing in nursing homes, and also drew upon the WPA ex-slave narratives (see **D.174**); the text features excerpts of their reminiscences as well as tales.

D.168. Gwaltney, John Langston. *Drylongso: A Self-Portrait of Black America.* New York: Random House, 1980.

Gwaltney, an African-American anthropologist, presents 41 narratives he recorded in the 1970s from "drylongso" (ordinary) black people, old and young, living in rural and urban communities in the U. S.; it constitutes a contemporary "folk history" of "the old ways," addressing such issues as the legacy of slavery, relations with whites, gender and identity.

D.168.a. Johnson, Elondust Patrick. "Performance, Cultural Identity and Feminist Practice in the Oral History of an African American Domestic Worker." Doctoral Dissertation, University of North Carolina, 1996.

This is a study of the narratives of the author's grandmother, Mary Rhyne (pseud.), born in York County, South Carolina, in 1914, with excerpts of interviews conducted in 1993, focusing on stories and anecdotes of her experience as a domestic worker, prefaced by a discussion of the interview process as "dialogic performance ethnography."

169. Jones-Jackson, Patricia. *When Roots Die: Endangered Traditions on the Sea Islands.* Athens: University of Georgia Press, 1987.

This is a study of the African-American Gullah culture of the sea islands of South Carolina and Georgia, featuring portraits of Gullah-speaking storytellers, most of them elders, and their repertoire of traditional narratives.

D.170. Morgan, Kathryn L. *The Children of Strangers: The Stories of a Black Family.* Philadelphia: Temple University Press, 1980.

A book about stories and storytelling in the author's family, how family members reacted to them, and how the stories functioned within her family; a central figure in this study is her mother Maggie, born at the turn of the century, who told Morgan and her brothers these stories during their formative years in Philadelphia.

D.170.a Mullen, Patrick B. "Two Courtship Stories from the Blue Ridge Mountains." *Folklore and Folklife in Virginia* 2 (1980-1981), 25-37.

Two couples from the same rural Black community near the Virginia-North Carolina border, relate stories of their courtship and marriage, told from the perspective of fifty and sixty-three years of married life.

D.171. Painter, Nell Irvin. *The Narrative of Hosea Hudson: His Life as a Negro Communist in the South.* Cambridge: Harvard University Press, 1979.

This is a unique "oral autobiography," recorded and edited by Painter, of a 78-year-old retired ironworker from Birmingham, Alabama, and longtime political radical, whose activism has always been rooted in southern working class African-American culture.

D.172. Perdue, Charles L., Jr., Thomas E. Barden, and Robert K. Phillips, eds. *Weevils in the Wheat: Interviews with Virginia Ex-Slaves.* Charlottesville: University Press of Virginia, 1976.

These are selections of narratives of ex-slaves recorded under the WPA Federal Writers' Project; most of them were over eighty at the time the interviews were conducted during the late 1930s. (see **D.174**)

D.173. Portelli, Alessandro. "History-Telling and Time: An Example from Kentucky." *Oral History Review* 20:1-2 (1992), 51-66.

Portelli distinguishes "history-telling" from other forms of traditional storytelling in that "the history-teller weaves personal recollections into a broader historical background"; he cites as an example the narratives of Reverend Hugh Cowans, and African-American minister, interviewed by Portelli in Lexington, Kentucky, in 1983, who told him about life in the coalfields of Harlan County, Kentucky, from the 1930s to the present.

D.174. Rawick, George P. *The American Slave: A Composite Autobiography. Volumes 1-19.* Westport, Connecticut: Greenwood Press, 1972-1976.

This multi-volume work constitutes the most comprehensive published body of ex-slave narratives from the WPA Federal Writers' Project Slave Narrative Collection; a mine of information on slavery, as well African-American folklore, they are also a resource for the study of aging and memory: most of the subjects were over eighty when interviewed in the 1930s (see also **D.162**, **D.164**, **D.172**, and **D.184**).

D.175. Rice, Sarah (Louise Westling, ed.). *He Included Me: The Autobiography of Sarah Rice.* Athens: University of Georgia Press, 1989.

Born in Clio, Alabama in 1909, to a schoolteacher mother and a minister father, who eventually resettled in Jacksonville, Florida, Rice told Westling stories of her rural upbringing, family, career as a schoolteacher, devotion to church, and the challenges of life as an African-American woman.

D.176. Robinson, Beverly J. "Life Narratives: A Structural Model for the Study of Black Women's Cultures." In Unruh, David R., and Gail S. Livings, eds. *Personal History Through the Life Course.* Greenwich, Connecticut: JAI Press, 1989, 127-140.

Folklorist Robinson presents a structural model for the study of personal experience narratives, in which life stories both reveal past experience and preserve the culture within which the teller has lived; the life narrative of Phyllis Carter, born in 1880, is presented as an illustration of the structural model.

D.177. Rosengarten, Theodore. *All God's Dangers: The Life of Nate Shaw.* New York: Alfred A. Knopf, 1974.

Rosengarten presents the oral history of Ned Cobb (assigned the pseudonym Nate Shaw for this book), a black tenant farmer from east-central Alabama, recorded in the early 1970s, when Cobb was in his mid-80s; he recalls life as a sharecropper who stood his ground to defend his community and way of life (see **D.178**).

D.178. Rosengarten, Theodore. "Stepping Over Cockleburs: Conversations with Ned Cobb." In Marc Pachter, ed. *Telling Lives: The Biographer's Art.* Washington, D.C.: New Republic Books, 1979, 105-131.

Rosengarten discusses the problems he encountered in the process of interviewing the aging sharecropper whose life story he edited into the classic oral history, *All God's Dangers* (see **D.177**).

D.179. Santino, Jack. *Miles of Smiles, Years of Struggle: Stories of Black Pullman Porters.* Urbana: University of Illinois Press, 1989.

Folklorist Santino interviewed about 30 retired porters in and around Washington, D. C., who talked about their lives on the railroad, labor struggles, racism, occupational folklore, and the contrast between the low status of porters on the trains and their high status within the African-American community (see **H.189**).

D.180. Seder, Jean. *Voices of Another Time: Three Memories.* Philadelphia: ISHI Publications, 1985.

These are the stories of three older African-American women, Eleanorah Hawkins, Thelma Sims and Lelia Palmer, all raised on farms in the rural South, whom the author met and interviewed in Philadelphia, and who presents their narratives in blank verse form in three sections, with a fourth section devoted to "recipes, cures, advice and sayings" of these three elders.

D.181. Simonsen, Thordis, ed. *You May Plow Here: The Narrative of Sara Brooks.* New York: W. W. Norton, 1986.

The author was a child of four in the late 1940s when Brooks came to work one day a week at her parents' home in Cleveland; in the mid-1970s she recorded the stories that Brooks, an African-American woman, born in 1911, told of life on her parents' subsistence farm in west Alabama.

D.182. Titon, Jeff Todd. "Reverend C. L. Franklin: Black American Preacher-Poet." In Alan Jabbour and James Hardin, eds. *Folklife Annual 1987.* Washington, D. C.: Library of Congress, 1988, 86-105.

Titon reviews the life and performance style of Franklin, born in Sunflower County, near Indianola, Mississippi, in 1915, and presents excerpts of sermons and personal experience narratives.

D.183. Wilson, Emily Herring. *Hope and Dignity: Older Black Women of the South.* Philadelphia: Temple University Press, 1983.

This book offers portraits of twenty-seven older black women from North Carolina, featuring excerpts of oral history interviews conducted by Wilson, with accompanying photographs by Susan Mullally; biographical sketches of an additional twenty women are contained in a final chapter.

D.184. Yetman, Norman R., ed. *Voices From Slavery.* New York: Holt, Rinehart and Winston, 1970.

This volume presents a selection of over 100 narratives of ex-slaves recorded for the WPA Federal Writers' Project; most of them were over eighty at the time the interviews were conducted during the late 1930s (see **D.174**).

Anglo-American

D.185. Armstrong, Roy II. "Miss Emily and Miss Olive and the Legend of the Devil's Hoof Prints of Bath." *North Carolina Folklore Journal* 36:2 (1989), 121-127.

Armstrong presents the accounts of Emily Padgett, 85, and her sister-in-law Olive Douglas, 93, residents of "The Crossroads" in Bath, North Carolina, who recall stories about one Jessie Elliot who, in 1813, rode off to a Sunday horse race near Bath and was thrown and killed by his horse, whose hoofprints miraculously restore themselves.

D.186. Attebery, Jennifer Eastman. "Storytelling Style in the Personal Narratives of Homer Spriggs." *Journal of the Folklore Institute* 14:1-2 (1971), 51-58.

While primarily offering an analysis of the narrative style of this rural Indiana storyteller, Attebery also provides commentary on how Spriggs's storytelling and narrative technique reflect the ways in which the 88-year-old former musician and blacksmith has compensated for the limitations imposed by arthritis.

D.187. Baldwin, Karen. "'Woof!': A Word on Women's Roles in Family Storytelling." In Rosan A. Jordan and Susan J. Kalcik, eds. *Women's Folklore, Women's Culture.* Philadelphia: University of Pennsylvania Press, 1985, 149-162.

Baldwin discusses family storytelling traditions among her mother's kin, the Solleys of Clearfield County in central Pennsylvania, and the narrative balance struck between the accounts of women and men, as exemplified in the different ways apple-butter making is remembered by Great-Uncle Roscoe Solley and his wife of 52 years, Great-Aunt Rheva Rowles Solley.

D.188. Bauman, Richard. "Ed Bell, Texas Storyteller: The Framing and Reframing of Life Experience." *Journal of Folklore Research* 24:3 (1987), 197-221.

In his personal experience stories, Ed Bell (1905-1986) of Luling, Texas, chronicled his own social development; but even the "tall tales" he told explored issues that came up in his own long life.

D.189. Beck, Jane C. "Just Keep the Saw Cutting." *Northeast Folklore* 30 (1995), 90-123.

Beck presents and discusses the life story of John Lamberton, born in 1912, in Cabot, Vermont, and presently residing in a farmhouse on the Winooski River, outside the village of Marshfield, who talks about growing up on a farm in Cabot, and working in logging camps and mills.

D.190. Beck, Jane C. *Vermont Recollections: Sifting Through the Interview Process.* Orono: Maine Folklife Center, 1995 [special issue: *Northeast Folklore* 30].

Beck presents a collection of essays consists of life stories of older Vermonters, as well as reflections on the process of collecting and editing oral histories in the state (see **D.189**, **D.231**, **D.236**, **D.240**, **D.245**, and **D.277**).

D.191. Bethke, Robert D. *Adirondack Voices: Woodsmen and Woods Lore.* Urbana: University of Ilinois Press, 1981.

A study of woodsmen in northern New York State, this book "is about a recoverable past, one recoverable through the storytelling and folksong heritages, the recollected experiences, and the personalities of elderly woodsmen."

D.192. Bethke, Robert D. "Storytelling at an Adirondack Inn." *Western Folklore* 35:2 (1976), 123-139.

Bethke reports and presents excerpts of a storytelling event on a summer evening in 1970 in the barroom at Ham's Inn, in St. Lawrence County, northern New York, featuring the tall tales and anecdotes of 66-year-old Ham Ferry.

D.193. Bird, Donald Allport, and James R. Dow. "Benjamin Kuhn: Life and Narratives of a Hoosier Farmer." *Indiana Folklore* 5:2 (1972), 143-263.

The authors present the recorded life history, reminiscences, anecdotes and repertoire of traditional narratives and folk medical beliefs of Kuhn (1888-1972), who lived and farmed his entire life in central and southern Indiana.

D.194. Brisco, Mary S. "Sister Sooky's Story: The Autobiography of Mary S. Brisco."*Mid-South Folklore* 5:3 (1977), 77-99.

Mary Susan Brisco (née High), born in High, Arkansas in 1875, and who died there in 1958, was a carpenter, healer and folksinger; in 1954, just before her 79th birthday, she wrote "The Story of My Life" with a big lead pencil in a Jumbo school tablet; it is presented with historical and folklore annotations.

D.195. Brittain, Robbie. "A Study of the Personal Experience Narratives of Ernest Luck, an Asheboro Raconteur." *North Carolina Folklore Journal* 40:1 (1993), 36-44.

Brittain looks at the interplay of memory, belief, and sometimes conflicting attitudes toward tradition and modernity reflected in the personal narratives of a North Carolina elder whose home, replete with gardens, an apiary, and a backyard petting zoo, is located about four miles from the Asheboro city limits.

D.196. Brown, Mary Ellen. "Personal Experience Stories, Autobiography, and Ideology." *Fabula* 31:3-4 (1990), 254-261.

> Brown analyzes a discussion between Mamie Koons, 90, and her husband's aunt, Ruth Williams, 80, visiting the homeplace in Indiana from Missouri, looking at personal narratives as not only reflective of individual women's lives, but also of "the cultural, political and ideological nexus in which we women live."

D.197. Burke, Carol, and Martin Light, eds. *Back in Those Days: Reminiscences and Stories of Indiana.* Bloomington: Indiana Writes, 1978.

> This is a collection of anecdotes and tales drawn from tape-recorded interviews with 130 people who live in west-central Indiana, as part of a project, "Tell Us Your Stories: Creative Storytelling with Senior Citizens of Indiana," sponsored by the Indiana Arts Commission, NEA and Purdue University.

D.198. Burrison, John A. "Cap'n George Wheatley, Oldest Tangier-Man." *Keystone Folklore Quarterly* 11 (1966), 27-41.

> On a song-collecting expedition, the author collected few songs, but did record a fair amount of commentary by the 88-year-old resident of Tangier Island, Virginia, in Chesapeake Bay (see also **D.199**).

D.199. Carey, George G. "'And Everyone of Them's Gone But Me': Another look at Tangier Island's Oldest Inhabitant." *Studies in the Literary Imagination* 3:1 (1970), 73-87. [Special issue on "Creativity and Southern Tradition"]

> Carey presents generous excerpts of interviews recorded in the late 1960s with George Allen "Cap'n Al" Wheatley, who sold his skiff and crab pots and retired from the trade at age 83; his personal experience narratives, tall tales, jests and anecdotes reflect the traditions of four generations of Chesapeake Bay watermen (see also **D.198**).

D.200. Chappell, Fred. "The Ninety-Ninth Foxfire Book." *Appalachian Journal* 11:3 (1984), 260-267.

> Chappell shares "a few skeptical thoughts about Foxfire," including a critique of the mystique surrounding one of Foxfire's most renowned subjects, the "old mountain woman" Aunt Arie (see **D.208**).

D.201. Curry, Jane. *The River's in My Blood: Riverboat Pilots Tell Their Stories.* Lincoln: University of Nebraska Press, 1983.

> Curry presents excerpts of oral history interviews with 50 retired and working river pilots and captains along the Ohio and Mississippi rivers, ranging in age from 22 to 102 (most of them born before the 1920s), and whose experience has covered steam packets, towboats and excursion boats.

D.202. Egerton, John. *Generations: An American Family.* Lexington: University Press of Kentucky, 1983.

> In the course of an ambitious (and unrealistic!) search for a family "whose collective life stories were sufficiently diverse to be typical or representative of the majority of Americans," Egerton found and interviewed, in 1978, Burnam Ledford, then 102, and his wife Addie, 93, who had lived most of their lives in Garrard County Kentucky (for a critique, see **D.239**).

D.203. Ferris, William R., Jr. "More of Ray Lum's Horse Sense." *Mid-South Folklore* 6:2 (1978), 43-50.

A continuation of Ferris's article in *Mid-South Folklore* 6:1 (see **D.205**).

D.204. Ferris, William R., Jr. "Ray Lum: Muletrader." *North Carolina Folklore Journal* 21:3 (1973), 105-119.

Ferris presents some of the stories of Lum, born in Rocky Springs, Mississippi, in 1891, and began trading in 1904; he eventually settled in Vicksburg, where he is renown not only as a trader but also as a raconteur (see **H.33**).

D.205. Ferris, William R., Jr. "Ray Lum's Horse and Mule Lore." *Mid-South Folklore* 6:1 (1978), 15-27.

Ferris presents personal experience narratives of Lum (1891-1976), trader, auctioneer of farm animals, and storyteller from Vicksburg, Mississippi (see **D.205**, **H.33**).

D.206. Foster, Stephen William. *The Past Is Another Country: Representation, Historical Consciousness and Resistance in the Blue Ridge.* Berkeley, University of California Press, 1988.

Among the many insights in this study of people who have lived their entire lives in Ashe County, North Carolina are Foster's characterizations of older and younger residents, including differences noted in self-presentation, self-understanding and memory between older and younger community members whose life histories he recorded.

D.207. French, Lawrence. "'When I Get Good and Ready.'" *Appalachian Journal* 16:1 (1988), 62-70.

French presents–as a sample of the interviews he and his students at the University of North Carolina have conducted–the personal narrative of "Hazel," (recorded in 1976) who has lived in Jackson County, North Carolina, since arriving there from Haywood County as a young married woman in 1921, and who describes herself as a "mountaineer born and mountain bred, and when I die, a mountaineer dead!"

D.208. Garland, Linda, and Eliot Wigginton. *Aunt Arie: A Foxfire Portrait.* New York: E. P. Dutton, 1983.

Produced as part of the Foxfire project, started by Wigginton, a rural Georgia high school teacher who sent his students out to collect the lore of mountain folk in their community (see **B.2-B.13**), this is a compilation of numerous narratives recorded by different students over several years, of the folk wisdom of Arie Carpenter (for critiques, see **D.200, D.239**).

D.209. Gluck, Sherna, ed. *From Parlor to Prison: Five Suffragists Talk About Their Lives—An Oral History.* New York: Vintage Books, 1976.

In the early 1970s, Gluck interviewed Sylvie Thygeson, 104; Jessie Haver Butler, 89; Miriam Allen deFord, 85; Laura Ellsworth Seilor, 82; and Ernestine Hara Kettler, 79, who recall their activism and discuss the diverse social circumstances that compelled them to join the suffrage movement in the U. S. in the early part of this century.

D.210. Goldberg, Linda S. *Here on This Hill: Conversations with Vermont Neighbors.* Middlebury: Vermont Folklife Center, 1991.

This is a collection of short transcripts of the author's interviews with 50 of her neighbors on Hollister Hill, in Marshfield, Vermont, ranging in age from 7 to 82 (10 of whom are over 60), who tell personal stories of life in this rural community.

D.211. Harrah-Conforth, Jeanne. "'And I Thank God for the Union Every Day': An Account of Women's Experiences Working in the Indiana Auto Industry." *Indiana Folklore* 14:2 (1985), 113-135.

In interviews conducted between 1982 and 1984 , women who participated in strikes at Anderson's Guide Lamp and the Studebaker plant in South Bend, Indiana, in 1936, recall the union and the strike–high points in their work life–and talk about the personal experience of the work they've done, revealing differences between men's and women's roles in their jobs (see also **D.261**).

D.212. Holmes, Tony. "Wind Out of Beech River Bottoms and Isanabelle's Last Visit with Henry." *Tennessee Folklore Society Bulletin* 55:2 (1991), 56-59.

This is a family story about Henry Holmes, whose wife "Isan" died in March, 1901 just before her 73rd birthday, and who appeared to him that August; for this account of a ghostly visitation the author interviewed his grandfather (Isan's grandson, who last visited her when he was 11), and other elder relatives.

D.213. Hufford, Mary. *Chaseworld: Foxhunting and Storytelling in New Jersey's Pine Barrens.* Philadelphia: University of Pennsylvania Press, 1992.

Hufford presents the lives of elder woodsmen, who tell stories of fox-hunting in the forests of south-central New Jersey, and also describes the ways in which they shape their own life stories into a variety of autobiographical projects, ranging from straightforward narratives to scrapbooks and folk-art.

D.214. Hufford, Mary. "Soundscape and Story: Foxhunting in New Jersey's Pine Barrens." In James Hardin and Alan Jabbour, eds. *Folklife Annual 88-89.* Washington, D.C.: American Folklife Center, Library of Congress, 1989, 12-33.

In a survey of working-class fox hunting in New Jersey's Lebanon State Forest, Hufford relates the experiences of several participants, mostly older self-described woodsmen whose lives and memories are linked to the foxhunting landscape.

D.215. Inscoe, John C. "Memories of a Presbyterian Mission Worker: An Interview with Rubie Ray Cunningham." *Appalachian Journal* 15:2 (1988), 145-160.

In an interview conducted in 1983, Cunningham (1897-1987), recalls her encounter over 60 years before with the mountain folk of Buckhorn, Kentucky, when she came, in 1918, to teach at the Witherspoon School, established by Edward O. Guerrant, a Presbyterian minister.

D.216. Jones, Lu Ann. "'Mama Learned Us to Work': An Oral History of Virgie St. John Redmond." *Oral History Review* 17:2 (1989), 63-90.

Jones presents transcripts of an interview with Redmond, born in 1919 in the North Carolina Piedmont, and who farmed in Iredell County, whose life story was recorded as part of a Smithsonian-sponsored project, "An Oral History of American Agriculture," in which 180 women and men who came of age during the period of the New Deal were asked to talk about changes in work, family and community life.

D.217. Jones-Eddy, Julie. *Homesteading Women: An Oral History of Colorado, 1890-1950.* New York: Twayne Publishers, 1992.

The author, a granddaughter of early settlers in Northwestern Colorado, interviewed 47 women, ranging in age from 54 to 95, who talk about their lives as homesteaders in remote rural areas in this region (and in a few cases, life in small communities in the area); excerpts of interviews, along with many of Jones-Eddy's interview questions, are arranged in such categories as "Starting a New Life," "Home and Family," "Community," and "Looking Back."

D.218. Joyce, Rosemary. "The Life of Sarah Penfield, Rural Ohio Grandmother: Tradition Maintained, Tradition Threatened." In Erika Bourguignon, ed. *A World of Women: Anthropological Studies of Women in the Societies of the World.* New York: Praeger, 1980, 271-303.

Joyce discusss the conservative and pervasive role of tradition in the life of a 74-year-old woman from a rural community in southeastern Ohio (see **D.219**).

D.219. Joyce, Rosemary O. *A Woman's Place: The Life History of a Rural Ohio Grandmother.* Columbus: Ohio State University Press, 1983.

Over a three-year period in the 1970s, Joyce recorded the life story of Sarah Flynn Penfield (pseud.); the book is divided into chapters on methodology, the personal and historical context of Sarah's life, and her contrasting views on family traditions and the treatment of women; narrative passages are framed by commentary and summaries by the author.

D.220. Kahn, Kathy. *Hillbilly Women.* Garden City, New York: Doubleday , 1973.

A sympathetic series of interviews was conducted with young and old Anglo-American women in southern Appalachia, who talk about life as miners' wives, as workers in factories and cotton mills, some as recipients of welfare; they address traditional community life and values, as well as social injustice.

D.221. Knoepfle, John. "Johnny Dobbs: A Pilot's Memories." *Tennessee Folklore Society Bulletin* 54:2 (1990), 49-55.

This is the transcript of an interview conducted by Knoepfle in 1957 with Dobbs, pilot of the *Joe Wheeler* and other boats on the Tennessee river, who started working on the river in 1903 and, after a hiatus in 1953, continued on the excursion Steamer *Avalon*.

D.222. Lawless, Elaine. *Handmaidens of the Lord: Pentecostal Women Preachers and Traditional Religion.* Philadelphia: University of Pennsylvania Press, 1988.

Lawless offers an analysis of the lives and ministry of Pentecostal women pastors and preachers in central Missouri, and includes the life stories of four women in their 50s to 80s, as well as transcriptions of sermons.

D.223. Lloyd, Timothy C., and Patrick B. Mullen. *Lake Erie Fishermen: Work, Identity, and Tradition.* Urbana: University of Illinois Press, 1990.

This book is based on interviews with active and retired fishermen and their wives, both at work and at leisure; one chapter, "the Past," is devoted to the reminiscences of retired fishermen; excerpts of transcribed interviews appear throughout the work.

D.224. Long, Terry L. "Occupational and Individual Identity Among Ohio Railroad Workers of the Steam Era." *Western Folklore* 51:3-4 (1992), 219-235.

Long analyzes the personal narratives of retired railroad workers in central and southern Ohio, recorded over a several year period beginning in the late 1970s, noting the retention of occupational identity as primary, even though removed from the workplace.

D.225. McDermitt, Barbara. "Storytelling and a Boy Named Jack." *North Carolina Folklore Journal* 31 (1983), 13-90.

McDermitt describes and presents the transcribed narratives of Ray Hicks, Blue Ridge Mountain storyteller, born in 1922, and best known for his "Jack Tales" (see **D.238, D.239**).

D.226. McMahon, Felicia (Faye). "Inside Millie's Kitchen: Voices of the Adirondacks." *New York Folklore* 16:1-2 (1990), 1-24.

McMahon presents and analyzes the personal narratives of Millie Geisler, a resident of Westport, New York, a village on the shore of Lake Champlain, recorded along with the comments of her friends in this Adirondack community.

D.227. McNeil, W. K., and Kathy Nicol. "Folk Narratives of Jessie Hubert Wilkes." *Tennessee Folklore Society Bulletin* 48:3 (1982), 68-82.

Wilkes, born in 1905, in Sidney, Arkansas, has lived much of his life in Cave City, Arkansas, where he is renowned as a teller of tall tales, several of which are presented here, in additional to one or two stories represented as "true."

D.228. Meader, John T. "Dell Turner: The Stories of His Life." *Northeast Folklore* 27 (1988), 1-126.

Labeled a "biography/autobiography" of Meader's grandfather Turner (1892-1980), of New Brunswick, Meader presents a portrait composed from interviews with Turner's friends and relatives, and his own personal knowledge about his grandfather.

D.229. Minister, Kristina. "Rehearsing for the Ultimate Audience." In Elizabeth C. Fine and Jean Haskell Speer, eds. *Performance, Culture and Identity*. Westport, Connecticut: Praeger, 1992.

Minister analyzes the narrative performances of Ili Harrison, 82, living in the Huachaca Mountains southeast of Tucson, Arizona, who spent much of her life hunting, working cattle, and lecturing about the wildlife of the Sonora Desert; an expert storyteller, she cultivates an image for her audience, and posterity, of a vigorous woman still riding the mountain trails and working with cowboys.

D.230. Mitchell, Roger E. "'I'm a Man That Works': The Biography of Don Mitchell of Merrill, Maine." *Northeast Folklore* 19 (1978), 1-130.

Don Mitchell, age 79, told the story of his life as a woodsman to his son Roger, age 51, who presents excerpts culled from over 2,000 pages of transcribed material, interspersed with his own comments about "woods work" drawn from his own experience.

D.231. Morse, Rebecca. "Weaving the Fabric of Our Lives: Collecting Oral History from Family Members." *Northeast Folklore* 30 (1995), 167-189.

Morse interviewed her grandmother, Dorothy Paulen Rogers, born in 1910, and who worked and ministered in a nursing home in central Vermont, also recorded the recollections of her mother, born in 1932, to provide generational continuity.

D.232. Mullen, Patrick B. "A Traditional Storyteller in Changing Contexts." In Richard Bauman and Roger D. Abrahams, eds. *'And Other Neighborly Names': Social Process and Cultural Change in Texas Folklore.* Austin: University of Texas Press, 1981, 266-279.

Mullen discusses the ways in which Ed Bell, who had developed as a storyteller over the forty years that he ran a bait camp on the Gulf Coast, adapted his performances in late life to accommodate changes in the nature of his audience.

D.233. New, Michael S. "Tales of a Southwestern Pioneer." *Southwest Folklore* 1:3 (1973), 29-40.

New presents transcripts of an interview with Henry Pollack, storyteller and singer born in 1910 in Kane County, Utah, who talks about life in the small Mormon farming communities of southern Utah.

D.234. Newby, Christine H. "Ray Hicks: A Storyteller's Story." *Tennessee Folklore Society Bulletin* 49:4 (1983), 155-167.

Newby presents a profile, with generous transcribed interview excerpts, of the life of traditional storyteller Hicks, of Beech Mountain, North Carolina, born in 1922, known for his ghost and spirit tales told as authentic personal experiences.

D.235. O'Farrell, M. Brigid, and Lydia Kleiner. "Anna Sullivan: Trade Union Organizer." *Frontiers* 2:2 (1977), 29-36.

This interview with Sullivan, of Holyoke, Massachussetts, born in 1904, who worked in textile mills from age 14 through the 1930s, and who talks about her family, life in the mills, and organizing for the Textile Workers Union of America in 1936, was part of an oral history project involving interviews with 50 trade union women activists throughout the country.

D.236. Ott, Eleanor. "Back There." *Northeast Folklore* 30 (1995), 15-43.

Ott met Bernice Vienna Angell Wheeler ("Grammy"), born in 1895 in South Woodbury, Vermont, through Bernice's daughter Lucille Cerutti; she recorded the life story of Grammy, then 95, at her farmhouse in North Montpelier, where she moved when she got married in the early 1900s; Ott discusses the nature of the interview (occasionally a three-way conversation including Lucille).

D.237. Oxford, Cheryl. "The Storyteller as Craftsman: Stanley Hicks Telling 'Jack and the Bull.'"*North Carolina Folklore Journal* 36:2 (1989), 73-120.

Oxford examines the performance style of Hicks, born in 1911, a traditional instrument maker, musician and storyteller from Beech Mountain, North Carolina (see also **D.225, D.238**).

D.238. Oxford, Cheryl. "The Storyteller as Shaman: Ray Hicks and His Jack Tales." *North Carolina Folklore Journal* 38:2 (1991), 74-186.

Oxford examines the performance style and personality of Hicks, born in 1922, a traditional storyteller from Banner Elk, North Carolina, in the Blue Ridge Mountains, who reveals much about himself as he tells stories from the popular Jack Tale cycle.

D.239. Perdue, Charles. "The Americanization of John Egerton and Aunt Arie." *Appalachian Journal* 11:4 (1984), 437-441.

Perdue critiques two published life histories of older Appalachians, one by Egerton, whose *Generations* chronicled the lives of Burnan and Addie Ledford (see **D.202**) and an oral history of "Aunt" Arie Carpenter, of *Foxfire* fame (see **D.208**); he describes them as presenting romanticized views of the past that "share a nostalgic concern for old people, old things and old times."

D.240. Post, Jennifer. "Family Song Tradition: The Pierce Spaulding Family." *Northeast Folklore* 30 (1995), 57-89.

Post presents excerpts of a recorded conversation with Marjorie Pierce, born in 1903, whose family has lived in Bridgewater, North Shrewsbury, Vermont, since the 18th century; Pierce discusses rural Vermont musical traditions at the turn of the century, and the legacy of her mother Gertrude Spaulding-Smith, with examples of the family song repertoire.

D.241. Pride, Fleetwood (David C. Smith and Edward D. Ives, eds.). "Fleetwood Pride 1864-1960: The Autobiography of a Maine Woodsman." *Northeast Folklore* 9 (1967), 1-60.

Folklorist Ives met Pride in 1959, and he and Smith present a written narrative by Pride, edited and footnoted by them, with added material transcribed from interviews conducted with Pride in 1959.

D.242. Riggins, Stephen Harold. "If Work Made People Rich: An Oral History of General Farming, 1905-1925." *Midwestern Folklore* 17:2 (1991), 73-109.

Riggins' main informant, Eithel (Ledgerwood) Riggins, born in 1905, and several others, describe family and agricultural lifestyles in the first quarter of this century, with a focus on Ledgerwood Farms, south of the town of Loogootee, Indiana.

D.243. Riley, Sheila. "Mam Ma: An Oral Life History of Mona Baldwin." Master's Thesis, Western Kentucky University, Bowling Green, 1986.

Riley presents a study of the personal experience narratives, traditional stories, and folk beliefs of her grandmother, "Mam Ma" Baldwin, of Owenton, Kentucky, with generous excerpts of interviews conducted between 1978 and 1985.

D.244. Shackelford, Laurel, and Bill Weinberg, eds. *Our Appalachia.* New York: Hill and Wang, 1977.

This is a collection of transcribed excerpts of interviews conducted under the auspices of the Appalachia Oral History Project in the early 1970s, and represents a cross section of young and old residents of Central Appalachia–"mountain people" living in the hills and valleys of eastern Kentucky, southwestern Virginia and western North Carolina.

D.245. Sharrow, Gregory. "Field Research Collaboration: Getting to Know George Daniels." *Northeast Folklore* 30 (1995), 124-167.

Sharrow presents, and discusses the process of recording, the life story of Daniels, born in 1910 on a hill farm near the village of Royalton, Vermont, and who has spent a lifetime largely engaged in the activity of subsistence farming.

D.246. Sharrow, Gregory, with Meg Ostrum and Stan Sherer. *Families on the Land: Profiles of Vermont Farm Families.* Middlebury: Vermont Folklife Center, 1995.

This is a collection of interviews by folklorist Sharrow, with photographs by Stan Sherer, from ten families, representing several generations, that were featured in the exhibit "Making and Remaking Vermont Farmsteads, as part of a project directed by Ostrum.

D.247. Silver, James L. "A Oral History of Underground Coal Mining: A Tape-Recorded Interview With A Retired Miner." *Midwestern Folklore* 19:1 (1993), 34-47.

In April, 1983, the author interviewed his grandfather Carl, 89, and grandmother Gladys, 87, in their home in Terre Haute, Indiana, about their memories of mining in Diamond, Indiana.

D.248. Smith, Winton S. "Escar Coe on the Upper Cumberland: Reminscences of a River Pilot." *Kentucky Folklore Record* 20:3 (1974), 59-83.

Coe, born in Russel County, Kentucky, in Puncheon Camp Bottom, on the Cumberland River, in 1899, recalls piloting steamboats on the Upper Cumberland in Kentucky and Tennessee from 1918-1929.

D.249. Storm, Carolyn. "Arizona Stories." *Southwest Folklore* 2:1 (1978), 32-39.

This is a collection of anecdotes "as told to Shirley Swan, Cave Creek Arizona" by Jim Hardy, 97, who talks about life in Cave Creek in the early part of this century, and his career as a cowpuncher.

D.250. Tilton, Tom (Gale Huntington, ed.) "Tom Tilton: Coaster and Fisherman." *Northeast Folklore* 23 (1982), 1-68.

Tilton, born in Chilmak on the island of Martha's Vineyard, Massachusetts, in 1887, tells of a life spent sailing the coastal waters of the U. S. and trapfishing in the waters around the Vineyard, to Huntington, who interviewed him in the 1970s.

D.251. Turley, Todd. "Grandad's Stories." *Southwest Folklore* 2:1 (1978), 49-54.

This is a brief collection of stories recorded in Flagstaff, Arizona, by the author from his grandfather, S. D. Allen, a former stone mason who has lived most of his life in Arizona, hunting, trapping, and building his own stone house.

D.252. Utech, Eugene. "J. Raymond Bear's Olde Tyme Ghost Tales of Cumberland County." *Keystone Folklore Quarterly* 12:4 (1967), 211-228.

Utech recorded several ghost stories from Bear, born in 1896, at the old Barnitz feed mill in Carlisle, Pennsylvania (as well a couple of others who walked into the conversation); Bear makes it clear that he has seen supernatural phenomena, attributing his ability to having been born with a caul (veil).

D.253. Wagner, Sally Roesch. "Oral History as a Biographical Tool." *Frontiers* 2:2 (1977), 87-92.

Wagner describes, with excerpts, her interview with Maltida Jewell Gage, 91, of Aberdeen, South Dakota, the only living grandchild of suffragist Matilda Josyln Gage, and who has kept letters and manuscripts, and tells family stories about the elder Gage, in order to keep alive the memory of a radical whose history was eclipsed by more conservative forces within the suffrage movement.

D.254. Walton, David A. "Lou Sesher Stories III" *Keystone Folklore Quarterly* 12:3 (1967), 177-186.

More tales by Sesher, retired riverboat engineer (see **D.256**).

D.255. Walton, David A. "Lou Sesher Stories IV" *Keystone Folklore Quarterly* 12:4 (1967), 229-232.

More tales by Sesher, retired riverboat engineer (see **D.256**).

D.256. Walton, David A. "Pennsylvania Riverboat Stories." *Keystone Folklore Quarterly* 11:4 (1966), 215-237.

Walton presents transcripts of an interview with Lou Sesher, 74, retired steamboat engineer living in Lock Four, Pennsylvania, who weaves personal experience and tall tales of life along the river.

D.257. Walton, David A. "Pennsylvania Riverboat Tales II" *Keystone Folklore Quarterly* 12:1 (1967), 81-93.

More stories by Lou Sesher, retired riverboat engineer (see **D.256**).

D.258. Warner, William S. "An Honest Woodsman: The Life and Opinions of Dave Priest–Maine Trapper, Guide and Game Warden." *Northeast Folklore* 22 (1981), 1-112.

Warner presents the life of Priest, born in 1913, retired game warden, largely through excerpts of interviews conducted at his home along the Penobscot River.

D.259. Wayne, Reuel Bean, ed. "Me and Annie: The Oral Autobiography of Ralph Thompson of Topsfield, Maine." *Northeast Folklore* 14 (1973), 1-94.

This is a self-portrait of the woodsman, born in 1885, lifelong resident of Topsfield, in Washington County, Maine, and his experiences with his wife Annie, with whom he was married from 1910 to 1969.

D.260. Wildridge, Aimee. "Performing Folklore at a Family Dinner: Transcription of a Tape-Recorded Interview." *Midwestern Folklore* 19:1 (1993), 43-60.

Wildridge recorded a storytelling session during a family gathering on Sunday, April 12, 1992, in her grandmother's house in Odeon, Indiana, with her two sisters, her parents, "Granny" (born 1925) and "Pap" (born 1918), which included stories of Pap and Granny's courting days.

D.261. Wolford, John B. "Memories, Dreams, Recollections: A Sampler From Studebaker Oral Histories." *Indiana Folklore* 14:2 (1985), 87-111.

Wolford presents excerpts of eight interviews, selected from 30 conducted in 1984 with former workers at the Studebaker auto plant in South Bend, Indiana, which closed in 1963; the excerpts (presented with both Wolford's questions and the interviewees'responses) focus on particular themes related to the experience of working at Studebaker (see also **D.211**).

Other European-American

D.262. Asplund, Arvid. "Via Dolorosa." In Alan Jabbour and James Hardin, eds. *Folklife Annual 1986*. Washington, D. C.: American Folklife Program, Library of Congress, 1987, 132-153.

Following his retirement in 1973, Asplund, born in 1908, a child of Finnish immigrants, composed a personal account of his early family life in northern Wisconsin, prompted by a desire to write a story for his children to read, and inspired by a creative writing class at the Senior Center, Manitowoc, Wisconsin.

D.263. Degh, Linda. "Dial a Story, Dial an Audience: Two Rural Women in an Urban Setting." In Rosan A. Jordan and Susan J. Kalcik, eds. *Women's Folklore, Women's Culture*. Philadelphia: University of Pennsylvania Press, 1985, 3-25.

Degh describes the ways in which "Aunt" Marge Kovács and "Aunt" Katie Kis, elder members of Gary, Indiana's Hungarian community and "born village storytellers," bring to bear Old World narrative skills when conversing on the telephone (this article was also published as "Two Old World Narrators on the Telephone,"[see **D.8**]).

D.264. Dieffenbach, Victor C. "Reminiscences of "Der Dumm Fattel." *Pennsylvania Folklife* 15:4 (1965), 44-49.

Dieffenbach (1882-1965), a frequent contributor to *Pennsylvania Folklife,* recalls his childhood in the "Dumb Quarter," a German community in the northwest corner of Berks County, Pennsylvania.

D.265. Huisingh, Valerie. "'The Nun in the Trash Can': The Personal Experience Narratives of Robert Jungers." *North Carolina Folklore Journal* 41:1 (1994), 44-54.

Huisingh presents the recorded narratives of her father, a retired chemist in his 60s, who recalls growing up in a small town in Montana in the 1930s and '40s.

D.266. Johnson, Colleen Leahy. *Growing Up and Growing Old in Italian-American Families.* New Brunswick, New Jersey: Rutgers University Press, 1985.

Middle-aged and elderly Italians describe family life both in its traditional immigrant form (from southern Italy) and its contemporary form; an analysis of intergenerational relations at a time of personal life transition and social change is presented, interspersed with interview excerpts.

D.267. Mathias, Elizabeth, and Richard Raspa. *Italian Folktales In America: The Verbal Art of an Immigrant Woman.* Detroit: Wayne State University Press, 1985.

This book reviews the repertoire of storyteller Clementina Todesco, as recorded by her daughter, Bruna, and rediscovered by Mathias and Raspa, who re-interviewed Todesco, and returned to the Italian village where she grew up, where they recorded the memories and stories of elders there as background to the stories and personal experience narratives of Todesco.

D.268. Moran, Joyce Demcher. *"Miz Ukraini:* "We Are from the Ukraine.'"*Pennsylvania Folklife* 28:2 (1978-79), 12-17.

Moran interweaves interviews with her grandparents, conducted in Forestville, Pennsylvania in 1966/67, with historical background.

D.269. Paris, Beltran, with William A. Douglas. *Beltran: Basque Sheepman of the American West.* Reno: University of Nevada Press, 1979.

Paris was born in 1888 in the town of Lasse, in the French Basque country near the Spanish border, and came to the American West in the early 1900s to herd sheep; shortly after Douglas became Coordinator of Basque Studies at the University of Nevada in 1967, he met Paris, and conducted interviews with him then, and again in the mid-1970s when Paris,was 89 and still "camptending" and directing the young herders.

D.270. Rauchle, Bob. "Reminiscences from the Germantown Settlement in Gibson County, Tennessee." *Tennessee Folklore Society Bulletin* 45:11 (1979), 62-67.

Rauchle interviewed Mrs. Louise Theresa Räuchle Casey, 81, "one of the matriarchs of the German colony," who recalled life in the Germantown Settlement near Milan, Tennessee, in the early 1900s.

D.271. Riegel, Lewis Edgar. "Reminiscences of a Boyhood in Reading 1883-1890." *Pennsylvania Folklife* 16:3 (1967).

This is the second installment of the author's autobiography, relating his adaptation as a "Dutch-speaking country boy" to school in Reading, Pennsylvania (see **D.272**).

D.272. Riegel, Lewis Edgar. "Reminiscences of Centerport, 1876-1885." *Pennsylvania Folklife* 14:2 (1964) 24-47.

The author recalls family stories, and visits to Grandmother during his childhood in Centerport, Berks County, Pennsylvania (see **D.271**).

D.273. Sehnsdorf, Henning K. "'I Went Through a Lot of Misery': The Stories of Fred Simonsen, Norwegian American Fisherman." *Northwest Folklore* 10:1 (1991), 5-42.

Simonsen (1890-1990), a fisherman who emigrated from Norway in 1910 to the Pacific Northwest, talks about fishing in the Bering Sea, logging in Portland, mining in Juneau, fighting fires in Idaho, and finally retiring, in 1960, to Ballard, a Scandinavian neighborhood in Seattle, where he gained a reputation as a storyteller.

D.274. Sevigny, Anna M. (Julia A. Hunter, ed.) "Anna May: Eighty Two Years in New England." *Northeast Folklore* 20 (1979), 1-106.

Sevigny (1895-1979), who spent much of her life in southern New Hampshire, told her life story to Hunter (then a student of anthropologist and author Michael Dorris at Dartmouth College, in 1978) at Sevigny's last residence at the Hanover Terrace Health Care Center.

D.275. Shakir, Evelyn. "Syrian-Lebanese Women Tell Their Story." *Frontiers* 7:1 (1983), 9-13.

Shakir interviewed her mother, who emigrated from Lebanon in 1907, and then spoke with "relatives, friends and friends of friends" in the Boston area, and a few in St. Paul, Minnesota; she summarizes, with excerpts, interviews she conducted with 20 women, aged 55 to 90, eight of them born in the U. S., who recall life in mountain villages of Syria and Lebanon as well as urban America.

D.276. Siporin, Steve. "Our Life was Very Clear." *Northwest Folklore* 8:2 (1990), 3-18.

Siporin interviewed members of the Nick family, Italian immigrants in the town of Price, in Carbon County, Utah, including matriarch Mary Nick Juliano, who recalls emigrating from southern Italy in 1909.

D.277. Sweterlitsch, Dick. "Sophia Bielli: A Vermont Storyteller." *Northeast Folklore* 30 (1995), 44-56.

Bielli, age 84, Barre, Vermont's "most celebrated ranconteur," shares her memories of life in the Italian North End among other immigrants and children of immigrants, many of whom worked in area granite quarries.

Asian/Pacific Americans

D.278. Gillenkirk, Jeff, and James Motlow. *Bitter Melon: Inside America's Last Rural Chinese Town.* Berkeley, California: Heyday Books, 1987.

This collection of thirteen oral histories (ten of them with elders), and accompanying photographs, documents the lives of residents of Locke, in California's Sacramento Delta, settled by Chinese immigrants in 1915, and the only town in North America built and inhabited exclusively by Chinese.

D.279. Glenn, Evelyn Nakano. *Issei, Nisei, War Bride: Three Generations of Japanese-American Women in Domestic Service.* Philadelphia: Temple University Press, 1986.

Glenn, a sansei (3rd generation Japanese-American), interviewed *issei* (1st generation) women aged 65 to 91, *nisei* (2nd generation) women aged 48-84, and war brides (women born in Japan who arrived after WWII) aged 41-55, to understand their relationship to family and community, and how they have adapted to domination at home and in the labor market; she attended church functions, senior centers and other informal social events; historical analysis is presented along with interview excerpts.

D.280. Kikamura, Akemi. *Through Harsh Winters: The Life of a Japanese Immigrant Woman.* Novato, California: Chandler & Sharp, 1981.

Anthropologist Kikamura presents the life history, from tape-recorded interviews, of her mother, Michiko Tanaka, born in 1904, along with essays by the author about her journey to Japan to gather background material on her mother's past, and reflections on her mother's past made after completing the life history.

D.281. Kim, Elaine, and Eui-Young Yu. *East to America: Korean American Life Stories.* New York: The New Press, 1996.

This is a collection of short, edited transcripts of 38 interviews chosen from over 100 recorded from Korean-Americans living in Los Angeles, as part of a project ironically inspired by the attention brought to the Korean community during the riots in 1993 in the wake of the acquittal of the police officers who beat Rodney King; while most of the narrators in the book are immigrants in their 20s to 40s, there are a number of older Koreans represented.

D.282. Lee, Helie. *Still Life With Rice: A Young American Woman Discovers the Life and Legacy of her Korean Grandmother.* New York: Scribner, 1996.

In an impressionistic work about the life of her 80-year-old grandmother, Baek Hongyong, Lee takes poetic license with oral history, opening with her description of the search for her grandmother's past, and her own self-reflection, and then constructing a narrative in the voice of her grandmother, with material based on interviews with her, as well as conversations with the author's mother, who is credited with "filling in the blanks when Grandmother's memory failed."

D.283. Lee, Joann Faung Jean. *Asian American Experiences in the United States: Oral Histories of First to Fourth Generation Americans from China, the Phillipines, Japan, India, the Pacific Islands, Vietnam and Cambodia.* Jefferson, North Carolina: McFarland & Co., 1991.

Lee conducted oral history interviews with over 50 people aged 11 to 82, ten of whom are elders; most of them live in the New York tri-state area, and range from newly arrived immigrants in New York's Chinatown to members of a senior citizens' center; the brief narratives are arranged in three major sections: "Living in America", "Americanization"; and "Aspects of Interracial Marriage."

D.284. Lee, Mary Paik (Sucheng Chan, ed.). *Quiet Odyssey: A Pioneer Korean Woman in America.* Seattle: University of Washington Press, 1990.

Chan edited the typewritten manscript of Lee, 86, who came with her family at age 5 to Hawaii, then settled a year and a half later in Southern California, following an immigrant occupational pattern of agricultural work and domestic service; in addition to descriptions of migration, farming, marriage and children, are accounts of discrimination and reflections on old age.

D.285. Masumoto, David Mas. *Country Voices: The Oral History of a Japanese American Family Farm Community.* Del Rey, California: Inaka Countryside Publications, 1987.

Masumoto, raised in a Japanese farming community in central California, combines oral history interviews of older *issei* (first generation Japanese American immigrants) as well as *nisei* (2nd gen.) and *sansei*, (3rd gen.), with essays and stories, recreating everyday life in Del Rey, just south of Fresno.

D.285.a. Nee, Victor G., and Brett De Bary Nee. *Long Time Californ'.* New York: Pantheon Books, 1973.

The authors present a study of San Francisco's Chinatown that includes the transcribed, edited excerpts of a number of oral history interviews with residents; one chapter is entitled "Oldtimers' Tales"; another is "Clans and Elders."

D.286. Tamura, Linda. *The Hood River Issei: An Oral History of Japanese Settlers in Oregon's Hood River Valley.* Urbana: University of Illinois Press, 1993.

Tamura presents the life stories of 14 first-generation Japanese immigrants who arrived in the U. S. between the late 1800s and the 1920s, and who settled in the rural Hood River Valley; reminiscences of childhood in Japan, life in the Valley on family farms, and memories of anti-Japanese feelings, internment, and the eventual return to their apple orchards, are interwoven with historical documentation.

D.287. Tsuchida, John Nobuya, ed. *Reflections: Memoirs of Japanese Amerian Women in Minnesota.* Covina, California: Pacific Asia Press, 1994.

Ironically, memories stirred by the 50th anniversary of Pearl Harbor inspired this collection of self-composed autobiographies of 14 elder *nisei* (1st generation Japanese-American) women born on the West Coast, interned in camps in 1942, then allowed to relocate to the midwest to attend college, and who later led varied professional lives; in their retirement, they look back upon their unusual odyssey, and reflect on their ties to the Japanese-American community.

D.288. Yung, Judy. "'A Bowlful of Tears': Chinese Women Immigrants on Angel Island." *Frontiers* 2:2 (1977), 52-55.

Yung describes, with interview excerpts, the experiences of Chinese-American women in their 70s and 80s who were among the thousands of Chinese immigrants detained on San Francisco's Angel Island Immigration Station between 1910 and 1941.

Hispanic-American

D.289. Benmayor, Rina, Ana Juarbe, Blanca Vazquez Erazo, and Celia Alvarez. "Stories to Live By: Continuity and Change in Three Generations of Puerto Rican Women." *Oral History Review* 16:2 (1988), 1-93.

This is a set of articles by each of the authors, part of a project initiated by the Center for Puerto Rican Studies of Hunter College, City University of New York, in which life stories were recorded of Puerto Rican women who have worked in the garment industry, including elders, whose identities and strategies for personal and cultural survival are revealed in their narratives.

D.290. Clark, M., and M. Mendelson. "Mexican-American Aged in San Francisco: A Case Study." *The Gerontologist* 9:2 (1969), 90-95.

This is a life portrait of Beatriz Chavez, a 71-year-old grandmother, and her family, living in San Francisco's Mission District.

D.291. Coles, Robert. *The Old Ones of New Mexico*. Albuquerque: University of New Mexico Press, 1973.

Coles, a child psychiatrist who came to New Mexico in search of young interview subjects for his *Children of Crisis* series, was told "if you want to know about the children, you must first speak with the old people; what they believe, the child soon believes," and so he recorded these life stories of Spanish-speaking elders.

D.291.a. deBuys, William, and Alex Harris. *River of Traps: A Village Life*. Albuquerque: University of New Mexico Press, 1990.

The life of Jacobo Romero, an old farmer living in the Sangre de Cristo Mountains of northern New Mexico, is documented by writer deBuys and photographer Harris, who met Romero when they became neighbors in the early 1970s while working for Robert Coles (see **D.291**).

D.292. Elsasser, Nan, Kyle MacKenzie, and Yvonne Tixier y Vigil. *Las Mujeres: Conversations From a Hispanic Community*. Old Westbury, New York: The Feminist Press, 1980.

This is a collection of 21 life stories told to the authors by Hispanic women of New Mexico, ranging in age from their 20s to their 80s, and divided into four sections, based on their ages, the first two sections featuring respectively five women aged 60 to 80, and five women in their 50s.

D.293. Garcia, Mario T. "Identity and Gender in the Mexican-American *Testimonio*: The Life and Narrative of Frances Esquivel Twyoniak." In Benmayor, Rina, and Andor Skotnes, eds. *Migration and Identity.* Oxford: Oxford University Press, 1994, 151-166.

Garcia defines the *testimonio* as "a Latin-American genre of autobiographical texts that are the result of oral history projects usually involving academic scholars or journalists, on the one hand, and grass-roots activists on the other"; he examines the *testimonio* of Fran Esquivel, born in 1931, whose family moved from New Mexico to California's San Joaquín Valley when she was 6, and who later taught in the San Francisco Bay area.

D.294. García, Nasario, ed. *Abuelitos: Stories of the Río Puerco Valley.* Albuquerque: University of New Mexico Press, 1992 .

The author presents a second bilingual volume featuring the voices of older Mexican-American residents of New Mexico's Rio Puerco Valley (see also **D.294.a, D.294.b**).

D.294.a. García, Nasario, ed. *Recuerdos de los Viejitos: Tales of the Río Puerco.* Albuquerque: University of New Mexico Press, 1987.

García presents, in a bilingual edition, the life stories and traditional tales of 15 former residents of four Spanish-speaking villages in the Río Puerco Valley of west-central New Mexico, ranging in age from 58 to 93, and including the author's paternal grandmother (see also **D.294, D.294.b**).

D.294.b. García, Nasario, ed. *Tata: A Voice from the Río Puerco.* Albuquerque: University of New Mexico Press, 1994.

This is the third volume in García's trilogy of the life and times of the people of New Mexico's Río Puerco valley; this book presents the personal narratives of the author's father, Nasario P. García, presented, as are the other two volumes, in a bilingual Spanish-English format (see **D.294, D.294.a**).

D.295. MacKenzie, Kyle, Yvonne Tixier y Vigil and Nan Elasser. "Grandmother's Stories." *Frontiers* 2:2 (1977), 56-58.

This is a description and presentation of a brief, partially bi-lingual conversation between 85-year-old Grandma Vigil and Yvonne Tixier y Vigil, about life as an Hispanic woman in the southwest U. S. in Grandma's day.

D.296. Martin, Patricia Preciado, and Louis Carlos Bernal. *Images and Conversations: Mexican Americans Recall a Southwestern Past.* Tucson: University of Arizona Press, 1983.

This is a collection of transcribed oral history interviews, conducted by Martin, with accompanying photographs by Bernal, of elders residing in Tucson, Arizona, whose reminiscences, folktales, and anecdotes comprise a narrative history of the town's oldest Mexican neighborhoods.

D.297. Martin, Patricia Preciado. *Songs My Mother Sang to Me: An Oral History of Mexican-American Women.* Tucson: University of Arizona Press, 1992.

In these oral histories of ten women in their sixties to eighties, "daughters of ranchers, cowhands, boarding-house keepers, laundresses and midwives," from rural southern Arizona who eventually moved to Tucson, are to be found accounts of family and community history and descriptions of folk traditions.

D.298. De Pellicano, Lilia Patricia Reade. *"Abuelitas de El Paso*: A Selective Cultural Study." Master's thesis, University of Texas at El Paso, 1989.

This is an analysis of the oral histories of five older Mexican-American women, *abuelitas* (grandmothers) whose stories chronicle changes in Mexican-American culture, women, and the city of El Paso, of whose history they have all been part.

D.299. Weber, Devra Anne. *"Raiz Fuerte*: Oral History and Mexican Farmworkers." *Oral History Review* 17:2 (1989), 47-62.

This essay focuses on the recollections of Mrs. Valdez (pseud.), daughter of a Mexican sharecropper, who, as an adolescent, fled with her family from the Mexican revolution of 1910, eventually settling in a small town in California's San Joaquin valley; Weber examines the content and style of her narrative and the nature of the memories she evokes, with a focus on her recollections of a strike by cotton workers in 1933.

D.300. Weigle, Marta. "'Some New Mexico Grandmothers': A Note on the WPA Writers' Program in New Mexico." In Marta Weigle, ed. *Hispanic Arts and Ethnohistory in the Southwest*. Santa Fe, New Mexico: Ancient City Press, 1983.

This article describes the work of Annette Hesch Thorp who, under the auspices of the WPA Writers' program, collected a number of personal experience narratives, including stories of saints, miracles, and witchcraft, told to her by elderly Hispanic women in northern New Mexico in 1940 and 1941.

Jewish

D.301. Kahn, Alison. *Listen While I Tell You: A Story of the Jews of St. John's, Newfoundland*. St. John's: Institute of Social and Economic Research, Memorial University of Newfoundland, 1987.

Based on the author's master's thesis in folklore at Memorial University, much of the book consists of the edited transcripts of oral history interviews with 27 people who represent the first, second, and third generations of the families that established the small Jewish community in St. John's at the turn of the century.

D.302. Kann, Kenneth. *Comrades and Chicken Ranchers: The Story of a California Jewish Community*. Ithaca, New York: Cornell University Press, 1993.

Over a 12-year period, Kann conducted oral history interviews with members of three generations of people who have lived in the small Jewish community of Petaluma California, founded by immigrant radicals who earned a living raising chickens, and who kept alive an enclave of the Yiddish-speaking left-wing subculture, lost on their children and grandchildren, and unknown to newcomers.

D.303. Kann, Kenneth L. *Joe Rapoport: The Life of a Jewish Radical*. Philadelphia: Temple University Press, 1981.

Kann presents the edited transcript of over 70 hours of oral history interviews with Rapoport, an elder Jewish immigrant political activist, and a longtime member of a unique community of Jewish chicken ranchers in Petaluma, California (see **D.302**).

D.304. Kramer, Sydelle, and Jenny Masur, eds. *Jewish Grandmothers*. Boston: Beacon Press, 1976.

These are oral histories, mostly recorded in Chicago, of ten older East European Jewish immigrant women, who talk about their lives, their cultural traditions, their adjustment to changing social conditions and to the aging process.

D.305. Kugelmass, Jack. *The Miracle of Intervale Avenue: The Story of a Jewish Congregation in the South Bronx*. New York: Schocken Books, 1986.

This is a study of cultural survival among a small group of mostly elderly Jews who frequent the Intervale Jewish Center in a former Jewish neighborhood in the Bronx, with a focus upon the personal narratives of Moise Sacks, the Center's "charismatic leader, acting rabbi, master baker, and storyteller" (see **H.190**).

D.306. Leviatin, David. *Followers of the Trail: Jewish Working-Class Radicals in America*. New Haven: Yale University Press, 1989.

Leviatin presents extracts of oral history interviews with–and accompanying photographs of–former members of "Followers of the Trail," a summer camp for Jewish Communist workers founded in the 1930s in Buchanan, New York; they review their political lives, culture and religion, talk about communal living, and reflect upon aging.

D.307. Myerhoff, Barbara. *Number Our Days*. New York: E. P. Dutton, 1978.

Anthropologist Myerhoff's landmark study of the lives of elderly Jews who congregate at a senior center on the boardwalk in Venice, California; she recorded their life stories both individually and in "living history" groups, and documented the ceremonies that hold this small, diminishing, but vibrant community together (see **D.13, H.193**).

D.308. Shuldiner, David. *Aging Political Activists: Personal Narratives from the Old Left*. Westport, Connecticut: Praeger, 1995.

Shuldiner presents the complete transcripts of conversations conducted with four political activists in their 60s and 70s, a married couple and their two closest friends, all raised in radical Jewish working-class families and all former members of the Communist Party in Connecticut, who talk about how the confluence of personal, political and cultural aspects of their identity have played out in lives that continue to be defined by their vision of a better world.

D.308.a. Shuldiner, David. "Of Moses and Marx: Folk Ideology Within the Jewish Labor Movement in the United States." Doctoral dissertation, University of California, Los Angeles, 1984.

This is a study of the Jewish left-wing subculture in the U. S., based to a large extent upon, and presenting excerpts of, oral history interviews conducted in the early 1980s with older Jewish immigrants and first-generation Jewish-Americans residing in Southern California, who had been active in Jewish communist, socialist, anarchist and labor zionist groups in the early part of this century (and several of whom were still active at the time they were interviewed).

Native American Indian

_____*Alaska Series*. Surrey, British Columbia: Hancock House, 1980-1981.

A series of nine "autobiographies," compiled from tape-recorded interviews (conducted and edited by Curt Madison and Yvonne Yarber) of elders residing in villages serviced by the Yukon-Koyukuk School District in Alaska; they were designed for upper elementary students living in rural Alaska. The series titles consist of the names and villages of residence of persons interviewed:

D.309. *Henry Beatus, Sr.—Hughes.*

D.310. *Joe Beetus—Hughes.*

D.311. *Roger Dayton—Koyukuk.*

D.312. *Moses Henzie—Allakaket.*

D.313. *John Honea—Ruby.*

D.314. *Oscar Nictune—Alatna.*

D.315. *Edwin Simon—Huslia.*

D.316. *Madeline Solomon—Koyukuk.*

D.317. *Frank Tobuk—Bettles.*

D.318. _____*Isahkaalaxpe [With Grandmother]: A Traditional Crow Story as Told by George Takes Gun*. Transcribed by Euna Rose He Does It. Crow Agency, Montana: Bilingual Materials Development Center, 1984.

Produced as a bilingual text for the school district serving the Crow Indians of Montana, this is an illustrated tale about an old woman who helps her grandson overcome the Two-Faces people who had massacred their relatives and friends.

D.318.a. Ahenakew, Freda, and H. C. Wolfart. *Kôhkominawak Otâcimowiniwâwa—Our Grandmothers' Lives as Told in Their Own Words*. Saskatoon, Saskatchewan: Fifth House Publishers, 1992.

This is a collection of the reminiscences and personal stories of seven Cree women elders, recorded in their own language, and presented in the original Cree, with English translations on facing pages.

D.319. Arden, Harvey, ed. *Noble Red Man: Lakota Wisdomkeeper Mathew King*. Hillsboro, Oregon: Beyond Words, 1994.

This book consists of transcripts of conversations with King (1902-1989) elder and spiritual leader of the Lakota (Sioux), recorded by Arden in the late 1980s.

D.320. Ashley, Yvonne. "'That's the Way We Were Raised': An Oral Interview with Ada Damon." *Frontiers* 2:2 (1977), 59-62.

Ashley presents excerpts of an oral history interview she conducted with Damon, her father's aunt, on the Navajo Reservation in Shiprock, New Mexico, just north of where Damon was born in 1900.

D.321. Austin, Alberta. *Ne Ho Niyo De No: That's What It Was Like.* Lackawanna, New York: Rebco Enterprises, 1986.

> Produced as part of the Seneca Nation Curriculum Project, Mrs. Austin, a member of the Seneca Nation, conducted interviews with several dozen Seneca elders; excerpts and summaries are presented, with the two-fold aim of preserving cultural heritage and developing a course on Seneca-Iroquois history and culture for schools on and bordering the Reservations in New York and Pennsylvania.

D.322. Bataille, Gretchen M. *American Indian Women: Telling Their Lives.* Lincoln: University of Nebraska, 1984.

> Among the chapters in this study of American Indian women's autobiography, are essays on Mountain Wolf Woman, a Winnebago Indian whose life story was recorded by Nancy Lurie (see **D.367**), and Maria Chona, a Papago Indian whose account was taken down by Ruth Underhill (see **D.398**).

Beatus, Henry, Sr. [see *Alaska Series* in this section]

Beetus, Joe. [see *Alaska Series* in this section]

D.323. Black-Rogers, Mary. "Dan Raincloud: 'Keeping Our Indian Way.'" In Clifton, James A., ed. *Being and Becoming Indian: Biographical Studies of North American Frontiers.* Chicago: The Dorsey Press, 1989, 226-248.

> During the mid-1960s, Raincloud (1903-1974), a Minnesota Ojibwa *Midewiwin* (Grand Medicine Lodge) priest, presented a carefully constructed "life-legend" to Black-Rogers, who sees Raincloud's narrative as a story he acted out in his effort to mediate between his traditional role and that of a "bridge to the new" (see **D.333**).

D.324. Black Elk, Wallace, and William S. Lyon. *Black Elk: The Sacred Ways of a Lakota.* New York: HarperCollins, 1990.

> This account, transcribed from tape-recorded narratives in English by Black Elk, presents the personal story and teachings of Black Elk, Lakota elder and shaman—born in 1921 on the Rosebud Reservation in South Dakota, and "spiritual" grandchild of Nicholas Black Elk (see **D.343**, **D.375**).

D.325. Blackman, Margaret B. *During My Time: Florence Edenshaw Davidson—A Haida Woman.* Seattle: University of Washington Press, 1992 (1982).

> The text of this book consists of the life story of Davidson, of the community of Masset on the Queen Charlotte Islands off the coast of British Columbia, recorded by Blackman in the early 1980s, preceded by chapters on the nature of life histories, Haida women, and a "biographical sketch"; following the personal narrative is a description of the celebration of Florence Davidson's ninety-fifth birthday.

D.326. Blackman, Margaret B. *Sadie Brower Neakok: An Iñupiaq Woman.* Seattle: University of Washington Press, 1989.

> Based on interviews conducted in the mid-1980s by ethnographer Blackman, this is the life story of Neakok, born in Barrow, Alaska in 1916, the daughter of Asiannggataq, an Eskimo woman, and Charles Brower, Barrow's first white settler; she speaks of her bi-cultural upbringing, her life as a teacher, nurse, social worker and judge, and her work as cultural/political mediator.

D.327. Blue, Helen M, and R. T. King, eds. *Albina Redner: A Shoshone Life.* Reno, Nevada: Oral History Program, University of Nevada, 1990.

Born in the central Nevada mining town of Austin in 1924, Albina Redner recalls her life as a Western Shoshone, describing the traditional way of life, her rejection and ultimate embrace once again of her Shoshone heritage.

D.328. Bodfish, Waldo Sr. (William Schneider, ed., in collaboration with Leona Kisautaq Okakok and James Mumigana Nageak). *Kusiq: An Eskimo Life History from the Arctic Coast of Alaska.* Fairbanks: University of Alaska Press, 1991.

This is an oral biography of Bodfish, Sr., an Iñupiaq elder from the village of Wainwright on the Arctic Coast of Alaska; Schneider who recorded and compiled Bodfish's account, with assistance from Okakok and Nageak, follows the narrative with an historical overview of the themes Bodfish raises.

D.329. Brant, Charles S. *The Autobiography of a Kiowa Apache Indian.* New York: Dover, 1991 [1969].

In the late 1940s, Brant recorded, through a translator, the life story of Jim Whitewolf, born circa 1878, presenting the perspective of one who had witnessed seventy years of dramatic social change (Whitewolf died in the mid 1950s).

D.330. Broker, Ignatia. *Night Flying Woman: An Ojibway Narrative.* St. Paul: Minnesota Historical Society Press, 1983.

Broker, an Ojibway elder, storyteller, and member of the White Earth Reservation, has written a narrative "in the tradition of the Ojibway people," chronicling the life of the mythological *Ni-bo-wi-se-gwe*, or Night Flying Woman, also known as Oona, from her birth during a solar eclipse to her old age, in a merging of traditional stories and Broker's own memories of her community's social and historical experiences.

D.331. Brown, Jennifer, and S. H. Brown. "'A Place in Your Mind for Them All': Chief William Berens." In Clifton, James A., ed. *Being and Becoming Indian: Biographical Studies of North American Frontiers.* Chicago: The Dorsey Press, 1989, 204-225.

In 1940, William Berens (1865-1947), chief of the Berens River band of Saulteaux Indians (Manitoba Ojibwa) shared his reminiscences with anthropologist Irving Hallowell, capping a ten-year period during which he had dictated stories, myths, anecdotes and accounts of dreams to Hallowell; Brown examines the motives each brought to their collaboration (see **D.333**).

D.332. Chief Henry [*Yugh Noholnigee*] (Eliza Jones, ed.). *The Stories That Chief Henry Told.* Fairbanks: Alaska Native Language Center, University of Alaska, 1979.

Eliza Jones [*Neltiloyineelno*] recorded, transcribed, and translated into English, stories told by her uncle, Chief Henry of Huslia, in his native Koyukon Athabaskan, about what traditional life was like in the Allakaket area, and ultimately in the village of Huslia, in interior Alaska.

D.333. Clifton, James A., ed. *Being and Becoming Indian: Biographical Studies of North American Frontiers.* Chicago: The Dorsey Press, 1989.

This work presents analyses of cultural, ethnic, and personal identity in the lives of fourteen individuals who have occupied the cultural margins between traditional Indian society and the dominant Anglo-European culture in North America; several elders are among those whose accounts are considered (see, e.g., **D.331**, **D.355**).

D.334. Colson, Elizabeth, ed. *Autobiographies of Three Pomo Women*. Berkeley, California: Archaeological Research Facility, Department of Anthropology, University of California, 1974.

This work belatedly presents and analyzes the life histories of Sophie Martinez, age 67, Ellen Wood, age 59, and Jane Adams, "slightly over sixty," when they were interviewed by Colson in 1941; to "give insight into the life of Pomo women of a particular generation," caught between traditional culture and white society.

D.335. Cowan, Susan, ed. *We Don't Live in Snow Houses Now: Reflections of Arctic Bay*. Ottowa: Canadian Arctic Producers Limited, 1976.

Canadian Arctic Producers, an art and craft marketing agency owned and operated by the Iñuit in the Northern Territories, produced this book, a bilingual collection (Inuktitut-English) of personal narratives by artists, mostly elders, who live and work in the community of Arctic Bay (Ikpiarjuk).

D.336. Cruikshank, Julie. *Life Lived Like a Story: Life Stories of Three Yukon Native Elders*. Lincoln: University of Nebraska Press, 1990.

These are the accounts of three Native American Indian elders, Angela Sidney, Kitty Smith, and Annie Ned, born in the southern Yukon Territory around the turn of the century, who recall personal and cultural events, and offer stories, songs and other folklore of the Tuchon, Tagish and Tlingit peoples.

D.337. Cruikshank, Julie. "Myth and Tradition as Narrative Framework: Oral Histories From Northern Canada." *International Journal of Oral History* 9:3 (1988), 198-214.

Cruikshank describes her experience interviewing Athabaskan women in the Yukon born during or shortly after the Klondike gold rush (1896-1898), and the challenge of confronting a Native narrative model in which personal history and traditional narratives were considered inseparable parts of one's life story (see **D.336**).

D.338. Cruikshank, Moses (William Schneider, ed.). *The Life I've Been Living*. Fairbanks: University of Alaska Press, 1986.

Cruikshank, an Athabaskan elder born at Fishhook Town, a Native village on the Black River in Northern Yukon sometime between 1902 and 1906, recalls family traditions, a life of hunting and trapping, and encounters between Athabaskans on the Yukon and Porcupine rivers and white fur traders.

D.339. Cunningham, Keith. *American Indians' Kitchen-Table Stories: Contemporary Conversations with Cherokee, Sioux, Hopi, Osage, Navajo, Zuni and Members of Other Nations*. Little Rock, Arkansas: August House, 1992.

This is a collection of narratives, including legends, descriptions of healing, and humor, recorded by folklorist Cunningham and his wife Kathy in the 1980s from Native American Indians ranging in age from 18 to 86; the age and tribe of the teller is recorded, along with contextual information.

D.340. Dauenhauer, Nora Marks, and Richard Dauenhauer, eds. *Haa Shuká, Our Culture: Tlingit Life Stories (Classics of Tlingit Oral Literature, Vol 3)*. Seattle: University of Washington Press, 1994.

Part of a monumental effort by the Dauenhauers to document the oral literature of the Tlingits of southeast coastal Alaska; this volume features biographies of over 50 men and women, most of them born between 1880 and 1910; these life histories follow a standard biographical format, but do incorporate oral and written material from the elders and their families as well as information from archival sources (see **D.341**, **D.342**).

D.341. Dauenhauer, Nora Marks, and Richard Dauenhauer, eds. *Haa Shuká, Our Ancestors: Tlingit Oral Narratives (C;Classics of Tlingit Oral Literature, Vol 1)*. Seattle: University of Washington Press, 1987.

These stories told by Tlingit elders about their forebears along the coast of southeast Alaska were recorded and transcribed in Tlingit, translated and presented in a bilingual edition; includes biographies of the narrators (see **D.340**, **D.342**).

D.342. Dauenhauer, Nora Marks, and Richard Dauenhauer, eds. *Haa Tuwundáagu Yís, for Healing Our Spirit: Tlingit Oratory (Classics of Tlingit Oral Literature, Vol 2)*. Seattle: University of Washington Press, 1990.

The speeches of Tlingit elders, mostly recorded between 1968 and 1988, are presented in the original Tlingit, with English translations on facing pages; the book features an extensive introduction and biographies of the orators (see **D.340**, **D.341**).

Dayton, Roger. [see *Alaska Series* in this section]

D.343. DeMallie, Raymond J., ed. *The Sixth Grandfather: Black Elk's Teachings Given to John G. Neihardt*. Lincoln: University of Nebraska Press, 1984.

This work makes available the original transcripts of interviews Neihardt conducted with Black Elk in 1931 and in 1944, when the Oglala elder and holy man was 67 and 80 years old respectively; in the former Black Elk tells his life story; in the latter, he presents, along with elder Eagle Elk, vignettes of his life and narratives relating to Lakota history and customs (see also **D.324**, **D.375**).

D.344. Eber, Dorothy. *Pitseolak: Pictures Out of My Life*. Seattle: University of Washington Press, 1971.

Designed for young readers, this book presents the life story of 70-year-old Pitseolak, an Eskimo woman artist from Cape Dorset on Baffin Island, as recorded by Eber, translated by interpreter Ann Hanson, and presented in a bilingual Eskimo/English edition, lavishly illustrated with Pitseolak's drawings.

D.345. Emerick, Richard G. *Man of the Canyon: An Old Indian Remembers His Life*. Orono, Maine: Northern Lights, 1992.

This is the life story of Mark Hanna, of the Havasupai of Cataract (Havasu) Canyon, a few miles above its confluence with Grand Canyon in Arizona, "as told to" anthropologist Emerick in 1953, who took down the account in writing when Hanna was 71 years old; this is its first publication.

D.346. Frey, Rodney, ed. *Stories That Make the World: Oral Literatures of the Indian Peoples of the Inland Northwest as Told by Lawrence Aripa, Tom Yellowtail and Other Elders*. Norman: University of Oklahoma Press, 1995.

Anthropologist Frey recorded these stories from members of the Coeur d'Alene, Crow, Klikitat, Kootenai, Nez Perce, Sanpoil and Wasco communities of Oregon, Washington, Idaho and Montana; features portraits of the storytellers and discussions of the role of oral literature and contexts of storytelling.

D.347. Hall, Edwin S. *The Eskimo Storyteller: Folktales From Noatak, Alaska.* Knoxville: University of Tennessee Press, 1975.

Both a study of oral literature and a collection of narratives, Hall not only presents stories collected from Noatak elders Edna Hunnicut and Paul Monroe, but he also presents short autobiographies of the storytellers, and examines what the tales meant to them as performers and as members of the Noatak Eskimo community.

Henzie, Moses [see *Alaska Series* in this section]

D.348. Herbert, Belle. *Shandaa: In My Lifetime.* Fairbanks: Alaska Native Language Center, University of Alaska Press, 1992.

Herbert is a Gwich'in Athabaskan woman from the village of Chalkyitsik, on the Black River in northeastern Alaska; she was at least 105 when interviewed through an interpreter; her life story, organized into a series of accounts, is presented in a bilingual Gwich'n/English format, with photographs.

D.349. Highwalking, Belle [Katherine M. Weist, ed.]. *Belle Highwalking: The Narrative of a Northern Cheyenne Woman.* Billings, Montana: Montana Council for Indian Education, 1979.

In 1970, Highwalking, then 78, described to Katherine Weist her life as a Cheyenne woman, wife, mother, and grandmother; dictated in Cheyenne, it was translated by her daughter-in-law, Helen Hiwalker, and edited by Weist, who met her while living on the Northern Cheyenne reservation for one year in the 1960s.

D.350. Hìtakonanu'laxk (Tree Beard). *The Grandfathers Speak: Native American Folk Tales of the Lenapé People.* New York: Interlink Books, 1994.

Hìtakonanu'laxk, chief of the Lenapé Nation, along the eastern seaboard of the present-day U. S., retells tales he collected among his people and from archival sources, including creation stories about the Grandmothers of the four directions and Nanapush, Grandfather and Spirit Helper of the Lenapé.

Honea, John. [see *Alaska Series* in this section]

D.351. Hungry Wolf, Beverly. *The Ways of My Grandmothers.* New York: Quill, 1982.

The best way to describe this book is to say that it is a collection of stories of, about and by the author's mother, Ruth Little Bear, her grandmother Hilda Strangling Wolf, and other elders of the Blood People of the Blackfoot Nation; it includes personal narratives, myths and legends, as well as teachings relating to everyday life.

D.352. Jahner, Elaine. "Woman Remembering: Life History as Exemplary Pattern." In Rosan A. Jordan and Susan J. Kalcik, eds. *Women's Folklore, Women's Culture.* Philadelphia: University of Pennsylvania Press, 1985, 214-233.

Jahner presents an analysis of the life story of Ann Keller, member of the Brule Sioux tribe, born in 1917 on the Rosebud Sioux Reservation; the essay includes a transcript of a brief life history interview with Keller, with the author's questions.

D.353. Jake, Lucille, Evelyn James and Pamela Bunte. "The Southern Paiute Woman in a Changing Society." *Frontiers* 7:1 (1983), 44-49.

Jake and James, Southern Paiutes (Jake an elder of the Kaibab-Paiute in northern Arizona, James from the San Juan Southern Paiute) who grew up hearing about the lives and activities of their grandmothers, joined with anthropologist Bunte to conduct oral histories of two grandmothers, Mabel Drye, a Kaibab-Paiute in her 90s, and Marie Lehi, a San Juan Paiute in her 80s; the reminiscences of the two are compared, with analysis and interview excerpts.

D.354. Johnson, Broderick H., ed. *Stories of Traditional Navajo Life and Culture.* Tsaile, Navajo Nation, Arizona: Navajo Community College Press, 1977.

Aimed at presenting the subject of Navajo traditional culture "from the purely Navajo point of view," this book, published on the Navajo reservation, presents the life stories of twenty-two Navajo women and men, aged 56 to 96, translated into English from interviews conducted in Navajo.

D.355. Johnson, Thomas H. "Maud L. Clairmont: Artist, Entrepreneur, and Cultural Mediator." In Clifton, James A., ed. *Being and Becoming Indian: Biographical Studies of North American Frontiers.* Chicago: The Dorsey Press, 1989, 249-275.

Johnson looks at the ways Clairmont (b. 1902) has dealt with her bicultural identity: raised in a "white" rural ranching culture but on the Wyoming Wind River Shoshone reservation; though an elder on the Shoshone tribal council and successful businesswoman, with her background she has had to struggle to have her grandchildren recognized as Shoshone (see **D.333**).

D.356. Johnson, Sandy, and Dan Budnik. *The Book of Elders: The Life Stories and Wisdom of Great American Indians.* San Francisco: HarperSanFrancisco, 1994.

This book presents the personal narratives and oral traditions of 30 elders from 19 different tribes, identified as "important spiritual, political and cultural figures in their own communities," recorded and edited by Johnson, with accompanying photographs by Budnik.

D.357. Katz, Jane, ed. *Messengers of the Wind: Native American Women Tell Their Life Stories.* New York: Ballantine Books, 1995.

Katz presents a collection of narratives by Native American women, young and old, from a variety of tribal communities, who talk about their lives and work as artists, activists, healers, grandmothers, mothers and daughters, and discuss their diverse traditions, roles, and ways of coping with present-day challenges.

D.358. Kegg, Maude. *Gabekanaansing—At the End of the Trail: Memories of Chippewa Childhood in Minnesota.* Greeley: University of Northern Colorado, Museum of Anthropology, 1978.

Kegg, a resident of the Mille Lacs Indian Reservation in Central Minnesota, reminisces about life with her grandmother, in a bilingual edition published in Ojibwe and English.

D.359. Kegg, Maude. *Nookomis Gaa-Inaajimotawid / What My Grandmother Told Me.* St. Paul: Minnesota Archaeological Society, 1983.

Maude Kegg, age 77, of the Mille Lacs Indian Reservation in Central Minnesota, retells stories told to her by her grandmother, Margaret Pine.

D.360. King, R. T. *An Interview With Winona James.* Reno, Nevada: Oral History Program, University of Nevada, 1984.

James, a Washo Indian born in 1903 in a *galesdangl* (winter house) built on a white man's property in Genoa, Nevada, and raised by traditional grandparents who lived alternately in Lake Tahoe fishing camps and the Van Sickle ranch in Carson Valley; she talks about the nature of Washo life early in this century.

D.361. Lame Deer, John (Fire), and Richard Erdoes. *Lame Deer: Seeker of Visions.* New York: Simon and Schuster, 1972.

In the late 1960s, Erdoes recorded the life story of *Tacha Ushte*–John (Fire) Lame Deer–a 70-year old Sioux medicine man, born on the Rosebud reservation in South Dakota; a short epilogue by Erdoes describes how he came to be the scribe for the memories and visions of this elder *wicasa wakan* (holy man) of the Lakotas.

D.362. Lee, Linda, Ruthie Sampson, Ed Tennant and Hannah Mendenhall, eds. *Lore of the Inupiat: The Elders Speak [Uquaaqtuanich Inupiat: Utuqqanaat Uqaaqtuaqtut].* Vol. II. Kotzebue, Alaska: Northwest Arctic Borough School District, 1990.

See description under **D.373.**

D.363. Linderman, Frank B. *Indian Old-Man Stories.* New York: Charles Scribner's Sons, 1920.

Linderman retells stories, collected from War Eagle, a Chippewa elder, about Napa, or "Old-Man," the deity who created the world and its inhabitants, echoing a common association of elders with the origin of things and dispensation of traditional knowledge in Native American Indian mythology.

D.364. Linderman, Frank B. *Plenty-Coups: Chief of the Crows.* Lincoln: University of Nebraska Press, 1957 [originally published in 1930 as *American: The Life Story of a Great Indian*].

This is presented as a "first person" account of a series of conversations conducted by Linderman, through an interpreter and sign language, with Plenty-Coups, then in his 80s; Linderman includes explanations of Crow customs and beliefs, recording not only his own comments, but also those of Coyote-Runs and Plain-Bull, old friends of Plenty-Coups, who joined them during these sessions.

D.365. Linderman, Frank B. *Pretty-Shield: Medicine Woman of the Crows.* Lincoln: University of Nebraska Press, 1972 [originally published in 1932 as *Red Mother*].

Much like his "autobiography" of Plenty-Coups (see **D.364**), the recorded narrative of Pretty-Shield, age 74, is presented in quotes, along with commentary by Linderman, and his occasional record of interruptions in the conversations when she checks up on or is engaged by her grandchildren.

D.366. Lucier, Charles V., and James W. VanStone. "An Iñupiaq Autobiography." *Études* 11:1 (1987), 149-172.

The authors present, with an introduction and extensive footnotes, the brief recorded life story of Della Keats (Puyuq), an Iñupiaq Eskimo born on the Upper Noatak River in the Kotzebue region of northwest Alaska in 1907.

D.367. Lurie, Nancy Oestreich. *Mountain Wolf Woman, Sister of Crashing Thunder: The Autobiography of a Winnebago Woman.* Ann Arbor: University of Michigan Press, 1981 [1961].

In the late 1950s, at age seventy-five, Mountain Wolf Woman told her life story to her adopted niece, anthropologist Nancy Lurie; in an appendix, Lurie provides a brief commentary on the nature of the autobiographical narrative she recorded (see also **D.322**).

D.368. Mails, Thomas E. (with Dallas Chief Eagle). *Fools Crow.* Lincoln: University of Nebraska Press, 1979.

Based on interviews conducted in the 1970s by Mails, this is an oral history of Fools Crow, who recounts his life as a medicine man, spiritual leader, and chief of the Teton Sioux; born around the time of the massacre at Wounded Knee, in 1890, he recalls his life from early vision quests to his role in the Sun Dance, and finally his role, in his 80s, as a mediator during the American Indian Movement's occupation of Wounded Knee on the Pine Ridge reservation in 1973.

D.369. Margolin, Malcolm, ed. Rev. ed. *The Way We Lived: California Indian Stories, Songs and Reminiscences.* Berkeley, California: Heyday Books, 1993 [1981].

Included in this collection are the narratives of elders of several California Indian communities, compiled, with commentary, by Margolin, co-founder of *News From Native California,* a quarterly devoted to history and cultural concerns that regularly features life stories by and about Native elders (see periodicals list in Chapter A).

D.370. McClanahan, A. J., ed. *Our Stories, Our Lives.* Anchorage, Alaska: The CIRI Foundation, 1986.

This is a collection of interviews with twenty-three elders–Eskimos, Indians and Aleuts–of the Cook Inlet Region in southern Alaska, conducted and transcribed by McClanahan, an Alaskan journalist.

D.371. McEwan, J. Richard [W. D. Hamilton, ed.]. *Memories of a Micmac Life.* Frederick, New Brunswick: The Micmac-Maliseet Institute, University of New Brunswick, 1988.

At age 77, McEwan told his life story to W.H. Hamilton; recounting his childhood on the Bear River Reserve in Nova Scotia; work in New England in the mid-1920s to mid-1930s; his return to the Reserve to raise a family; and his lifelong "love affair with the fiddle," an art learned from his father.

D.372. McFadden, Steven. *Profiles in Wisdom: Native Elders Speak About the Earth.* Santa Fe, New Mexico: Bear & Company, 1991.

McFadden interviewed 17 elders, six from North American communities, one from Peru; he alternates short commentary with interview excerpts in which elders talk about their lives and views about the fate of the Earth.

D.373. Mendenhall, Hannah, Ruthie Sampson, and Edward Tennant, eds. *Lore of the Inupiat: The Elders Speak [Uquaaqtuanich Inupiat: Utuqqanaat Uqaaqtuaqtut].* Vol. I. Kotzebue, Alaska: Northwest Arctic Borough School District, 1989.

This collection of transcriptions of Inupiat elders' narratives was inspired by a series of Elders Conferences in the 1970s and '80s; elders wanted to pass their knowledge and experience to younger generations, and the local school district complied by printing the stories, with author portraits, in a bilingual book (see also **D.362**).

D.373.a. Moran, Bridget. *Stoney Creek Woman: The Story of Mary John*. Vancouver, British Columbia: Tillacum Library, 1988.

> Mary John, born around 1914 to the Carrier Indian band living on the Stoney Creek Reservation in northern British Columbia, tells of a life struggling for cultural survival and facing adversity as an independent Native woman.

D.374. Morrow, Phyllis, and William Schneider, eds. *When Our Words Return: Writing, Hearing and Remembering Oral Traditions of Alaska and the Yukon*. Logan: Utah State University Press, 1995.

> This is a group of essays by non-native scholars who examine the challenges of accurately recording the oral narratives of predominantly elder tradition bearers, addressing issues such as the influences of the relationship between these elders and their audiences, including those who record and study their narratives.

D.375. Neihardt, John G. *Black Elk Speaks: Being the Life Story of a Holy Man of the Oglala Sioux*. Lincoln: University of Nebraska Press, 1979 [1932]

> This life history of Nicholas Black Elk, born in 1863, as told through an interpreter to Neihardt in 1931, has faced some controversy over how much license Neihardt, a poet and novelist, took in his literary interpretation of Black Elk's oral account; nevertheless, it is apparently accepted by many Lakota as an accurate record of his life and teachings (see also**D.324, D.343**).

D.376. Neihardt, John G. *When the Tree Flowered: An Authentic Tale of the Old Sioux World*. New York: Macmillan, 1951.

> This book is based on interviews conducted by the author, largely with Black Elk (see **D.375**) and another elder, Eagle Elk, who share their teachings through personal experience narratives and stories relating to Lakota history and culture (**D.343**).

Nictune, Oscar. [see *Alaska Series* in this section]

D.377. Philips, Donna, Robert Troff and Harvey Whitecalf, eds. *Kataayuk: Saskatchewan Indian Elders*. Saskatoon: Saskatchewan Indian Cultural College, 1976.

> A book of photographic portraits and excerpts of interviews with Cree elders residing in the "Treaty Six" region of Saskatchewan province; narratives in this bilingual collection have been rendered in English as well as Cree "syllabics."

D.378. Pitseolak, Peter, and Dorothy Eber. *People From Our Side: An Eskimo Life Story in Words and photographs*. Bloomington: Indiana University Press, 1975.

> Eber edited the text for this book, based on a manuscript written in Eskimo syllabics by Pitseolak, of Cape Dorset on Baffin Island, when he was 71 years old, translated by Ann Hanson of Frobisher Bay, augmented with excerpts of oral history interviews, and accompanied by selected photographs from among over 2,000 that Pitseolak has taken since the 1930s.

D.379. Plummer, Stephen, and Suzanne Julin. "Lucy Swan, Sioux Woman: An Oral History." *Frontiers* 6:3 (1982), 29-32.

> Born on the Rosebud Reservation in south central South Dakota in 1900, Swan, interviewed by Plummer in 1971, reflects upon her childhood, and her life with her husband on the Cheyenne River Reservation in Cherry Creek, where they moved in 1918, and where she remains.

D.380. Powers, Marla N. *Oglala Women: Myth, Ritual and Reality.* Chicago: University of Chicago Press, 1986.

Based on interviews conducted during the course of over twenty-five years of study on the Pine Ridge reservation in South Dakota, Powers offers an in-depth look at women in Oglala life; featuring excerpts of conversations with old women as well as young, it looks at religion, politics, economics, medicine and old age.

D.381. Rice, Julian. *Lakota Storytelling: Black Elk, Ella Deloria and Frank Fools Crow.* New York: Peter Lang, 1989.

Rice examines the narrative styles and strategies of three well-known Lakota elders; for example, as spiritual leaders these elders invoke their age and acknowledge their own elders as emblematic of the longevity promised by the ancestral spirits.

D.382. Ridington, Robin. *Trail to Heaven: Knowledge and Narrative in a Northern Native Community.* Iowa City: University of Iowa Press, 1988.

Ridington has spent over twenty years studying the *Dunne-za,* or Beaver Indians of northeastern British Columbia; here he presents translations of personal narratives and traditional stories of *Dunne-za* elders, and relates a parallel narrative of his own development, as influenced by these elders.

D.383. Robinson, Harry (Wendy Wickwire, ed.). *Nature Power: In the Spirit of an Okanagan Storyteller.* Vancouver, British Columbia: Douglas & McIntyre, 1992.

This second collection of narratives by master storyteller Robinson (1900-1990), member of the Lower Similkameen Indian Band, in the Oganagan Valley in British Columbia's southern interior, focuses on stories about the spiritual relationship between humans and their nature helpers (see **D.384**).

D.384. Robinson, Harry (Wendy Wickwire, ed.). *Write it on Your Heart: The Epic World of an Okanagan Storyteller.* Vancouver, British Columbia: Talonbooks, 1989.

A collection of mythological tales and tales of contact with whites, recorded and transcribed by ethnographer Wickwire, these stories by Robinson are in some ways an "autobiographical" account, in that they are memories of a life of listening to and telling traditional narratives, and follow a Native tradition of merging personal accounts with community history and legend (see also **D.383**).

D.385. Sands, Kathleen Mullen. "Telling 'A Good One': Creating a Papago Autobiography." *Melus* 10:3 (1983), 55-65.

Sands discusses, with tape-recorded excerpts, the narratives of Papago storyteller Theodore Rios, born in 1915 at San Xavier del Bac, educated in the boarding school system, forced to seek work off the reservation, and compelled to redefine his role in tribal society, whose stories reinforced ties with a culture from which he has been estranged during his lifetime.

D.386. Sarris, Greg. *Mabel McCay: Weaving the Dream.* Berkeley: University of California Press, 1994.

In this unique portrait of McCay, Pomo basketmaker and medicine woman, Sarris, an English professor and elected chief of the Coast Miwok tribe, interweaves personal experience narratives of McCay with an account of his coming to terms with his own life in the process of recording her stories.

D.387. Scarberry, Susan J. "Grandmother Spider's Lifeline." In Paula Allen Gunn, ed. *Studies in American Indian Literature.: Critical Essays and Course Designs.* New York, Modern Language Association of America, 1983, 100-107.

This short essay describes the identity and role of Grandmother Spider, an important figure in Native American Indian mythology and culture, and the use of "Grandmother" imagery among American Indian writers.

D.388. Schneider, William. "A Sense of Context and Voice in an Oral Biography." *Northwest Folklore* 6:1 (1987), 31-38.

Describing oral history as a collaborative effort, Schneider recalls the challenges of preparing, for publication, his interviews with Moses Cruikshank, Athabaskan elder, as "our struggle to find ways to preserve in text form a strong sense of his voice and the context of his personal history" (see **D.338**).

D.389. Shulimson, Judith Ann. "Eskimo Verbal Art and the Teachings of the Elders." Doctoral dissertation, University of Texas at Austin, 1986.

While not about storytelling per se, this study examines the ways in which elder members of the Eskimo community of Nome, Alaska, have adapted features of traditional verbal art, including storytelling, rooted in their cultural past, to the forms of social interaction demanded in the present.

Simon, Edwin. [see *Alaska Series* in this section]

D.390. Simpson, Richard. *Ooti: A Maidu Legacy.* Milbrae, California: Celestial Arts, 1977.

A blend of mythology and personal experience narrative, this is a unique depiction of the cultural legacy of the Maidu Indians of north central California, with text and photographs by Simpson framing the words of Lizzie Enos, one of the last traditional Maidu, who, in her 80s, tells the story of *ooti*, the acorn.

D.391. Sneve, Virginia Driving Hawk. *Completing the Circle.* Lincoln: University of Nebraska Press, 1995.

In searching her own family roots, Sneve, a Dakota Sioux, drew from her own memories of "oral histories: legends, facts and family stories that were a mixture of legend and fact" along with historical research, in preparing a portrait of her grandmothers and "other women of the circle."

Solomon, Madeline. [see *Alaska Series* in this section]

D.392. Speare, Jean E., ed. *The Days of Augusta.* Vancouver: Douglas & McIntyre, 1992.

Mary Augusta Tappage, born in 1899 at Soda Creek in British Columbia's Cariboo country and the granddaughter of a Shuswap chief, told Speare stories about her life, which are presented as vignettes with accompanying photographs by Robert Keziere.

D.393. Starita, Joe. *The Dull Knifes of Pine Ridge: A Lakota Odyssey.* New York: G. P. Putnam's Sons, 1995.

Starita interviewed members of the Dull Knife family of Pine Ridge, North Dakota, and their friends in preparing this chronicle of a century of Lakota Sioux life through their memories, framed by the reminiscences of Guy Dull Knife, Sr., born in 1899, one of the oldest living Oglala Sioux.

D.394. Stewart, Irene [Doris Ostrander Dawdy, ed.]. *A Voice in Her Tribe: A Navajo Woman's Own Story*. Novato, California: Ballena Press, 1980.

Anthropologist Mary Shepardson first met Stewart (b. 1907) at the latter's home in Chinle, Arizona, on the Navajo reservation, in 1955, and they became friends; in the mid 1960s, Shepardson asked her to write her life story, which she did in a series of letters, edited for publication by Dawdy.

D.395. Swann, Brian, ed. *Coming to Light: Contemporary Translations of the Native Literatures of North America*. New York: Random House, 1994.

A sampling of tales from many different Native American communities, showcasing several collections of narratives of Native elders, recorded by several contemporary scholars, native and non-native, who offer profiles of the tellers and translations that try to capture the tales as presented in their original contexts.

D.396. Thompson, Lucy. *To the American Indian: Reminiscences of a Yurok Woman*. Berkeley, California: Heyday Books, 1991 [1916].

Thompson, born to an aristocratic family of the Klamath River Yurok in the mid-1800s, published this narrative in her late 60s; a personal and tribal history, it is written in the style of a traditional, nonlinear oral account.

Tobuk, Frank. [see *Alaska Series* in this section]

D.397. Trafzer, Clifford E. "Grandmother, Grandfather, and the First History of the Americas." In Arnold Krupat, ed. *New Voices in Native American Literary Criticism*. Washington, D. C.: Smithsonian Institution Press, 1993, 474-487.

The author treats Native American storytellers as oral historians, citing, among others, Andrew George who, interviewed in 1980, discussed his life as a Palouse Indian in the Inland Pacific Northwest U. S., merging his own life story, which began at the turn of the century, with traditional stories of his people.

D.398. Underhill, Ruth. *Papago Woman*. Prospect Heights, Illinois: Waveland Press, 1979.

During visits to the Papago reservation near Tuscon, Arizona, from 1931-1933, Underhill recorded the life story of 90-year-old Maria Chona, first published in 1936 as *Autobiography of a Papago Woman*. Forty-five years later she wrote, from memory, her impressions of her encounter with Chona, for this reprint (see also **D.322**).

D.399. Wall, Steve. *Shadowcatchers: A Journey in Search of the Teachings of Native American Healers*. New York: HarperCollins, 1994.

This book documents the meetings photojournalist Wall had with elders from thirteen Native communities throughout the Americas; descriptions of his encounters are interspersed with recorded narratives of these "wise women and men: tribal leaders, healers, high priests and sorcerers."

D.400. Wall, Steve. *Wisdom's Daughters: Conversations With Women Elders of Native America*. New York: HarperCollins, 1993.

Photojournalist Wall describes his meetings with thirteen Native women and their families, from ten North American tribes, and presents a collection of narratives highlighting the philosophy and teachings of these spiritual leaders.

D.401. Wall, Steve, and Harvey Arden. *Wisdomkeepers: Meetings With Native American Spiritual Elders.* Hillsboro, Oregon: Beyond Words Publishing, 1990.

This book as the title implies, describes the encounters of the authors with eighteen Native American elders from fourteen tribes; photographs of the elders and their communities accompany selected short narratives by each elder.

D.402. Wallis, Velma. *Two Old Women: An Alaska Tale of Betrayal, Courage and Survival.* New York: HarperPerennial, 1993.

Wallis, an Alaskan Native of the *Gwich'in* band living in the Fort Yukon area, retells an Athabaskan Indian legend of two old women abandoned by their tribe, who survive a harsh winter and end up saving their community.

D.403. Webster, Peter S. *As Far As I Know: Reminiscences of an Ahousat Elder.* Campbell River, British Columbia: Campbell River Museum and Archives, 1983.

Born in Clayoquot Sound, on the west coast of Vancouver Island, British Columbia, in 1905, Webster recalls growing up (including memories of his grandparents) and growing old; he also tells several traditional stories.

D.404. Weibel-Orlando, Joan. "Indians, Ethnicity as a Resource, and Aging: You Can Go Home Again." *Journal of Cross-Cultural Gerontology* 3:4 (1988), 323-348.

As part of a study of 28 Native American Indians living most of their lives in urban areas who returned to their traditional homelands following retirement, this article focuses on the life story of one older Sioux woman who retired to her childhood reservation home in South Dakota after living in Los Angeles for 26 years; her narrative demonstrates that ethnicity may serve as a resource throughout the life-span, providing a source of well-being in late life.

D.405. Wong, Hertha Dawn Wong. *Sending My Heart Back Across the Years: Tradition an Innovation in Native American Autobiography.* New York: Oxford University Press, 1992.

Wong discusses problems of interpreting the life stories of Native American Indians; among the autobiographies she discusses in detail are the accounts of Black Elk, Plenty-Coups and Pretty Shield, elders at the time they collaborated with Euro-American authors who recorded their life experiences (see **D.343, D.364, D.365**).

D.406. Yarber, Yvonne, and Curt Madison, eds. *Walter Northway.* Fairbanks: Alaska Native Language Center, University of Alaska, 1987.

Age 111 when this book was published, Walter Northway, an Athabaskan Indian from the village of Northway in interior Alaska, shared his memories and teachings with family members and others who recorded, translated, and transcribed them.

E

Traditional Arts

Once again, as with other sections of this bibliography, I have drawn from a broad palette, citing works about older artists engaged in a wide variety of creative endeavors based on traditional concepts, methods and subjects, and/or personal visions tied in some way to a history and experience shared with some community. I also have included a few other works on material culture, such as vernacular architecture and traditional gardens, because of their aesthetic elements. I leave it to others to haggle over particular labels–"self-taught," "outsider," "environmental," etcetera–that have been applied to some artists and their works, or to debate whether the works of some elders fall outside the canons of the traditional arts. For the most part this list is a survey of works which focus upon, or offer some references to, the aesthetic practices and memories of elders working within established traditions of creativity, craft and performance, or at the very least playing at the boundaries of tradition.

****

E.1. Hufford, Mary, Marjorie Hunt and Steven J. Zeitlin. *The Grand Generation: Memory, Mastery, Legacy.* Washington, D. C.: Smithsonian Institution, 1987.

Special mention must be made of this book, which accompanied the groundbreaking Smithsonian traveling exhibit, "The Grand Generation," featuring the creative traditions of elder Americans: painters, quiltmakers, weavers, lacemakers, story-tellers and others; it describes how their works embody living history, mastery of their respective traditional art forms, and strategies for coping with age. It features chapters on "Traditional Culture and the Stages of Life"; "Memory: The Living Past"; "Mastery: A Lifetime of Knowledge and Experience"; and "Legacy: The Human Unit of Time."

****

The following three works also go to the top of the heap, for while they are not exclusively devoted to aging and traditional arts, they provide lists of individual folk artists, many of whom are elders, with additional biographical and other information, making them excellent points of departure for research in traditional arts and aging.

E.2. Bronner, Simon J., ed. *American Folk Art: A Guide to Sources.* New York: Garland, 1984.

This is a first-stop for anyone searching for material on American folk art issued before 1984. It is a fully annotated list of works on the subject, and is divided into a number of sections, prepared by Bronner and a host of folk art scholars, covering a variety of concerns and subjects, including theory, genres, biographies, regions, ethnicity, Afro-Americans, occupations, collectors and museums, education, films, and "Topics on the Horizon," featuring sections on public folk arts, folk art and gender, and one devoted to folk art and aging.

E.3. Rosenak, Chuck and Jan. *Museum of American Folk Art Encyclopedia of Twentieth-Century American Folk Arts and Artists.* New York: Abbeville Publishers, 1990.

This monumental work features 255 illustrated descriptions of folk artists in the U. S., using a broad definition of folk art and encompassing a wide range of forms, including paintings, drawings, sculpture, pottery and environmental works; each entry incudes biographical data, in addition to descriptions of subjects and materials; appendices include lists of exhibitions and public collections, and there are endnotes on each artist, as well as a bibliography; this is a recommended first stop for research on individual older folk artists.

E.3.a. Siporin, Steve. *American Folk Masters: The National Heritage Fellows.* New York: Harry N. Abrams, 1992.

This book was published in conjunction with the exhibition, "America's Living Folk Traditions," which celebrates the life and work of 150 recipients, mostly elders, of National Heritage Fellow awards, presented each year since 1982 by the Folk Arts Program of the National Endowment for the Arts to outstanding folk artists. It features not only descriptions of the variety of traditions represented, it also contains a directory of all National Heritage Fellows from 1982 to 1991, with bibliographic, discographic and/or filmographic references for those listed through 1990, and biographical summaries for those Fellows not fully discussed elsewhere in the text.

GENERAL

E.4. Hawes, Bess Lomax. "Folk Arts and the Elderly." In Thomas Venum, ed. *1984 Festival of American Folklife.* Washington, D. C.: Smithsonian Institution and the National Park Service, 1984, 28-31.

Hawes reflects upon the concentration of elders among the recipients of the annual National Heritage Fellowships offered by the Folk Arts Program at the National Endowment for the Arts (see E.3), remarking on traditional arts as a "second career" and elders as "aesthetic resources" for succeeding generations.

E.5. Hufford, Mary. "All of Life's a Stage: The Aesthetics of Life Review." In Thomas Venum, ed. *1984 Festival of American Folklife.* Washington, D. C.: Smithsonian Institution and the National Park Service, 1984, 32-35.

In this essay, Hufford explores the autobiographical quality of the traditional arts of elders, noting that "folk art exhibits are filled with life-review projects that comprise a kind of three-dimensional reminiscence for their makers, whereby the past bursts into a tangible being."

E.6. Kirshenblatt-Gimblett, Barbara. "Objects of Memory: Material Culture as Life Review." In Elliott Oring, ed. *Folk Groups and Folklore Genres: A Reader.* Logan: Utah State University Press, 1989, 329-338.

Kirshenblatt-Gimblett reviews "the ways objects encode memories and stimulate life review," including a discussion of the memory art of elders, in such media as quilts, embroidery, and folk sculpture.

E.7. Whisnant, David E. "Old Men and New Schools: Rationalizing Change in the Southern Mountains." In James Hardin and Alan Jabbour, eds. *Folklife Annual 88-89.* Washington, D.C.: American Folklife Center, Library of Congress, 1989, 74-85.

Whisnant examines the work of a group of college-educated women who created and promoted the myth of an aged mountaineer who "inspires" them to establish missionary schools for mountain children, and whose cabin is moved to the school grounds to serve as a museum for the "old ways."

MISCELLANEOUS TRADITIONAL ARTS
(including surveys, anthologies, mixed genre works, and odds and ends).

E.8. Daniel, Ana. *Bali: Behind the Mask.* New York: Alfred A. Knopf, 1981.

Daniel, a photographer and student of Balinese theater, documents her encounter and study with I Nyoman Kakul, "teacher, farmer, philosopher, father and grand-father," and a master of classical Balinese dance.

E.9. Doucette, Laurel. *Creative Elders and Traditional Culture in Contemporary Newfoundland: The Development of Expressive Skills in Retirement and Later Life.* Ottawa: National Library of Canada, 1988 [microfiche copy of Ph.D. thesis, Memorial University of Newfoundland, 1986].

Doucette's study of "late-bloomers" in traditional or tradition-related skills, is based on interviews with ten women and men, age 54 to 84, who have, in later life, adopted a wide range of expressive activities reflecting aspects of rural Newfoundland culture, such as writing personal histories, composing poetry or songs, sculpt-ing, making models, painting pictures, reciting or singing in public, or taking up a variety of needle and textile crafts.

E.10. Ferris, William. *Local Color: A Sense of Place in Folk Art.* New York: McGraw-Hill, 1982.

Ferris presents excerpts of recorded conversations with nine older Southern folk artists: Victor "Hickory Stick Vic" Bobb, cane maker, Leon "Peck" Clark, basket-maker (see **H.31**), Louis Dotson, one-string guitar maker, Theora Hamblett, painter (see **H.25**, **H.234**), Ethel Wright Mohamed, needleworker (see **H.25**, **H.81**, **H.256**), James "Son Ford" Thomas, sculptor, Othar Turner, cane fife maker (see **H.26**), Pecolia Warner, quilt maker (see **H.25**), and Luster Willis, painter and cane maker.

E.11. Glassie, Henry. *Passing the Time in Ballymenone: Culture and History of an Ulster Community.* Philadelphia: University of Pennsylvania, 1982.

Glassie's survey of folklife in Ballymenone, County Fermanagh, Ireland, includes extensive excerpts of recorded stories, songs and reminiscences of its residents, prominent among them elders Michael Boyle, Ellen Cutler, Peter Flanagan and Hugh Nolan (see also **E.37**).

E.12. Govenar, Alan. "The Photographs of Benny Joseph: African-American Life and Community in Houston." In James Hardin, ed. *Folklife Annual 90.* Washington, D. C.: American Folklife Center, Library of Congress, 1991, 82-99.

Joseph, born in Lake Charles, Louisiana, in 1924, moved to Houston at age two, and worked as a photographer in Houston's African-American communities from 1950 to 1982, when he retired; this article presents several of his photographs and excerpts from oral history interviews conducted in the mid to late 1980s.

E.13. Holtzberg-Call, Maggie. *The Lost World of the Craft Printer.* Urbana: University of Illinois Press, 1992.

This study of traditional craftspeople in the printing trade is based on interviews conducted with older printers, at work and at a retirement home for printers, who talk about the lost world of the hot-metal printers, "compositors, stonehands, and Linotype operators engaged in the physical production of printed words."

E.14. Hubbard, Ethan. *Faces of Wisdom: Elders of the World.* Washington Depot, Connecticut: Craftsbury Common Books, 1993.

I list this work, consisting almost exclusively of photographs, because it is a veritable international gallery of "folk portraits" of traditional elders, each one a proverbial "thousand word" essay; Hubbard, formerly with the Vermont Historical Society, has organized his photographs into sections on "Family," "The Generations," "Working," "Leisure," and "Spirituality."

E.15. Mathias, Elizabeth. "The Game as Creator of the Group in an Italian-American Community." *Pennsylvania Folklife* 23:4 (1974), 22-30.

Mathias discusses the role of the pastime of *bocce* among male immigrants from southern Italy, pensioners from the local garment district in Philadelphia, aged 65-85, in the continuation of the communal relations and leisure patterns of southern Italian men.

E.16. McDaniel, George W. *Hearth and Home: Preserving a People's Culture.* Philadelphia: Temple University Press, 1982.

This is a social and architectural history of the homes of rural African-Americans in the old South, based on architectural fieldwork and interviews with elders who recall the living spaces of their youth.

E.17. Pisarski, Sherry. "A Porter County Seer." In Linda Degh, ed. *Indiana Folklore: A Reader.* Bloomington: Indiana University Press, 1980, 130-146.

Pisarski describes the practice of Mrs. Weeks (pseud.), 66, a fortune teller, originally from Iowa, part Blackfoot Indian, who presently lives in Valparaiso, Indiana; features excerpts of interviews with her and several of her clients, three women who believe, and one who is somewhat skeptical.

E.18. Rankin, Tom. "The Photographs of Maggie Lee Sayre: A Personal Vision of Household Life." In James Hardin, ed. *Folklife Annual 90.* Washington, D. C.: American Folklife Center, Library of Congress, 1991, 100-121.

Sayre, born deaf near Paducah, Kentucky, in 1920, grew up with her parents in a 3-room houseboat on Click Cree; this article presents several of her photographs, chronicling her family's life on the river, a short life story she typed in 1982, and excerpts of her remarks as presented through sign interpreter Jean Lindquist.

E.19. Safa, Michele Franklin. "Emblems of Identity: The Changing Meanings of the Traditional Arts in a Northern Yemenite Community in Israel." Doctoral dissertation, University of California, Los Angeles, 1993.

A feature of this study of the use and significance of traditional arts among Yemenite immigrants living in Tamar, Israel, is an exploration of the differences among three generations within this community in terms of their ethnicity and the meaning they attach to basketmaking, silversmithing, dance, bridedressing, and the culinary arts.

E.20. Sodei, T. "Japanese Aging: A Living Tradition." *Perspective on Aging* 10:2 (1981), 8-11.

Within the context of a discussion on the position of elders in Japanese society, Sodei observes that their status is embodied in traditional art forms; that the practice of traditional Japanese arts is emblematic of old age, providing elders with psychological stability and spiritual well-being

E.21. Stewart, Dana, ed. *A Fine Age: Creativity as a Key to Successful Aging.* Little Rock, Arkansas: August House, 1984.

This book is a survey of creative older persons, and includes descriptions of some traditional artists, such as blues musician Cedell Davis, quilter Hope Shoaf, woodcarver John Arnold, and basketmaker Helen Morgan.

E.22. Theophano, Janet S. "Expressions of Love, Acts of Labor: Women's Work in an Italian-American Community." *Pennsylvania Folklife* 45:1 (1995), 43-49.

Theophano examines the complex relationship mid-life Italian-American women have with food, as demonstrated in domestic life.

E.23. Theophano, Janet S. "'I Gave Him a Cake': An Interpretation of Two Italian-American Weddings." In Stephen Stern and John Allan Cicala, ed. *Creative Ethnicity: Symbols and Strategies of Contemporary Ethnic Life.* Logan: Utah State University Press, 1991, 44-54.

Marcella, a woman in her fifties, and a prominent member of the Italian-American community of Maryton in the northeastern U. S., confronts the changes of midlife using food and ritual as expressive media.

E.24. Tullos, Allen, ed. *Long Journey Home: Folklife in the South.* Special Issue of *Southern Exposure* (5:2-3, 1977), 1-224.

This special issue of *Southern Exposure* features over 25 short articles on various aspects of southern folklife; included are descriptions of older musicians, fishermen, potters, quiltmakers and metalworkers, as well as descriptions of a number of organizations offering Southern folklife resources, many of which are still active.

E.25. Westmacott, Richard. *African-American Gardens and Yards in the Rural South.* Knoxville: University of Tennessee Press, 1992.

A feature of this book, "the first extensive survey of African-American gardening traditions in the rural South," that makes it relevant to this bibliographic listing is that, aside from the physical descriptions of the gardens, Westmacott presents excerpts of interviews conducted with the gardeners, most of them elders, who talk about their aesthetic values, beliefs, and sense of purpose in the yards and gardens that they have designed and maintained.

E.26. Zeitlin, Steven J. "The Wedding Dance." In Steven J. Zeitlin, Amy J. Kotkin and Holly Cutting Baker. *A Celebration of Family Folklore: Tales and Traditions from the Smithsonian Collection*. New York: Pantheon, 1982, 213-221.

Zeitlin describes a traditional Russian dance passed through generations of his family by his grandparents, Eastern European Jewish immigrants who settled in Philadelphia, and still performed by such family members as Uncle Oscar, 65, and his sons, at weddings and bar mitzvahs.

E.27. Zeitlin, Steven J., Amy J. Kotkin and Holly Cutting Baker. *A Celebration of Family Folklore: Tales and Traditions from the Smithsonian Collection*. New York: Pantheon, 1982.

This is, in part, a collection of photographs and stories recorded during the course of four summers at the Family Folklore Tent at the annual Smithsonian Folklife Festival in Washington, D. C.; in addition to excerpts of personal narratives representing several generations of family members there are essays on the traditions of several American families (see **E.26**, **E.31**, **E.33**, and **E.36**), a chapter on "How to Collect Your Own Family Folklore," and an appendix on the Smithsonians's Family Folklore Program.

VERBAL ARTS (SPOKEN WORD)

E.28. Briggs, Charles L. *Competence in Performance: The Creativity of Tradition in Mexicano Verbal Art*. Philadelphia: University of Pennsylvania Press, 1988.

This is a study of oral performances among members of rural Hispanic communities in northern New Mexico, particularly among older persons, whose competence in the presentation of proverbs, scriptural allusions, jokes, legends, treasure tales, hymns and prayers earn respect for their creative abilities.

E.29. Crandell, Horace (Keith Cunningham, ed.) "Uncle Horace Talks About His Recitations." *Southwest Folklore* 2:4 (1978), 20-25.

This is a transcript of an interview with Crandell, 84, who talks about his performances of narrative poetry, part of a special issue devoted to Crandell, featuring transcripts of his recitations that appear on an AFF Archive recording, a brief life history (see **E.30**), and a discussion by Cunningham about recitation as a folk genre.

E.30. Crandell, Horace (Keith Cunningham, ed.) "Uncle Horace's Life Story." *Southwest Folklore* 2:4 (1978), 26-31.

This is a brief oral history of Crandell, born in Pinedale, Arizona, in 1984, profiled in this special issue for his "recitations" of memorized self-composed narratives (see **E.29**); here he talks about a life of sheep shearing, prospecting, hunting, and playing fiddle at dances.

E.31. Dargan, Amanda. "She Comes By It Honestly: Characterization in Family Folklore." In Steven J. Zeitlin, Amy J. Kotkin and Holly Cutting Baker. *A Celebration of Family Folklore: Tales and Traditions from the Smithsonian Collection*. New York: Pantheon, 1982, 222-231.

Dargan describes the art of characterizing family members, as performed by various of the author's family members, in particular Tuga Peterson, 78, "who had nursed a generation of our relatives," and who "performed for us in the small kitchen that had always been her stage."

E.32. Davis, Gerald L. *I Got the Word in Me and I Can Sing It, You Know: A Study of the Performed African-American Sermon.* Philadelphia: University of Pennsylvania Press, 1985.

Davis examines the performance styles of African-American ministers, with a special focus on the sermons of 80-year-old Bishop Elmer. E. Cleveland, Pastor of Ephesians Church of God in Christ in Berkeley and Los Angeles, and bishop of the Northern California Jursidiction of the Church of God in Christ.

E.33. Folly, Dennis W. "Getting the Butter from the Duck: Proverbs and Proverbial Expressions in an Afro-American Family." In Steven J. Zeitlin, Amy J. Kotkin and Holly Cutting Baker. *A Celebration of Family Folklore: Tales and Traditions from the Smithsonian Collection.* New York: Pantheon, 1982, 232-241.

Folly describes proverbs in his family, as recorded and presented in excerpts of conversations with his great-grandmother, Mrs. Clara Abrams (né Clara Wilson Tolliver), born in 1898 in Hanover County, Virginia, and his mother, Mrs. Jean Folly, born in 1934, also in Hanover County.

E.34. Renwick, Roger deV. *English Folk Poetry: Structure and Meaning.* Philadelphia: University of Pennsylvania Press, 1980.

In this study of working-class poets and singers in Yorkshire, England, one chapter is devoted to the poetry of Martha Bairstow, a retired factory worker, born in the village of West Hartford, two miles from her present home in Millington, whose verse draws upon such subjects as work experience, local characters, childhood memories, kinship and old age.

E.35. Renwick, Roger deV. "Two Yorkshire Poets: A Comparative Study." *Southern Folklore Quarterly* 40 (1976), 239-281.

Renwick presents and analyzes the folk poetry of two residents of Batley, in the West Riding area of England's County Yorkshire, one of them a young man in his 30s, the other, Emma Kittredge (pseud.), born in 1901, who, after she retired in 1968 as a doffer in the local textile mill, began composing Yorkshire dialect poems, vernacular narrative verses with references to local places and characters.

E.36. Yocum, Margaret. "Blessing the Ties That Bind: Storytelling at Family Festivals." In Steven J. Zeitlin, Amy J. Kotkin and Holly Cutting Baker. *A Celebration of Family Folklore: Tales and Traditions from the Smithsonian Collection.* New York: Pantheon, 1982, 250-259.

Yocum discusses storytelling in her Pennsylvania German family at life-cycle celebrations; she also describes the stories evoked by the selling of the home of Grandmother and Grandfather Yocum in 1976, and the auction of its contents when Grandfather Isaac moved into a nursing home and Grandmother Bertha went to live next door with her daughter Gladys and family.

FOLK DRAMA

E.37. Glassie,Henry. *All Silver and No Brass: An Irish Christmas Mumming.* Philadelphia: University of Pennsylvania Press, 1976.

Glassie's study features transcripts of four conversations he recorded with elders Michael Boyle, Ellen Cutler, Peter and Joseph Flanagan, and Hugh Nolan, who recalled days of mumming in Ballymenone, County Fermanagh, Ireland (see also **E.11**).

E.38. Porter, John A. "The Solitary Memory: A Greek-American's Recollections of the Folk Play *Panáretos*." In Daniel W. Patterson and Charles G. Zug III, eds. *Arts in Earnest: North Carolina Folklife*. Durham, North Carolina: Duke University Press, 1990, 117-134.

In 1977, the author met an old Greek man living in relative isolation in Asheville, North Carolina, who, since he arrived in the U.S. in 1900, kept alive a connection to his homeland through his repertoire of Greek song and poetry, in particular a village play whose recitation evokes memories of his native land.

TRADITIONAL SINGERS/MUSICIANS

African American

E.39. Alyn, Glen, ed. *I Say Me for a Parable: The Oral Autobiography of Mance Lipscomb, Texas Bluesman*. New York: W. W. Norton, 1993.

Alyn compiled this oral history from hundreds of hours of tape-recorded interviews he conducted between 1973 and 1976 with Lipscomb (1895-1976), the legendary songster from Navasota, Texas, who talks about his life as a sharecropper, and his "discovery" in the 1960s by folk music fans and musicians (see also **H.105**).

E.40. Bastin, Bruce. *Red River Blues: The Blues Tradition in the Southeast*. Urbana: University of Illinois Press, 1986.

A history of the blues in the southeastern U. S., this book draws in good measure upon the recollections of older blues musicians .

E.41. Dargan, William Thomas, and Kathy White Bullock. "Willie Mae Ford Smith of St. Louis: A Shaping Influence Upon Black Gospel Singing Style." In Judith Weisenfeld and Richard Newman, eds. *This Far By Faith: Readings in African-American Women's Religious Biography*. New York: Routledge, 1996, 32-55.

This analysis of the singing style of Smith, born in Rolling Fork, Mississippi, in 1904, discusses not only her innovations in gospel in the 1930s and '40s, but also the maturation of her style and the force of her presence as the matriarch "Mother Smith," and features excerpts of the recollections of her contemporaries and the observations of her children, recorded in the late 1980s.

E.42. Evans, David. *Big Road Blues: Tradition and Creativity in the Folk Blues*. Berkeley: University of California Press, 1982.

This study of the musical culture of the blues includes descriptions of the lives and songs of a number of bluesmen and women, and features excerpts of interviews with several older musicians.

E.42.a. Fulcher, Bobby. "Cuje Bertram: Excerpts from an Interview." *Tennessee Folklore Society Bulletin* 53:2 (1987), 58-70.

Fulcher tracked down the legendary African-American fiddler, born in 1894 in the Cumberland Plateau region in north central Tennessee, to his present home in Indianapolis, where he was interviewed in 1980.

E.43. Guida, Louis; Lorenzo Thomas, and Cheryl Cohen. *Blues Music in Arkansas.* Philadelphia, Pennsylvania: Porfolio Associates, 1982.

This booklet, based in large part on extensive interviews with musicians, many of them elders, is essentially an oral history of the state's blues traditions, with accompanying photographs, produced as part of a University of Arkansas at Pine Bluff bicentennial project.

E.44. Jarmon, Laura C. "From Blues to Gospel: The Case of W. B. 'Hop' Hopson." *Tennessee Folklore Society Bulletin* 54:2 (1990), 38-44.

This is a short biography, with song samples and an interview excerpt, of Hopson, a former blues singer turned gospel performer, in his 70s, from Haywood County, Tennessee, and a longtime friend and neighbor of the author's grandparents.

E.45. Jones, Bessie (John Stewart, ed.) *For the Ancestors: Autobiographical Memories.* Urbana: University of Illinois Press, 1983.

This is a collection of edited transcripts of conversations recorded by anthropologist Stewart with Jones, born in Smithville, Georgia in 1902, and later settled in the St. Simon Island community, where she was active in the Georgia Sea Island Singers, preserving some of the earliest African-American spirituals and secular songs (see also **E.46**).

E.46. Jones, Bessie, and Bess Lomax Hawes. *Step It Down: Games, Play Songs and Stories from the Afro-American Heritage.* Athens: The University of Georgia Press, 1972.

This is both a collection of children's songs and a memoir of "days coming up" in rural Georgia, as recorded by folklorist Hawes; Jones (1902-1984), recipient of a National Heritage Fellowship award from the National Endowment for the Arts, also shares her teaching methods and ideas about child development (see also **E.45**).

E.47. Lomax, Alan. *The Land Where Blues Began.* New York: Pantheon Books, 1993.

This is an anecdotal book in which the legendary collector of traditional music in the southern U. S. recalls his forays into the field, quoting generously from elder statesmen of the blues whose lives and music he has documented.

E.48. Pearson, Barry Lee. *"Sounds So Good To Me": The Bluesman's Story.* Philadelphia: University of Pennsylvania Press, 1984.

This collective portrait of the lives of blues singers and musicians, presents long and short excerpts of field interviews and published autobiographies, including personal narratives many of the elder statesmen (and one woman) of the blues.

E.49. Pearson, Barry Lee. *Virginia Piedmont Blues: The Lives and Art of Two Virginia Bluesmen.* Philadelphia: University of Pennsylvania Press, 1990.

This book, based on extensive oral history interviews, presents detailed studies of the lives and performance styles of Archie Edwards, born in Franklin City, Virginia, in 1918, and John Cephas, born in the Foggy Bottom District of Washington, D. C., in 1930.

E.50. Rankin, Thomas Settle. "'And I'm Still Here': The Oral Autobiography of Andrew Jones." Master's Thesis, University of North Carolina at Chapel Hill, 1983.

This is a presentation and analysis of the narratives of Jones, an African-American musician born in 1908 in Gibson County, Tennessee, recorded in interviews with the author, as well as self-recorded tapes made by Jones, whose songs and stories incorporating traditional motifs and personal experience reflect his transformation from secular to sacred musician.

E.51. Schroeder, Rebecca B., and Donald M. Lance. "John L. Handcock: 'There Is Still Mean Things Happening.'" In Archie Green, ed. *Songs About Work: Essays In Occupational Culture for Richard Reuss.* Bloomington: Folklore Institute, Indiana University, 1993, 184-205.

Handcock (1904-1992), a "sharecropper, union organizer, and composer of folk songs of the Southern Tenant Farmers Union in 1935-37," recalls his activism, poems, and old and new songs in interviews with Schroeder in 1989 and Lance in 1989 and 1990.

E.52. Tullos, Allen, Daniel W. Patterson and Tom Davenport. "'A Singing Stream: A Black Family Chronicle': Background and Commentary." *North Carolina Folklore Journal* 36:1 (1989), 1-36.

This article is a discussion of the documentary, "A Singing Stream" (see **H.49**), chronicling the African-American religious song traditions of four generations of the Landis family of rural Granville County, North Carolina, anchored by Bertha Landis, born in 1898; a transcript of the film follows the article.

Anglo and other European American

E.53. Abrahams, Roger D. "Creativity, Individuality, and the Traditional Singer." *Studies in the Literary Imagination* 3:1 (1970), 5-34. [Special issue on "Creativity and Southern Tradition"]

The author examines the nature of individual creativity within a tradition-oriented community, citing the case of Almeda "Granny" Riddle [1898-1986], an Anglo-American traditional ballad singer living in the White-Cleburn County area of Arkansas.

E.54. Abrahams, Roger D. *A Singer and Her Songs: Almeda Riddle's Ballad Book.* Baton Rouge: Louisiana State University Press, 1970.

Abrahams presents a study of the relationship between Riddle's life and her songs, based on several hours of interviews with the then-71 year old Ozark folksinger; features numerous selections from her repertoire of Anglo-American ballads.

E.55. Abrams, W. Amos. "Horton Barker: Folk Singer Supreme." *North Carolina Folklore Journal* 22:4 (1974), 141-153.

Abrams first recorded Barker, of Chilhowis, Virginia, born in 1889, when the balladeer was 53; he reminisces about this and subsequent encounters, and presents samples from Barker's repertoire of folksongs and English ballads.

E.56. Bronner, Simon J. "'I Kicked Three Slats Out of My Cradle First Time I Heard That': Ken Kane, Country Music, and American Life." *New York Folklore* 3:1-4 (1977), 53-81.

Bronner presents a study, based on interviews and observation, of the life, cultural and historical contexts, and repertoire of traditional country music performer Ken Kane, of Hartwick, New York, who was born in the area in 1914.

E.57. Cauthen, Joyce H. *With Fiddle and Well-Rosined Bow: Old Time Fiddling in Alabama.* Tuscaloosa: University of Alabama Press, 1989.

This survey of the fiddle in Alabama history includes stories and reminiscences of older musicians, among them William Everis Campbell, of Troy, Alabama, born in 1909, whose narrative begins with a recollection of his great-grandmother, Caroline Steel Johnson: "I would set on the porch a lot of nights in the summer and she would fiddle and tell tall tales."

E.58. Ellington, Richard. "Fellow Worker, Guy Askew: A Reminiscence." In Archie Green, ed. *Songs About Work: Essays In Occupational Culture for Richard Reuss.* Bloomington: Folklore Institute, Indiana University, 1993, 303-315.

Ellington presents excerpts of correspondence he received during the years 1956-1966 from Askew (1896-1996), a fellow member of the Industrial Workers of the World (IWW), in which he shared with the author his memories, including the lyrics of early "Wobbly" songs in addition to those appearing in the IWW's famous "Little Red Songbook."

E.59. Feintuch, Burt Howard. "Pop Ziegler, Fiddler: A Study of Folkloric Performance." Doctoral dissertation, University of Pennsylvania, 1975.

While focusing primarily on the performance style of Ziegler, an 83-year-old fiddler from Bucks County, Pennsylvania, Feintuch devotes a chapter to his life history, featuring generous excerpts from tape-recorded interviews.

E.60. Garland, Jim (Julia S. Ardery, ed.) *Welcome the Traveler Home: Jim Garland's Story of the Kentucky Mountains.* Lexington: University Press of Kentucky, 1983.

In a posthumously edited memoir, Garland (1905-1978) looks back at a life that began in the coalfields of Harlan County; steeped in family traditions, especially folksongs, he brought his singing tradition to bear in the labor and political protest movement of the 1930s; recorded by the Library of Congress, he was also sent by them to collect traditional songs in his home state of Kentucky.

E.61. Ives, Edward D. *Joe Scott, The Woodsman-Songmaker.* Urbana: University of Ilinois Press, 1978.

Of relevance to aging in this life history of Scott (1867-1917), Maine woodsman and songster, is that, in addition to drawing from Scott's autobiographical ballads, as well as letters, Ives recorded the reminscences of elders who recall him or stories about him, including singers such as Jim Brown of New Brunswick, in his 70s when Ives met him in 1959, and whose repertoire included songs by Scott.

E.62. Kartchner, Kenner C. (Larry V. Shumway, ed.) *Frontier Fiddler: The Life of a Northern Arizona Pioneer.* Tucson: University of Arizona Press, 1990.

Born to Mormon pioneers in Snowflake, Arizona, Kartchner (1886-1970) held various occupations, from cowpuncher and sheepshearer to store clerk and forest ranger, but was best-known as an old-time fiddler; his hand-written memoirs were typed by his daughter Merle Kartchner Shumway and, and edited posthumously by his grandson Larry Shumway.

E.63. Minton, John. "'The Waterman Train Wreck': Tracking a Folksong in Deep East Texas." In Archie Green, ed. *Songs About Work: Essays In Occupational Culture for Richard Reuss.*. Bloomington: Folklore Institute, Indiana University, 1993, 37-76.

As part of his search for extant versions of a folksong commemorating a turn-of-the-century train wreck, Minton plumbed the memories of local elders for accounts of the event, the ballad that it inspired, and those who created and recreated it.

E.64. Moloney, Michael. "Medicine for Life: A Study of a Folk Composer and His Music." *Keystone Folklore* 20:1-2 (1975), 5-37.

Based on interviews and conversations, Moloney describes the life and work of Ed Reavy, born in the village of Barnagrove, county Cavan, Ireland in 1897, and who now resides in Philadelphia, where his family came in 1912; transcripts of comments on several songs Reavy composed are also presented.

E.65. Newman, Katherine D. *Never Without a Song: The Years and Songs of Jennie Devlin, 1865-1952.* Urbana: University of Illinois Press, 1995.

This unique work about the Irish-American songster was written, as the author puts it: "in three voices in two different time frames": when she, as Kay Dealy, recorded the stories and songs of an elder Devlin in 1936-38, and fifty years later, as Dr. Katherine Dealy Newman, remembering, as an elder herself, the singer and her songs.

E.66. Parsons, Jack, and Jim Sagel. *Straight From the Heart: Portraits of Traditional Hispanic Musicians.* Albuquerque: University of New Mexico Press, 1990.

This is essentially a collection of photographs by Parsons of traditional Mexican-American musicians, most of them elders, living in New Mexico, inspired by his work on a documentary film, "*La Música de los Viejos*—Music of the Old Ones" (see **H.231.a**), with an essay by Sagel on the musicians and musical culture of Hispanic New Mexico.

E.67. Taylor, Jay. "Bradley Kincaid: Still the 'Kentucky Mountain Boy' at 81." *Keystone Folklore Quarterly* 24:1 (1978), 10-14.

Taylor presents excerpts of an interview conducted with Kincaid, veteran Appalachian guitar player, singer and collector of traditional mountain ballads and songs.

E.68. Warner, Anne and Frank. "'That's the Way They Lived.'" *New York Folklore Quarterly* 22:2 (1966), 104-113.

The Warners interviewed Yankee John Galusha, a traditional singer living on a farm in the Adirondacks near Minerva, New York in 1950, shortly before his death at age 91; Galusha talked about his life as a lumberjack, game and fishing guide, and forest ranger, and shared songs from his repertoire.

British, Irish, Canadian

E.69. Cox, Gordon. "'I've Changed from That Type of Life to Another': Some Individual Responses to Social Change by Singers in a Newfoundland Outport." *Folk Music Journal* 4:4 (1983), 385-400.

Among Cox's informants for this study was "Sam" (whose response to a request for "the old songs" inspired the title for this article), who declined to sing those songs associated with his youth and a lifestyle he had abandoned 40-50 years back.

E.69.a. Kodish, Deborah. "Fair and Tender Ladies and Bonnie Irish Boys: Pattern in Vernacular Poetics." *Journal of American Folklore* 96:380 (1983), 131-150.

Kodish examines the ballad books of Mary Caul, a Newfoundland elder, whose songs reflect the issues–courtship, women leaving their families of origin to establish a new place in the community, and other social situations of adult life–with which she dealt when, in the early 1900s, she came into adulthood, a status with which she must continually grapple, and defend, as an older woman.

E.70. Kodish, Deborah Gail. "'Never Had a Word Between Us': Pattern in the Verbal Art of a Newfoundland Woman." Dissertation, University of Texas at Austin, 1981.

In a study of performance traditions in Newfoundland, Kodish examines the lifestyle, personal narratives and repertoire of Mary Caul, of Placentia Bay, a singer and storyteller, and looks at several occasions in which Mrs. Caul and Mrs. Ellen Hepditch, friends for over seventy years, talk and sing together.

E.71. Morton, Robin, ed. *Come Day, Go Day, God Send Sunday.* London: Routledge & Kegan Paul, 1973.

Subtitled "The songs and life story, told in his own words, of John Maguire, traditional singer and farmer from Co. Fermanagh," this is both an oral history of the Irish songster, and a generous sample of his songs, collected by Morton, a founding member of the Celtic folksong revival band, Boys of the Lough.

E.72. Palmer, Roy, ed. "The Minstrel of Quarry Bank: The Reminiscences of George Dunn (1887-1975)" [Part One], *Oral History* 11:1 (1983), 62-68.

Palmer and Charles Parker recorded the life story of Dunn, chainmaker and traditional singer, in the early 1970s; in the first of two articles, Palmer presents interview excerpts in which Dunn speaks of childhood and family in the village of Quarry Bank in South Staffordshire, England, and the first songs he learned.

E.73. Palmer, Roy, ed. "The Minstrel of Quarry Bank: The Reminiscences of George Dunn (1887-1975)" [Part Two], *Oral History* 11:2 (1983), 61-68.

In this second article featuring excerpts of interviews with Dunn (see E.72), he describes his working life in the Midlands chainmaking industry, and talks about leisure time, often spent singing, like his father before him (an LP of his songs [*George Dunn,* Leader LEE 4042] was issued shortly before his death).

E.74. Poicus, Gerald L. "'The First Day That I Thought of It Since I Got Wed': Role Expectations and Singer Status in a Newfoundland Outport." *Western Folklore* 35:2 (1976), 109-122.

In this study of Vince and Monica Ledwell, born in 1888 and 1889 respectively, a couple living in Calvert, a small Irish Catholic community 60 miles south of St.

John's, Newfoundland, and both traditional singers, Poicus discusses the difference in status accorded them as singers during their lifetimes, partly attributed to the male-female role system in the "outport" (coastal villages outside St. John's).

E.75. Richards, Sam. "Bill Hingston: A Biography in Song." *Oral History* 10:1 (1982), 24-46.

Hingston, a traditional English singer and musician, born in 1914 in Modbury, Yorkshire, England, and who has lived in Dittisham, some 25 miles away, for the past 40 years, has chronicled in song his own experiences, observations of life around him, and the life and repertoire of local bards he has known.

E.76. Swing, Pamela. "Teaching Traditional Fiddle in Shetland Isles Schools." In James Hardin and Alan Jabbour, eds. *Folklife Annual 88-89.* Washington, D.C.: American Folklife Center, Library of Congress, 1989, 86-99.

Swing describes the late-life career of Tom Anderson who, after retiring from the insurance business, inaugurated a program in which traditional fiddling is taught in the Shetland school system.

E.76.a. Szwed, John F. "Paul E. Hall: A Newfoundland Song-Maker and His Community of Song." In Henry Glassie, Edward D. Ives and John F. Szwed. *Folksongs and Their Makers.* Bowling Green, Ohio: Bowling Green University Popular Press, 1970, 149-169.

Based in part on fieldwork conducted in the early 1960s, Szwed presents a portrait of Hall, born in southwestern Newfoundland in 1897, who remained in the area and never married, with a focus on one of his compositions, "A Bachelor's Song."

CRAFT TRADITIONS

Surveys: By Culture/Region/Gender

E.77. _____"Women's Traditional Arts: The Politics of Aesthetics." Special issue of *Heresies: A Feminist Publication on Art and Politics* 1:4 (1977-78), 1-126.

This special issue consists of a series of short articles exploring "the interrelationships between art objects and the conditions in which they are produced," and features several descriptions of older traditional women artists.

E.78. _____*Keepers of Beauty: Master Craftsmen of the Russian Federation, the Ukraine, Lithuania, Azerbaijan and Central Asia.* Leningrad: Aurora Art Publishers, 1983.

This book is a tribute to the then-Soviet Union's "national treasures," predominantly older craftspeople keeping alive longstanding local traditions, including a carver of wooden figures of birds, figurative potter, decorative painter, and makers of birch vessels, decorative tiles, straw dolls, chimney caps, *pysankas* (Ukranian decorated eggs), decorative ironwork, *shebeke* (Azerbaijanian glass mosaics), *ganch* (Uzbek decorative alabaster moulding), and others.

E.79. Birdsell, Derek, ed. *The Living Treasures of Japan.* London: Wildwood House, 1973.

Portraits of fourteen older traditional craftspeople, honored in Japan as "holders of Intangible Cultural Properties" for their skills as potters, weavers, woodworkers and the like; photographs by Peccinotti, and texts by Barbara Adachi, including excerpts of interviews she conducted with these "Living National Treasures."

E.80. Dewhurst, C. Kurt, Betty McDowell and Marsha MacDowell. *Artists in Aprons: Folk Art by American Women.* New York: E. P. Dutton, 1979.

This book was prepared in conjunction with an exhibition on art in the everyday life of American women; statements by artists appear throughout the work; one chapter lists brief biographies of about 75 women, active from the 1600s to the present–these include a number of contemporary elder folk artists, such as Minnie Evans, Theora Hamblett, Clementine Hunter, Ethel Wright Mohamed, Sister Gertrude Morgan, Inez Nathaniel, Anna Mary Robertson "Grandma" Moses, Mattie Lou O'Kelley, Tressa "Grandma" Prisbrey, Gertrude Rogers, Fannie Lou Spelce, Queena Stovall and Clara McDonald Williamson.

E.81. Ferris, William, ed. *Afro-American Folk Art and Crafts.* Boston: G. K. Hall, 1983.

This landmark work pairs scholarly articles with biographies of artists, including quiltmakers, basket makers, musicians, blacksmiths and potters, several of whom are over fifty years old; it has an extensive bibliography, as well as a list of documentary films, including several about older folk artists.

E.82. Glassie, Henry. *Turkish Traditional Art Today.* Bloomington: Indiana University Press, 1993.

This ethnographic study of contemporary Turkish folk art features regional surveys and portraits of individual craftspeople, including elders such as calligrapher Mahmut Öncü, woodworkers Mustafa Kesici, Mustafa Sargin and Ahmet Sefa, potter Sabri Yasar, calligraphic tile painter Ahmet Sahin, and others.

E.83. Shaw-Smith, David. *Ireland's Traditional Crafts.* London: Thames and Hudson, 1984.

This survey and social history of crafts in Ireland, features chapters on textiles, stonework, woodwork, willow, rush and straw, leather, metalwork, pottery, and glassware, and includes portraits (with occasional interview excerpts) of older masters of traditional crafts.

E.84. Sugimura, Tsune, Tsuneari Ogawa, et al. *The Enduring Crafts of Japan: 33 Living National Treasures.* New York: Walker/Weatherhill, 1968.

A photographic record by Sugimura, with commentary by Ogawa, of thirty-three Japanese craftspeople (all but three in their 60s to 80s) in their workshops; features potters, textile artists, doll makers, and those working in lacquer, metal and bamboo.

Miscellaneous Crafts

E.85. Clayton, Lawrence "Bill Barton: Putting Art in Saddlemaking." In Francis Edward Abernethy, ed. *Folk Art in Texas.* Dallas, Texas: Southern Methodist University Press, 1985, 115-121.

Clayton presents a portrait–with photographs by Larry Fink–of Barton, former "roughneck," Army wrangler, cowboy on ranches and rodeos, who took up a late life career as leather craftsman.

E.86. Cochran, Robert and Martha, with Christopher Pierle. "The Preparation and Use of Bear Grass Rope: An Interview with Robert Simmons, Mississippi Folk Craftsman." *New York Folklore Quarterly* 30:3 (1974), 185-196.

Simmons was born in Washington Parish, Louisiana, in 1904, and later moved to Mississippi, where he was interviewed in his home and woodworking shop; he recalls the versatility of bear grass, used for a variety of purposes in his youth, and describes how to prepare and use it for making chair bottoms.

E.87. Dyen, Doris J. "Frank Valentich: Croatian *Tamburitza* Maker." In Shalom D. Staub, ed. *Craft and Community: Traditional Arts in Contemporary Society.* Philadelphia: Balch Institute for Ethnic Studies and the Pennsylvania Heritage Affairs Commission, 1988, 57-62.

Dyen discusses the work of second-generation Croatian-American Frank Valentich, who has played his part in a 50-year tradition of instrument making and performing by the Valentich brothers in southwestern Pennsylvania.

E.88. Edgette, J. Joseph. "The Wood Family: Generations of Stone Carvers in Delaware County." In Shalom D. Staub, ed. *Craft and Community: Traditional Arts in Contemporary Society.* Philadelphia: Balch Institute for Ethnic Studies and the Pennsylvania Heritage Affairs Commission, 1988, 35-42.

Based in part on interviews with family members, Edgette looks at four generations of gravestone carvers, noting the transmission of knowledge and skills from elders to younger family members through apprenticeship.

E.89. Gallegos, Esperanza. "The Piñata-Making Tradition in Laredo." In Joe S. Graham, ed. *Hecho en Tejas: Texas-Mexican Folk Arts and Crafts* [*Publications of the Texas Folklore Society, Vol. 50*]. Denton: University of North Texas Press, 1991, 188-203.

Gallegos focuses on two piñata-making families; one of them consists of Cipriano Cedillo, 76, and his four brothers, who have been making piñatas in Laredo since the 1930s.

E.90. Graves, Thomas E. "Robert Moore: Native American Craftsman." In Shalom D. Staub, ed. *Craft and Community: Traditional Arts in Contemporary Society.* Philadelphia: Balch Institute for Ethnic Studies and the Pennsylvania Heritage Affairs Commission, 1988, 43-48.

Graves describes the work of Moore, a Cherokee craftsman born in 1929, who practices traditional styles of Native American tanning, leatherwork, and decoration with quills, wampum and glass beads; Graves notes that some of Moore's skills are innovations, and others are revivals of aspects of Native American craft that had not been practiced for some time

E.91. Hester, Elizabeth Allen. "Vadie Williams, Folk Artist: Drawnwork as a Reflection of Personal Identity in Rural Kentucky." Master's thesis, Western Kentucky University, Bowling Green, 1989.

Based on interviews and observation of her work, this is a study of the significance of needlework in the everyday life of an older farm woman in rural Allen County, Kentucky, in particular the ways in which her drawnwork reflects her beliefs and identity as an individual and as a member of her community.

E.92. Johnson, Geraldine Niva. "It's a Sin to Waste a Rag: Rug-Weaving in Western Maryland." In Rosana A. Jordan and Susan J. Kalcik, eds. *Women's Folklore, Women's Culture.* Philadelphia: University of Pennsylvania Press, 1985, 65-96.

Johnson describes the life and work Elaine (pseud.), born in 1907 on a farm in western Maryland, who practices the art of rag-rug weaving; features interview excerpts and photographs.

E.93. Lornell, Christopher. "Coy Thompson, Afro-American Corn Shuck Mop Maker: 'We Make Them Now to Show the Younger People How the Older Ones Come Up.'" *Tennessee Folklore Society Bulletin* 42:2 (1976), 175-180.

Lornell describes, with interview excerpts, the work of Thompson, 76, of Piedmont, North Carolina, who also talks about his role in preserving and transmitting "old-timey ways" and his views of his practical knowledge as a potential supplement to formal schooling for young people.

E.94. McNutt, James C. "Miguel Acosta, *Instrumentista.*" In Joe S. Graham, ed. *Hecho en Tejas: Texas-Mexican Folk Arts and Crafts* [*Publications of the Texas Folklore Society, Vol. 50*]. Denton: University of North Texas Press, 1991, 172-187.

This portait of Acosta, instrument maker and musician from San Antonio, born in 1918, focuses on his construction of the *bajo sexto*, the "bass guitar" of Texas-Mexican *conjunto* music.

E.95. Shea, Lark A. "Mrs. Annie Watson: A Maker of Appalachian Knotted Bedspreads." *North Carolina Folklore Journal* 30:1 (1982), 34-42.

In 1981, Shea interviewed Watson, of Deep Gap, North Carolina, who recalled deriving income from this Appalachian craft along with her mother and many mountain women, back in the lean 1920s and even leaner 1930s; she still maintains her craft as a hobby, giving pleasure and relieving isolation.

E.96. Snyder, Mabel. "How I Make Soap." *Pennsylvania Folklife* 17:4 (1968), 12-15.

Snyder, born in 1902 in Perry Township, Berks County, Pennsylvania, and a native Pennsylvania German speaker recalls a life of soap-making in a bilingual article.

Basketmaking

E.96.a. Abel-Vidor, Suzanne, Dot Brovarney and Susan Billy. *Remember Your Relations: The Elsie Allen Baskets, Family & Friends.* Berkeley, California: Heyday Books [with the Grace Hudson Museum and the Oakland Museum of California], 1996.

This is a catalogue of an exhibit researched and curated by the authors for the Grace Hudson Museum in Ukiah, California, in 1993; it pays tribute to Pomo elder Elsie Commanche Allen (1899-1990), as well as 26 other native weavers past and present; the text features reminiscences and statements from several elders.

E.97. Allen, Elsie [Vinson Brown, ed.] *Basketmaking: A Supreme Art for the Weaver.* Happy Camp, California: Naturegraph Publishers, 1972.

In a brief autobiographical essay, 73-year-old Pomo basketmaker Elsie Allen describes her efforts to "bring back an understanding of our own background and the beautiful things our old people did"; this precedes a detailed description, with accompanying photographs, of Pomo basketmaking techniques (see also **E.96.a**).

E.98. Cort, Louise Allison, and Nakamura Kenjii. *A Basketmaker in Rural Japan.* New York: Weatherhill, 1994.

> Published in conjunction with a Smithsonian Institution exhibit, this book documents the life and work of Hiroshima Kazuo, born in 1915, the last professional basketmaker from the mountainous Hinokage region on the island of Kyushu.

E.99. Davis, Gerald L. "Afro-American Coil Basketry in Charleston County, South Carolina: Affective Characteristics of an Artistic Craft in a Social Context." In Don Yoder, ed. *American Folklife.* Austin: University of Texas Press, 1976, 151-184.

> Davis presents excerpts of interviews with basket makers Peter Alston and Margaret Wilson, ages identified as "fifty years, plus..."

E.100. Glassie, Henry. "William Houck, Maker of Pounded Ash Adirondack Pack-Baskets." *Keystone Folklore Quarterly* 12:1 (1967), 23-54.

> Glassie describes the life and work of Houck, born to a German farming family in West Leyden County, New York, in 1884, and whose father made baskets; however, Houck doesn't remember being taught: "I just figgered it out by myself."

E.101. Hinson, Glenn. "An Interview with Leon Berry, Maker of Baskets." *North Carolina Folklore Journal* 27:2 (1979), 56-60.

> Hinson presents a short transcript of an interview he conducted with Berry, 92, a white oak basketmaker, at the craftsman's home in Mecklenburg County, North Carolina, in 1976.

E.102. Joyce, Rosemary O. *A Bearer of Tradition: Dwight Stump, Basketmaker.* Athens: University of Georgia Press, 1989.

> Joyce presents, through photographs and transcripts of interviews she conducted from 1977 to 1985, the life and work of Stump, born in 1900, who has made white-oak round-rod baskets in Hocking County, Ohio, since he was 17.

E.103. Marshall, Howard Wright. "Mr. Westfall's Baskets: Traditional Craftsmanship in Northcentral Missouri. *Mid-South Folklore* 2:2 (1974), 43-60.

> Marshall presents, with interview excerpts, the work of Joseph Earl Westfall, 72, residing near Higbee, Missouri, who makes hand-riven white oak farm and market baskets using techniques practiced in his family for several generations.

E.104. McBride, Bunny. *Our Lives in Our Hands: Micmac Indian Basketmakers.* Gardiner, Maine: Tilbury House, 1990.

> This book, the product of a tribal effort to gather and document a museum collection, tells the story of several generations of basketmaking among the Micmac of Aroostook County, Maine, and features biographies, with photographs by Donald Sanipass, of eleven basketmakers, most of them elders (see **H.137**).

E.105. Peterson, Sally. "Plastic Strap Baskets: Containers for a Changing Context." In James Hardin and Alan Jabbour, eds. *Folklife Annual 88-89.* Washington, D. C.: American Folklife Center, Library of Congress, 1989, 138-147.

> This articles focuses on the work of Chia Ker Lor, a Loatian Hmong elder now living in North Philadelphia, who adapted his skills as a bamboo basket weaver to the creation of baskets made of plastic strapping salvaged from workplace waste.

E.106. Rosengarten, Dale. "'Bulrush is Silver, Sweetgrass is Gold': The Enduring Art of Sea Grass Basketry." In James Hardin and Alan Jabbour, eds. *Folklife Annual 88-89.* Washington, D.C.: American Folklife Center, Library of Congress, 1989, 148-163.

Rosengarten reviews the history of sea grass basketry among African-Americans living along the South Carolina seacoast, and draws attention to several elder basket makers and their role in preserving this traditional art.

E.107. Schlick, Mary Dodds. *Columbia River Basketry: Gift of the Ancestors, Gift of the Earth.* Seattle: University of Washington Press, 1994.

Schlick presents the baskets of Indians living along the Columbia river within the context of the lives of the people who created and used them; history, mythology and descriptions of basket construction are integrated with personal narratives, including the reminiscences of elder basketmakers.

E.108. Shaner, Richard H. "The Oleg Valley Barkmaster." *Pennsylvania Folklife* 14:1 (1964), 2-9.

Shaner describes the life and work of Pennsylvania German farmer Freddie Bieber, 79, who lives in Oleg Valley, Berks County, Pennsylvania, and makes white oak baskets with his wife Annie, who helps him weave.

Metalwork

E.109. Borden, Elizabeth. "Blacksmith Lore: Joe Hansberry, Master Blacksmith." *Tennessee Folklore Society Bulletin* 51:1 (1985).

Borden presents excerpts of interviews conducted in 1984 with Hansberry, lifelong smith ("I ain't never retired") who quit work in 1978 only to return as resident village blacksmith in an outdoor museum replica of Anderson's Blacksmith Shop, a long-standing institution in Murfreesboro, Tennessee.

E.110. Harper, Douglas. *Working Knowledge: Skill and Community in a Small Shop.* Berkeley: University of California Press, 1987.

A unique study "of material and folk culture," this book describes, with extensive interview excerpts, the application of traditional craft methods and concepts in the work of Willie, a metalsmith and Saab repair man in rural north New York.

E.111. O'Connor, Malachi. "Bob Rock: Blacksmith." In Shalom D. Staub, ed. *Craft and Community: Traditional Arts in Contemporary Society.* Philadelphia: Balch Institute for Ethnic Studies and the Pennsylvania Heritage Affairs Commission, 1988, 71-78.

O'Connor presents a portrait of Rock, born in 1906, who has been a blacksmith and tool maker for over 60 years in Bedford County, Pennsylvania, and also makes three styles of five-string banjos.

E.112. Shuldiner, David. "The Art of Sheet Metal Work: Traditional Craft in a Modern Industrial Setting." *Southwest Folklore* 4 (1980), 37-41.

This is a brief portrait of the author's father, Max Shuldiner, born in 1918, a sheet metal worker who, for the past 30 years, had worked in small shops that retained aspects of an older craft tradition where artisans make products from start to finish; he also recalls a legend about Abraham Lincoln that came to mind at a work site and led to the solution of an installation problem.

E.113. Stinson, Craig M. "Bea Hensley and the Redefinition of the Blacksmith in the North Carolina Mountains." *North Carolina Folklore Journal* 40:1 (1993), 19-29.

Stinson offers a brief portrait of Hensley, born in 1919, an ornamental blacksmith who owns a shop off the Blue Ridge Parkway in Spruce Pine, including interview excerpts in which Hensley reminisces and describes the development of his craft.

E.114. Vlach, John Michael. *Charlestown Blacksmith: The Work of Philip Simmons.* Athens: University of Georgia Press, 1981.

This is a detailed study of the life and work of Simmons, with generous excerpts of tape-recorded interviews with the blacksmith, born in 1912 on Daniel Island, between the Wando and Cooper Rivers north of Charlestown, South Carolina.

E.115. Vrooman, Nicholas Curchin, and Patrice Avon Marvin, eds. *Iron Spirits.* Fargo: North Dakota Council on the Arts, 1982.

This work documents the tradition of blacksmith-created iron grave crosses brought by Catholic immigrants from Russia's Black Sea region into North Dakota from the late 1800s to the 1940s; accompanying photographs of the crosses are the voices of these immigrants and their descendants, reflecting the perspectives of several generations on the life and work of the cross makers and their friends and families.

Pottery

E.116. Babcock, Barbara A. "'At Home, No Womens Are Storytellers': Potteries, Stories and Politics in Cochiti Pueblo." In Joan Newlon Radner, ed. *Feminist Messages: Coding in Women's Folk Culture.* Urbana: University of Illinois Press, 1993, 221-248.

Babcock describes the work of Cochiti pueblo elder Helen Cordero, who reinvented a traditional form of figurative pottery, encouraging a generation of women potters who defy traditional gender roles by creating a livelihood from their "potteries."

E.117. Babcock, Barbara A. "Modeled Selves: Helen Cordero's 'Little People.'" In Victor W. Turner and Edward M Bruner, eds. *The Anthropology of Experience.* Urbana: University of Illinois Press, 1986.

Babcock describes the clay "Storyteller" figures created by 65-year-old Cordero, a Cochiti Pueblo woman, seeing them as "modeled selves" reflecting images from her personal history, family life, the Pueblo community, ritual and mythology.

E.118. Babcock, Barbara, and Guy and Doris Monthan. *The Pueblo Storyteller: Development of a Figurative Ceramic Tradition.* Tucson: University of Arizona Press, 1986.

The central figure in this richly illustrated text is Helen Cordero, born in 1915 to the Pumpkin group, Fox clan, of Cochiti Pueblo, New Mexico, and considered largely responsible for the revival of Pueblo figurative pottery; a potrait of her life and work is presented along with a biographical survey of 110 artists who have made Storyteller figures or related objects between the mid-1960s and the mid-1980s.

E.119. Lau, Barbara A. "A Woman at the Wheel: Issues of Gender in a North Carolina Pottery Tradition." *North Carolina Folklore Journal* 41:1 (1994), 1-13.

Lau presents, with interview excerpts, a portrait of seventh-generation potter Nell Cole Graves of Seagrove, North Carolina, presently in her 80s, and the first woman "turner" on a pottery wheel in the eastern Piedmont pottery community.

E.120. Mulryan, Leonore Hoag. *Mexican Figural Ceramists and Their Works* [*Monograph Series Number 16*]. Los Angeles: Musuem of Cultural History, University of California, Los Angeles, 1982.

This monograph accompanied an exhibit of the works of five Mexican potters working with traditional figurative forms and motifs; descriptions of the lives and work of these middle-aged and older craftspeople feature statements, including personal experience narratives, of the artists.

E.121. Peterson, Susan. *The Living Tradition of Maria Martinez*. Tokyo: Kodansha International, 1977.

This is a richly detailed portrait, in words and photographs, of the work of Martinez, a potter from the pueblo of San Ildefonso, New Mexico, well into her 90s when the author met the artist and her family in the 1970s; Peterson discusses the elder potter's influence on her family and community.

E.122. Peterson, Susan. *Lucy M. Lewis: American Indian Potter*. Tokyo: Kodansha International, 1984.

Like the book about Maria Martinez above, this is a detailed and richly illustrated portrait of Lewis, a potter from Acoma Pueblo, New Mexico, in her eighties when studied by Peterson, who draws upon her conversations with the artist and family members.

E.123. Peterson, Susan. *Shoji Hamada: A Potter's Way & Work*. New York: Weatherhill: 1995 [1974].

This book presents, in text and photographs, an intimate portrait of Hamada, (1894-1978), declared a "Living National Treasure" in 1955, and a major figure in Japan's folkcraft movement; he was 76 when Peterson documented his work during a four-month stay at his home in the town of Mashiko, Tochigi Prefecture.

E.124. Rinzler, Ralph, and Robert Sayers.*The Meaders Family: North Georgia Potters* [*Smithsonian Folklife Studies, Number 1*]. Washington, D. C.: Smithsonian Institution Press, 1980.

This monograph, along with a documentary film produced by the Smithsonian Office of Folklife Programs, presents portraits of members of the Meaders family, including elders Cheever Meader and his wife Arie, along with descriptions of their folk pottery enterprise (see **H.247**).

E.125. Seriff, Suzanne. "Homages in Clay: The Figural Ceramics of José Varela." In Joe S. Graham, ed. *Hecho en Tejas: Texas-Mexican Folk Arts and Crafts* [*Publications of the Texas Folklore Society, Vol. 50*]. Denton: University of North Texas Press, 1991, 146-171.

Seriff describes the life and work of Varela, born in 1907 in the border state of Coahuila, Mexico, and who moved with his family in the wake of the Mexican Revolution to the South Texas town of D'Hanis, where he began to make ceramic figures at age 15, and continues the tradition of *retratos* (portrait busts) and other representational figures in clay.

E.126. Spivey, Richard L. *Maria*. Flagstaff, Arizona: Northland Press, 1979.

This is not so much a biography of the legendary Pueblo potter Maria Martinez as it is a photo-essay, presented with statements by and about Maria, including excerpts of conversations with the author recorded when she was 90 (see also **E.121**).

E.127. Trimble, Stephen. *Talking With the Clay: The Art of Pueblo Pottery.* Santa Fe, New Mexico: School of American Research Press, 1993 [1987].

The title refers to the narrative impulse in Pueblo pottery designs; Trimble offers portraits in photographs and texts, of the work of several generations of Pueblo storytellers in clay, including excerpts of conversations with the artists.

E.128. Zug, Charles G. III. "'New' Pots for Old: Burlon Craig's Strategy for Success." In James Hardin and Alan Jabbour, eds. *Folklife Annual 88-89.* Washington, D. C.: American Folklife Center, Library of Congress, 1989, 126-137.

Craig, born in 1914, is a traditional potter from Catawba County, North Carolina, who has revived old forms and made innovations in order to keep making a living producing pottery in the North Carolina regional style.

Quilting

[NOTE: Many of the entries in this special section are to be found in the pages of *Uncoverings,* annual volumes of the Research Papers of the American Quilt Study Group (600 Mission Street, Suite 400, San Francisco, CA, 94105), published since 1980; this is a recommended first stop for anyone searching for material on older quilters (I have not listed every article in *Uncoverings* mentioning elders, so there's more to uncover in these volumes!).]

E.129. _____*A Patchwork of Our Lives: Stories from the Cambridge Women's Quilt.* Boston: The Oral History Center, 1982.

This is a collection of the personal narratives that accompanied the "Cambridge Women's Quilt Exhibit," in which women and girls ages 8 to 80 from 15 ethnic communities each contributed a quilt block that tells a story from the sewer's life.

E.130. Burdick, Nancilu B. "Talula Gilbert Bottoms and Her Quilts." In Sally Garoute, ed. *Uncoverings 1984 [Vol 5]* San Francisco: American Quilt Study Group, 1985, 7-28.

Burdick tells the story of her grandmother, Talula Bottoms (1862-1946), of Atlanta, Georgia, through her quilts, correspondence, and "a little book of memories" written when she was 81.

E.131. Cantú, Norma, and Ofelia Zapata Vela. "The Mexican-American Quilting Traditions of Laredo, San Ygnacio and Zapata." In Joe S. Graham, ed. *Hecho en Tejas: Texas-Mexican Folk Arts and Crafts [Publications of the Texas Folklore Society, Vol. 50].* Denton: University of North Texas Press, 1991, 77-92.

This essay draws upon interviews with 18 quiltmakers in Zapata County and Laredo, Texas, focusing on the lives and work of older women; brief biographical information on the quilters who were interviewed, 10 of whom are over 60, is given at the end of the article.

E.132. Caudle, Nancy Habersat. "Quilts and Quiltmakers of the Penobscot Peninsula, Downeast Maine." In Sally Garoute, ed. *Uncoverings 1983 [Vol 4].* San Francisco: American Quilt Study Group, 1984, 45-57.

This portrait of several older quiltmakers living along coastal Maine–the oldest of them celebrated her 100th birthday in 1984–features generous excerpts from oral history interviews.

E.133. Cerny, Catherine A. "A Quilt Guild: Its Role in the Elaboration of Female Identity." In Laurel Horton, ed. *Uncoverings 1991 [Vol 12]*. San Francisco: American Quilt Study Group, 1992, 32-49.

Focusing on the Minnesota Quilters, whose members range from late 20s to over 70, Cerny describes the ways in which quilt guilds provide mutual support, while reconciling traditional female roles with contemporary "post-industrial" feminist sensibilities; she notes members' self-identification as homemakers, and their preferences for patterns reflecting an earlier rural life centered on home and family, reflecting a "feminine culture" that, while Cerny doesn't discuss it in terms of age, embodies the milieu in which the older members were raised.

E.134. Cooper, Patricia, and Norma Bradley Allen. *The Quilters–Women and Domestic Art: An Oral History*. New York: Anchor/Doubleday, 1989 [1977].

This book is a composite of oral histories, with photographs, of several dozen women, average age 73, who grew up in rural homesteads in Texas and New Mexico; arranged in chapters from "Childhood" to "Old Age," these women describe the role of quilts in their lives (the book inspired a Broadway play).

E.135. Cunningham, Joe. "Fourteen Quilts Begun by One Woman and Finished by Another." In Sally Garoute, ed. *Uncoverings 1986 [Vol 7]*. San Francisco: American Quilt Study Group, 1987, 61-72.

The author describes the work of two Midwest quiltmakers, Betty Harriman (b. 1890) and Mary Schafer (b. 1910), who began corresponding with each other in the 1960s; following Betty's death at age 81, Mary acquired her unfinished quilts and completed them.

E.136. Dyen, Doris J. "The Allison Park Quiltmakers." In Shalom D. Staub, ed. *Craft and Community: Traditional Arts in Contemporary Society*. Philadelphia: Balch Institute for Ethnic Studies and the Pennsylvania Heritage Affairs Commission, 1988, 63-70.

Dyen describes an intergenerational quilting group (mid-30s to mid-70s) in Hampton Township near Pittsburgh, one of many sparked by a quilting revival in the 1970s; at least two members completed quilts started by older women relatives with skills they picked up in the quilting group.

E.137. Farb, Joanne. "Piecin' and Quiltin': Two Quiltmakers in Southwest Arkansas." *Southern Folklore Quarterly* 39 (1975), 363-375.

Rushie, 75, and Stella, 70, have been quilting for over 50 years; they recall their lifetimes of quiltmaking, and Farb describes some of the techniques and patterns they have used.

E.138. Galvin, Seán (edited by Linda Cross and Pamela Richardson). *What's This Got to Do With Quilting?: Nine Stories of Southern Women Quilters Living in New York City*. Albany, New York: Lane Press, 1994.

This illustrated booklet features stories of nine older African-American women who participated in the Elder Craftsmen Textile Project (1989-1994), under the auspices of Elder Craftsmen, Inc., an organization started in 1955 that both offers crafts workshops for women and men age fifty-five and older and also seeks broader public recognition for the creative skills of older persons.

E.139. Gebel, Carol Williams. "Quilts in the Final Rite of Passage: A Multicultural Study." In Virginia Gunn, ed. *Uncoverings 1995 [Vol 16]*. San Francisco: American Quilt Study Group, 1995, 199-227.

> Gebel looks at the function of quilts in ceremonial rites and customs related to death in selected European-American, Polynesian, Native American Indian, African and Asian cultures.

E.140. Hall-Patton, Colleen. "Innovation Among Southern California Quiltmakers." In Laurel Horton and Sally Garoutte, eds. *Uncoverings 1987 [Vol 8]*. San Francisco: American Quilt Study Group, 1989, 73-86.

> Hall-Patton compares the work and life-histories of members of two suburban quilting groups in the greater Los Angeles area; one is intergenerational, the members of the other range in age from 74 to 93; among the latter, the social aspects of quilting (interaction with other quilters and reinforcement of self-image) are at least as important as the aesthetic (creativity and innovation).

E.141. Hilty, Lucille. "A Passion for Quiltmaking." In Sally Garoute, ed. *Uncoverings 1980 [Vol 1]*. San Francisco: American Quilt Study Group, 1981, 13-17.

> A quiltmaker since her college years, the author reflects on the intensification of her feelings about the craft of quiltmaking and the community of quilters as she approached retirement age.

E.142. Hindman, Jane E. "Quilt Talk: Verbal Performance Among a Group of African-American Quilters." In Laurel Horton, ed. *Uncoverings 1992 [Vol 13]*. San Francisco: American Quilt Study Group, 1993, 85-108.

> Based on participant observation in a racially mixed sewing group in Tucson, Arizona, Hindman discusses the "social and oral context" within which the African-American women in the group, all elders, "teach and perform quilting."

E.143. Ice, Joyce. "Women's Aesthetics and the Quilt Process." In Susan Tower Hollis, Linda Pershing, and M. Jane Young, eds. *Feminist Theory and the Study of Folklore*. Urbana: University of Illinois Press, 1993, 166-177.

> Ice studied members of the Lytton Springs quilting club in central Texas, ranging in age from mid-40s to 80s; the author explores the interaction of personal experience and shared identity of women working together in a group.

E.144. Johnson, Geraldine N. "'More for Warmth Than for Looks': Quilts of the Blue Ridge Mountains." *North Carolina Folklore Journal* 30:2 (1983), 55-84.

> Johnson, a fieldworker for the Blue Ridge Project of the American Folklife Center, interviewed 16 quilters, "plain" and "fancy"; she describes their work and presents excerpts of interviews with several of them.

E.145. Kendra, Caryn M. "Hard Times and Home Crafts: The Economics of Contemporary Appalachian Quilting." In Laurel Horton, ed. *Uncoverings 1991 [Vol 12]*. San Francisco: American Quilt Study Group, 1992, 177-189.

> As part of a discussion of quilt production by individuals and craft cooperatives as part of an Appalachian mountain handicraft industry that emerged as a response to impoverishment and economic exploitation, Kendra cites the example of Cora Vest, born in Ezel, Kentucky, in 1915 and a lifelong quilter, who relies on quilt sales to supplement her monthly Social Security check.

E.146. Langellier, Kristin M. "Contemporary Quiltmaking in Maine: Refashioning Femininity." In Laurel Horton, ed. *Uncoverings 1990 [Vol 11].* San Francisco: American Quilt Study Group, 1991, 29-55.

Langellier describes the Pine Tree Quilters Guild, most of whose members are recent quilters (ten years or less), with the two largest age groups in their forties and sixties; the author notes that quilting continues to be highly gendered, and that "quiltmaking is most easily accommodated when women's other responsibilities, notably child-bearing and paid labor, diminish."

E.147. Lasansky, Jeanette. "Southwestern Quilts and Quiltmakers in Context." In Laurel Horton, ed. *Uncoverings 1993 [Vol 14].* San Francisco: American Quilt Study Group, 1994, 97-118.

Lasansky presents and analyzes selected stories from among oral histories of over 200 older rural women living in New Mexico who learned quilting from relatives or friends, conducted as part of a survey commissioned by the Museum of International Folk Art in 1985 (see also **E.152**).

E.148. McDonald, Mary Anne. "'Because I Needed Some Cover': Afro-American Quiltmakers of Chatham County, North Carolina." Master's thesis, University of North Carolina at Chapel Hill, 1985.

This study of a group of largely elder African-American women documents quiltmaking styles, the role of quiltmaking in promoting social solidarity and strengthening family ties, and the ways in which the quilts serve as symbolic reminders of people and events.

E.149. McDonald, Mary Anne. "Lillie Lee and Jennie Burnett: Afro-American Quilters." *North Carolina Folklore Journal* 32:2 (1984), 46-49.

This is a brief profile of the two 1984 Brown-Hudson Award winners, both in their 80s, and lifelong residents of northern Chatham County, North Carolina.

E.150. McDonald, Mary Anne. "Symbols from Ribbons: Afro-American Funeral-Ribbon Quilts in Chatham County, North Carolina." In Daniel W. Patterson and Charles G. Zug III, eds. *Arts in Earnest: North Carolina Folklife.* Durham: Duke University, 1990, 164-178.

McDonald reports on her conversations with several elderly black women for whom quilts made of funeral-ribbons are symbolic of people, experiences and ideals in their lives; they may commemorate the departed, or evoke memories of happier times and places, helping them cope with loss and change.

E.151. Metzler-Smith, Sandra J. "Quilts in Pomo Culture." In Sally Garoute, ed. *Uncoverings 1980 [Vol 1].* San Francisco: American Quilt Study Group, 1981, 41-47.

In a brief description of quilting as adopted by the Pomo Indians of Northern California from local white families, the author cites excerpts from interviews of Pomo women in their 60s collected around 1940 (see **D.334**), and women born at the turn of the century (recorded in 1980 for the Mendocino County Museum).

E.152. Pickens, Nora. "Scrap Quilts of New Mexico." In Sally Garoute, ed. *Uncoverings 1986 [Vol 7].* San Francisco: American Quilt Study Group, 1987, 39-45.

Pickens reports on the New Mexico Quilt Survey, conducted in 1985 for the Museum of International Folk Art (Santa Fe), in which over 200 quiltmakers were interviewed, most of them having lived in New Mexico since the 1920s or 1930s (see also **E.147**).

E.153. Ramsey, Bets. "The Land of Cotton: Quiltmaking by African-American Women in Three Southern States." In Laurel Horton, ed. *Uncoverings 1986 [Vol 7]*. San Francisco: American Quilt Study Group, 1987, 9-28.

This article is based on interviews conducted with 35 older African-American women in Alabama, Georgia and Tennessee, who talked about the role of quiltmaking in their lives; they note significant changes: 60 years before, their first quilts were made of necessity; now they make quilts for pleasure, learn more new patterns, and take pride in exhibiting their quilts.

E.154. Ramsey, Bets. "Recollections of Childhood Recorded in a Tennessee Quilt." In Sally Garoute, ed. *Uncoverings 1983 [Vol 4]*. San Francisco: American Quilt Study Group, 1984, 27-37.

Ramsey describes a collaborative life review project, the "Recollections of Childhood Quilt," that she carried out with several older women as part of her job as craft specialist for Senior Neighbors of Chattanooga (Tennessee).

E.155. Shea, Elizabeth Weyrauch, and Patricia Cox Crews. "Nebraska Quiltmakers: 1870-1940." In Laurel Horton, ed. *Uncoverings 1986 [Vol 7]*. San Francisco: American Quilt Study Group, 1987, 54-68.

This historical essay is based on data conducted during the project Nebraska Quilt History Days and tape-recorded interviews conducted with elders who recalled their early quiltmaking days and those of their families and communities.

E.156. Stahl, Sandra K. D. "A Quiltmaker and Her Art." In Linda Degh, ed. *Indiana Folklore: A Reader*. Bloomington: Indiana University Press, 1980, 46-73.

This is a portrait of Bessie DeVault of Darke County, Ohio, born in 1903 in Middletown, Michigan, who recalls quilting as a social event, and talks about the aesthetics of quilting.

E.157. Stewart, Susan. "Sociological Aspects of Quilting in Three Brethren Churches of Southeastern Pennsylvania." *Pennsylvania Folklife* 23:3 (1974), 15-29.

Stewart discusses the meaning of quilts in terms of craft and social function, based on interviews with several older women church members who quilt.

E.158. Weatherford, Sally E. "Profile of a Murfreesboro Quiltmaker." *Tennessee Folklore Society Bulletin* 44:3 (1978), 108-114.

Weatherford describes the work of Nellie Virge, 96, of Murfreesboro, Tennessee, a daughter of slaves who later became sharecroppers, who has quilted since childhood largely as a utilitarian activity until the death of her husband 20 years ago, after which quiltmaking became a hobby pursued more for aesthetic reasons.

Woodwork

E.159. Archbold, Annelen. "Percy Beeson, A Kentucky Broommaker." *Mid-South Folklore* 3:2 (1975), 41-45.

This is a short study of Beeson, 81, the last member of an African-American family of farmer-craftspeople who made brooms to support the family, based on fieldwork and interviews conducted in Butler and Warren Counties, Kentucky, in 1973.

E.160. Bethke, Robert D. *Americana Crafted: Jehu Camper, Delaware Whittler.* Jackson: University Press of Mississippi, 1995.

Text and photographs commemorate the life and work of Camper (1897-1989), who constructed miniature replicas depicting Delaware farm life of an earlier era; in his essay, Bethke discusses the role of retirement in folk art production, and the fascination with miniatures among older folk artists.

E.161. Bethke, Robert. "Farm Folklife in Wood: Jehu F. Camper, Delaware Whittler." In Roger D. Abrahams, Kenneth S. Goldstein, and Wayland Hand, eds. *By Land and By Sea: Studies in the Folklore of Work and Leisure Honoring Horace P. Beck on His Sixty-Fifth Birthday.* Hatboro, Pennsylvania: Legacy Books, 1985, 20-31.

Bethke describes the life and work of Camper, presents excerpts of interviews conducted between 1980 and 1984 at his farm in rural Kent County, Delaware, and discusses his miniatures depicting farm life as a form of life review (see also **E.160**).

E.162. Briggs, Charles L. "A Conversation with Saint Isidore: The Teachings of the Elders." In Marta Weigle, ed. *Hispanic Arts and Ethnohistory in the Southwest.* Santa Fe, New Mexico: Ancient City Press, 1983.

In 1972 Briggs was "adopted" by a family of wood carvers in Cordova, New Mexico, who, in addition to teaching him about the art of carving saints, told didactic stories by Cordovan elders about*"los viejitos de antes"* ("the elders of bygone days"), including a hymn about one of the saints they carved.

E.163. Briggs, Charles L. "The Role of *Mexicano* Artists and the Anglo Elite in the Emergence of a Contemporary Folk Art." In John Michael Vlach and Simon J. Bronner, eds. *Folk Art and Art Worlds.* Logan: Utah State University Press, 1992 [1986], 195-224.

In the context of a survey of the role of Anglo art patrons in the image-carving industry in Cordova, New Mexico, Briggs describes the life of José Dolores Lopez (1868-1937), who began whittling at age 50 when his eldest son was called up to serve in WWI and who, in late life, carved to supplement the family income while his sons tended the farm, making religious figures, and creating works for the tourist trade.

E.164. Bronner, Simon J. *The Carver's Art: Crafting Meaning From Wood.* Lexington, Kentucky: University Press of Kentucky, 1996 [originally published as *Chain Carvers: Old Men Crafting Meaning* (1985)].

Bronner's study is based on conversations with several older men in Indiana who, in their retirement, carve linked chains from single blocks of wood, a traditional craft remembered from their childhood; he sees this creative late-life activity as a form of adjustment to changing life situtations.

E.165. Bronner, Simon J. "An Experiential Portrait of a Woodcarver." *Indiana Folklore* 13:1-2 (1980), 30-45.

Bronner describes the life and work of George Bloom, born in 1898 outside Schnellville, in Dubois County, Indiana, into a German Catholic family; around age 60, he took up whittling, inspired by a wooden chair made by an elderly man.

E.166. Davis, Gerald L. "Elijah Pierce, Woodcarver: Doves and Pain in Life Fulfilled." In Michael D. Hall and Eugene W. Metcalf, Jr., eds. *The Artist Outsider: Creativity and the Boundaries of Culture.* Washington, D. C.: Smithsonian Institution Press, 1994, 291-311.

Davis discusses the problem of situating Pierce (1892-1984)–a Mississippi-born resident of Columbus, Ohio, who whittled figures and created wood relief portraits on social and religious themes–within the tradition of African-American Southern rural folk art; includes excerpts of an interview with Pierce, recorded by Michael Hall in 1971 (see also **E.213, E.34**).

E.167. Feintuch, Burt. "Frank Boccardo: Toward an Ethnography of a Chairmaker." *Pennsylvania Folklife* 22 (1973), 2-9.

Feintuch presents the life and work of Boccardo, a craftsman of Newtown, Pennsylvania, born in 1885 in a farm Italy's Adriatic coast, and who emigrated to the U. S. at age 21.

E.168. Henry, Bill. "Alex Stewart: A Personal Reminiscence." *Tennessee Folklore Society Bulletin* 47:2 (1981), 48-86.

The author, born in 1929, who has lived in East Tennessee since the early 1930s, presents a portrait, with interview excerpts, of Stewart, a 90-year-old craftsman living in Hancock County, Tennessee, best known as a cooper, who the author befriended in 1968, and to whom he was briefly apprenticed in the mid-1970s.

E.169. Hinson, Glenn. "'The Lord Gave Me the Gift of Carving': The Artistry of George and Donnis SerVance." *North Carolina Folklore Journal* 40:2 (1993), 82-86.

Hinson describes the collaborative work of George SerVance, 73, of Thomasville, North Carolina, who carves dolls, walking sticks, Biblical figures, animals, and other pieces, and his wife Donnis, who paints them.

E.170. James, A. Everette, and Pattie Virginia Royster James. "Artful Arliss Watford: North Carolina Wood Carver." *North Carolina Folklore Journal* 39:2 (1992), 72-76.

The James's provide a brief portrait of Watford, born in 1924 and raised near Winton in Hereford County, North Carolina, who uses a mixture of machine tools and hand carving to create angels, farmers, animals and other figures.

E.171. Johnson, Rhonda S. "Harmon Young, Georgia Wood Sculptor." *Southern Folklore Quarterly* 42 (1979), 243-256.

Young, a former construction worker born in south Alabama, has, since his retirement, carved walking sticks, small figures and other wood objects; Johnson presents excerpts of an interview conducted with Young in his present home in Forest Park, Georgia.

E.172. Jones, Michael Owen. *Craftsman of the Cumberlands: Tradition & Creativity.* Lexington: University Press of Kentucky, 1989].

In this revised edition of *The Handmade Object and Its Maker* [1975], Jones explores the life and work of Chester Cornett (1913-1981), a woodworker and chairmaker whose creations were also a means of coping with the problems that he encountered in life; features excerpts of interviews with the artist (see also **H.6**).

E.173. Kalb, Laurie Beth. *Crafting Devotions: Tradition in Contemporary New Mexico Santos.* Albuquerque: University of New Mexico Press, 1994.

Based on fieldwork conducted in northern New Mexico, this illustrated study of *santos*, Hispano Catholic images of saints, and the *santeros* who make them, wood carvers and painters; a chapter is devoted to Enrique Rendón (1923-1987), who began carving saints after retiring at age 51 on a disability pension.

E.174. Kiah, Virginia. "Ulysses Davis: Savannah Folk Sculptor." *Southern Folklore Quarterly* 42 (1978), 271-285.

Kiah presents, with interview excerpts the life and work of Davis, born in Fitzgerald, Georgia, in 1914, who has carved wood since his youth, and whose barbershop, built in the rear of his home in Savannah, Georgia, where he moved in 1942, also includes his workshop, where he works on and displays his sculptures and bas-relief panels, many on biblical themes.

E.175. Ladenheim, Melissa. *Birds in Wood: The Carvings of Andrew Zergenyi.* Jackson: University Press of Mississippi, 1996.

This book presents the life and work of Zergenyi, an Eastern European immigrant in his 90s, whose carvings of birds "bring him artistic pleasure, consolation, and a place in mainstream America."

E.176. Mordoh, Alice Morrison. "Two Woodcarvers: Jasper, Dubois City, Indiana." *Indiana Folklore* 13:1-2 (1980), 17-29.

Mordoh presents excerpts of interviews with Mr. Lamperd, in his early 60s, from the German community of Jasper, furniture factory worker who quit, then took to carving mostly toys in late life; and Aloysius Schuch, in his 70s, a cabinet maker and assembler for 43 years, who also took to carving in late life; both use discarded hard wood remnants.

E.177. Reuter, Frank. "John Arnold's Link Chains: A Study in Folk Art." *Mid-South Folklore* 5:2 (1977), 41-52.

Reuter describes the work of Arnold, born in Otwell, Indiana, in 1897, presently residing in Monticello, Arkansas; once a winter pastime, Arnold now whittles year round and earns extra income in his retirement.

E.178. Tebbetts, Diane. "Marvin E. May: 'I Made That From Scratch.'" *Indiana Folklore* 13:1-2 (1980), 1-16.

May, born in 1910 near Allen's Creek in Monroe County, Indiana, makes fiddles, chairs, and toy wagons; he held a variety of jobs in his life, from farm to sawmill to stone quarry, before retiring in 1962, when he took to gardening, fishing, and woodworking.

E.179. Van Horn, Donald. "'Carve Wood': The Vision of Jesse Aaron." *Southern Folklore Quarterly* 42 (1978), 257-270.

Van Horn presents a personal narrative by Aaron, born in 1887, part African-American and part Seminole Indian, a nurseryman who has grown flowers and vegetables on a plot of land near Gainseville, Florida; he tells the story of a vision that came to him in the late 1960s to carve wood sculptures.

E.180. Van Horn, Donald. *Carved in Wood: Folk Sculpture in the Arkansas Ozarks.* Batesville, Arkansas: Arkansas College Folklore Archive Publications, 1979.

This book offers both a study of the tradition of woodcarving in the Ozarks, and portraits of four carvers, one of them elder Marvin Warren, born in 1895 on his family's farm near Oxley, Arkansas; the chapter devoted to his life and work features excerpts of interviews conducted by the author in 1977.

VISUAL ARTS: "FOLK"/"NAIVE"/"OUTSIDER"/"ENVIRONMENTAL"/ETC.

E.181. Adele, Lynne. "Frank Jones: The Psychology and Belief System of a Black Folk Artist." Master's thesis, University of Texas at Austin, 1987.

Adele examines the work of Frank Albert Jones (c.1900-1969), born near Clarkesdale, Texas, and an inmate of the Texas Department of Corrections for over twenty years; in the last five years of his life he created colored-pencil drawings reflecting beliefs he was exposed to as an African-American in the rural South.

E.182. Atkins, Jacqueline M. "Joseph Yoakum: Visionary Traveler." *The Clarion* 15:1 (1990), 50-57.

This is a brief portrait of folk artist Yoakum, born in Window Rock, the Navajo Nation, Arizona, between 1886 and 1888, and who has alternately described himself as an "old black man" and a full-blooded "Nava-joe Indian," who began making pictures in his 70s after a dream revealed to him that the Lord wanted him to draw.

E.183. Bousquet, Woodward S. "Work, Family and Faith: Marshall Fleming's Folk Art." *Appalachian Journal* 19:3 (1992), 298-307.

This is a portrait of Marshall, 75, who lives in rural Mineral County, West Virginia, and who, following an early retirement in 1973, has created a folk art environment, "Little Hidden Valley," with miniature buildings, animal cutouts, windmills, and other small pieces.

E.184. Burgess, Karen E. *Home Is Where the Dog Is: Art in the Back Yard.* Jackson: University Press of Mississippi, 1996.

Burgess describes the work of her father, in his 70s, and relates "how the story of a family's decorative wooden dog defines the significance of yard art in America."

E.185. Chittenden, Varick A. "Veronica Terrillion's 'Woman-Made' House and Garden." In Daniel Franklin Ward, ed. *Personal Places: Perspectives on Informal Art Environments.* Bowling Green, Ohio: Bowling Green State University Popular Press, 1984, 41-61.

Terrillion, born in 1900 at Indian River in Northern Lewis County, New York, less than a mile from her present home, constructed life-size painted concrete statues of animals and people on the grounds of her ranch house.

E.186. Fenn, Elizabeth A. "'So Simple Yet So Complicated': Folk Artist William Young of Pantego." *North Carolina Folklore Journal* 32:1 (1984), 56-69.

Fenn surveys the life and work of Young, an African-American water color painter and wood sculptor, born around 1912 in Portsmouth, Virginia, and presently residing in Pantego, North Carolina.

E.187. Fetterman, William B. "Paul R. Wieland, Lehigh County Folk Artist." *Pennsylvania Folklife* 30:2 (1980-81), 87-93.

Fetterman reviews the life and work of Wieland, born in 1907 in Guth's Station, near Allentown, a "leader of Pennsylvania-German folk culture in Lehigh County for fifty years," and presents generous excerpts of interviews conducted by the author in 1979 and 1980.

E.188. Finster, Howard. *Howard Finster, Man of Vision*. Atlanta, Georgia: Peachtree Publishers, 1989.

This a collection of the visionary memory paintings of Finster, born in 1916, whose works contain religious and biographical texts with drawings and photographs; it features an interview and afterword, both by Susie Mee (see also **E.218, H.253**).

E.189. Francis, Doris. "Artistic Creations from the Work Years: The New York World of Work." In John Calagione, Doris Francis and Daniel Nugent, eds. *Workers' Expressions: Beyond Accommodation and Resistance*. Albany: State University of New Press, 1992, 48-67.

Francis explores the folk art created by several retired workers: sculptures, drawings and paintings that evoke memories of their work experiences and occupational roles (see also **G.117**).

E.190. Fussel, Fred C. *Memory Paintings of an Alabama Farm: The Art and Remembrances of Jessie DuBose Rhoads, Alabama Folk Artist*. Saint Petersburg, Florida: Byron Kennedy and Co., 1983.

This book, sponsored by the Historic Chattahoochie Commission, consists of paintings and reminiscences by Rhoads (1900-1972), who recalls her life growing up in southeastern Alabama (see also **E.221**).

E.191. Gilman, Deborah Ann. "A Study of Four Contemporary Untrained Artists From Southern Louisiana." Master's thesis, Louisiana State University, 1989.

Drawing from observation and personal interviews, Gilman explored sources of inspiration of four African-American folk artists, three of them elders: David Butler, 94, nursing home resident and creator of tin sculptures; Royal Robertson, visionary painter in his late 50s; and James Scott, 67, fishing boat model-maker.

E.192. Goldstein, Kenneth. "William Robbie: Folk Artist of the Buchan District, Aberdeenshire." In Horace P. Beck, ed. *Folklore in Action: Essays for Discussion in Honor of MacEdward Leach*. Philadelphia: American Folklore Society, 1962, 101-111.

Based on interviews conducted in 1959-60, Goldstein presents a portrait of Robbie, born in 1887 in Old Deer Parish in Scotland's Buchan District, a painter of farm animals with a special interest in Clydesdale horses.

E.193. Greenfield, Verni. *Making Do or Making Art: A Study of American Recycling*. Ann Arbor, Michigan, 1986.

In a work addressing the use of found objects in works of art, Greenfield devotes chapters to two older folk artists: Leo Dante, born of Sicilian parents in Tunis, North Africa, who owns a tailor shop in Southern Caifornia and who makes assemblages from tailors' materials; and Tressa Prisbrey, another Southern California resident, who has constructed several buildings with bottles and other recycled materials, to house her various collections of pencils, dolls and other discards (see **H.108**).

E.194. Greenfield, Verni. "Silk Purses From Sows Ears: An Aesthetic Approach to Recycling." In Daniel Franklin Ward, ed. *Personal Places: Perspectives on Informal Art Environments.* Bowling Green, Ohio: Bowling Green State University Popular Press, 1984, 131-147.

Greenfield presents portraits of two older folk artists, Emmanuel Damonte and Tressa Prisbrey, both of whom make ample use of discarded materials (see **E.193**).

E.195. Hollander, Stacy C. *Harry Lieberman: A Journey of Remembrance.* New York: Dutton Studio Books, in association with the Museum of American Folk Art, 1991.

This is an annotated gallery of reproductions of the work of Lieberman (1880-1983), who began his career as folk artist at age 80, inspired by a class he took at a senior center in Great Neck, New York; his paintings depict Jewish religious scenes and memories of the Eastern European *shtetl* where he was born and raised (see **H.109**).

E.196. Hood, John. "Jimmy Lee Sudduth." *Folk Art* 18:4 (1993/94), 47-51.

Hood offers a brief description of Sudduth, an African-American folk artist born near Fayette, Alabama, in 1910, and who has lived most of his life in the area, where he has made paintings with unusual combinations of materials, such as mud and housepaint.

E.197. Jordan, Sandra. "Alice Dickerson Montemayor of Laredo." In Francis Edward Abernethy, ed. *Folk Art in Texas*. Dallas, Texas: Southern Methodist University Press, 1985, 185-187.

Jordan offers a brief portrait of Montemayor, an 81-year-old South Texas folk artist of Irish, Indian, and Mexican ancestry, whose work is described as "a mixture of actual memory and vivid flights of imagination."

E.198. Kallir, Jane. *Grandma Moses: The Artist Behind the Myth.* New York: Clarkson N. Potter, 1982.

Kallir, the granddaughter of Otto Kallir, who first exhibited the work of Moses, discusses the nature of her appeal, her notoriety, her place in the art world and art history, the development of her style, and the nature of folk art (see also **E.208**, **H.241**).

E.199. Kangas, Gene. "Zoratti's Garden." *Folk Art* 17:3 (1992), 42-47.

Silvio Peter Zoratti (1896-1992), was born in Undine in northern Italy, arriving in the U. S. in 1919, and eventually settling in the Lake Erie town of Conneaut, Ohio, where he worked for the Nickel Platte Railroad, repairing roundhouses, stone fences, bridges and other railroad-related architectural forms; in the 1950s, he took his skills into his vegetable garden, where he created garden sculptures of stone, concrete and wood for over 30 years.

E.200. Kogan, Lee. "Mose Tolliver: Picture Maker." *Folk Art* 18:3 (1993), 44-52.

Tolliver, born in 1914 in the Pike Road Community near Montgomery, Alabama, a sharecropper's son, a tenant farmer and gardener, and who was encouraged to paint by a former employer in the early 1970s, makes fantastic images based on traditional folk beliefs, the Bible and other sources.

E.201. Leroux, Odette, Marion E. Jackson and Minnie Adola Freeman. *Inuit Women Artists: Voices From Cape Dorset.* Vancouver, British Columbia: Douglas & McIntyre, 1994.

This collection features the work of nine Inuit women artists, five of whom are elders; personal experience narratives of each artist accompany photographs of drawings, paintings and sculptures reflecting traditional Inuit themes.

E.202. Lomax, Joseph P. "The Orange Show." In Francis Edward Abernethy, ed. *Folk Art in Texas.* Dallas, Texas: Southern Methodist University Press, 1985, 39-46.

In text and photographs, Lomax presents a portrait of Jeff McKissick (1901-1979) who, over a 25 year period, constructed an elaborate personal shrine to the orange, and who wrote a book on *How You Can Live to Be One Hundred Years Old and Still Be Spry;* ironically he died 7 months after opening his "show" to the public.

E.203. Machann, Clinton. "'Uncle Pete' Drgac, Czech-American Folk Artist." In Abernethy, Francis Edward, ed. *Folk Art in Texas.* Dallas, Texas: Southern Methodist University Press, 1985, 172-177.

Machann presents, in text and photographs, the life and work of Peter Paul Drgac (1883-1976), a retired grocery-store owner from Caldwell, Texas who, at age 85, took up a late life "career" decorating yard and household objects and painting.

E.204. Maduro, Renaldo. "Artistic Creativity and Aging in India." *International Journal of Aging and Human Development* 5:4 (1974), 303-329. [Reprinted in Robert Kastenbaum, ed. *Old Age on the New Scene.* New York: Springer, 1981].

Life history and psychological data were collected from 110 male Brahmin folk painters at Nathdwara, an orthodox sacred pilgrimage center in Rajasthan, Western India; Maduro discusses "Hindu folk theories " as well as contemporary western notions of lifespan development, creativity and aging.

E.205. Mai, Annie. "Aaron Birnbaum: A Little Pepper, a Little Salt." *Folk Art* 20:3 (1995), 48-55.

Mai describes the life and work of 100-year-old Birnbaum, a Jewish immigrant born in Scola, in Eastern Galicia, then a region of Austria-Hungary, presently residing in Brooklyn, who paints scenes from his life in the U. S.

E.206. Maresca, Frank, and Roger Ricco. *Bill Traylor: His Art, His Life.* New York: Knopf, 1991.

Traylor (1856-1947), born a slave on a farm near the village of Benton, Alabama, remained there until the 1930s, when at the age of 80, he settled in Montgomery, Alabama, where he began drawing scenes of city life, as well as images from his early memories of rural life; he completed over 1200 pictures, mostly in the late 1930s and early '40s. [Traylor is also the subject of a marvelous children's book, *Deep Blues: Bill Traylor, Self-Taught Artist,* by Mary E. Lyons (New York: Charles Scribner's Sons, 1994).]

E.207. Moore, Ross. *Sam Byrne: Folk Painter of the Silver City.* Ringwood, Victoria: Penguin Books Australia, 1985.

Moore documents the life and work of Byrne (1883-1978), an Anglo-Australian folk artist whose paintings recall scenes from a life spent in the Broken Hill silver mining district of New South Wales; included are excerpts of personal narratives of Byrnes, as well as the reminiscences of several close relatives and friends.

E.208. Moses, Grandma [Otto Kallir, ed.]. *Grandma Moses: My Life Story.* New York: Harper & Brothers, 1951.

Moses (1860-1961) was first brought to prominence in the 1940s by Kallir, a modern art dealer, who compiled this collaborative autobiography from her own handwritten sketches, as well as taped-recorded conversations (see also **E.198**).

E.209. Mott, Michael. "Johnny W. Banks, Black, Man, Texan, Artist." In Francis Edward Abernethy, ed. *Folk Art in Texas.* Dallas, Texas: Southern Methodist University Press, 1985, 179-183.

Mott presents a brief portrait of Banks, a 71-year-old San Antonio folk artist, whose work ranges from memory paintings depicting life in Texas in the early part of the twentieth century to political caricatures.

E.210. Ohrn, Steven. "Visual History and Biography on Jolly Ridge: The Inspiration of Paul Friedlein." In Daniel Franklin Ward, ed. *Personal Places: Perspectives on Informal Art Environments.* Bowling Green, Ohio: Bowling Green State University Popular Press, 1984, 31-40.

On Jolly Ridge, south of Guttenberg, Iowa, Friedlein built Inspiration Point, overlooking the Mississippi River, a folk art envrioment consisting of a house and shrine with grotto, begun when he was 68.

E.211. O'Kelley, Mattie Lou. *From the Hills of Georgia: An Autobiography in Paintings.* Boston: Little, Brown, 1983.

This book is, indeed, a visual personal history of folk painter O'Kelley, from Maysville, Georgia, whose depictions of scenes from her life, including one of her birth in 1908, are each accompanied by her own illustrative comments.

E.212. Poole, Jerry Dwayne. "An Historical and Biographical Study of Ten Arkansas Folk Painters During the Decade 1960-1970." Doctoral Dissertation, University of Arkansas, 1974.

Poole conducted oral history interviews with ten Arkansas folk painters, half of whom were elders at the time he recorded their life stories, as well as their views on art; the body of this work is analytical and descriptive, with transcripts of each interview, as well as a list of interview questions, in appendices.

E.213. Roberts, Norma J., ed. *Elijah Pierce, Woodcarver.* Seattle: University of Washington Press, 1992.

Published in conjunction with an exhibit at the Columbus Museum of Art, this catalogue features essays on, and photographs of, the relief carvings of Pierce (1892-1984), born on a farm near Baldwin, Mississippi, and whose works reflect a narrative impulse, and feature animals, and biblical and historical scenes (see also **E. 166, H.34**).

E.214. Sackton, Alexander. "Eddie Arning: Texas Folk Artist." In Francis Edward Abernethy, ed. *Folk Art in Texas.* Dallas, Texas: Southern Methodist University Press, 1985, 189-195.

Sackton presents a brief overview of the life and work of Arning, born in Germania, Texas, in 1898, and confined to a mental hospital most of his adult life, who began painting from memory and magazine images in his mid-60s (see also **E.270**).

E.215. Stanley, Tim. "Two South Carolina Folk Art Environments." In Daniel Franklin Ward, ed. *Personal Places: Perspectives on Informal Art Environments.* Bowling Green, Ohio: Bowling Green State University Popular Press, 1984.

Stanley describes the work of Joshua Samuel, 68, of Walterboro, South Carolina, who has dedicated the past six years of his life to building and promoting his "Can City"; and L. L. Carson, 70, retired contractor from Orangeburg, who constructed a miniature "City" with a variety of themes, from Hanging Gardens to Aztec temples.

E.216. Starr, Nina Howell. "Minnie Evans and Me." *Folk Art* 19:4 (1994/95), 50-57.

Starr, a close friend of Evans, and who represented her for over 20 years, spent years photographing Evans and recording their conversations; here she recalls her friendship with the African-American visionary artist from North Carolina (see **E.273**).

E.217. Stuttgen, Joanne Raetz. "Enlarging Life Through Miniatures: Bill Austin's Roadside Carnival." *Western Folklore* 51:3-4 (1992), 303-315.

Stuttgen describes the miniature carnival rides constructed by Bill and Martha Austin on the roadside near their mobile home northwest of Wisconsin Dells, Wisconsin, made of discards reinvested with value, as a response to the anxieties and loss of identity and purpose following retirement 11 years prior, through which they recreated themselves and reshaped their experiences.

E.218. Turner, John F. *Howard Finster, Man of Visions: The Life and Work of a Self-Taught Artist.* New York: Alfred A. Knopf, 1989.

Turner reviews the life and work of Finster, born in 1916, a Baptist minister whose eclectic visionary paintings ("sermon art") feature biblical quotations and autobiographical passages; he also constructed a *Paradise Garden*, made from various discarded materials, in the swampland around his repair shop (see also **E.188**).

E.219. Weatherford, Claudine. "In My Mind's Eye: The Genre Painting of Queena Stovall." *Folklore and Folklife in Virginia* 3 (1984), 7-30.

Weatherford examines the work of Stovall–born in Campbell County, Virginia in 1887, and who produced oil paintings between age 62 and 86–within the context of her life as an African-American country woman; the article focuses upon "Swing Low, Sweet Chariot," a painting of a funeral that Stovall did in 1953.

E.220. Wilson, James L. *Clementine Hunter: American Folk Artist.* Gretna, Louisiana: Pelican Publishing, 1988.

Born around 1886 on Hidden Hill Plantation, near Cloutierville, Louisiana, Hunter began painting about 1940, creating several thousand works, the last completed just a few months before her death in 1988; this book features a biography of the artist and comments by Hunter accompanying several of the reproductions of her works.

E.221. Yocum, Margaret. "A Past Created for the Present: Selectivity and the Folk Paintings of Jessie Rhoads. A Review Essay." *Kentucky Folklore Record* 30:1 (1984), 34-46.

This essay reviews the book *Memory Paintings*, which features the work of Alabama folk artist Jessie Rhoads (see **E.190**), discusses challenges to the interpretation of "memory painting," often highly selective and "predominantly cheerful"; and presents excerpts of interviews Yocum conducted with Rolf, 76, and Dorothy Tullos, 75, of northeastern Alabama, as they reminisced and reacted to Rhoads's painting.

TRADITIONAL ARTS: STATE AND REGIONAL SURVEYS IN THE U. S.

The selections below are books and exhibit catalogues focusing on traditional arts in specific states and regions in the United States, produced by state folk arts programs, universities, libraries, museums, folklore societies, and the like.

E. 222. [COLORADO] "Master/Apprentice: Colorado Folk Arts and Artists, 1986-1990." Arvata Center for the Arts and Humanities, Arvata, Colorado, and the Museum of Western Colorado, Grand Junction.

> This is "a retrospective exhibit of the work of recipients of the Colorado Council on the Arts and Humanities Master/Apprentice Grants in the folk arts"; the catalogue profiles each of the masters, most of whom are elders, along with the apprentices, and catalogue essays describe the arts represented, from Native American Indian leatherwork, quilling, drum making and other forms, Hispanic weaving, stitchery, and woodcarving, African-American woodcarving, Ukranian *pysanky*, quilting and saddlemaking.

E. 223. [CONNECTICUT] "Living Legends: Connecticut Master Traditional Artists." Institute for Community Research, Hartford, Connecticut, 1994. Curated by Lynn Williamson, Director, Connecticut Cultural Heritage Arts Program.

> This catalogue documents an exhibit of twelve traditional artists, seven of whom are elders; articles by Williamson, Salvatore Scalora and David Shuldiner discuss the diversity of folk art in Connecticut, and the role of elders as teachers, often supplanted by younger community members when generational continuity is lost; traditions of elders include those of Norwegian rosemaling, German *scherenschnitt*, a Pequot basketmaker, African-American quilter, Greek instrument maker, Puerto Rican lacemaker, and an Irish-American blacksmith .

E.224. [FLORIDA] "Expressions of Everyday Life: Traditional Folk Arts in Florida." Florida Department of State, Bureau of Florida Folklife Programs, 1989. Compiled and edited by Deborah S. Fant.

> Among the elders featured in this booklet are, Anglo-American quilters, Czech and Hungarian embroiderers, Anglo- and African-American, as well as Vietnamese, basketmakers, chair makers and corn shuck chair seat makers.

E.225. [IDAHO] Siporin, Steve, ed. *"We Came to Where We Were Supposed to Be": Folk Art of Idaho.* Boise: Idaho Commission on the Arts, 1984.

> An exhibit catalogue, this work features photographs of the works exhibited, along with portraits of individual artists, organized into sections on "Beauty in the Home," "Working on the Land," "Whimsey and Recreation," and "Ceremony and Celebration"; among the elders featured are a silversmith, rawhider, saddle maker, quilter, lace maker, sculptor, woodcarver, basket maker, and bead worker.

E.226. [ILLINOIS] "Expressions: Folkways in Southern Illinois." Carbondale: Southern Illinois Folk Arts Project, Southern Illinois University, 1979. Terry Alliband, Project Director.

> A survey of the folk arts of the 16 southernmost counties of Illinois, a region known as "Little Egypt," this booklet profiles the lives and work of such elders as an Anglo-American fiddler, a model maker, a basketmaker, woodcarvers, storytellers, and a weaver.

E.227. [ILLINOIS] "Straight from the Heart: A Folk Art Sampler of Western Illinois." Quincy: Gardner Museum of Architecture & Design, 1990. Exhibit Direction and catalogue text by Sherry Pardee.

This exhibit catalogue features portraits of several folk artists from West Central Illinois, including an elder quiltmaker, decoy carver, crocheter, wood carver, basketmaker, model maker, a loom weaver and a rag rug weaver.

E.228. [ILLINOIS] McClain, Margy. *A Feeling For Life: Cultural Identity, Community and the Arts.* Chicago, Illinois: Urban Traditions, 1988.

McClain is Director of Urban Traditions, and this publication presents traditions across the generations that she and her colleagues have explored in several Illinois communities: Gibson City, Melvin and Sibley in central Illinois, the African-American community of Cairo, and the Polish-, Mexican-, Jewish- and Japanese-American communities in Chicago.

E.229. [INDIANA] Rawles-Heiser, Carolyn. *Pieces of Our Lives: Folk Arts in Vermillion County Indiana.* Clinton, Indiana: Clinton Public Library, 1985.

A follow-up to a Local Libraries Folk Arts Project of the Indiana Arts Commission, which identified tradition bearers in Vermillion County, interviews were conducted with them, transcribed and edited for presentation in this booklet; elders featured describe Italian foodways, Anglo-American woodcarving, river lore, storytelling, maple syruping, farming, and other aspects of local folklife.

E.230. [IOWA] Ohrn, Steven, ed. *Passing Time and Traditions: Contemporary Iowa Folk Artists.* Ames: Iowa State University Press, 1984 [published for the Iowa Arts Council].

This is an anthology of writings and photographs documenting a wide range of forms and communities, from roadside and yard art, grottoes and monuments, to traditional music, folk toys, "Easter eggs and fine lace"; a number of older artists are featured; one article is "As I Remember: Visual Histories and Narratives."

E.231. [KANSAS] Chinn, Jennie, and Carl Magnuson. *Kansas Folk Arts Apprenticeship Program: Selected Portraits.* Topeka: Kansas State Historical Society, 1989.

These are profiles of recipients of Kansas Folk Arts Apprenticeship awards, a program with counterparts in several states, supported by grants from the National Endowment for the Arts, Folk Arts Program, providing for study with acknowledged elder craftspeople; several recipients are themselves elders.

E.232. [KENTUCKY] "Local Visions." Sponsored in part by a grant from the Kentucky Arts Council with funds from the National Endowment for the Arts, 1991.

This exhibit documents the work and lives of 16 middle-aged and older Anglo-American folk artists in rural eastern Kentucky; curator Adrian Swain contributes portraits of the artists–painters and makers of wood carvings, cutouts and sculptures–and one section of her catalogue essay is devoted to a discussion of "reflective yearning" and storytelling in the works of older folk artists.

E.233. [LOUISIANA] "Doing It Right and Passing It On: North Louisiana Crafts." An exhibition organized by the Alexandria Museum/Visual Art Center and partially supported by a grant from the Louisiana State Arts Council.

This exhibit featured the work of about thirty regional folk artists, most of them elders, documented by field workers Douglas Raymand and Melissa Green;

catalogue portraits of the artists feature interview excerpts; work and media featured include a walking stick, blowing horn, quilt, corn shuck, ladder-back chair, woodworking, carving, net-making, metalwork, and gourd dippers.

E.234. [MICHIGAN] Kamuda, Alan R. *Hands Across Michigan: Tradition Bearers.* Detroit: Detroit Free Press, 1993. Introduction by C. Kurt Dewhurst.

Produced in cooperation with Michigan State University Museum and the Historical Society of Michigan, this profusely illustrated book documents the works of over sixty-five folk artists from all regions of the state, and a wide range of ethnic communities; artists' remarks are woven into each profile.

E.235. [MINNESOTA] *Circles of Tradition: Folk Arts of Minnesota.* St. Paul: Minnesota Historical Society (produced for the University of Minnesota Art Musem), 1989.

Among contributors to this book, two focus on older folk artists: Johannes Riedel on "Nicolás Castillo and the Mexican-American Corrido Tradition," and M. Catherine Daly on "Anna Mizens, Latvian Mitten Knitter"; Marion J. Nelson writes about Norwegian folk artists, including older quilters and rosemalers; other elders featured include a Dakota Indian pipe carver, and a stone carver.

E.236. [MINNESOTA] *Minnesota Folk.* St. Paul: Minnesota Historical Society, 1993.

This book was published in conjunction with "Minnesota Folk," the first annual folk festival sponsored by the Minnesota Historical Society and the Minnesota State Arts Board at the Minnesota History Center in St. Paul; among the elders featured are an Anglo-American quilter, Norwegian woodworker, German-American concertina player, and Ojibway black ash and birch bark basketmakers.

E.237. [MISSISSIPPI] "Made By Hand: Mississippi Folk Art." An exhibition at the Mississippi State Historical Museum, Mississippi Department of Archives and History, Jackson, Mississippi, 1980.

While the catalogue for this exhibit does not feature portraits of each of the artists, descriptions of several older artists are to found in the catalogue essays, notably "Local Color: Memory and Sense of Place in Folk Art," by William Ferris; " Black Creativity in Mississippi: Origins and Horizons," by John Michael Vlach; "Choctaw Arts and Crafts," by Kennith H. York; and "The Folk Pottery of Mississippi," by Georgeanna H. Greer.

E.238. [MISSOURI] "Missouri Folk: Their Creative Images." Department of Art, University of Missouri-Columbia, 1982. Catalogue designed and edited by R. F. Bussbarger.

This catalogue consists of a listing of exhibited works, photographs of some, and brief descriptions of the artists; among the elders featured are Hank Williams, painter on wood, Jesse Howard, sign artist; Charles R. Skelton, basketmaker; Harold Beasley, violin maker; Daisy Cook, painter; and Frank Schmidt, model builder.

E.239. [NEW JERSEY] Moonsammy, Rita Zorn. *Passing It On: Folk Artists and Education in Cumberland County, New Jersey.* Trenton: New Jersey State Council on the Arts, 1992.

This book documents the experiences and works of participants in the Folk Arts in Education program of the New Jersey State Council on the Arts in Cumberland County; among the participating elder folk artists are an African-American gospel singer, farmer, fisherman, Estonian-American painter and jewelry maker, oyster planter, Ukrainian-American embroiderer, woodsman and a quilter.

E.240. [NEW YORK] *Between the Branches: Folk Art of Delaware County, New York.* N.p: Delaware County Historical Association, Roxbury Arts Group, 1985. Curated by Douglas A. DeNatale.

This exhibit catalogue features an introductory essay by DeNatale, and biographical sketches of about fifteen folk artists; of the dozen living artists whose lives are profiled, half of them are elders; of the three deceased artists profiled, one lived into his late 70s, the other two well into their 80s.

E.241. [NEW YORK] "Festival of the Adirondacks: Celebrating Living Cultural Traditions." Crandall Library, City Park, Glens Falls, New York, 1990. Todd DeGarmo, Director, Department of Folklife Programs, Crandall Library.

This is a program book for the Festival, produced annually since 1989 with funds from the Folk Arts Program of the New York State Council on the Arts; features short portraits of twenty-one folk artists, half of whom are elders, with articles on folk arts, foodways, storytelling and country music.

E.242. [NEW YORK] "Living Traditions in Genesee County: A One Day Celebration of Genesee Folk Artists and Traditions at Genesee Arts Council's Annual Fourth of July 'Picnic in the Park.'" Batavia, New York, 1990.

This commemorative booklet, edited by festival organizer Kathy Kimiecik, features an essay by James Kimball, "Clarence Maher: An Old-Time Fiddler Remembers," featuring the reminiscences of Maher, born in Stone Church, New York, in 1899.

E.243. [NORTH DAKOTA] "Faces of Identity, Hands of Skills: Folk Arts in North Dakota." North Dakota Council on the Arts, 1995. Curated by Troyd A. Geist, State Folklorist.

Fourteen artists are featured, with portraits that include excerpts of oral history interviews; the six elders exhibited include a Sioux drum and whistle maker, a Belcourt fiddler, German lacemaker, and German-Russian folk singer.

E.244. [NORTH DAKOTA] Martin, Christopher. *Prairie Patterns: Folk Arts in North Dakota.* Bismarck: North Dakota Council on the Arts, 1989.

This book was produced in conjunction with an exhibit produced for the State Historical Society of North Dakota; individual artists from across the state are profiled; elders featured include a Ojibway pipe maker, and a willow basketmaker; German-Russian grave cross maker; Ukrainian dulcimer maker, and a *pysanky* artist; Lakota quiltmaker; Anglo-American blacksmith, carver, and model makers; Bavarian bobbin lace maker; and a Norwegian *rosemaler* (enamel painting).

E.245. [OKLAHOMA] "Folk Art in Oklahoma." Oklahoma City: Oklahoma Museums Association, 1981. Mary Ann Anders, Project Director.

This catalogue documents an exhibition presenting the fruits of a survey conducted of folk art in the state; short profiles of the 14 artists featured, most of them in their 70s and 80s, are provided following several essays on the history and social context of Oklahoma folk arts and artists.

E.246. [OREGON] "Webfoots and Bunchgrassers: Folk Art of the Oregon Country." An exhibition organized by the Oregon Arts Commission, in cooperation with the University of Oregon Museum of Art, 1980. Curated by Suzi Jones.

The catalogue essays for this exhibit consist of an overview of Oregon folk art, and articles on "Native Americans," "Pioneers," "Buckaroos," and "Ethnic Arts"; among the descriptions of the works featured in the exhibit are brief portraits of elder artists George Winkler, who took up carving when he retired as a mill hand; W. B. Edmonson, a retired logger whose works include logging tableaus in wood; whittler Walt "Chris" Christiansen; quiltmaker Nina Miller Weinhard; saddlemaker Mark F. "Sandy" Anderson, and others.

E.247. [PENNSYLVANIA] Staub, Shalom D., ed. *Craft and Community: Traditional Arts in Contemporary Society*. Phildadelphia: Museum of the Balch Institute for Ethnic Studies and the Pennsylvania Heritage Affairs Commission, 1988.

This is a collection of catalogue essays focusing on the work of Pennsylvania folk artists, and features several portraits of older artists individually and within family and community settings (see **E.87**, **E.88**, **E.11**, and **E.136**).

E.248. [RHODE ISLAND] "Hand to Hand, Heart to Heart: Folk Arts in Rhode Island." Rhode Island State Council on the Arts, 1985. Michael E. Bell, Project Director.

This catalogue documents the work and lives of thirty folk artists in the state, over half of whom are elder craftspeople; an introductory article addresses the role of personal experience, community and generational transmission in folk art.

E.249. [SOUTH DAKOTA] "South Dakota Folk Arts: Maps and Markers of Cultural Heritage." South Dakota Folk Arts Program, South Dakota State Historical Society, and the Department of Education & Cultural Affairs, Pierre, South Dakota, 1992. Text by Michael F. Miller.

Intended as "an introduction to the folk cultural resources of the state," this brief survey features several captioned photographs of elders, including quilters, a willow basketmaker, a guitar and violin maker, and a *wycinanki* (Polish paper cutting) artist.

E.250. [TEXAS] Abernethy, Francis Edward, ed. *Folk Art in Texas*. Dallas, Texas: Southern Methodist University Press, 1985.

This 45th publication of the Texas Folklore Society celebrates the traditional arts of the Lone Star state; articles on cemeteries, tattooing, cowboy craft traditions, quilting, whittling, painting and other expressive forms feature portraits of several older folk artists (see **E.85**, **E.202**, **E.203**, **E.197**, **E.209**, and **E.214**).

E.251. [TEXAS] "The Eyes of Texas: An Exhibition of Living Texas Folk Artists." Houston: University of Texas/Lawndale Annex, 1980. Curated by Gaye Hall and David Hickman.

This exhibit featured the work of over a dozen artists, all but one in their late fifties to age 91, including Reverend Johnnie Swearingen, paintings; Eddie Arning, drawings; Ezekiel Gibbs, paintings; Nan McGarity, woodcarving; Ernest "Spider" Hewit, crochet; Earl Cabaniss, iron sculpture; Willard Watson, sculpture garden; Timoteo Martinez, paintings and constructions; Mildred and Floyd Clark, painting and framing; Ann Montalbano, collages; Eddie Jackson, paintings; and Inez Unger, painted sculptures.

E.252. [TEXAS] "Tejano Folk Arts & Crafts in South Texas/Artesanía Tejana." Kingsville: Texas A & I University, 1992. Text by Joe S. Graham, Research Associate, John E. Conner Museum.

This exhibit catalogue documents the folk arts of Texas-Mexicans; mention is made within the several catalogue essays on aspects of Tejano material culture of the traditional crafts of elder *vaqueros* (cowboys), blacksmiths, musical instrument makers and quiltmakers.

E.253. [UTAH] "Southern Utah Folklife Festival." Janice F. DeMille, ed. Hurricane, Utah: Homestead Publishers, 1985.

Over 30 interviews with craftspeople, musicians, food preparers and a Native American Indian spiritual leader, most of them elders, were recorded at the 1984 Southern Utah Folklife Festival by DeMille and Miriam C. Force, excerpts of which are presented in this book, part of Homestead's Desert Tapestry Heritage Series.

E.254. [UTAH] "Utah's Living Treasures: Ten Years of the Governor's Folk Art Awards." An exhibition at the Chase Home Museum of Utah Folk Art, Salt Lake City. A project of the Utah Arts Council, Folk Arts Program, 1991.

Among the elder folk artists whose profiles appear in the exhibit catalogue are members of the Utah Travelers gospel group; Patty Dutchie, Ute cradleboard-maker; Catalina Reyes, Mexican piñata-maker; Merle Kartchner Shumway, old-time fiddler; Tamae Kogita Sauki, Japanese flower arranger; A DeWitt Palmer, rawhide braider; Mollie Bonamont and Molley McCurdy, Goshute basketmakers; John Costello and Tony Kokal, Jr., Slovenian accordianists; Nina Grimes, quilter; and Kenneth Ward Atwood, Sr., storyteller.

E.255. [VERMONT] Jane Beck, ed. *Always in Season: Folk Art and Traditional Culture in Vermont.* Montpelier: Vermont Council on the Arts, 1982.

This book accompanied "Vermont's first folk art exhibition"; scattered throughout the work are portraits of and quotes from several older folk artists, including makers of quilts, rugs, paintings, collages, lacework, ash baskets; also featured are excerpts of personal experience narratives of farmers, mill workers, Native American Indians, and others.

E.256. [WASHINGTON] Jens Lund, ed. *Folk Arts of Washington State: A Survey of Contemporary Folk Arts and Artists in the State of Washington.* Tumwater, Washington: Washington State Folklife Council, 1989.

This book features articles by Lund, Phyllis Harrison, Janet Gilmore and Harry Gammerdinger on such topics as folk arts and community, the resourcefulness of folk artists, and occupational folk art, as well as a bibliography and "Ethnic Resource Guide"; elders profiled include Native, German, and Anglo-American basketmakers, a Finnish carver and Norwegian needleworker.

E.257. [WEST VIRGINIA] *Passing It On: An Introduction to the Folk Art & Folk Life of West Virginia, & to the West Virginia Folk Arts Apprenticeship Program.* Elkins, West Virginia: Augusta Heritage Center of Davis & Elkins College, 1994.

This survey includes several portraits, in text and photographs of local elders representing sections on folk music, dance, craft, decorative folk art, foodways, rural living, ethnic traditions, folk speech, folk songs, tales, and beliefs, and a description of Augusta Heritage Center's research activities, publications, community outreach, public presentations and workshops.

E.258. [WISCONSIN] *From Hardangers to Harleys: A Survey of Wisconsin Folk Art.* Sheboygan, Wisconsin: John Michael Kohler Arts Center, 1987. Robert T. Teske, Curator.

The exhibit was assembled from the work of folklorists Janet C. Gilmore and James P. Leary, who spent a year interviewing artists throughout the state and documenting their work; the catalogue features essays by Teske, Gilmore and Leary, and biographical notes on the 75 featured artists, over 40 of whom are elders.

E.259. [WISCONSIN] Robert T. Teske, ed. and curator. *Passed to the Present: Folk Arts Along Wisconsin's Ethnic Settlement Trail.* Cedarburg, Wisconsin: Cedarburg Cultural Center, 1994.

This exhibit catalogue features the work of folk artists living along Wisconsin's Lake Michigan shoreline; among the elders profiled are a Danish heart basketmaker and a cross-stitch embroider; a Slovenian wood carver; African-American quiltmakers; Puerto Rican piñata maker and a carver; Armenian lacemaker; Dutch shoemaker; Oneida corn-husk dollmaker; Czech basketmaker, and a Ukranian *pysanky* (egg decoration) artist; includes articles on ethnic identity and craft by Teske, James P. Leary and Mary A. Zwolinski.

TRADITONAL ARTS EXHIBITION/FESTIVAL/PROJECT CATALOGUES

Exhibits with Aging as an Overall Theme

E.260. "The Elders: Passing It On." Organized by the Origins Program, Minneapolis, under a grant from the Minnesota Humanities Commission, 1989. Linda Crawford, Curator.

"Before the institution of schools, how did people share what they knew from one generation to the next? And what is left of that system of 'passing it on' today?" asks Crawford; this exhibit responds with five Native American Indian artists who depict elders, and the *wigwas*, or birch bark bitings of elder Angelique Merasty from Beaver Lake, Manitoba; Native Americans Ron Libertus and Roberta Hill Whiteman contribute catalogue essays on oral history and the wisdom of elders.

E.261. "Everybody in My Family Has Something From Me: Older Cleveland Folk Artists." Sponsored by the Department of Aging, City of Cleveland, with the support of the Ohio Arts Council and the Ohio Humanities Council, 1981. Curated by Doris Francis-Erhard.

This exhibit featured the work of 23 folk artists, including painting, embroidery, quilting, carver, lace making, calligraphy, crochet, jewelry, paper cutting, and costume-making; the catalogue features statements from each artist.

E.262. "From Old Timer to New Timer: The Life and Work of Mark M. Walker." Monterey Peninsula Museum of Art, 1989. Curated by Jo Farb Hernandez.

This exhibit documented the folkways of Walker, born in 1892 in DeHaven, a redwood mill town in Mendocino County along California's north coast, chronicling the work of this homesteader, barn builder, folk sculptor, fiddle maker and folk historian, who shared his memories of rural northern California life.

E.262.a "Grand Pa Wiener." New York State Historical Commission, Cooperstown, New York, 1970. Curated by Joanne Bock.

This is a catalogue for a loan exhibition of the works of Isidor Wiener, born in Kishinev, Russia, in 1886, and settled in New York in 1903; from age 64, he created memory paintings depicting the "Old Country," Biblical scenes, portraits of birds and beasts, still lifes and impressions of the "New Country."

E.263. "Images of Experience: Untutored Older Artists." Pratt Institute, New York, 1982. Curated by Ellen Schwartz, Amy Snider and Don Sunseri.

The exhibit features the work of eleven elderly artists, all of whom began painting or sculpting in late life; the catalague features an essay by Snider on "The Education of the Elderly Artist," and brief life histories of each artist accompany reproductions of their works.

E.264. "10 Years of Grace: An Exhibition of Vermont Grass Roots Art." A traveling exhibition of the New England Foundation for the Arts, organized by the Catamount Film & Arts Company and Grass Roots Art and Community Effort (GRACE), 1987. Don Sunseri, Project Director.

Working in Vermont nursing homes in the 1970s, Sunseri, encouraged older people to create works of art; the exhibit documents the work of 21 of these elders; in a catalogue essay, Lucy R. Lippard eschews the term "folk art" for these works, preferring the word "vernacular, made at home, for art like that of GRACE."

E.265. "A Time to Reap: Late Blooming Artists." Cosponsored by Seton Hall University, The Museum of American Folk Art, and the New Jersey Council on the Arts. Co-curated by Barbara Wahl Kaufman and Didi Barrett, 1985.

Held at Seton Hall University, New Jersey, this exhibit featured the works of fifty older folk artists; the catalogue contains a brief essay by Barrett, "On Memories and Memory Art," with profiles of each artist and reproductions of their work.

Other Exhibits/Festivals/Projects Featuring Older Folk Artists

E.265.a. "All Roads Are Good: Native Voices on Life and Culture." New York: Smithsonian Institution, National Museum of the American Indian, 1994.

Published in conjunction with an exhibit at the National Museum of the American Indian in New York City, this catalogue features statements by 22 contemporary Native American Indians; among these are statements of two elders notable for present purposes: Joseph Medicine Crow, Crow storyteller ("Mysterious Powers"), and Abe Conklin, Ponca-Osage dancer and storyteller ("Made With Prayer").

E.266. "Artesanos Mexicanos." Los Angeles, California: Craft and Folk Art Museum, 1978. Curated by Judith Bronowski.

This bilingual catalogue accompanied both an exhibit and a film trilogy, "Mexico's Folk Artists," produced by Bronowski and Robert Grant, highlighting the work of Pedro Linares, papier-mâché artist, Sabina Sánchez, embroidery artist, and Manuel Jiménez, woodcarver; the narrative for each artist is presented in two sections, "Self-Portrait "(transcribed excerpts of filmed interviews) and "Cultural Context" (see **H.246, H.252, and H.255**).

E.267. "The Artworks of William Dawson." Randolph Gallery of the Chicago Public Library Cultural Center, 1990. Curated by David Kargl and Michael Noland.

The catalogue essay by Ruth Ann Stewart describes the life and work of Dawson, born in 1901, who grew up on a farm in Huntsville, Alabama, moved to Chicago in the early 20s and, after retiring from a career as one of the first Black produce workers at the South Water Market, began carving wooden figures at age 74.

E.268. "Ben George: A Woodcarver's World." Casper, Wyoming: Nicolaysen Art Museum, 1989. Curated by Margery M. Barber.

This exhibit catalogue documents the life and work of George (1895-1987), born in Tserovitza, Bulgaria, whose family emigrated to the U.S. in 1912, and who eventually settled in Wyoming to the life of a miner, and taking up woodcarving in earnest when he retired at age 74; he carved figures evoking community life, work, childhood, nature and religion.

E.269. *Black Folk Art in America: 1930-1980.* Published for the Corcoran Gallery of Art, Washington, D.C., by the University of Mississippi, Jackson, and the Center for the Study of Southern Culture, 1982. Curated by Jane Livingston and John Beardsley.

More a book than catalogue, this work documents, in photographs and life portraits, the works of twenty major African-American folk artists from throughout the U.S., most of whom who came to their art and/or prominence in late life. Articles by Livingston, Regina Perry and Beardsley explore the nature of African-American folk art and the visionary quality of much of the creations.

E.270. "Eddie Arning: Selected Drawings, 1964-1973." Abby Aldrich Rockefeller Folk Art Center, Williamsburg, Virginia, 1985 [Catalogue published by the Colonial Williamsburg Foundation]. Curated by Barbara Luck .

Born in 1898, in Germania, Texas, of German immigrant parents, Arning was confined much of his adult life in the Austin State Hospital for the mentally ill; from 1964 when he was transferred to a nursing home, until his discharge in 1973, he drew some 2,000 pictures inspired by childhood memories and images in old magazines; there are short essays by Luck and Alexander Sackton, longtime friend of Arning.

E.271. "Fine Folk: Art 'n' Facts from the Rural South." Piedmont Arts Association, Martinsville, Virginia, 1989. Curated by Howard and Anne Smith.

This exhibit featured the work of 8 artists, 4 black and 4 white, from five southern states; the six elders featured, whose works range from painting to sculpting to metal work, are Reuben Miller (b. 1912) and Ralph Griffin (b. 1925) of Georgia; James Harold Jennings (b 1931) of North Carolina; Rev. B. F. Perkins (b.1904) of Alabama; Oscar L. Spencer (b. 1908) of Virginia; and Willie Massey (b. 1906) of Kentucky; the catalogue presents biographical portraits of each artist.

E.272. "Folk Art in Canada." Plattsburgh, New York: Clinton County Historical Museum, 1981.

The catalogue for this exhibit on traditional arts of Canada features an essay by Joan I. Mattie, who notes that "many folk works have been created by older people who, in their art, recapture the places in which they haved lived, the way they used to do things, and the occupations they had in their younger years."

E.273. "Heavenly Visions: The Art of Minnie Evans." North Carolina Museum of Art, Raleigh, North Carolina, 1986. Curated by Mitchell D. Kahan.

Evans, an African-American woman born at Long Creek, Pender County, North Carolina, in 1892, began creating visionary drawings in the mid-1930s, turned to more conventional paintings during the '40s and '50s, then in late life returned to visionary images inspired by her religious faith, nature, and personal visions she has experienced; Kahan addresses her life and the nature of her visionary art.

E.274. "Home and Yard: Black Folk Life Expressions in Los Angeles." California Afro-American Museum, Los Angeles, California, 1987. Curated by Lizzetta LeFalle-Collins.

In the title article of this exhibit catalogue, LeFalle-Collins presents a compelling argument for an African-American folk aesthetic, brought from the southern U. S., as reflected in the interiors and yards of migrants to Los Angeles, most of them elders; an essay by folklorist Beverly Robinson is on "Vernacular Spaces and Folklife Within Los Angeles's African-American Community."

E.275. "Made in Troy: Folk Arts from the Collar City." Rensselaer County Council for the Arts, Troy, New York, 1989. Curated by Ellen McHale.

Commemorating the bicentennial of the naming of Troy, the exhibit featured the work of 18 traditional artists; elders include a quiltmaker, painter, Easter palm braider, icon maker, wood carver, fly tier, and embroiderer; the catalogue features articles by McHale, as well as Douglas DeNatale and Peggy LaPoint Orman.

E.276. "Missouri Artist Jesse Howard, With a Contemplation on Idiosyncratic Art." Columbia: Department of Art, University of Missouri, 1983. Curated by Ann Klesener.

Jesse Howard, noted for his topical and religious roadside signs, was born in Shamrock, Missouri, in 1885, and died in 1983, in "Sorehead Hill" near Fulton, making this exhibit catalogue a memorial book, with essays by Klesener and Howard W. Marshall.

E.277. "1984 Festival of American Folklife." Smithsonian Institution and the National Park Service, Washington, D. C. Catalogue edited by Thomas Vennum.

This is a Program Book of the Festival of American Folklife, produced in the National Mall every year since 1967; while every issue is worth reviewing, the 1984 program book includes essays by Bess Lomax Hawes on folk arts and elders (see **E.4**), Mary Hufford on life review (see **E.5**), and Barbara Myerhoff on elderly Jews in Venice, California, inaugurating the Smithsonian traveling exhibit "The Grand Generation" (see**E.1**); also of note are "Grandmotherly Knowledge, Grandfatherly Knowledge: Alaska's Traditional Native Arts," by Suzi Jones, and "Alaska Native Oral Tradition," by Nora and Richard Dauenhauer.

E.278. "Pioneers in Paradise: Folk and Outsider Artists of the West Coast." Cosponsored by the Long Beach Museum of Art, Long Beach, California, Henry Art Gallery, University of Washington, Seattle, and the San Jose Museum of Art, San Jose, California, 1984. Curated by Susan Larsen-Martin and Lauri Robert Martin.

This exhibit was a broad historical survey of self-taught local artists who lived in California, Oregon and Washington in the 19th and 20th centuries; biographical sketches of each artist are presented in the catalogue (most of the living artists are elders), and an introductory essay includes a discussion of the role these artists have played in their respective communities, especially in their old age.

E.279. "A Rural Life: The Art of Laverne Kelley." Hamilton College, New York, 1989. Curated by William Salzillo.

Kelley, age sixty at the time of this exhibit, still lived on the farm in upstate New York where he was born; he carves wooden trucks, farming equipment and other pieces reflecting his knowledge and experience; an essay by Joyce Ice discusses Kelley's carving within the context of his rural life.

E.280. "Stories to Tell: The Narrative Impulse in Contemporary New England Folk Art." DeCordova and Dana Museum and Park, Lincoln, Massachusetts, 1988. Curated by Lisa Weber Greenberg.

Prefaced with essays by Greenberg, Jane Beck, Dillon Bustin, and Edward D. Ives, on folk art and its reflection of personal life, communal experience and New England history, profiles of 31 folk artists are divided into categories of "Family Narratives," "Local History," "Narratives of Work," and "Ethnic Expressions"; the featured artists range in age from 31 to 100; 20 of them are over 60 years old.

E.281. "Traditional Folk Art of Montgomery County, New York." Montgomery County Historical Society, Fort Johnson, New York, 1989. Curated by Field Horne.

Among the elders profiled for this catalogue exhibit are Anglo-American quilters, a Ukrainian iconographer, an Anglo-American "celebratory" painter, a Dominican cabinet-maker, an Anglo-American quilter, a Puerto Rican gourd carver, and an Anglo-American decoy carver.

E.282. "Two Black Folk Artists: Clementine Hunter, Nellie Mae Rowe." Miami University Art Museum, Oxford, Ohio, 1987. Curated by Sterling Cook.

This exhibit features the work of painters Hunter (b. 1886), raised on Melrose Plantation, near Natchitoches, Louisiana (see also **E.220**) and Rowe (b. 1900), who lived in rural Georgia, near Atlanta.

E.283. "Two Black Mississippi Folk Artists: Mary Tilman Smith, Sarah Mary Taylor." Lexington: Folk Art Society of Kentucky in cooperation with the Center for Contemporary Art at the University of Kentucky., 1986. Curated by Larry Hackley and James Pierce Smith.

This exhibit featured the work of two folk artists who began late in life: Tilman, born in 1904, who paints on discarded metal and plywood and Taylor, born in 1916, a quiltmaker who uses a variety of traditional motifs; catalogue essays by Smith include excerpts of conversations with the artists.

E.284. "Women's Work: Carrying the Culture." Southern Appalachian Historical Association, 1991. Produced by Sharon Fairweather.

This booklet accompanied a series of folk music and art performances and presentations by about twenty women representing three generations of ballad singers, musicians, weavers, quilters, basketmakers and storytellers; Fairweather describes the background of each woman; with photographs by Debbie DeVita.

F

Health and Healing

This section lists readings with a focus on folk beliefs and practices related to health and healing among the aging, organized by region, with some subdivisions by ethnic group, and a section organized by gender-related subjects. This section includes works describing customs and beliefs of the elderly regarding health, folk healing practices related to conditions of age, and portraits of older traditional healers. Much of the literature on traditional medicine and aging has been written by health professionals and researchers with practical concerns about health care delivery among elders. For the benefit of practitioners, there is a complementary section on health and healing in Chapter G: "Applied Folklore."

[NOTE: A chapter of *Anthropology of Aging: A Partially Annotated Bibliography* (see **B.1**) is devoted to "Medical Aspects of Aging" with sub-headings on "Health and Social Services," and "Institutionalization," and is well worth consulting as a companion to the list of works below.]

GENERAL/CROSS CULTURAL

F.1. _____*Religion, Aging and Health: A Global Perspective.* New York: Haworth Press, 1988 [special issue of *Journal of Religion and Aging* 4:3-4 (1988)].

This is a cross-cultural collection of articles on the relationship of religious lifestyles and beliefs to aging and the aged (see **F.3**, **F.9**, **F.13**, **F.16**, **F.19**, and **F.20**)

F.2. Barrettt, Sondra. "Complementary Self-Care Strategies for Healthy Aging." *Generations* 17:3 (1993), 49-52.

Barrett addresses alternative healing techniques for the treatment of chronic illness among elders, looking at homeopathy, as well as traditional Chinese medicine, including the concept of *Qi* (energy or vital force), seen as a key to health and longevity; she describes *qi gong,* a series of exercises linking breathing and the body, and often practiced by persons in their 80s and 90s in China.

F.3. Davis, A. Michael. "Judaism: Lifestyles Leading to Physical, Mental and Social Well-Being in Old Age." *Journal of Religion and Aging* 4:3-4 (1988), 87-100.

Davis presents a brief overview of Jewish beliefs and customs related to health and aging ranging from biblical observations to descriptions of life on the kibbutz.

F.4. Ducey, Charles. "The Life History and Creative Psychopathology of the Shaman: Psychoanalytic Perspectives." *Psychoanalytic Study of Society* 7:1 (1976), 73-230.

A psychological profile of the shaman, with case histories of older healers.

F.5. Halifax, Joan. *Shamanic Voices: A Survey of Visionary Narratives.* New York: Arkana/Penguin, 1979.

Halifax, a medical anthropologist specializing in psychiatry and religion, presents the words of about 35 shamans, mostly elders, and all but two from traditional communities throughout the world, who tell of their visionary experiences.

F.6. Halifax, Joan. "Shamanism and Aging." in John-Raphael Staube, ed. *Wisdom and Age: The Adventure of Later Life.* Berkeley, California: Ross Books, 1981, 40-59.

In one of a series of symposia presentations conducted by the Proteus Institute in Big Sur and the Wright Institute in Berkeley, California, Halifax discusses the centrality of elderhood and the wisdom of age in shamanistic practice.

F.7. Laderman, Carol, and Marina Roseman, eds. *The Performance of Meaning.* New York: Routledge, 1996.

In this collection of essays by anthropologists, who discuss the role of dramatic performance in healing practices among a wide range of cultures, are numerous references to older healers (see, e.g., **F.15**).

F.8. O'Connor, Bonnie Blair. *Healing Traditions: Alternative Medicine and the Health Professions.* Philadelphia: University of Pennsylvania Press, 1995.

Based largely on participant observation and field interviews with clients, healers and teachers, young and old, folklorist O'Connor discusses the nature of traditional health beliefs systems, addressing the relation of health beliefs to larger cultural systems, the role of personal experience, the ways in which people learn about, enter into, and evaluate health belief systems, and how people negotiate the relation between traditional healing and biomedical practices.

F.9. Said, Hakim Mohammed. "Islam and the Health of the Elderly." *Journal of Religion and Aging* 4:3-4 (1988), 27-38.

This is a brief overview of those aspects of Islamic society and teachings relating to the aging, with references to the Quran and other traditional literature.

AFRICA

F.10. Ferreira, Monica. "Medicinal Use Of Indigenous Plants by Elderly Coloureds: A Sociological Study of Folk Medicine." *South African Journal of Sociology* 18:4 (1987), 139-143.

Based on data collected from a sample of 90 subjects aged 65 and over, the author describes the use, as well as cultural and symbolic significance of indigenous plant remedies among the elderly colored population in rural areas of Cape Province, South Africa; also discussed are reasons why herbal healing persists in light of the availability of modern health care services, and suggestions are offered for integrating traditional and biomedical systems.

F.11. Sheldon, Sherman W. "Curing Tales From Teso." *Journal of the Folklore Institute* 13:2 (1976), 137-154.

Sheldon collected 54 stories of curing rituals of Iteso witch doctors in the Teso District of Uganda; these accounts reinforce faith in the healer and native theories of disease causation; recurring themes are that the dead live on, and that one must respect the elderly, especially those near death, or their spirits may seek revenge by causing sickness.

F.12. Turner, Edith L. B. "Philip Kabwita, Ghost Doctor: The Ndembu in 1985." *The Drama Review* 30 (1985), 12-35.

Turner reports on her encounter with an elder healer when she revisited the Ndembu of Southern Africa, whom she had studied many years before.

ASIA/PACIFIC

F.13. Chit-Daw, Khin Myo. "Add Years to Life the Buddhist Way." *Journal of Religion and Aging* 4:3-4 (1988), 39-67.

In his review of Burmese Buddhist beliefs and practices related to aging and health, the author discusses traditional stories and sayings, rituals and festivals.

F.14. Connor, Linda, Patsy Asch, and Timothy Asch. *Jero Tapakan: Balinese Healer: An Ethnographic Film Monograph.* 2nd ed. Los Angeles: University of Southern California, 1995 [1986].

Description and script of an ethnographic film presenting the life story of Jero, an elder spirit medium practicing within the framework of Hindu-Balinese religious philosophy (see **H.62**).

F.15. Desjarlais, Robert R. "Presence." In Carol Laderman and Marina Roseman, eds. *The Performance of Meaning.* New York: Routledge, 1996, 143-164.

Desjarlais discusses the healing practices of Membe Yombo, "grandfather shaman," of the Helambu region of north-central Nepal, to whom he was apprenticed in the late 1980s (see **F.7**).

F.16. Fukui, Fumimaso. "On Perennial Youth and Longevity: A Taoist View on Health of the Elderly." *Journal of Religion and Aging* 4:3-4 (1988), 119-126.

Fukui looks at the history of Taoist views on health and aging, the core of which revolves around the injunction to follow the Tao, or way, of living according to natural law, by which route one might attain not only health and long life but immortality as well.

F.17. Laderman, Carol. "Ambiguity of Symbols in the Structure of Healing." *Social Science and Medicine* 24:4 (1987), 293-301.

Laderman discusses the nature of symbols in the healing practice of an elder Malay shaman.

F.18. Laderman, Carol. *Taming the Winds of Desire: Psychology, Medicine and Aesthetics in Malay Shamanistic Performance.* Berkeley: University of California Press, 1991.

Laderman presents a study of the healing performances she recorded and learned as an apprentice to an elder Malay shaman, comparing the ceremonies to traditional dramas of Southeast Asia and other cultures.

F.19. Mitsuhashi, Takeshi. "Study of the Health of the Elderly from the Standpoint of Shinto." *Journal of Religion and Aging* 4:3-4 (1988), 127-131.

Mitsuhashi examines those aspects of the Shinto religion and lifestyle that contribute to well-being in late life; the author reviews ceremonial rites and festivals that promote social engagement, the teachings of Shinto, such as the notion of a kindred spirit of all things, that help to overcome loneliness, and the belief that people and ancestors coexist with mutual respect, mitigating the fear of death.

F.20. Okada, Takehiko. "The Teachings of Confucianism on Health and Old Age." *Journal of Religion and Aging* 4:3-4 (1988), 101-107.

Okada provides an overview of Confucian teachings related to health care and old age, and compares them to the views of Taoism and Buddhism on how to maintain well being and achieve longevity ; the author quotes extensively from the writings of Ekiken Kaibara, a Japanese Confucianist of the Tokugawa era, in particular, the *Yojokun* (Motto for Health).

F.21. Sachdev, Perminder S. "Maori Elder-Patient Relationship as a Therapeutic Paradigm." *Psychiatry* 52:4 (1989), 393-403.

Sachdev observed the practice of a traditional Maori elder healer in a New Zealand psychiatric unit; he compares and contrasts the healer-patient relationship with that of conventional psychotherapy.

EUROPE

F.22. _____*Health Remedies and Healthy Recipes.* London: Age Exchange, 1987.

This booklet is a collection of narratives by Carribean elders in London who reflect upon health and diet practices as recalled from their lives in Jamaica and their experiences in Britain.

F.23. Kerewsky-Halper, Barbara. "Trust, Talk and Touch in Balkan Folk Healing." *Social Science and Medicine* 21:3 (1985), 319-325.

Kerewsky-Halper discusses the role of extra-medical factors in the practice of elder folk healers in Serbia (see also **F.92**).

F.24. Lovelace, Martin J. "The Life History of a Dorset Folk Healer." *Talking Folklore* 8 (1990), 13-23.

In an extract of his thesis on the life and work of Les Ollerton, of Dorset, England, Lovelace discusses the fieldwork experience, noting that Ollerton's narrating of his traditional healing knowledge and practices to the interviewer differs from the way he would normally teach his craft, by having his "students" observe him at work; Ollerton discusses the primary importance of learning from elder practitioners in this manner, as he has.

LATIN AMERICA

F.25. Bastien, Joseph W. "Metaphysical Relations Between Sickness, Society and Land in a Quollahuaya Ritual." In Joseph W. Bastien and John M. Donahue, eds. *Health in the Andes.* Washington, D.C.: American Anthropological Association, 1981, 19-37

Based on fieldwork conducted in the 1970s, Bastien describes the curing rituals of Sarito, an elder Quollahuayan (Aymara) diviner from Kaata, Bolivia.

F.26. Garro, Linda C. "Intracultural Variation in Folk Medical Knowledge: A Comparison Between Curers and Noncurers." *American Anthropologist* 88:2 (1986), 351-370.

This paper, which examines folk medical beliefs in a rural Tarascan community in west-central Mexico, notes a high agreement in beliefs between the group of ten curers studied and older community members who share similar levels of knowledge by virtue of their long experience dealing with, and talking about, illness.

NORTH AMERICA

F.27. _____"Remedies, Herb Doctors and Healers." In Eliot Wigginton and Margie Bennett, eds. *Foxfire 9.* New York: Doubleday, 1985, 12-82.

This selection present the folk beliefs, practices, and reminiscences of Flora Youngblood, born in 1906, and others, as collected by high school students in Rabun Gap, Georgia (see **B.2-B.13**).

F.28. Baldwin, Karen. "Aesthetic Agency in the Folk Medical Practices and Remembrances of North Carolinians." In James Kirkland, Holly F. Mathews, C. W. Sulivan III, and Karen Baldwin, eds. *Herbal and Magical Medicine: Traditional Healing Today.* Durham, North Carolina: Duke University Press, 1992, 180-195.

Baldwin discusses the artistry of folk healing traditions and the role of personal experience narratives in the exchange of folk medical knowledge, citing, among other sources, the life and work of Emma Dupree, African-American herbalist (see also **F.34, F.40, H.264**).

F.29. Gopalan, Gopalan V. (Bruce Nickerson, ed.). "Faith Healing in Indiana and Illinois." *Indiana Folklore* 6:1 (1973), 33-99.

Gopalan interviewed a number of practitioners and those treated by them, including African-Americans Rev. Edgar Roberston, 68, pastor of the New Jerusalem International Interdenominational Church, Danville, Illinois; Anna Simmons, 89, of the Danville Union Baptist Church; and Rev. Mrs. Hattie Ryan, 81, assistant pastor of the Spiritual Healing Church; and Anglo-Americans Rev. Clara Johnson, 65, pastor of the Golden Hour Universal Church in Terre Haute, Indiana, and Mrs. Sarah Holt, 65, a medium who hosts seances in her home.

F.30. Kirkland, James, Holly F. Mathews, C. W. Sullivan III, and Karen Baldwin, eds. *Herbal and Magical Medicine: Traditional Healing Today.* Durham, North Carolina: Duke University Press, 1992.

This collections of essays on traditional medical beliefs and practices among Native, Anglo- and African-Americans in North Carolina and Virginia features descriptions of, and statements from, practitioners and patients, old and young.

F.31. Spicer, Edward H., ed. *Ethnic Medicine in the Southwest.* Tucson: University of Arizona Press, 1977.

This is a survey of traditional health beliefs and practices of Native Americans, African-Americans, Anglo-Americans and Mexican-Americans in the southwest U. S., practiced to a greater extent among older community members.

F.32. Vestal, Paul K., Jr. "Herb Workers in Scotland and Robeson Counties." *North Carolina Folklore Journal* 21:4 (1973), 166-170.

Vestal interviewed four herb-doctors in North Carolina–two Lumbee Indians and two Anglo-Americans–about a vanishing art practiced in most cases by elders; he presents short statements by them about herbal healing and lists the herbal medicines they use.

F.33. Wilkinson, Doris Y. "Traditional Medicine in American Families: Reliance on the Wisdom of Elders." *Marriage and Family Review* 11:3-4 (1987), 65-76.

In examining the social history and prevalence of folk medicine in selected ethnic communities, Wilkinson looks at the "health maintenance wisdom" of elders and their key role in "maintaining a healing legacy" as part of basic family values.

African-American

F.34. Baldwin, Karen. "Mrs. Emma Dupree: 'That Medicine Thing.'" *North Carolina Folklore Journal* 32:2 (1984), 50-53

This is a brief portrait of Dupree, born in 1897, an herbalist living in Fountain, North Carolina, with excerpts of personal experience narratives (see also **F.28**, **F.40**, and **H.264**).

F.35. Bell, Michael Edward. *Roots and Remedies: Afro-American Folk Medicine in Rhode Island* [Report of Joint Project: Rhode Island Black Heritage Society, St. Martin DePorres Center, Rhode Island Folklife Project, and Brown University Long Term Gerontology Center]. Providence, Rhode Island, 1981.

Bell describes healing lore collected among African-American elders in and around Providence, Rhode Island.

F.36. Blake, J. Herman. "'Doctor Can't Do Me No Good': Social Concomitants of Health Care Attitudes and Practices Among Elderly Blacks in Isolated Rural Populations." *Black Sociologist* 8:1-4 (1978-1979), 6-13.

In a study of older residents of the Sea Islands of South Carolina, the author notes that traditional attitudes about health in the Islands, including faith, attention to nature, looking at health not as the absence of disease, but by whether one can still live independently, must be respected by rural health services providers.

F.37. Boyd, Eddie L., Leslie A. Shimp, and Marvie Jarmon Hackney. *Home Remedies and the Black Elderly: A Reference Manual for Health Care Providers.* Ann Arbor: Institute of Gerontology and College of Pharmacy, University of Michigan, 1984.

Essentially this is a list, compiled from interviews with 50 elders living in the Detroit-Ann Arbor area, of specific substances, natural and manufactured, their pharmacological background and sources in folk medical practice.

F.38. Fontenot, Wonda L. *Secret Doctors: Ethnomedicine of African Americans.* Westport, Connecticut: Bergin & Garvey, 1994.

Fontenot examines the folk medical practices of African-Americans in rural southwest Louisiana; she presents excerpts of interviews with nine practitioners–three women and six men–ranging from 36 to 88 in age, and devotes a chapter to Madame Neau (pseud.), a spiritualist in her late seventies.

F.39. Lee, John, and Arvilla C. Payne-Price. "John Lee: An African-American Folk Healer." In Brett Williams, ed. *The Politics of Culture.* Washington, D. C.: Smithsonian Institution Press, 1991, 155-173.

This is a brief portrait of Lee, of Moncure, North Carolina, who learned the healing arts from his mother, a midwife "of mixed descent: American Indian (Lumbo-Cherokee), British-Irish and African," and his father, an herbalist who had certain magical abilities; with excerpts of interviews with Lee.

F.40. Mathews, Holly F. "Doctors and Root Doctors: Patients Who Use Both." In James Kirkland, Holly F. Mathews, C. W. Sullivan III, and Karen Baldwin, eds. *Herbal and Magical Medicine: Traditional Healing Today.* Durham, North Carolina: Duke University Press, 1992, 68-98.

Mathews discusses the role of "root medicine," herbal healing now practiced mostly by elder African-Americans, and the experiences of patients who have received both traditional and biomedical care; Mathews cites the work of Mrs. Emma Dupree, 94-year-old herbalist (see also **F.28**, **F.34**, and **H.264**).

F.41. McLean, Patricia S. "Conjure Doctors in Eastern North Carolina." *North Carolina Folklore Journal* 20:1 (1972), 21-29.

McLean desribes conjure, or hoodoo, doctors, drawing from African voodoo, Native and Anglo-American healing practices, and presents excerts of interviews with practitioners, including Lewis Lee Jones, born in 1896, whose clients include many believers from North Carolina who come to his house near Boykins, Virginia, about ten miles from the state line.

F.42. Morson, Donald, Frank Reuter and Wayne Viitanen. "Negro Folk Remedies Collected in Eudro, Arkansas, 1974-1975. *Mid-South Folklore* 4:1 (1976), 11-24.

Four individuals, two women and two men, age 57-84, describe their knowledge of folk remedies; features interview excerpts (see also **F.49**).

F.43. Payne-Jackson, Arvilla, and John Lee. *Folk Wisdom and Mother Wit: John Lee–An African American Herbal Healer.* Westport, Connecticut: Greenwood Press, 1993.

Brief descriptions of African-American folk medicine, and a profile of Lee preface what is essentially an illustrated "repertoire" of the herbs he has used (see also **F.39**).

F.44. Sexton, Rocky. "Cajun and Creole Treaters: Magico-Religious Folk Healing in French Louisiana." *Western Folklore* 51:3-4 (1992), 237-248.

Sexton describes the *traiteur* who heals ailments through prayer, laying on of hands and, on occasion, herbal medicine, citing, with interview excerpts, the practice of Pop Cliff, and elderly Creole from rural St. Landry Parish, in southwest Louisiana.

F.45. Snow, Loudell F. "I Was Born Just Exactly with the Gift." *Journal of American Folklore* 86:341 (1973), 272-281.

Snow describes, with interview excerpts, the work of Mother D., an African-American folk healer with multi-ethnic clientele who practices in a residential enclave near downtown Tucson, Arizona.

F.46. Snow, Loudell F. "Sorcerers, Saints and Charaltans: Black Folk Healers in Urban America." *Medicine and Psychiatry* 2 (1978), 69-106.

Snow discusses the role of folk healers in African-American communities, many of them elders.

F.47. Snow, Loudell F. *Walkin' Over Medicine.* Boulder, Colorado: Westview Press, 1993.

Drawing from community-based studies in Arizona and Michigan, as well as data collected from the author's students, this work features descriptions of beliefs and practices of African-American traditional medicine, and includes excerpts of interviews with patients and practitioners, old and young.

F.48. Terrell, Suzanne J. *This Other Kind of Doctors: Traditional Medical Systems in Black Neighborhoods in Austin, Texas.* New York: AMS Press, 1990.

Terrell interviewed older residents of East Austin's African-American community, relying heavily on data collected from five "key consultants" ranging in age from late 50s to 87 years old; their comments are excerpted throughout the book; a single chapter is devoted to one of these, 87-year-old herbalist "Mama Doc."

F.49. Vaugh, Freddie, and Frank Reuter. "Negro Folk Remedies Collected in Southeast Arkansas, 1976." *Mid-South Folklore* 4:2 (1976) 61-74.

The authors present folk remedies recorded from African-American elders (see **F.42**).

F.50. Watson, Wilbur H. "Folk Medicine and Older Blacks in Southern United States." In Wilbur H. Watson, ed. *Black Folk Medicine: The Therapeutic Significance of Faith and Trust.* New Brunswick, New Jersey: Transaction, 1984, 53-66.

Noting that "modern scientific" and folk medicine act as "parallel systems of health care intervention" among older blacks that often properly defer to each other, Watson addresses the need for information to avoid harmful interactions between the two, and suggests further research on the social organization of folk medicine.

Anglo and Other European American

F.51. Babb, Jewel, with Pat Ellis Taylor. *Border Healing Woman: The Story of Jewel Babb.* Austin: University of Texas Press, 1981.

Taylor recorded and transcribed the life story of Jewel Babb, an 80-year-old Anglo-American woman living alone in the desert near El Paso, Texas, who treats people with a combination of herbs, spring water and "mind healing."

F.52. Bryan, William J. "Folk Medicine in Butler County, Pennsylvania." *Pennsylvania Folklife* 17:4 (1968), 40-43.

Bryan presents excerpts of interviews with longtime residents of Prospect, in western Pennsylvania, about folk medical practices in the years 1875-1900.

F.53. Crellin, John K., and Jane Philpott. *Herbal Medicine Past and Present. Volume I: Trying to Give Ease.* Durham, North Carolina: Duke University Press, 1990.

"This book emerged out of an invitation from Allen Tullos [see **F.64**] to evaluate the reputation of the herbs known to and used by A. L. Tommie Bass," born in 1908 in Cherokee County, northeast Alabama, where he continues to practice herbal medicine; the book is based in large part on interviews with Bass (one chapter presents excerpts of his life story), as well as his friends, neighbors, and people in his community.

F.54. Evans, E. Raymond, Clive Klileff and Karen Shelley. *'That Was All We Ever Knew': Herbal Medicine, a Living Force in the Appalachians.* Durham, North Carolina: Duke University Medical Center, 1982.

Appalachians elders recall the primacy of herbal medicine in traditional healing practices.

F.55. Green, Edward C. "A Modern Appalachian Folk Healer." *Appalachian Journal* 6:1 (1978), 2-15.

Green describes the life, outlook, and practice of Clarence Gray, better known as "Catfish, Man of the Woods," born in 1917 in Jackson County, West Virginia, who has an extensive knowledge of herbal medicine learned from his mother, from Germans during a stay in Ohio, and from blacks and Indians in and around his West Virginia home (see **H.2**).

F.56. Harris, Bernice Kelly, ed. *Southern Home Remedies.* Murfreesboro, North Carolina, 1968.

Members of the Creative Writing Group of Chowan College interviewed elders in North Carolina, who recalled traditional healing methods and the circumstances under which they were administered.

F.57. Horwatt, Karin. "The Shamanic Complex in the Pentacostal Church." *Ethos* 16:2 (1988), 128-145.

Horwatt discusses the nature of spirituality and healing in the Pentacostal Church in the southern U. S. among congregants old and young.

F.58. Lornell, Kip. "'Sod' Rogers: Tipton County Herbalist." *Tennessee Folklore Society Bulletin* 47:2 (1982).

Lornell presents, with generous interview excerpts, the work and philosophy of Rogers, born in 1911, whose knowledge of herbal medicine was acquired through his mother's side of the family and by reading Cherokee Indian herb books.

F.59. Macklin, June. "A Connecticut Yankee in Summer Land." In Vincent Crapanzano and Vivian Garrison, eds. *Case Studies in Spirit Possession.* New York: John Wiley & Sons, 1977, 41-85.

Macklin presents a study, with interview excerpts, of Mrs. Rita M., a possession trance-medium and ordained minister of the National Spiritualist Association of Churches of the United States of America (NSAC), born in Vermont in 1909 of first-generation immigrant parents, a French-Canadian mother and an Italian father; Mrs. M. was one of nine Spiritualists whose life histories Macklin recorded.

F.60. Raichelson, Richard M. "Belief and Effectivity: Folk Medicine in Tennessee." *Tennessee Folklore Society Bulletin* 49:3 (1983), 103-119.

Raichelson discusses the role of belief in the effectiveness of traditional healing practices, in a survey of rural Tennessee, with references to beliefs among elders.

F.61. Shaner, Richard H. "Uni Day's Herb Garden." *Pennsylvania Folklife* 14:3 (1965), 46-48.

Day is described as a "Dutchman" in his 70s living in the forest of Rockland Township, Berks County, preserving the "Dutch" [Pennsylvania German] tradition of herbal folk medicine.

F.62. Snellenburg, Betty. "Four Interviews with Powwowers." *Pennsylvania Folklife* 18:4 (1969), 40-45.

Snellenburg presents excerpts of interviews with four practitioners of this Pennsylvania German form of healing through charms, all in their in their 70s, living in the vicinity of York and Lancaster in western Pennsylvania.

F.63. Steckert, Ellen J. "Southern Mountain Medical Beliefs in Detroit: Focus for Conflict." In Otto Feinstein, ed. *Ethnic Groups in the City*. Lexington, Massachusetts: Lexington Books, 1971.

Steckert discusses the retention of folk medical beliefs among Southern migrants in a northern city who, bitter about the harsh realities of urban poverty, turn back to traditional beliefs and customs, as embodied in skilled practitioners of "home medicine," usually older women familiar with folk remedies.

F.64. Tullos, Allen. "Tommie Bass: A Life in the Ridge and Valley Country." Master's thesis, University of North Carolina, 1976.

Tullos presents the recorded life history of Bass, born and raised in Cherokee County, northeastern Alabama, and a practitioner of herbal medicine (see also **F.53**).

Asian-American

F.65. Chen, Pauline. "The Ritual Process of Aging and the Chinese American Elder." A. B. Honors thesis, Harvard University, 1986.

Chen examines rituals of aging among Chinese-Americans in San Francisco who have been served by On Lok Senior Health Services, a community agency operating in the city's Chinese community.

F.66. Handelman, Lauren. *Cambodian Elderly Explanatory Models for Illness and Help Seeking Behavior*. Washington, D. C.: Gerontological Society of America, 1991.

Handelman presents a study of elderly Cambodian refugees in San Jose, California, with a focus on the relation between culture and psychosomatic aspects of illness.

F.67. Lew-Ting, Chih-yin. "Health, Perceptions of Aging and Self-Care of Chinese Elderly Residing in Retirement Homes." Doctoral dissertation, University of California at Los Angeles, 1992.

Lew-Ting investigates health beliefs, attitudes toward aging, and self-care, including folk medical remedies, among Chinese-Americans in housing for the elderly.

F.68. Pang Keum, Young Chung. "Hwabyung: The Construction of a Korean Popular Illness Among Korean Elderly Immigrant Women in the United States." *Culture, Medicine and Psychiatry* 14:4 (1990), 495-512.

> The author examines *hwabyung*, a cultural construction based on traditional Korean medical beliefs, and employed by older Korean women to explain their reactions to stressful life situations.

Hispanic

F.69. Applewhite, Steven Lozano. "Curanderismo: Demystifying Health Beliefs and Practices of Elderly Mexican Americans." *Health and Social Work* 20:4 (1995), 247-253.

> Applewhite examines folk healing among older Mexican-Americans from two senior centers in a major metropolitian area of Arizona; he argues that folk healing is a time-honored alternative to conventional biomedicine and can help maintain healthy lifestyles among those with strong traditional cultural ties.

F.69.a. Dodson, Ruth. "Don Pedrito Jaramillo: The Curandero of Los Olmos." In Wilson M. Hudson, ed. *The Healer of Los Olmos and Other Mexican Lore* [*Publications of the Texas Folklore Society Number XXIV*] Dallas: Southern Methodist University Press, 1951, 9-70.

> Dodson reviews the life and practice of Don Pedrito (1829-1907), a Mexican emigre who achieved a legendary status through a mid to late life career as a healer in South Texas; Dodson, who belongs to one of the oldest ranching families in South Texas, first heard about Don Pedrito in the early 1890s; she records stories about the healer, including the reminiscences of several elders who recall his exploits (see also **F. 73**)

F.70. Gafner, George, and Stephane Duckett. "Treating the Sequelae of a Curse in Elderly Mexican-Americans." *Clinical Gerontologist* 11:3-4 (1992), 145-153.

> The authors look at the role of *curanderismo* in treating a culture-specific medical complaint among Mexican-American elders.

F.71. Hardwood, Alan. *Rx: Spiritist as Needed: A Study of a Puerto Rican Community Health Resource.* Ithaca, New York: Cornell University Press, 1987 [orig. pub. by John Wiley, 1977].

> This is a study of *espiritismo,* or healing through a spirit medium, as practiced by old and young specialists in the Puerto Rican community, but disproportionately sought out as a treatment modality by older community members.

F.72. Hubbard, Richard. *Psychological Factors in Drug Abuse Among Hispanic and Non-Hispanic Elderly: Final Report.* Notre Dame, Indiana: University of Notre Dame, 1984.

> Among the findings of in-home interviews conducted with Anglo and Mexican-American women and men age 60 and over were that Hispanic females relied the most on folk medicines, while Anglo females used the most prescription drugs; a bibliography and recommendations for drug education are included.

F.73. Romano, Octavio. *Don Pedrito Jaramillo: The Emergence of a Mexican-American Folk Saint.* Doctoral dissertation, University of California, Berkeley, 1964.

> This work is relevant to the study of folklore and aging on several counts: "Don Pedrito" (1829-1907), who came to be known as the "Saint of Los Olmos," the South Texas village to which he migrated from Guadalajara, Mexico, in 1881, earned

his legendary status largely through his late life practice, from his early 50s to his late 70s; Romano identifies the "healing hierarchy" in Mexican-American culture, in which the grandmother is "the ultimate familial recourse in questions of medical requirements or recommendations"; he also observes that neighborhood healers are characteristically middle-aged or older; finally, he quotes the testimony of several elders who recall Don Pedrito's practice (see also **F.69.a**).

F.74. Trotter, Robert T., and Juan Antonio Chavira. *Curanderismo: Mexican-American Folk Healing.* Athens: University of Georgia Press, 1981.

The authors examine folk healing among Mexican Americans in the Southwest U. S., where many of the practitioners and a large proportion of the patients are elders.

Native American Indian

F.75. Bergman, Robert L. "A School for Medicine Men." *American Journal of Psychiatry* 130:6 (1973), 663-666.

Bergman discusses the training of medicine men among the Navajo, for many of whom the practice of traditional medicine is a vocation taken up in mid to late life.

F.76. Boyer, L. Bryce. "Folk Psychiatry of the Apaches of the Mescalero Indian Reservation." In Ari Kiev, ed. *Magic, Faith and Healing: Studies in Primitive Psychiatry Today.* New York: The Free Press, 1964, 384-419.

This study is notable here not only for its descriptions of shamanistic practice but for its reference to age with regard to witchcraft (those identified as witches among the Apache are characteristically over 60), echoing other reports linking elders with witchcraft (see, e.g., **C.113-C.118**).

F.77. Boyer, L. Bryce, and Ruth M. Boyer. "Understanding the Individual Through Folklore." *Contemporary Psychoanalysis* 13:1 (1977), 30-51.

This article is a case history of the cultural components of illness in an elderly Mescalero Apache woman.

F.78. Boyer, L. Bryce, Ruth M. Boyer and George A. DeVos. "An Apache Woman's Account of Her Recent Acquisition of the Shamanistic Status." *Journal of Psychoanalytic Anthropology* 5:3 (1982), 299-331.

This is account of an Apache woman who assumes the responsibilities of a shaman as she enters older adulthood.

F.79. Grant, Richard Earl. "Tuukiya: The Hopi Healer." *American Indian Quarterly* 6:3-4 (1982), 291-304.

Grant discusses the characteristics of the Hopi *Tuukiya*, or "True Healer"; the most important visual attribute is his grey hair, symbolizing life experience, level of religious and ritual knowledge, and a degree of maturity and wisdom essential for success as a traditional healer.

F.80. Lewis, Thomas H. *The Medicine Men: Oglala Sioux Ceremony and Healing.* Lincoln: University of Nebraska Press, 1990.

Lewis, a physician and medical anthropologist, lived on the Pine Ridge Sioux reservation in South Dakota from 1969-1972, observing elder healers, and recording their personal lives and traditional medical practices.

F.81. Topper, Martin D. "Becoming a Medicine Man: A Means to Successful Midlife Transition Among Traditional Navajo Men." In Robert A. Nemiroff and Calvin A. Colarusso, eds. *New Dimensions in Adult Development.* New York: Basic Books, 1990, 443-466.

Topper argues that, the Navajo medicine man embodies not only healing skills, but also those qualities of social, economic and political leadership that emerge with the mature wisdom of mid to late life; this is contrasted with professional training in Western culture, usually marking a transition to young adulthood.

F.82. Topper, Martin D. "The Traditional Navajo Medicine Man: Therapist, Counselor, and Community Leader." *Journal of Psychoanalytic Anthropology* 10:3 (1987), 217-249.

Topper notes the relationship of communal authority and healing, which converge among Navajo medicine men in mid to late life.

F.83. Turner, Edith. "From Shamans to Healers: The Survival of an Inupiaq Eskimo Skill." *Anthropologica* 31:1 (1989), 3-24.

This article is a summary of findings from 11 months of fieldwork conducted in the late 1980s among the Inupiaq Eskimos of Point Hope, where nine adults practice traditional healing, five of them between 40 and 70, four of them over 70; she gathered accounts of 151 healings, and was a participant-observer in 46 of them.

F.84. Walker, Willard. "Cherokee Curing and Conjuring, Identity, and the Southeastern Co-Tradition." In George Pierre Castile and Gilbert Kushner, eds. *Persistent Peoples: Cultural Enclaves in Perspective.* Tucson: University of Arizona Press, 1981, 86-105.

While not discussing aging per se, Walker relates a revealing instance of generational loss of belief in traditional healing practices, in which an afflicted girl, submitting to parental pressure, agrees to go to an elder healer, but the treatment fails, to a large extent due to her skepticism about the efficacy of the treatment.

GENDER

F.84.a. Cattell, Maria G. "Gender, Aging and Health." In Carolyn F. Sargent, ed. *Gender and Health: An International Perspective.* Upper Saddle River, New Jersey: Prentice Hall, 1996.

This essay presents a cross-cutural perspective on the relationship of gender and aging as cultural constructs.

F.85. Chamberlain, Mary. *Old Wives Tales: Their History, Remedies and Spells.* London: Virago, 1981.

This book, based on interviews with women at "elderly people's homes" in Lambeth, London and Suffolk, England, discusses the role of women as healers in their respective communites.

F.86. Counts, Dorothy Ayers. "Aging, Health and Women in West New Britain." *Journal of Cross-Cultural Gerontology* 6:3 (1991), 277-285.

Counts, in addition to discussing demographic changes accompanying modernization that have left elders deprived of care traditionally provided by co-resident children, notes that the authority of elderly female healers has declined with the loss of their skills and knowledge; she presents a case study of an old blind woman.

F.87. Harvey, Youngsook Kim. *Six Korean Women: The Socialization of Shamans.* St. Paul, Minnesota: West Publishing, 1979.

Between 1971-1973, Harvey recorded the life stories of six female shamans—most of them 50 to 60 years old—who practiced in Seoul, Korea; she presents biographies of these women in separate chapters, with extensive interview excerpts.

F.88. Hubbard, Richard, and Carmen Portillo. "*Nervios* and Dysphoria in Mexican American Widows." In Dona L. Davis and Setha M. Low, eds. *Gender, Health and Illness: The Case Of Nerves.* New York: Hemisphere, 1989, 181-201.

This is a study of culture-specific ailments among older Mexican American women.

F.89. Hutheesing, Ottome K. "Facework of a Female Elder in a Lisu Field, Thailand." In Diane Bell, Pat Caplan and Wazir Jahan Karim, eds. *Gendered Fields: Women, Men and Ethnography.* London: Routledge, 1993.

Two currents are followed in this article: the deference given to *tsu-mo* ("people old"), whose age and knowledge of healing give them greater behavioral license, and the danger of loss of face presented by the depletion of cultural healing resources and exploitation of women in the modern capitalist market economy.

F.90. Jones, David E. *Sanapia: Comanche Medicine Woman.* Prospect Heights, Illinois: Waveland Press, 1984 [1972].

This is an ethnographic account of the life and practice of Sanapia, born in 1895, "the last Comanche Eagle doctor," with generous excerpts of oral history interviews conducted in English by Jones in the late 1960s.

F.91. Kendall, Laurel. *Shamans, Housewives, and Other Restless Spirits: Women in Korean Ritual Life.* Honolulu: University of Hawaii Press, 1985.

Kendall discusses the role of spiritual healing among Korean women, carrying some authority for female shamans into mid and late life.

F.92. Kerewsky-Halper, Barbara. "Healing With Mother Metaphors: Serbian Conjurers' Word Magic." In Carol Shepard McClain, ed. *Women as Healers: Cross-Cultural Perspectives.* New Brunswick, New Jersey: Rutgers University Press, 1989, 115-137.

This essay describes the charms recited by elderly women curers in Serbia who practice healing rituals drawing upon the associative qualities of sounds, words and other utterances (see also **F.23**).

F.93. Koss-Chioino, Joan. *Women as Healers, Women as Patients: Mental Health Care and Traditional Healing in Puerto Rico.* Boulder, Colorado: Westview, 1992.

Psychotherapist Koss-Chioino describes her Therapist-Spiritist Project, in which she brought *espiritistas* (female spiritual healers) and mental health workers together to develop a holistic approach to healing; she notes life experiences that generally bring Spiritists to their calling later in life (the health workers in the Project were college-educated and in their 20s-40s, the Spiritists were 40 to 72).

F.94. Lake, Robert G. "Shamanism in Northwestern California: A Female Perspective on Sickness, Healing, Health." *White Cloud Journal* 3:1 (1983), 31-42.

This is a discussion of the outlook and role of female traditional healers, often elders, among Native Americans in northern California.

F.95. Mayers, Raymond Sanchez. "Use of Folk Medicine by Elderly Mexican-American Women." *Journal of Drug Issues* 19:2 (1989), 283-295.

This article reviews studies on *curanderismo*, a folk healing practice, that point to its continued widespread use by Mexican-Americans, especially elderly women; Mayers notes that women have traditionally been responsible for family health care decisions, including what conditions are appropriate for folk or biomedical treatment.

F.96. Pang-Keum, Young Chung. *Korean Elderly Women in America: Everyday Life, Health and Illness.* New York: AMS Press, 1991.

This work is based on a study of health beliefs and practices conducted among 20 elderly Korean women aged 64-80, who had been in the U. S. an average of seven years, and who were currently living in the Washington, D. C., area, and discusses their use of *hanbang*, traditional Korean medicine, as well as American biomedical treatments, and describes such concepts as *ki*, or vital energy, considered key to health and longevity.

F.97. Perron, Bobette, H. Henrietta Stockel and Victoria Krueger. *Medicine Women, Curanderas, and Women Doctors.* Norman: University of Oklahoma Press, 1989.

Featuring excerpts of interviews with ten women, half of whom are elders, including Native American and Hispanic southwest traditional healers, and several M.D.s, this book raises such issues as the cultural aspects of healing and the nature of trust in the healing relationship.

F.98. St. Pierre, Mark, and Tilda Long Soldier. *Walking in the Sacred Manner: Healers, Dreamers and Pipe Carriers—Medicine Women of the Plains Indians.* New York: Touchstone/Simon & Schuster, 1995.

This survey presents generous excerpts of interviews with young and old medicine women among the Lakota, Cheyenne, Crow and Assiniboine, including elders Lucy Swan, Good Lifeways Woman, Louise Plenty Holes and Darlene Young Bear, as well as reminiscences of family members about elder healers among their forebears, such as Blue Earring Woman, Lightning Bug Woman, Martha Bad Warrior, Lucy Looking Horse, Iron Woman, and Isabel Ten Fingers.

F.99. Wedenoja, William. "Mothering and the Practice of 'Balm' in Jamaica." In Carol Shepard McClain, ed. *Women as Healers: Cross-Cultural Perspectives.* New Brunswick, New Jersey: Rutgers University Press, 1989.

This discussion of the role of gender in the folk-medical practice of Balm healing in Jamaica features a portrait of one of its practitioners, 64-year-old Reverend Martha "Mother" Jones.

F.100. Welch, Alice Z. "Concepts of Health, Illness, Caring, Aging and Problems of Adjustment Among Elderly Filipinas Residing in Hampton Road, Virginia."Doctoral dissertation, College of Nursing, University of Utah; 1987.

Welch describes health beliefs and practices, and attitudes toward aging, of older Filipino-American women.

Granny Midwives

F.101. _____ "Midwives and Granny Women." In Eliot Wigginton, ed. *Foxfire 2*. New York: Anchor Press/Doubleday, 1973, 274-303.

Under the guidance of Wigginton, a teacher at Rabun Gap-Nacoochee School in Georgia, students interviewed several local granny midwives, who told stories about their role and experiences.

F.102. Buss, Fran Leeper. *La Partera: Story of a Midwife.* Ann Arbor: University of Michigan Press, 1980.

Buss presents the life history of 70-year-old Jesusita Aragón of the town of Las Vegas in northeastern New Mexico, one of the last Hispanic midwives in the region, transcribed and edited from tape recorded conversations with Aragón.

F.103. Davis, Shelia P., and Cora A. Ingram. "Empowered Caretakers: An Historical Perspective on the Roles of Granny Midwives in Rural Alabama." In Barbara Bair and Susan E. Cayleff, eds. *Wings of Gauze: Women of Color and the Experience of Health and Illness.* Detroit: Wayne State University Press, 1993, 191-201.

The authors point to the important social role of granny midwives as independent figures of authority; features excerpts of interviews conducted by the authors with elder midwives and women who were attended by them.

F.104. Dunn, Ella Ingenthron, with Elmo Ingenthron. *Granny Woman of the Hills.* Branson, Missouri: The Ozarks Mountaineer, 1978.

Born in 1890 in Forsyth, Missouri, Dunn, whose own mother was a "granny-woman," wrote her memoirs, mostly describing everyday life in the Ozarks, with additional biographical information provided by her nephew Elmo.

F.105. Logan, Onnie Lee, with Katherine Clark. *Motherwit: An Alabama Midwife's Story.* New York: E. P. Dutton, 1989.

This an oral history, transcribed and edited by Clark, of Logan, an African-American midwife, born around 1910 in Sweetwater, Marengo County, Alabama, who, inspired by stories of her grandmother–a former slave and midwife–and the example of her mother, also a "granny," decided to become one herself.

F.106. Mulcahy, Joanne B. "'How They Knew': Women's Talk About Healing on Kodiak Island, Alaska." In Joan Newlon Radner, ed. *Feminist Messages: Coding in Women's Folk Culture.* Urbana: University of Illinois Press, 1993, 182-202.

In a study based on oral history interviews conducted with Kodiak Native American women elders between 1979 and 1988, Mulcahy describes the ways in which they have preserved important aspects of Native values and identity through their stories of healing as midwife/herbalists.

F.107. Mulcahy, Joanne B., with Mary Petersen. "Mary Petersen: A Life of Healing and Renewal." In Barbara Bair and Susan E. Cayleff, eds. *Wings of Gauze: Women of Color and the Experience of Health and Illness.* Detroit: Wayne State University Press, 1993, 148-168.

Mulcahy interviewed Petersen, a Native Alaskan in her mid fifties living on Kodiak Island, who told stories about her life, her knowledge of traditional healing and her practice as a midwife.

F.107.a. Smith, Margaret Charles, and Linda Janet Holmes. *Listen to Me Good: The Life Story of an Alabama Midwife.* Columbus: Ohio State University Press, 1996.

This is an oral history, recorded and edited by Holmes, of 91-year-old Smith, who recalls a career lasting nearly five decades and describes the traditions, beliefs and pharmacopeia of midwifery in rural Greene County, Alabama.

F.108. Susie, Debra Anne. *In the Way of Our Grandmothers: A Cultural View of Twentieth-Century Midwifery in Florida.* Athens: University of Georgia Press, 1988.

Between 1981 and 1984, Susie conducted interviews with older traditional African-American midwives; the book presents an historical overview with interview excerpts, and transcripts of recorded conversations with eight midwives.

F.109. Ulrich, Laurel Thatcher. *A Midwife's Tale: The Life of Martha Ballard, Based on Her Diary, 1785-1812.* New York: Vintage, 1990.

Born in Oxford, Massachusetts in 1735, Martha Ballard moved in 1777 to Hallowell, Maine where, at age 42, she was a relative elder in a fairly youthful community; over the next 27 years, she kept a diary of her work as a midwife, performing over 800 births; Ulrich closely examines selected diary passages.

Menopause

F.110. Beyene, Yewoubdar. "An Ethnography of Menopause: Menopausal Experiences of Mayan Women in a Yucatan Village." Doctoral dissertation, Department of Anthropology, Case Western Reserve University, 1985.

Based on interviews with over 100 Mayan village women, Beyene observes that they perceive menopause as a stage of life free of taboos and restrictions, and do not report having hot flashes or other common "symptoms" of menopause; a comparison is made to a group of Greek women studied by the author.

F.111. Davis, Donna Lee. "The Newfoundland Change of Life: Insights Into the Medicalization of Menopause." *Journal of Cross-Cultural Gerontology* 4 (1989), 49-73.

Davis observes that in a rural Newfoundland fishing village, women's notions of menopause as a natural part of the aging process have not yet been eclipsed by the biomedical model; she discusses the role of women's support networks in conditioning their experience of menopause.

F.112. Davis, Donna Lee. "The Meaning of Menopause in a Newfoundland Fishing Village." *Culture, Medicine and Psychiatry* 10 (1986), 73-94.

Davis presents "a comparison of etic and emic options for climacteric research" by using standard testing, as well as examining the folk health views among women in the Newfoundland outport village of Grey Rock Harbour to determine how they experience menopause.

F.112.a. Horrigan, Bonnie J., ed. *Red Moon Passage: The Power and Wisdom of Menopause.* New York: Harmony Books, 1996.

Horrigan, publisher of the journal *Alternative Therapies in Health and Medicine,* presents a collection of essays providing a cross-cultural perspective on menopause, and featuring contributions by Paula Gunn Allen, scholar of Laguna Pueblo and Sioux heritage, (see **C.87, C.87.a**); Kachinas Kutenai, Apache medicine woman, Barbara Walker (see **G.62**), and others.

F.113. Kearns, Bessie Jean Ruley. "Perceptions of Menopause by Papago Women." In Ann M. Voda, Myra Dinnerstein and Sheryl R. O'Donnell, eds. *Changing Perspectives on Menopause.* Austin: University of Texas Press, 1982, 70-83.

Kearns notes contrasts between traditional and "acculturated women" in their response to menopause; her study showed that while half of the women surveyed went to the Indian Health Service, a much smaller, more traditional, group reported seeking the advice of older women and medicine men.

F.114. Lock, Margaret. *Encounters with Aging: Mythologies of Menopause in Japan and North America.* Berkeley: University of California Press, 1993.

Lock examines *konenki* (menopause) as a cultural construct in which subjective experience and interpretation reflect differences between Japanese and American views of women in general; features extensive excerpts of interviews with midlife and older Japanese women.

F.115. Weed, Susan S. *Menopausal Years: The Wise Woman Way.* Woodstock, New York: Ash Tree, 1992.

Herbalist Weed offers a "new age" approach to menopause, offering a healing regimen involving natural remedies and rituals drawing heavily from Native American beliefs and practices.

F.116. Wright, Ann L. "Variation in Navajo Menopause: Toward an Explanation." In Ann M. Voda, Myra Dinnerstein and Sheryl R. O'Donnell, eds. *Changing Perspectives on Menopause.* Austin: University of Texas Press, 1982, 84-99.

Wright notes that "traditional" Navajo women and those in ill-health tend to suffer more from physical complaints associated with menopause, while "acculturated" women tended to manifest more psychological symptoms, reflecting differing lifestyle patterns.

G

Applied Folklore

The works listed below describe the practical applications of concepts, content and/or methodologies in folklore studies to some form of social intervention by or on behalf of older persons. There are probably more articles and books by nonspecialists in this listing than in other chapters. Many of them offer behavioral observations as well as practical suggestions; their placement in this chapter is based on the assumption that the content of the work is directed primarily toward practical concerns. They are cited for what they reveal about the ways in which specialists and nonspecialists view the nature and value of aspects of traditional culture in terms of their contribution to the well-being of elders. (Applied insights may also be found in works cited in other chapters, in particular, "Beliefs and Customs" and "Health and Healing.")

GENERAL

G.1. Jabbour, Alan. "Some Thoughts from a Folk Cultural Perspective." In Priscilla W. Johnston, ed. *Perspectives on Aging: Exploding the Myths.* Cambridge, Massachusetts: Ballinger, 1981, 139-149.

> Jabbour makes some observations on the value of folklife as a form of "spiritual nourishment" in old age, and as a means of cultural exchange between young and old; he also cites several stories that illustrate the tenacity of folklife that often thrives, and even flowers in old age despite physical and cognitive losses.

G.2. Kastenbaum, Robert. "Saints, Sages and Sons of Bitches: Three Models for the Grand Old Man." *Journal of Geriatric Psychiatry* 27:1 (1994), 61-78.

> Kastenbaum looks at three alternative models for successful aging that society has offered over the centuries; he argues for new models for the "grand old man" that transcend these cultural stereotypes and the expectations that they imply.

G.3. Kos, B. A. *Relationship Between Valuing of Time and Self Perceived Activity Levels in Healthy Aging Individuals: A Q Study.* Hempstead, New York: Hofstra University, 1979.

> In a study of 50 suburban individuals aged 65 to 85, to test the hypothesis that the valuing of time was correlated with self-perceived levels of activity among healthy older persons, participants were administered a "42-item Q-sort," consisting of time-related folk sayings and proverbs.

ARCHITECTURE

G.4. Gostoli, Francesco. "Progetto Casa del Pescatore, Chioggia." *Domus* 697 (1988), 6-8.

> Briefly describes a project named "Casa del Pescatore" (Fishermans Dwelling), a residential building for the elderly, singles and couples, in Chioggia (near Venice), designed by architect F. Gostoli, based on the vernacular architecture of an Italian fishing village.

G.5. Ley, Robert A. "'A City Set Apart' for the Elderly." *Architecture* 78:7 (1989), 60-63.

> Describes a 400-unit life care community, designed by Cook Douglas Farr and Samuel Mockbee, in conjunction with a gerontologist; commissioned by the Dominican Sisters, it is designed as a village, inspired by the Italian city of Sienna.

G.6. Okada, S. "Yokohama Municipal Nase Home for the Elderly, 1979." *Japan Architect* 56:1 (1981).

> Describes a residential compound for elders conceived and designed to reflect the ambience (particularly the sense of space) of a dwelling in a traditional Japanese village.

CUSTOMS AND BELIEFS

G.7 ____*Project to Develop, Test, and Apply a Methodology for Designing and Implementing Tribal Operated Multi-Service Delivery Systems for Elderly Native Americans: Final Report.* Albuquerque: Gerontology Center, University of New Mexico, 1984.

> Among the aims of this study, conducted in eight Pueblo Indian communities in New Mexico, and prepared jointly by the University of New Mexico and the All Indian Pueblo Council for the U. S. Administration on Aging, is the development of service delivery systems consistent with tribal customs and values.

G.8. Baum, Martha, and Mary Page. "Caregiving and Multigenerational Families." *The Gerontologist* 31:6 (1991), 762-769.

> In this study linking expanded caregiving systems with the extension of traditional family household boundaries, among the "predictor variables" used in the research project were the presence, nature, and extent of family proverbs and family rituals.

G.8.a. Blaakilde, Anne Leonora. "Old People in Rural Areas, Fighting Against Symbolic Death." *Folklore in Use* 3:1 (1995), 31-34.

> In a study of a small Danish island of 100 inhabitants, 25 percent of whom are over 65, Blaakilde notes a "cultural antagonism" of older islanders to social service providers and other representatives of urban culture; she explores their worldview, as reflected in certain verbal expressions, and points to the need to understand and respect the sense of identity of these rural elders.

G.9. Bolton, Christopher, and Delpha J. Camp. "Post-Funeral Ritual in Bereavement Counseling and Grief Work." *Journal of Gerontological Social Work* 14:3-4 (1989), 49-59.

> The authors describe a study conducted among 50 widowed persons (all but three female) participating in a bereavement counseling program in which certain reported post-funeral rituals, such as gatherings of family and friends, gift exchanges,

sympathy cards and letter writing, were correlated with higher degrees of grief adjustment; implications for grief counselors are discussed.

G.10. Chae, Myungye. "Older Asians." *Journal of Gerontological Nursing* 13:11 (1987), 11-17.

The author describes Asian cultural traditions, in particular ceremonies and traditional beliefs retained by first-generation immigrants, offers two case studies in which nurses misunderstood the behaviors and attitudes of Asian patients, and suggests that nurses use interventions that respect cultural traditions.

G.11. Cheng, E., and M. J. Hong. *Elder Chinese: A Cross-Cultural Study of Minority Elders in San Diego.* San Diego: Center on Aging, School of Social Work, San Diego State University, 1978.

The authors examine the relationship between the lifestyles and customs of Chinese elders and their perceptions of, and interaction with, social services agencies.

G.12. Damron-Rodriguez, Joann. "Commentary: Multicultural Aspects of Aging in the U. S.: Implications for Health and Human Services." *Journal of Cross-Cultural Gerontology* 6:2 (1991), 135-143.

This article summarizes a symposium on the cultural diversity of the aging and the need for culturally appropriate services; among the issues discussed are the role of culture in the search for meaning in late life, and the importance of ritual for ethnic identity and social interchange.

G.13. Dukepoo, Frank. *Elder American Indian: A Cross-Cultural Study of Minority Elders in San Diego.* San Diego: Center on Aging, School of Social Work, San Diego State University, 1978.

Dukepoo examines the relationship between the lifestyles and customs of Native American Indian elders and their perceptions of, and interaction with, social services agencies.

G.14. Eisenberg, A. "Nursing Home as a Community." In D. Blau and A. O. Freed, eds. *Mental Health in the Nursing Home: An Educational Approach for Staff.* Boston: Boston Society for Gerontological Psychiatry, 1979, 52-78.

Eisenberg encourages activities in nursing homes that generate a sense of community among residents, including informal communal rituals, as well as mourning ceremonies to openly deal with the passage from life.

G.15. Facio, Elisa. *Understanding Older Chicanas: Sociological and Policy Perspectives.* Thousand Oaks, California: Sage Publications, 1996.

Based on participant observation and oral history interviewing, Facio examines the lives and gender roles of older Chicanas; most of them are poor, and they are also stereotyped as widows and grandmothers, reflecting cultural values in the Mexican-American community; their stories show them to be actively engaged in determining the character of their old age and using community resources, such as senior centers, to do so; public policy implications of the social meaning of old age for Chicanas are discussed.

G.16. Fried, Hedi, and Howard M. Waxman. "Stockholm's Cafe 84: A Unique Day Program for Jewish Survivors of Concentration Camps." *The Gerontologist* 28:2 (1988), 253-255.

The authors describe a day program, designed in the spirit of a European cafe, and run by a psychiatrist who is herself a survivor, to deal with the delayed symptoms experienced by concentration camp survivors, through informal discussion, reminisce, and a variety of cultural activities, including a traditional Friday night ceremony.

G.17. Gubrium, Jaber F., and Andrea Sanker, eds. *Home Care Experience: Ethnography and Policy*. Newbury Park, California: Sage Publications, 1990.

This book, in providing an overview of research strategies and policy issues concerning the socio-cultural settings of home care and the regulatory interests and interventions of the state, offers insights into boundaries of custom and ritual surrounding care that is given within the household.

G.18. Hilgendorf, Lucy. *Laguna Demonstration Project: Reviving A Traditional Day Care System While Preserving a Community's Culture; Final Report*. Santa Fe: New Mexico Human Services Department, Planning and Evaluation Bureau, 1986.

This report describes a child care center set up on the grounds of a congregate housing facility at the Laguna Pueblo near Albuquerque, New Mexico; project staff and elder aides supervised the children, and a number of elders spent time with them each day, teaching about Laguna culture and language; children learned about their heritage and elders regained a sense of self-worth (see also **H.195**).

G.19. Ishikawa, W. H. *Elder Guamanian: A Cross-Cultural Study of Minority Elders in San Diego*. San Diego: Center on Aging, School of Social Work, San Diego State University, 1978.

Ishikawa examines the relationship between the lifestyles and customs of Guamanian elders and their perceptions of, and interaction with, social services agencies.

G.20. Ishikawa, W. H. *Elder Samoan: A Cross-Cultural Study of Minority Elders in San Diego*. San Diego: Center on Aging, School of Social Work, San Diego State University, 1978.

Ishikawa examines the relationship between the lifestyles and customs of Samoan elders and their perceptions of, and interaction with, social services agencies.

G.21. Ishizuka, K. C. *Elder Japanese: A Cross-Cultural Study of Minority Elders in San Diego*. San Diego: Center on Aging, School of Social Work, San Diego State University, 1978.

Ishizuka examines the relationship between the lifestyles and customs of Japanese elders and their perceptions of, and interaction with, social services agencies.

G.22. Martin, Diane S.; and Wendy G. Fuller. "Spirituality and Aging: Activity Key to 'Holiest' Health Care."*Activities, Adaptation and Aging* 15:4 (1991), 37-50.

The authors address the role of activities professionals in providing for the spiritual needs of institutionalized elders, noting the importance of symbol and ritual in reinforcing religious faith among elders, and they describe the formation of a faith discussion group at a nursing home.

G.23. Meske, Carolyn; Gregory F. Sanders, William H. Meredith, and Douglas A. Abbott. "Perceptions of Rituals and Traditions Among Elderly Persons." *Activities, Adaptation and Aging* 18:2 (1994), 13-26.

> The authors studied the importance of holidays and their attendant family traditions for a sample of 231 American grandparents of college students, who responded to a self-report survey, including such measures as the Family Strength Scale, a Ritual Activities Checklist, Ritual Importance measure, and Ritual Evaluation scale.

G.24. Peterson, R. *Elder Filipino: A Cross-Cultural Study of Minority Elders in San Diego.* San Diego: Center on Aging, School of Social Work, San Diego State University, 1978.

> Peterson examines the relationship between the lifestyles and customs of Filipino elders and their perceptions of, and interaction with, social services agencies.

G.25. Pett, Marjorie A.; Nancy Lang and Anita Gander. "Late-Life Divorce." *Journal of Family Issues* 13:4 (1992), 526-552.

> Through interviews with selected offspring of 111 divorced older persons, the authors assess the effects of late-life divorce on the nature of family rituals; it was found that the divorce itself was only the culmination of a process in which, over the years, family rituals were continually renegotiated and restructured; implications for therapeutic intervention are discussed.

G.26. Red Horse, J. G. "American Indian Elders: Unifiers of Indian Families." *Social Casework* 61:8 (1980), 490-493.

> Red Horse addresses the role of elders in preserving the family through tribal wisdom and guidance, providing spiritual continuity across generations, and advises social service providers to develop programs reflecting the Indian model of inter-generational integration rather than isolation.

G.27. Red Horse, J. G., R. Lewis, M. Feit, and J. Decker. "Family Behavior of Urban American Indians." *Social Casework* 59:2 (1978), 67-72.

> The authors argue that understanding urban Indian family networks, in which elders are the final arbiters of family behavior, including adherence to traditional language, religion and customs, is crucial in planning and delivering services.

G.28. Reingold, Jacob, Audrey S. Weiner, and Douglas Holmes. "Analysis of the Jewishness of Services to the Aged in the United States." *Journal of Aging and Judaism* 5:3 (1991), 177-189.

> In a study of long-term care and housing facilities, programs and services listed in the North American Association of Jewish Homes and Housing for the Aged directory, they conclude that while most facilities under Jewish auspices have kept their commitment to providing a Jewish religious, ritual and spiritual environment, few offer training beyond the basics of Jewish holidays and laws; they argue for training in Jewish languages, history and current events related to Jewish life.

F.29. Rempusheski, Veronica F. "The Role of Ethnicity in Elder Care." *Nursing Clinics of North America* 24:3 (1989), 717-724.

> The author discusses the role of ethnicity in elders' perceptions of care received in nursing homes, and suggests ways of designing culturally sensitive care programs by eliciting rituals, beliefs and other ethnic symbols related to care activities.

G.30. Robb, Thomas B. *Growing Up: Pastoral Nurture for the Later Years.* New York: Haworth Press, 1991.

> The author, a minister, discusses the spiritual aspects of aging, points to biblical stories of heroic elders as models for spiritual growth, discusses the importance of ritual, and the responsibility of the church for the "pastoral nurture" of elders.

G.31. Robb, Thomas B. "Liturgical Rites of Passage for the Later Years." *Journal of Religious Gerontology* 7:3 (1991), 1-9.

> In the absence of rites of passage for older adults following retirement or facing the "empty nest" syndrome, the author suggests the creation of liturgical rituals designed to help elders through these life transitions.

G.32. Sandel, Susan, and Jane Fisher. "Re-creation of Life Rituals in Long-Term Facilities." *Journal of Long-Term Care Administration* 19:1 (1991), 2-4.

> The authors address the importance of community rituals in providing engaging and meaningful activity for residents at long-term care facilities; they describe the re-creation, at a nursing home site, of the wedding of the assistant administrator, seeing it as an opportunity to be involved in a familiar ritual and as a stimulus to reminiscence.

G.33. Sankar, Andrea. "Ritual and Dying: A Cultural Analysis of Social Support for Caregivers." *The Gerontologist* 31:1 (1991, 43-50.

> Sankar reports about an ethnographic study of social support for caregivers of dying persons at home; ritual patterns followed those of other rites of passage; the author looks at rituals addressed to the dying person, and those whose purpose is to provide support for the caregiver; she observes that ritual support for caregivers is most effective when it provides a respite from other social roles.

G.34. Sardana, Ranjana. "Spiritual Care for the Elderly: An Integral Part of the Nursing Process." *Nursing Homes* 39:1 (1990), 30-31.

> The author suggests that care plans for nursing home residents should include an assessment of their spiritual needs, including querying them about beliefs and rituals, and the roles they have played in their lives.

G.35. Simmons, Henry C. "Countering Cultural Metaphors of Aging." *Journal of Religious Gerontology* 7:1-2 (1990), 153-165.

> In order to counteract cultural images that tend to marginalize older adults, the author suggests the creation of new images of aging within communities and religious rituals that publicly project these positive valuations of aging.

F.36. Wallace, Steven P. "Community Formation as an Activity of Daily Living: The Case of Nicaraguan Immigrant Elderly." *Journal of Aging Studies* 6:4 (1992), 365-383.

> This study examines the efforts of elders in the Nicaraguan immigrant community in San Francisco to strengthen cultural ties by instructing younger community members in the Spanish language and Nicaraguan culture, and maintaining the symbolism of traditional Nicaraguan church services.

EDUCATION

G.37. _____ "Education and the Elderly in Nations at Different Stages of Development."
Ageing International 13:1 (1986), 12-15.

The article presents a brief review of educational programs involving the elderly in
Ghana, Singapore and France; of note here is a project in Ghana, in which young
people were trained to tape-record the oral traditions of elders; among other
applications, this traditional material will be used in a local literacy drive.

G.38. Adams, Patricia L. "Primary Sources and Senior Citizens in the Classroom."
American Archivist 50:2 (1987), 239-242.

Adams describes a pilot project in St. Louis, Missouri, "Past and Future Coming
Together," in which elders shared their experiences with public school students to
demonstrate the effects of historical events on the lives of everyday people; among
the "unit topics" addressed were education, transportation, work, recreation, health,
religion and rituals, and family.

G.39. Adejumo, Dayo. "Education About Aging for Nigerian Adolescents." *Educational
Gerontology* 8:4 (1982), 353-358.

Adejumo discusses sources of information about aging among young Nigerians
attending secondary schools and universities, largely personal observation
supplemented by stories about aging told by elders; most information comes from
nonliterate traditional elders; while 55 percent of the students queried in a survey
said they would prefer to be an educated member of a traditional community, the
second largest group favored the role of the nonliterate traditional elder.

G.40. Aggor, Reuben A., and Chris Akwayena. "Young People Carry Out Ghana Project
to Collect Traditional Wisdom of the Elders." *Convergence: International Journal of Adult
Education.* 18:1-2 (1985), 50-57.

The authors describe a project initiated by the Adult Education Section of UNESCO,
in which they trained 12 young people from the Awudome community of the Volta
region of Ghana to collect customs and folklore from local elders through tape-
recorded interviews; from the information they gathered, materials were to be
assembled for a literacy campaign in this region.

G.41. Allen, Katherine R. "Promoting Family Awareness and Intergenerational Exchange:
An Informal Life History Program." *Educational Gerontology* 13:1 (1987), 43-52.

The author describes a program designed for "gerontologists, family practitioners,
senior citizen organizations, church groups and informal gatherings of family and
friends," to encourage communication and break down barriers between generations
by sharing family heritage.

G.42. Alvarez, Ronald A. F.; Susan Calhoun Kline, and Priscilla Brown McCutcheon.
Exploring Local History. Washington, D. C.: National Council on the Aging, 1978.

One of a series of reading anthologies, "Self-Discovery Through the Humanities,"
designed to promote opportunities for "lifelong learning" for older adults, this work
invites participants in an 8-week program to read about local history and investigate
their own communities, through visits to local historical societies, oral history
interviewing, looking at household inventories, and sharing photographs,
memorabilia and family stories (see also **G.44**).

G.43. Chasse, Emily S. "Chinese Folktales: A Librarian's Contribution to the Elderhostel." *Activities, Adaptation and Aging* 16:4 (1992), 1-6.

Chasse discusses a class on the moral and religious beliefs of common folk in Chinese society as reflected in their folktales, which she conducted as part of an Elderhostel program at Central Connecticut State University; similar classes have been conducted, focusing on Japanese, Korean and Russian folktales.

G.44. Davis, Allen Freeman, and Linda Funk Place, eds. *In the Old Ways.* Washington, D. C.: National Council on the Aging, 1981.

This is an eight-session study unit that, through selected readings on ethnic heritage in the U. S., invites participants to reflect on traditions within their own families and communities, and how these have changed during their lives; it is part of the series "Self-Discovery Through the Humanities," designed to promote opportunities for "lifelong learning" for older adults (see also **G.42**).

G.45. Davis, Shari, and Benny Ferdman. *Nourishing the Heart: A Guide to Intergenerational Programs.* New York: City Lore, 1993.

This "how-to" book is based on intergenerational workshops sponsored by New York City's Arts Partners between 1985 and 1991; among the participating organizations, City Lore provided oral history and folklore training for the artists and teachers involved with the program; model projects described include "Living History Theater" (see also **G.122-G.124**), "We Belong Here," involving a puppet/variety show incorporating community history and neighborhood folklore, "Family Story Quilts," and "Tradition Trees," designed to explore family traditions.

G.46. Jarvis, Peter. "Retirement: An Incomplete Ritual." *Journal of Educational Gerontology* 4:2 (1989), 79-84.

The author argues that retirement is an incomplete rite of passage, in which one goes through a rite of transition, of separation, but not incorporation in to a new status and set of social roles, and that this should be addressed by bringing retirees back to pre-retirement courses to provide counseling and support.

G.47. Johnson, Arleen H. "Humor as an Innovative Method for Teaching Sensitive Topics." *Educational Gerontology* 16:6 (1990), 547-559.

Johnson suggests ways that humor, in the form of jokes, stories, cartoons, personal experiences, and the like can be used to teach subjects such as aging, death, grieving and suicide, and also to prepare students to use humor as a therapeutic tool in clinical practice.

G.48. Kabwasa, Nsang O'khan, and Ashem Tem Kawata. "Elderly and the Media: The Case of Zaire." *African Gerontology* 3 (1985), 41-44.

The authors describe prime-time television programs in Zaire relating to the aging, including one where an actor plays a grandfather telling children traditional tales, and another in which the host talks about the customs of Zairean elders; they note that these programs present caricatures of aging, and that media should provide a forum where elders themselves transmit wisdom to the young.

G.49. O'Conner, Maureen. *Generation to Generation.* London: Cassell Educational, 1993.

This monograph presents case studies of intergenerational programs of LinkAge, a charitable trust in the United Kingdom that links clubs for older persons, nursing homes and hospitals with schools and youth groups; among the educational programs described are classroom craft and history lessons taught by seniors, local history projects drawing on the knowledge and experience of community elders, and oral history and reminiscence projects.

G.50. Powers, William, Brenda Bailey-Hughes, and Mathew Ranft. "Senior Citizens as Educational Resources." *Educational Gerontology* 15:5 1989), 481-487.

The authors describe a pilot project in the Muncie, Indiana, school district in which elders were invited into classrooms to share stories of instructional value to the children; story content and storytelling delivery were evaluated and found to have an overall positive effect in imparting information and values to the children.

G.51. Safford, Florence. "Humor as an Aid in Gerontological Education." *Gerontology and Geriatrics Education.* 11:3 (1991), 27-33.

Safford presents selected examples of humorous anecdotes, riddles, and jokes related to various gerontological subjects, and notes the effectiveness of the incongruity of humor as a pedagogical device.

G.52. Schwitters, S. Y., and I. Ashdown. "Elderly Hawaiians in a Changing Society." *Aging* 319-320 (1981), 10-19.

The authors observe that elderly Hawaiians have benefitted from a revival of traditional culture, including the role that elders have played as *kumu* or sources of cultural wisdom; they note projects in which elders teach Hawaiian language and culture in local schools.

G.53. Sharpe, Elizabeth M. *Senior Series Program: A Case Study With Implications for Adoption.* Washington, D. C.: Smithsonian Institution, 1982.

This report describes an outreach program, begun in 1978, for older adults who have trouble traveling to the Smithsonian; programs on various subjects, including traditional folk music and dance, are brought to local senior day centers, nursing and retirement homes, and nutrition sites.

G.54. Shuldiner, David. *Humanities for Older Adults: A Guide to Resources and Program Development.* 4th ed. Hartford: Connecticut State Department of Social Services, 1997.

This is an inventory of resources and models for educational programs for elders; much of the material and institutions cited relate to aspects of traditional culture and local history in the state; it also contains a chapter on intergenerational projects, a brief guide to oral history interviewing, and ideas for programs on traditional arts and aging (see **G. 55**).

G.55. Shuldiner, David. "Promoting Self-Worth Among the Aging." In Michael Owen Jones, ed. *Putting Folklore to Use.* Lexington: University Press of Kentucky, 1994, 214-225.

The author describes the ways in which his training and perspective as a folklorist were put to use as a "scholar in residence" developing community-based educational programs for older adults through a state agency on aging in Connecticut.

G.56. Sullivan. G., and C. Florio. "Senior Citizens in Education." In F. Riessman. *Older Persons: Unused Resources for Unmet Needs.* Beverly Hills, California: Sage, 1977, 146-151.

Sullivan reports on a survey conducted by the Academy for Educational Development on older adults employed or volunteering their services at public school, colleges and universities in the U.S.; one notable example is the Heritage Arts Program at Salem College, in Virginia, where 10-20 artisans are employed each year to teach quilting, chair caning and other traditional crafts.

G.57. Wigginton, Eliot. *Moments: The Foxfire Experience.* Washington, D.C.: Institutional Development and Economic Affairs Service (IDEAS), 1975.

Wigginton reviews the history and benefits of the "Foxfire learning concept," which he developed as a high school English teacher in Rabun Gap, Georgia, who sent his journalism students into the local hill community to interview residents, mostly elders, about traditional beliefs, customs and crafts (see also **B.1-B.13**).

GENDER

G.58. Bell, Marilyn J. *Women as Elders: Images,Visions and Issues.* New York: Haworth Press, 1986. [Published simultaneously as *Women as Elders: The Feminist Politics of Aging* by Harrington Park Press, and as a special issue of *Women and Politics* 6:2 (1986)].

This collection of essays reviews images of older women in North American cultural life and literature; included is an article by the Crone's Nest Committee, part of a St. Augustine, Florida women's residential community, the Pagoda, "an inter-generational and interracial space where elder women are honored and respected for their experience and wisdom."

G.59. Chaney, Elsa M. *Empowering Older Women: Cross-Cultural Views: A Guide for Discussion and Training.* Washington, D. C.: American Association of Retired Persons, Women's Initiative, 1990.

This is a training model inspired by empowerment workshops in Acapulco, Mexico and Washington, D. C.; citing references from anthropology, sociology, history and psychology, sources of power for women are identified, including their roles as keepers of lineages, guardians of religion and ritual authorities.

G.60. Fine, Irene. *Midlife and Its Rite of Passage Ceremony.* San Diego: Women's Institute for Continuing Jewish Education, 1983.

This book offers a rationale and set of guidelines for a mid-life rite of passage ceremony based on Jewish traditions; the complete text, with photographs, of a mid-life ceremony of one woman is presented, and an appendix contains an outline for a course preparing one for such a ceremony.

G.61. Radner, Joan N. "Coming of Age: The Creative Rituals of Older Women." *Southern Folklore* 50:2 (1993), 113-125.

Radner looks at rituals of aging, primarily among white, middle-class women, within the context of the contemporary women's movement, as ways of empowering themselves by drawing upon traditional symbols, such as the Crone, that reflect a positive valuation of older women.

G.62. Walker, Barbara G. *The Crone: Woman of Age, Wisdom and Power*. San Francisco: HarperSanFrancisco, 1985.

Walker surveys images of the Crone, or Wise Old Woman in world cultures, and argues for their cultivation by women to survive against patriarchal systems that have not only constrained them, but threaten to destroy humanity.

HEALTH CARE

G.63. Allen, Carol. "Cultural Diversity Training in a Multidisciplinary Geriatric Fellowship Program." *Gerontology and Geriatrics Education* 15:1 (1994), 83-100.

This article describes one component of a program developed by the University of California, San Francisco and the Mt. Zion Institute on Aging, involving seminars for physician fellows on ethnic and cultural diversity; these included sessions led by minority practitioners on folk medical beliefs and practices in ethnic communities.

G.64. Brenes-Jette, Carmen C. "Hispanic Geriatric Residents in a Long-Term Care Setting." *Journal of Applied Gerontology* 7:3 (1988), 350-366.

The author notes that barriers to such traditional forms of expression as language, religion, folk beliefs, and traditional values–such as *obligacion, respecto,* and *personalismo*–may compromise quality of life in a skilled-nursing facility, and that strategies to improve care must consider these cultural factors.

G.65. Castro, F. G. "The Chicano Community and Its Aged." In A. M. Reinhardt and M. D. Quinn, eds. *Current Practice in Gerontological Nursing*. St. Louis, Missouri: C. V. Mosby, 1979.

Castro examines the beliefs and customs of Chicanos, or Mexican-Americans, including attitudes toward aging , dating back to the Aztecs and Mayas, and death, as reflected in the Day of the Dead celebration, and suggests that health care workers consider cultural practices before imposing changes in health behavior.

G66. Clavon, Annie. "Black Elderly." *Journal of Gerontological Nursing* 12:5 (1986), 6-12.

In an article on cultural factors affecting behavior and health needs among black elderly, Clavon discusses the effects of traditional customs and values, along with poverty, chronic illness, and the legacy of slavery, and stresses the importance of taking into account a patient's beliefs and values in providing appropriate care.

G.67. Cooley, R. C., D. Ostendorf and D. Bickerton. "Outreach Services for Elderly Native Americans." *Social Work* 24:2 (1979), 151-153.

The authors describe a mental health outreach program for Apache elders in nursing homes in Phoenix, Arizona, offered through the Apache Tribal Guidance Center; including the presentation of taped performances of traditional music and song, serving foods prepared on the reservation, visits with relatives and transportation to special events in which tribal leaders take part.

G.68. Dicharry, Elizabeth K. "Delivering Home Health Care to the Elderly in Zuni Pueblo." *Journal of Gerontological Nursing* 12:2 (1986), 25-29.

Dicharry addresses the importance of sensitivity among health care workers to the role of beliefs and rituals among elders for whom care is being provided in their homes on the Zuni Indian Reservation in western New Mexico.

G.69. Fulder, Stephen. *End to Ageing: Remedies for Life Extension*. New York: Destiny Books, 1982.

This book offers advice from the fields of medicine, psychology and nutrition on countering the effects of the aging process; the author reviews herbal remedies from folk medical practice worldwide, and compares them with allopathic treatments; includes lifestyle recommendations and a bibliography.

G.70. Lew, Lillian. "Elderly Cambodians in Long Beach: Creating Cultural Access to Health Care." *Journal of Cross-Cultural Gerontology* 6:2 (1991) 199-203.

Lew describes the work of the Older Southeast Asian Health Project (OSEAHP) to improve access to health for Cambodian elders in Long Beach, California; the health beliefs and practices within the Cambodian community are described, as well as efforts to mediate between traditional and conventional medicine.

G.71. Lewis, Susan, Roberta Messner and William A. McDowell. "Unchanging Culture." *Journal of Gerontological Nursing* 11:8 (1985), 20-26.

While viewing folk medical beliefs as hindrances to modern health care, the authors discuss the need to acknowledge the culture of Appalachian elders facing care needs, the respect held for them, and their desire to remain home, whatever the cost.

G.72. Lock, Margaret M. "East Asian Medicine and Health Care for the Japanese Elderly." *Pacific Affairs* 57:1 (1984), 65-73.

Lock notes that in contemporary Japan, neither traditional or Western medicine can adequately address the issue of universal access to adequate social welfare for elders; however, the philosophy and practice of traditional medicine, which involves family members and uses herbal remedies tailored to each individual, can, if applied correctly, be beneficial in geriatric care.

G.73. Loughran, Diane. "Challenge of Aging in the Peruvian Andes." *Ageing International* 15:1 (1988), 9-12.

In a report on the health status of elders in the Department of Justin in the central Peruvian Andes, based on interviews with over 70 people in their 50s to 90s, Loughran notes that many still rely on traditional healing practices but have come to use the services of both traditional and biomedical practitioners.

G.74. McGuire, Francis A., Roseangela K. Boyd, and Ann James, eds. "Therapeutic Humor With the Elderly." Special issue of *Activities, Adaptation and Aging* 17:1 (1992), 1-96.

The articles brought together here examine the role of humor in activities for the elderly in long term care facilities, including a review of the literature, a theoretical overview, and a report on a study conducted by Clemson University about the effectiveness of humor in improving quality of life.

G.75. Newton, F. C. R. "Issues in Research and Services Delivery Among Mexican American Elderly: A Concise Statement With Recommendations." *The Gerontologist* 20:2 (1980), 208-213.

Among its recommendations, this article stresses the need to take into account folk medical beliefs, which vary from region to region, along with the cultural model of *personalismo*, conveying pride, dignity and respect, as important factors when planning health care services.

G.76. Padgett, Deborah K., ed. *Handbook on Ethnicity, Aging and Mental Health.* Westport, Connecticut: Greenwood Press, 1995.

Intended for clinical researchers, mental health practitioners, community service providers and the like, this anthology includes cross-cultural surveys as well as articles on African-American, Hispanic, Native American and Asian-American elders; among the essays devoted to such issues as mental health status, use of mental health services and care delivery systems, there are discussions of cultural perceptions of mental illness and traditional healing practices.

G.77. Primeaux, Martha. "Health Care and the Aging American Indian." In A. M. Reinhardt and M. D. Quinn, eds. *Current Practices in Gerontological Nursing.* St. Louis, Missouri: C. V. Mosby, 1979, 130-138.

Stressing the importance of understanding cultural influences in health care delivery, Primeaux discusses the nature of Native American Indian health care beliefs and practices in general, and those of elderly Indians in particular.

G.78. Rosenbaum, Janet N. "Health Meanings and Practices of Older Greek-Canadian Widows." *Journal of Advanced Nursing* 16:11 (1991), 1320-1327.

Rosenbaum interviewed Greek- and Turkish-born immigrants, aged 50-81, widowed for 6 months or longer; among reported health practices were the use of folk remedies while relying more on professional caregivers; nursing implications are discussed, specifically the need to consider family values and folk medical practices in providing culturally relevant care.

G.78.a. Rowles, Graham D. "Changing Health Culture in Rural Appalachia: Implications for Serving the Elderly." *Journal of Aging Studies* 5:4 (1991), 375-389.

Rowles looks at ways of reconciling traditional health care practices among rural Appalachian elders with conventional "professional" health care models by adopting a more expansive view of health care delivery that sets health care within a community-wide context.

G.79. Sakauye, Kenneth. "Elderly Asian Patient." *Journal of Geriatric Psychiatry* 25:1 (1992), 85-104.

Sakauye reviews the literature on mental health among Asian elders, and suggests, among other things, culturally sensitive outreach and projects involving alternative health care practices, such as traditional folk cures.

G.80. Sanders, Valisa. "Profiles of Elderly Armenians." *Journal of Gerontological Nursing* 10:11 (1984), 26-29.

Drawing from interviews with Armenian health care professionals, patients, families and students in the Los Angeles area, Sanders discusses factors relevant to nursing home care for elderly Armenians, including care for the elderly with the extended family system, dietary customs, language and other cultural customs and beliefs related to such things as modesty and formal manners.

G.81. Shomaker, Diana M. "Navajo Nursing Homes: Conflict of Philosophies." *Journal of Gerontological Nursing* 7:9 (1981), 531-536.

Shomaker discusses an apparent conflict between the role of elders as integral members of traditional Navajo families and their institutionalization; the Navajo have adapted nursing homes to meet cultural expectations, where elders may retain

Navajo customs, surrounded by Navajo-speaking community members, in settings much like the traditional extended family.

G.82. Sneve, Virginia Driving Hawk. *Three Lakota Grandmother Stories: Health Lessons for Young People.* New York: Association on American Indian Affairs, 1975.

This is not a collection of traditional narratives, but rather a trio of contemporary didactic stories which use the character–and traditional voice of authority–of the Lakota "Grandma," who offers health lessons to her grandchildren, occasionally invoking folk wisdom, including mythological figures and knowledge of healing.

G.83. Snyder, Patricia. "Health Service Implications of Folk Healing Among Older Asian Americans and Hawaiians in Honolulu." *The Gerontologist* 24:5 (1984), 471-486.

Through participant observation and interviews, Synder presents a survey of traditional healers and their clients, and argues that learning about both traditional healing and the social network within which it is practiced can improve the nature of conventional health care delivery to the elderly.

G.84. Stokes, L. G. "Growing Old in the Black Community." In A. M. Reinhardt and M. D. Quinn, eds. *Current Practice in Gerontological Nursing.* St. Louis, Missouri: C. V. Mosby, 1979.

Stokes looks at health problems of elderly blacks, within the context of culture and personal experience, including the role of religion, and discusses customs and beliefs related to aging and death, including the wake, funeral service and burial.

G.85. Weaver, Rix. *The Old Wise Woman: A Study of Active Imagination.* Boston: Shambhala, 1991 [1973].

This book is based on Carl Jung's method of "active imagination"–using elements of traditional narratives as frameworks for identifying and working through "personal myths" for therapeutic purposes; Weaver presents commentary on the psychology of stories of wise old women and men.

G.86. Weibel-Orlando, Joan. "Elders and Elderlies: Well-Being in Indian Old Age." *American Indian Culture and Research Journal* 13:3-4 (1989), 149-170.

Demographic and life history data collected from forty Indian elders who have lived in the Los Angeles area argue for the importance of engagement with ethnic community life as a key to success in managing their lives; the article title points to a distinction made among Indians between "elderlies" (the stereotypic aged: non-productive, frail and dependent) and "elders" (those embodying exemplary cultural traits and who make contributions to family and community).

G.87. Wieland, Darryl; Donna Benton, and B. Josea Kramer, eds. *Cultural Diversity and Geriatric Care: Challenges to the Health Care Professions.* Binghamton, New York: Haworth Press, 1994.

Among the articles in this collection are those addressing diverse cultural beliefs and practices about death and dying among the elderly, recognizing cultural differences, providing culturally appropriate care, and diversity training.

G.88. Wood, Joan. "Communication with Older Adults in Health Care Settings: Cultural and Ethnic Considerations." *Educational Gerontology.* 15:4 (1989), 351-362.

This article notes the tendency of minority elders to have difficulty both communicating openly with health care providers and dealing with the health system bureaucracy; greater sensitivity by health care workers to folk beliefs concerning etiology and treatment of illness may improve communication.

G.89. Yee, Barbara W. K., and Gayle D. Weaver. "Ethnic Minorities and Health Promotion: Developing a Culturally Competent' Agenda." *Generations* 18:1 (1994), 39-44.

An argument is made here for developing national health promotion goals that take into account the needs of minority elders; folk medical beliefs of Native American, Asian and Hispanic elders are discussed; it is cautioned that these beliefs and practices are manifest to varying degrees among minority elders.

NARRATIVE

G.90. Adams, Cynthia, Gisela Labouvie-Vief, Cathy J. Hobart, and Mary Dorosz. "Adult Age Group Differences in Story Recall Style." *Journals of Gerontology* 45:1 (1990), P17-P27.

The authors report a study in which groups of younger and older adults were presented with two narratives–a fable and a "nonfable"; their responses suggest a relationship between the style of recall (interpretive versus text-based) and age.

G.91. Averill, T. B. "Resident-Inspired Drama." *Nursing Homes* 29:1 (1980), 2-4.

Averill reports on a study conducted in three Wisconsin nursing homes, in which folk and fairy tales were read to residents over a one-month period, to encourage them to share personal experiences with staff and each other; staff at one site recorded these exchanges, yielding several oral historical narratives.

G.92. Carlton-LaNey, Iris. "Elderly Black Farm Women: A Population at Risk." *Social Work* 37:6 (1992), 517-523.

Ten elderly African-American farm women in Duplin County, North Carolina, talk about their lives, revealing their resourcefulness and reliance on mutual aid; the author suggests that programs and services to these elders should reflect a sensitivity to these feelings of sisterhood and cooperation that have enabled these older women to survive, and may be lacking as they face social isolation and dependence.

G.93. Chasse, Emily S. "Sharing Folktales with Seniors." *Activities, Adaptation and Aging* 15:3 (1991),109-113.

Chasse, a state university librarian and storyteller, relates her experience leading a program at a Connecticut senior center in which she presented folktales, legends and personal experience narratives to stimulate their memories and encourage them to share tales and life stories with each other.

G.94. Disch, Robert. "The Young, the Old, and the Life Review: Report on a Brookdale Project." *Journal of Gerontological Social Work* 12:3-4 (1988), 125-135.

Disch reports on a project of the Brookdale Institute of Hunter College in New York City, in which 103 teenagers conducted interviews with 447 frail elderly people in a variety of institutions and private homes; the project encouraged "mutually positive attitudes and fostered intergenerational transmission of ethnic heritages and cultural legacies," and resulted in a videotape, a life-stories manual and anthologies of selected interviews.

G.95. Engelsman, Joan Chamberlain. *Queen's Cloak: A Myth for Mid-Life.* Wilmette, Illinois: Chiron Publications, 1994.

Designed as a personal guide to mid-life, this book examines a fairy tale that reflects a number of issues facing women in mid-life; the author discusses her own experiences and those of other women for whom elements of the fairy tale may serve as archetypal models for life stage development and relationships.

G.96. Gothoni, Raili. "From Chaos to Cosmos: The Telling of a Life Story Reconsidered." *Journal of Cross-Cultural Gerontology* 5:1 (1990), 65-76.

Gothoni, a pastoral counselor at a city hospital in Helsinki, Finland, describes life review work with chronic patients aged 65-85, in which elders are guided into fashioning the apparent chaos of their personal experiences into an integrated whole (cosmos), in the manner of traditional storytelling.

G.97. John, Martha Tyler. "Story Writing in a Nursing Home: A Patchwork of Memories." *Activities, Adaptation and Aging* 16:1 (1991), 1-133.

The "Patchwork Storybook" is a nursing home reminiscence and learning program, in which, to encourage life storytelling, topics for study are chosen, such as myths and legends, historical fiction and adventure, and residents compile inventories of memories about families, personal experiences, and other subjects.

G.98. Mergler, Nancy. "Why Are There Old People." *Human Development* 26 (1983), 72-90.

Viewing physical and cognitive changes in older adults as adaptive rather than solely degenerative, Mergler argues that tasks enabling survival among elders often involve oral transmission of information, characteristically within storytelling contexts, and that memory for both story content and evaluation of the story's message actually increases with age.

G.99. Mergler, Nancy L., Marion Faust and Michael D. Goldstein. "Storytelling as an Age-Dependent Skill: Oral Recall of Orally Presented Stories." *International Journal of Aging and Human Development* 20:3 (1984-1985), 205-228.

The authors describe experiments testing listener recall and evaluation of orally presented stories; among the findings were that the physical qualities of older adults' voices made for better oral transmission, and that listeners had certain expectations about the type of oral information received from older adults.

G.100. Newbern, Virginia B. "Sharing the Memories: The Value of Reminiscence as a Research Tool." *Journal of Gerontological Nursing* 18:5 (1992), 13-18.

Newbern presents vignettes culled from interviews with 60 elders aged 65-96 who have lived in North Carolina, Mississippi and Texas, and notes the value of personal narratives as research tools for nurses: beyond its therapeutic value as life review, they can be sources of information used to enable elders to cope with health issues and avoid institutionalization.

G.101. Pratt, Michael W., and Susan L. Robins. "That's the Way It Was: Age Differences in the Structure and Quality of Adults' Personal Narratives." *Discourse Processes* 14:1 (1991), 73-85.

In a Canadian study, eighty adults from 18 to 87 participated in a study of the structure and style of storytelling; the narratives of the older adults were rated best in quality; explanations were offered by age (older adults have more experience in storytelling and larger repertoires) and by cohort effect (younger adults are products of a culture which has inhibited the development of storytelling).

G.102. Prétat, Jane R. *Coming to Age: The Croning Years and Late-Life Transformation.* Toronto, Ontario: Inner City Books, 1994.

Prétat, a Jungian analyst, offers a therapeutic model for understanding and negotiating middle and old age, drawing upon folk tales, legends and mythological figures as vehicles for engaging the "active imagination" in releasing the creativity and "life energy" contained within the aging body.

G.103. Reinharz, Shulamit. "Loving and Hating One's Elders: Twin Themes in Legend and Literature." In Karl A. Pillimer and Rosalie S. Wolf, eds. *Elder Abuse: Conflict in the Family.* Dover, Massachusetts: Auburn House, 1986, 25-48.

Reinharz looks at tensions across generations, reflected in rituals and beliefs relating to elders in traditional societies, in Greek mythology, fairy tales, and literature, and in actual cases of parricide; she points to contrasting themes of love and hate, whose recognition may help in the understanding of elder abuse.

G.104. Schram, Penninah. "Storytelling: A Practical Approach to Life Review." *Journal of Aging and Judaism* 2:3 (1988), 187-190.

Schram describes the use of storytelling in life review among Jewish elders as a means not only of recalling personal memories but also passing on a cultural and spiritual legacy to the next generation; elders are encouraged to use all senses in the recall of events, places, people, and feelings as sources for personal narratives.

G.105. Winkler, Mary G. "Walking to the Stars: Kathe Kollwitz and the Artist's Pilgrimage." *Generations* 14:4 (1990), 39-44.

In discussing issues of spiritual growth, aging, and art, Winkler looks at diary entries and self-portraits painted over the years by Kollwitz (1867-1945), likening her pilgrimage toward self-knowledge to that of the heroine in a Grimm's fairy tale who meets tests and temptations as she goes through the stages of her journey.

G.106. Wright, Mel. "Priming the Past." *Oral History Journal* 14:1 (1986), 60-65.

Wright, a social worker in the London Borough of Lewisham, discusses the importance of reminiscence among the elderly and describes the Bellingham History Group, which participated in the "Exploring Living Memory Festival" in London in 1985, and organized a local exhibit, "A View of Bellingham."

TRADITIONAL ARTS

G.107. Ambrosius, G. Richard, Margot Hood-Rogers and Curtis Cook. *"Buy Native American": A Step Toward Self-Sufficiency.* Final Report. U. S. Administration on Aging, Administration for Native Americans, 1986.

This report describes "Buy Native American," an initiative in which the National Indian Council on Aging collaborated with a private marketing firm to distribute Native American Indian artwork and crafts, and to develop a national network of cottage industries for elder craftspeople.

G.108. Andrada, Patsy A., and Alvin O. Korte. "En Aquellos Tiempo: A Reminiscing Group With Hispanic Elderly." *Journal of Gerontological Social Work* 20:3-4 (1993), 25-42.

The authors suggest ways of stimulating reminiscence among Hispanic nursing home residents through culturally appropriate multisensory activities, including singing Spanish folksongs, listening to folk tales, and eating ethnic food.

G.109. Angelil, Muriel M. "Teaching Coiling, An Ancient American Indian Basket Technique, to Nursing Home Residents." *Activities, Adaptation and Aging* 1:2 (1980), 27-34.

Angelil describes a project in which 24 female nursing home residents, aged 55 to 94 years old, were instructed in the traditional Native American Indian craft of basket making, using the fiber coiling technique; among the benefits were instilling a sense of self-worth as well as a bond of affection with the instructor.

G.110. Bailey, Chris Howard. "Precious Blood: Encountering Inter-Ethnic Issues in Oral History Research, Reconstruction and Representation." *Oral History Review* 18:2 (1990), 61-108.

Bailey, a dramaturge and oral historian, hired as scholar-in-residence at the Massachusetts Heritage State Park in Holyoke under the project, "Shifting Gears: The Changing Meaning of Work in Massachusetts, 1920-1980," produced a play based on the oral histories of old and young members of Holyoke's ethnic neighborhoods, along with archival research, and enacted by an intergenerational cast from the same communities; included in the article are interview excerpts and a transcript of the play. (see **G.111**).

G.111. Bailey, Christine Howard. "Soul Clap Its Hands and Sing: Living History Theatre as a Process of Creation." *Activities, Adaptation and Aging* 9:4 (1987), 1-43.

The author, a playwright and theater historian, studied with Susan Perlstein, founder of Elders Share the Arts (see **G.122-G.124**), and developed several plays based on oral history interviews with older residents of local ethnic neighborhoods, who then performed in the plays before community audiences; she discusses the social and therapeutic value of living history theater.

G.112. Carlton-LaNey, Iris. "The Last Quilting Bee." *Generations* 17:2 (1993), 55-58.

The author describes a quilting bee in which her mother and several female friends and relatives met to share their craft and personal stories; these elders talk about relationships, loss, and strength through family and religion; the author suggests female-centered, culturally sensitive outreach that acknowledges the resources valued and shared by these rural Southern African-American women.

G.113. Coombs-Ficke, Susan, and Helen K. Kershner. *New Worlds for Senior Enterprise: An International Survey and Analysis.* Washington, D. C.: American Association for International Aging, 1990.

This "white paper" presents a survey of local "senior enterprises" in Africa, Asia, Europe and the Americas; many of them take advantage of elders' traditional craft skills, operating small-scale cottage industries with flexible work conditions designed to meet the needs of elders in local communities.

G.114. Evanchuk, Roberta J. "Creating, Preserving and Communicating Traditions: A Role for Retirees of a Dance Company." In Michael Owen Jones, Michael Dane Moore and Richard Christopher Snyder, eds. *Inside Organizations: Understanding the Human Dimension.* Newbury Park, California: Sage, 1988.

Somewhat unique in this bibliography is this study of alumni of the Aman Folk Ensemble, a Los Angeles-based dance company, since these alumni are mostly midlife "retirees"; nevertheless, Evanchuk fruitfully explores the roles that former employees may play in sharing knowledge of an organization's traditions.

G.115. Glass, J. Conrad, Jr., and Judy L. Smith. "Crafts Marketing Programs for Older Adults: A Role for Education." *Educational Gerontology* 10:4-5 (1984), 325-334.

The authors discuss the educational and practical value of older adults learning to market crafts they produce; they look at the marketing programs of Elder Craftsmen shops nationwide, and local programs in Washington, D. C., North Carolina, and Delaware, that promote the sale of crafts by elders.

G.116. Hayes, Gaile. "Music and Myth: Drawing from the Past to Enhance the Present." *Nursing Homes* 38:3 (1989), 29-31.

In describing the value of music therapy in nursing homes, Hayes describes one program model in which the traditional music and dance of different cultures are presented along with legends and stories to encourage reminiscence.

G.117. Francis, Doris. "Images from the Occupational Years: The Reminiscences of Retirees and Their Implications for Social Work Practice." In Robert Disch, ed. *Twenty-Five Years of the Life Review: Theoretical and Practical Considerations.* New York: Haworth Press, 1988. [Published simultaneouly as *Journal of Gerontological Social Work* 12:3-4 (1988)].

Francis examines the folk art of retired workers whose pieces, depicting their occupational experiences, were featured in the exhibit "The Word of Work"; she suggests to social workers that they encourage elders to use such images of the past to facilitate personal growth (see **E.189**).

G.118. Keller, Jean M. "Intergenerational Sharing: Teens and Elderly for the Arts." *Journal of Applied Gerontology* 9:3 (1990), 312-324.

Keller describes a program developed in rural Georgia called Teens and Elderly for the Arts (TEA), in which elders from a senior center share their knowledge of traditional arts, including caning, rugmaking, candling, soapmaking, quilting, whittling, and basketmaking, with "latchkey" teenagers.

G.119. Kivnick, Helen Q. "Adulthood and Old Age Under Apartheid: A Psychosocial Consideration." *Ageing and Society* 8:4 (1988), 425-440.

Using Erikson's life stage developmental model, Kivnick observes how South Africans are able to draw upon traditional culture in adulthood and old age, in particular singing, offering a source of psychosocial strength throughout the life cycle and providing generational continuity, even under apartheid.

G.120. Lieberman, Leslie, and Leonard Lieberman. "Second Careers in Art and Craft Fairs." *The Gerontologist* 23:3 (1983), 266-272.

This essay reports on the results of interviews with 70 women and men aged 50 to 87 who left former occupations to take up second careers as artists and craftspeople. While the article discusses creativity and aging, what is missing is a survey of personal, family and cultural background as factors in the choice of a specific craft.

G.121. Nelson, Randy F. "George Black: A New Folk Hero." *North Carolina Folklore Journal* 20:1 (1972), 30-35.

This is a short article about an 83-year-old African-American brick maker from Winston-Salem, North Carolina, who was enlisted by the federal Agency for International Development to teach traditional hand brickmaking methods to villagers in Victoria, Guyana.

G122. Pearlstein, Susan. "Elders Share the Arts." *Generations* 15:2 (1991), 55-57.

Pearlstein is the founder of Elders Share the Arts (ESTA), a program based in New York City in which elders and intergenerational groups produce plays, journals, dances, collages and multimedia works based on personal experience narratives of program participants from various ethnic communities and neighborhoods.

G.123. Pearlstein, Susan, and Jeff Bliss. *Generating Community: Intergenerational Partnerships Through the Expressive Arts.* Brooklyn, New York: Elders Share the Arts, 1994.

This book distills the wisdom, gathered from years of experience, of Elders Share the Arts (ESTA), founded in 1979 to develop "Living History" projects among the elderly reflecting the diverse cultural traditions of New York City, and branching out to programs involving the collaboration of elders and public school students in community projects drawing from oral history and the creative arts; this is essentially a "how to" guide for community-based groups on creating partnerships among schools, senior centers and arts groups to "generate community" across boundaries of age and culture (see also **G.122, G.124, H.74-H.76,** and **H.78**).

G.124. Pearlstein, Susan. *A Stage For Memory: Life History Plays by Older Adults.* New York: Teachers and Writers Collaborative, 1981.

This booklet documents one of the earliest "living history theater" projects of Pearlstein, conducted at the Hodson Senior Center in New York City's South Bronx; it features a history of the troupe, portraits of participants (Jewish, African-American and Caribbean), and several dramatic sketches developed by the troupe, in which they recall holiday preparations, home remedies, and urban and rural life.

G.125. Roach, Susan. 'The Journey of David Allen, Cane Carver: Transformations through Public Folklore." In Robert Baron and Nicholas Spitzer, eds. *Public Folklore.* Washington, D.C.: Smithsonian Institution Press, 1992, 159-182.

Roach discusses change and continuity in the work of Allen, an elder African-American walking stick carver from rural north Louisiana, over the course of several years as a participant in public folklife presentations.

G.126. Sandel, Susan L., and David Reed Johnson. "Waiting at the Gate: Creativity and Hope in the Nursing Home."*Activities, Adaptation and Aging* 9:3 (1987), 3-178.

This special issue of *Activities, Adaptation and Aging* describes the contribution of creative arts therapies to quality of life among nursing home residents; while focusing on movement and drama therapy rather than traditional arts, they do address the therapeutic role of rituals based on holidays, birthdays and other events, and role of the arts in generating a communal spirit within the nursing home.

G.127. Schreter, Carol A. "Industrialization Spawns the Elder Craftsmen Shop." *International Journal of Aging and Human Development* 19:4 (1984), 301-309.

While this study of the Wilmington (Delaware) Senior Center Elder Craftsmen Shop focuses primarily upon the social value of craft production as a late-life activity, it is also an argument in favor of the revival of the methods and social organization of traditional craft guilds as a model for retired workers.

G.128. Weber, B. L. "Folk Art as Therapy With a Group of Old People." *American Journal of Art Therapy* 20:2 (1981), 47-52.

Weber describes an art therapy program at a municipal day care center serving a lower income group of elders, most of the African-American, in which participants were encouraged to make a mural of their community with cloth figures, to reinforce identity and stimulate mutual support.

G.129. Weiss, Caroline R., Mary Markve-Patch, and Janice M. Thurn. "Remembrance of Repasts Past: Culinary Reminiscence." *Journal of Long Term Care Administration* 20:2 (1992), 6-9.

The authors describe a project with implications for applied foodways research, the Culinary Reminiscence Project, in which recreation students encouraged recall of food-related experiences among confused residents of a nursing home, and included the preparation of an illustrated culinary autobiography, constructing creative culinary artifacts, kitchen-testing recipes from the past, producing a cookbook of residents' favorite recipes, and organizing a celebratory event at project's end.

H

Films

SEARCHING FOR FILMS

There are a vast number of films and videotapes featuring traditional elders, ranging from student-produced videos to professionally produced programs. Many of the latter are available through existing film and distribution companies. However, they are notorious for disappearing from circulation after awhile. Distribution may be spotty or non-existent, and even among professional distributors they may often change hands, making them hard to trace. Nevertheless, there are ways to find them.

1. World Catalogue, an electronic database accessible through most college and university libraries (as well as many public libraries), lists, in addition to books and other printed materials, films and videos in the permanent holdings of lending institutions; this is one way of locating films/videos that have gone out of print or for which you have no current information on producers/distributors.

2. Another way to track down films is through the institutions that might have sponsored their production. These include the National Endowment for the Arts (NEA), the National Endowment for the Humanities (NEH), state and regional folklife programs, state humanities or arts councils, museums, universities, historical societies or other cultural institutions, local PBS television stations (see PBS listing below), or local public access community TV stations, among others (an individual citation in World Catalogue may provide this information).

3. For folklore films and videotapes produced before 1982, there is *American Folklore Films and Videotapes: An Index,* published by the Center for Southern Folklore (Memphis, Tennessee, 1976), containing over 1800 titles, with a fair number of aging subjects (none of them indexed as such); and a supplement, *American Folklore Films and Videotapes: A Catalogue, Volume II* (R. R. Bowker, 1982). Also worth considering are: *Films: The Visualization of Anthropology* (1000 titles), and *Films for Sociology* (2000 titles), prepared by Pennsylvania State University AV Services; Bronner's *American Folk Art: A Guide to Sources* (see **E.2**), which has a section devoted to folk art on film; and a dissertation by Gammerdinger (see **A.54**), which contains a "Filmography of American Folklore Film and Videotape."

4. Educational Film Library, Brookdale Center on Aging, Hunter College, 425 East 25th Street, New York, NY 10010. (212) 481-4350.

> This is a clearinghouse for films relating to aging. They are not a lending library; what they do provide are sources of information on film and videos on aging subjects, including suggestions for places to continue your search for particular films and film subjects.

****

The selection listed below is by no means exhaustive but rather is a fairly representative sample of what is available (that is to say, accessible to most researchers). For convenience, the first section lists groups of films available through institutions that distribute (for sale or rental) a number of titles related to traditional culture and aging, while the second section lists single titles organized by subject. Where available, running time, filmmakers, and release date are noted.

ALL TITLES LISTED ARE AVAILABLE IN VHS VIDEO FORMAT UNLESS NOTED.

FILMS LISTED BY DISTRIBUTOR

Appalshop
306 Madison Street
Whitesburg, KY 41858
(606) 633-0108   Fax (606) 633-1009

Appalshop not only produces and distributes films on Appalachian culture, but it also conducts community projects and has been active in environmental and social justice issues in the hill communities of southeastern U. S.

H.1. "Artus Moser of Buckeye Cove" (29 min). By Anne Johnson, 1985.

> Born in 1894, Moser grew up on the Biltmore Estate near Asheville, North Carolina, where his father was a forester; this film explores his life as a collector of ballads for the Library of Congress, and as "a teacher, singer, storyteller, actor, painter, gardener, naturalist, and husband and father."

H.2. "Catfish: Man of the Woods" (27 min). By Alan Bennett, 1974.

> Portrait of Clarence "Catfish" Gray, a fifth-generation herb doctor living near Glenwood, West Virginia, who gathers herbs and roots from the woods around his house, receives visitors, and reads letters from around the world asking advice on health matters; he discusses his healing techniques and philosophy of life.

H.3. "Chairmaker" (22 min). By Rick DiClemente, 1975.

> This portrait of 80-year-old Dewey Thompson, of Sugarloaf Hollow, Kentucky, features him making a rough-hewn rocking chair, and conversing with the camera, sharing his philosophy of life.

H.4. "Dreadful Memories: The Life of Sarah Ogan Gunning" (38 min). By Mimi Pickering, 1988.

> Born in the eastern Kentucky coalfields in 1910, Gunning lived through organizing drives and coal mine strikes in the 1920s and 1930s; Sarah, her brother Jim Garland, and half-sister Aunt Molly Jackson moved their families to New York City, where

they influenced the folk music revival.

H.5. "Fixin' to Tell About Jack" (25 min). By Elizabeth Barret, 1975.

Ray Hicks, a mountain farmer from Beech Mountain, North Carolina, tells stories passed down through several generations in his family; interspersed with scenes of him gathering herbs, and describing his family's tradition of storytelling is his telling of a Jack tale, "Whickity-Whack, Into my Sack" (a.k.a. "Soldier Jack").

H.6. "Hand Carved" (88 min). By Herb E. Smith, 1981.

Chairmaker Chester Cornett tells the story of his apprenticeship with his grandfather and uncle, and reveals the life of a struggling artist; the film follows him from felling a tree on his family's homestead to the completion of an 8-legged "two-in-one" rocker (see also **E.172**).

H.7. "Homemade Tales: The Life of Florida Sloane" (29 min). 1993.

Presents the story of a singer, storyteller and "home-grown philosopher" who married at an early age and raised a large family in a remote mountain region in eastern Kentucky.

H.8. "John Jacob Niles" (32 min). By Bill Richardson, 1978.

Niles, whose career began as an adding machine repairman who came to eastern Kentucky in 1909, recalls, at age 86, a life spent collecting, recording and performing traditional Appalachian ballads.

H.9. "Lily Mae Ledford" (29 min). By Anne Johnson, 1988.

Ledford, a veteran banjo player, and recipient of a National Endowment for the Arts National Heritage Award shortly before her death in 1985, talks about growing up in Kentucky's Red River Gorge, and her life in music, notably as leader of the Coon Creek Girls, the first all-woman stringband on the radio.

H.10. "Mabel Parker Hardison Smith" (29 min). By Anne Johnson, 1985.

Smith, a Black Appalachian who taught school for over 35 years in the coalfields of eastern Kentucky, and known in her home region as a church organist and member of a local gospel group, recalls life in an African-American miner's family.

H.11. "Minnie Black's Gourd Band" (29 min). By Anne Johnson, 1988.

Black, who at 90 was still making music and art out of gourds grown in her own backyard garden in East Bernstadt, Kentucky, is featured playing unique versions of hymns and "old favorites" with her senior citizen gourd band.

H.12. "Morgan Sexton: Banjo Player From Bull Creek" (28 min). By Anne Johnson, 1991.

A National Heritage Award winner, 80-year-old Sexton recalls a life of farming, logging and coal mining; he and his nephew Lee Sexton recall learning music from their elders and each other, and the days when, after a hard days' work, they would play music and dance with their neighbors.

H.13. "Nature's Way" (22 min). By John Long and Elizabeth Barre, 1974.

Profiles several practitioners of folk medicine in Appalachia, including elders who practice midwifery, herbal healing, Indian healing methods, and the preparation of home remedies.

H.14. "Nimrod Workman: To Fit My Own Category" (35 min). By Scott Faulkner and Anthony Stone, 1975.

Workman, born in 1895, recalls life as miner and union organizer in the coalfields of West Virginia, and performs traditional ballads and originals songs which earned him a National Heritage Award.

H.15. "Oaksie" (22 min). By Anthony Stone, 1979.

This is a portrait of Oaksie Caudill, white oak basketmaker, fiddler and harp player from eastern Kentucky; in the film scenes of his fiddle and harp playing are interspersed with those of him weaving a basket.

H.16. "Quilting Women" (28 min). By Elizabeth Barret, 1976.

This film documents the work of traditional Appalachian quilters, featuring their comments on traditional patterns, the art of quilting, and the companionship of women working together over a quilting frame.

H.17. "The Ramsey Trade Fair" (18 min). By Scott Faulkner, 1973.

The camera visits the trade fair day held on Wednesdays in the coalfield community of Ramsey, Virginia, looking at the flea market as a microcosm of rural living where residents and local merchants, many of them elders, gather to sell, barter, tell tall tales, and play old time country music.

H.18. "Sarah Bailey" (29 min). By Anne Johnson, 1991.

Bailey is a renowned Appalachian weaver and corn shuck artist; in the film she talks about her beginnings as an artist "in the Hoover days," and is seen working on corn shuck dolls and flowers, and teaching corn shuck art and weaving at an Elderhostel program at the Pine Mountain Settlement School, which years back had helped her market her work.

H.19. "Sourwood Mountain Dulcimers" (28 min). By Gene DuBey, 1976.

J. D. Stamper, a master dulcimer maker and player from eastern Kentucky, and John McCutcheon, a young musician, play together, swap tunes, and discuss musical traditions.

H.20. "Tradition" (20 min). By Hill Hatton, 1973.

Logan Adams, who started his life's career in the coalfields, but broke his back mining, recalls his decision during the Depression to earn an income through the time-honored–but illegal–mountain tradition of whiskey-making; he and a federal revenue agent each offer a history of moonshining and the forces that motivate people like Adams.

Center for Southern Folklore
130 Beale Street
Memphis, TN 38103
(901) 525-3655   Fax (901) 525-3945

The Center is a research facility, with archival photographs and slides, field recordings, films and videos, and collections of traditional artifacts.

H.21. "Alabama Departure" (9 min). By Bryan Elson and Peter Bundy, 1978.

Described as "a poetic meditation upon the South" with "rich and disquieting ambiguity," this film presents images of land, water, and an old man, which are revisited a number of times.

H.22. "All Day and All Night: Memories From Beale Street Musicians" (30 min). By Robert Gordon and Louis Guida. Memphis: WETA-TV, 1990.

Blues musicians who performed on Beale Street in Memphis from the 1920s through the 1950s reminisce about Beale street lifestyle and culture; features B. B. King, Rufus Thomas, Evelyn Young and Fred Ford.

H.23. "Bukka White and Son House" (60 min).

Features performances by two elder statesmen of Mississippi Delta blues, with an introduction by blues revivalist Taj Mahal.

H.24. "Fannie Bell Chapman: Gospel Singer" (42 min). By Bill Ferris, Judy Peiser and Bobby Taylor. 1975.

This portrait of Chapman, gospel singer, faith healer and family leader from Centreville, Mississippi, presents her singing as well as her comments on music, faith and healing power in three generations of her family.

H.25. "Four Women Artists" (25 min). 1977.

Of the four older Southern women depicted in this film, three are folk artists: quilter Pecolia Warner, embroiderer Ethel Mohamed and painter Theora Hamblett (the fourth is novelist Eudora Welty, whose novels included folklore themes).

H.26. "Gravel Springs Fife and Drum" (11 min). By Bill Ferris and Judy Peiser, 1973.

Through the words and music of Othar Turner, a farmer, musician and cane fife maker from Gravel Springs, Mississippi, this short film focuses on town lifestyles, and compares African-American fife-and-drum music with its counterparts in West Africa.

H.27. "Green Valley Grandparents" (10 min).

This film looks at the Foster Grandparent Program initiated by Green Valley Development Center, where retired citizens share their lives with severely retarded children, emblematic of a tradition of caring in rural communities whose residents see themselves as one extended family.

H.28. "Legends of Bottleneck Blues Guitar"

This film focuses on Mississippi Delta bottleneck blues styles, and features the playing of Son House, Johnny Shines, Fred McDowell, Furry Lewis and Jesse Fuller.

H.29. "Legends of Country Blues Guitar"

Features rare footage from a variety of sources depicting some of the great blues musicians, including elder statesmen Mississippi John Hurt, Son House and Mance Lipscomb.

H.30. "Legends of Country Blues Guitar, Vol. 2"

More footage of some of the veteran artists of the "Golden Age" of country blues, including Bukka White, Sam Chatmon, Houston Stackhouse and Big Joe Williams, with rare footage of Huddie Lebetter, a.k.a. Leadbelly.

H.31. "Leon 'Peck' Clark: Basketmaker" (15 min). 1981.

This film portrait of a craftsperson within the setting of daily life in the rural South features scenes of basketmaking interwoven with reminiscences by Leon and Ada Clark about their long life together.

G.32. "Nellie's Playhouse" (14 min). By Linda Connelly Armstrong, 1982.

This film explores the creative output of Nellie Mae Rowe (1900-1982) of Fayetteville, Georgia, including sculptures, dolls and paintings, and presents her comments on the motivations behind her art.

H.33. "Ray Lum: Mule Trader" (18 min). By Bobby Taylor, Bill Ferris and Judy Peiser, 1973.

Lum, a veteran farm animal trader and legendary auctioneer from Vicksburg, Mississippi, tells stories going back to the early decades of the century in his native state and in Texas (see **D.203-D.205**).

H.34. "Sermons in Wood" (27 min). By Carolyn A. Jones, 1975.

Elijah Pierce (1892-1984), African-American woodcarver from Mississippi, describes his life and work, relief carvings commemorating scenes, including his father's tales of slavery, his own near-lynching, and his religious conversion (see **E.166, E.213**).

The Cinema Guild
1697 Broadway, Suite 506
New York, NY 10019-5904
(212) 246-5522 (800) 723-5522   Fax (212) 246-5525

The Guild distributes works of independent filmmakers, mostly in the area of politics and culture (traditional and popular).

H.35. "Alberta Hunter: My Castle's Rockin'" (60 min). By Stuart Goldman, 1988.

This film chronicles the life of the great blues singer Alberta Hunter, from her first hit, "Down Hearted Blues," in 1922 through a long career, and a late-life comeback in the late 1970s and 80s; features reminiscences of Hunter as well as scenes of her performing in late life.

H.36. "...All Our Lives" (54 min). By Lisa Berger and Carol Mazer, 1986.

This film examines the lives of several women, now in their 80s, who actively took part in the social revolution of the left subculture during the Spanish Civil War of the

1930s, and whose remembered lives form a bridge with the present, in which they perpetuate the traditions of lifetimes of commitment.

H.37. "Blood Memory: The Legend of Beanie Short" (56 min). By Robby Henson, 1992.

A survey of oral history and local storytelling, it is a study of the selective memory of older residents of Turkey Neck Bend, just above the Tennessee border in Kentucky, about Short, a Confederate Army deserter and robber of 100 years back.

H.38. "Catching Up With Yesterday: Andrew F. Boarman–Craftsman, Musician, Teacher" (29 min). By Stephen Plumlee and & Stephen T. Eckard, 1989.

Documents the life of Boarman, 78-year-old West Virginia instrument-maker and folk musician, who is shown in his workshop where he repairs, restores and builds instruments, and playing the banjo and autoharp.

H.39. "The End of an Old Song" By John Cohen, 1990 [1972].

Cohen presents a portrait of elder ballad singer Dillard Chandler, who plays the mountain music of an earlier era in the hills of North Carolina.

H.40. "The Flapper Story" (29 min). By Lauren Lazin.

This look at the "flapper," symbol of women who challenged prevailing social mores of the 1920s, features interviews with older women who recalled participating in the flapper movement, and explores the contradictions and limitations of the independent lifestyle of the flapper.

H.41. "My Yiddishe Momme McCoy" (20 min). By Bob Giges, 1991.

This film celebrates the half-century romance of 90-year-old Belle Demner, an Orthodox Jew from Vienna, with Irish Catholic Bernie McCoy; features Belle singing songs ranging from sacred prayers to World War II parodies.

H.42. "Plena is Work, Plena is Song" (29 min). By Pedro A. Rivera and Susan Zeig, 1989.

Examines the cultural and political history of the *plena,* and features some of the elder practitioners of this Puerto Rican topical song form, a blend of African and Spanish influences.

H.43. "Raananah: A World of Our Own" (28 min). By Marlene Booth, 1982.

This survey of Raananah Park, a Jewish summer colony in New York founded in 1937 by young Eastern European immigrants, features interviews with surviving members.

H.44. "The Voice of Free Labor: The Jewish Anarchists" (55 min). By Steven Fischler and Joel Sucher, 1980.

This study of the history and culture of the Jewish anarchist movement, which flourished between 1900 and World War I, features the reminiscences of participants in the movement, Yiddish songs and poems, and archival photos and newsreel footage.

H.45. "We've Got Rhythm" (30 min, 16mm). By Sara Gomez, 1967.

> Interviews with elderly local musicians trace the history of Cuban music and its basic instruments [part of the series "Cuba: A View From the Inside"].

Davenport Films
Route 1, Box 527
Delphane, VA 22025
(703) 592-3701

This is a distributor largely for the films of Tom Davenport, ethnographic filmmaker. The films listed below were produced with the support of the University of North Carolina.

H.46. Being a Joines: Life in the Brushy Mountains" (55 min). 1976.

> Presents the life and and tales of John E. Joines and his family from the Brushy Mountains of western North Carolina, and offers a glimpse of life in Appalachia in the first part of the 20th century.

H.47. "Born for Hard Luck: 'Peg Leg Sam' Jackson" (29 min). 1976.

> A biographical study of Arthur Jackson, an African-American street corner musician, who talks about his life as a hobo and performer with patent medicine shows in the South.

H.48. "The Shakers" (30 min). 1974

> This film reviews the history and culture of the Shaker's experiment in communal living through the memories and songs of one small group of surviving members, all women.

H.49. "A Singing Stream: A Black Family Chronicle" (57 min). 1987.

> Documents the religious song traditions of the Landis family of North Carolina family, focusing on Bertha M. Landis, 86, and her children and grandchildren, showing how they used music to hold the family together through years of tenant farming, depression, war, and the migration of some family members to jobs in the North (see **E.52**).

Documentary Educational Resources
101 Morse Street
Watertown, MA 02171
(617) 926-0491 Fax (617) 926-9519

DER produces, distributes and promotes the use of ethnographic and documentary films, and administers grants for independent filmmakers.

H.50. "Add and Mabel's Punkin Center" (16 min). By Richard Kane and Dillon Bustin, 1984.

> Add and Mabel run a homespun folk museum, the Punkin Center in Southern Indiana, filled with hundreds of thousands of antiques and curios that they have been collecting since the 1920s, each of which inspires reminiscences (see also **H.73**).

H.51. "Amir: An Afghan Refugee Musician's Life in Peshawar, Pakistan" (52 min). By John Baily [no date].

Between 1973 and 1977 Baily conducted fieldwork among urban musicians in Afghanistan; in 1985, while filming Afghan refugee musicians in Peshawar, he met an old friend, Amir Mohammad, and in "Amir" Baily portrays his life as a refugee and his relationship with other musicians.

H.52. "Ben's Mill" (59 min). By Michel Chalfour and John Karol, 1981.

Ben Thresher runs a water-powered, wood-working mill in rural Vermont that has operated since 1848, and is one of the few left in the U. S.; he uses his machines and hand tools to turn out a watering tub and horsedrawn sled for his neighbors in the farming community.

H.53. "Dadi's Family" (59 min). By James MacDonald, Rina Gill and Michael Camerini, [no date].

Dadi is the grandmother and mother-in-law of an extended family in the Haryana region of Northern India; the film explores the tensions created by her authority and by social and economic changes outside the village that threaten traditional family roles and relationships.

H.54. "The Drums of Winter (*Uksuum Cauyai*)" (90 min). By Sarah Elder and Leonard Kamerling, 1988.

Part of a series, "The Alaskan Eskimo," by Elder and Kamerling, this film explores the traditional dance, music and spiritual world of the Yup'ik Eskimos of Emonak, a village at the mouth of the Yukon River on the Bering Sea coast; the elders of Emonak are shown preparing for a potlatch with a neighboring village, practicing songs and dances in the Kashim (*qasgiq* or omen's house).

"From the Elders." By Katrina Waters, Sarah Elder and Leonard Kamerling, 1988.

This is a series of three films:

H.55. "Joe Sun" (19 min)

Immaluuraq (Joe Sun), a resident of Shungnak who grew up moving among seasonal camps in the Kobuk River region of Alaska, tells of the legendary Inupiaq prophet, Maniilaq, his great uncle, in a narrative form called *uqaaqtuaq* (a talk given by elders to young people seeking advice).

H.56. "In Iirgu's Time" (20 min)

Iirgu is an elder from the Siberian Yup'ik Eskimo village of Gambell on St. Lawrence Island; as two grandchildren listen, Iirgu recalls events in Gambell from the time the first missionaries arrived, in a narrative form called *unigipamsuk* (true historical narrative).

H.57. "The Reindeer Thief" (13 min)

Pelaasi, an elder from Gambell, tells a mythical story about a man who goes out in search of a reindeer thief, in a narrative form called *ungipaghaq* (a tale passed down unchanged through generations and believed to be based in fact).

H.58. "Hajari Bhand of Rajasthan: Jester Without Court" (40 min). By John and Ulrike Emigh.

> Bhand, of Chittogarh, Rajasthan is renowned for his skill as a *bahurupiya,* one of a host of wandering mimics who offer a vast assortment characters from the sacred to the profane, performing their routines in streets, market places and courtyards throughout Northern India.

"Inhabitants of the Land of Grace." By John Dickinson.

> This series documents the complexity of Caribbean cultural traditions in eastern Venezuela, each focusing on a folk artist who lives in or around the city of Cumana; two of the films in the series feature elders.

H.59. "The Mandolin King (El Rey de Bandolin)" (28 min), 1985.

> This is a portrait of Cruz Quinal, who makes a variety of musical instruments, including his own creation, a mandolin with two fretboards; an accomplished musician, he compares himself to a decaying colonial church across the street, revered yet neglected.

H.60. "Peasant Painter (Pintor Campesino)" (18 min), 1984.

> Cleto Rojas paints memories of his journey to Caracas, as well as visionary scenes inspired by mythology, the local cinema, and his rural surroundings.

H.61. "Jakub" (65 min). By. Jana Sevcikova, 1992.

> This is a study of the Ruthenians, living in the Maramuresh mountains of northern Romania and Western Bohemia, as seen primarily through the life of Jakub Popovich, whose story is followed from 1947 to the present (1992).

H.62. "Jero Tapakan: Stories in the Life of a Balinese Healer" (25 min). By Linda Connor, Patsy Asch and Timothy Asch, 1983.

> Jero talks with Connor about her life, recalling her poverty and despair as a farmer twenty five years earlier, and her conversion, following illness and mystical visions, into a spirit medium who through possession by ancestral spirits may determine the origin of afflictions, indicate auspicious days for ceremonies, and perform other healing functions (see **F.14**).

H.63. "A Joking Relationship" (13 min). By John Marshall.

> Part of a series, "The San (Ju/Wasi)," by Marshall, recording the daily lives of the !Kung, a hunting and gathering people in Namibia, this film depicts a moment of flirtation in a joking relationship between N!ai, the young wife of /Gunda, and her great-uncle /Ti!kay.

H.64. "Louisa Allamand" (17 min). By Aline Luque, 1991.

> Part of a series, "Portraits en Altitude (Portraits From On High)," in French with English subtitles, featuring women and their families commenting on life in the mountain communities of Haute-Savoie, France, this film presents Louisa, a retired farmer, who speaks about the paradox of a solitary life in the midst of a large family.

H.65. "The Ona People: Life and Death in Tierra del Fuego" (55 min). By Anne Chapman and Ana Montes de Gonzales, 1977.

This film chronicles the life and death of the Selk'nam Indians (also known as the Ona); much of the film is based on the personal accounts of Kiepja, a shaman who was almost 90 when ethnographer Chapman first met her in 1964, and who died in 1966, and Angela Loji, born at the turn of the century, the last surviving Ona Indian, who died in 1974.

H.66. "Our Lives in Our Hands" (49 min). By Haral Prins and Karen Carter, 1986.

Examines the traditional Native American craft of split-ash basketmaking as a means of economic and cultural survival for Aroostook Micmac Indians of northern Maine; Indian artisans are filmed at their craft in their homes, at work on local potato farms and at business meetings of the Basket Bank, a cooperative formed by the Aroostook Micmac Council (see **E.104**).

H.67. "The Pearl Fisher" (28 min). By Dillon Bustin, 1985.

This film follows Barnett Bass as he fishes for fresh-water mollusks in the White River of southern Indiana, seeking gem-quality pearls and the mother-of-pearl shell lining; the film explores issues as far ranging as international trade, the environment, the traditional symbolism of the pearl and the romance of everyday life.

H.68. "Perico the Bowlmaker" (45 min). By Jerome Mintz, 1987.

This film looks at the changing role of a traditional craftsman in Andalusia, Spain, and the social and personal factors that have shaped his occupation.

H.69. "Portrait of George Hardy" (30 min). By Gabriel Coakley, 1995.

Hardy, born on the island of Deer Isle, Maine, in 1917 and still residing there, began his career as a folk artist at the age of 60 after retiring from work as a mason; he creates wooden animal sculptures, and supplements his income with sales to summer visitors.

H.70. "Saudade (Nostalgia)" (57 min). By Bela Feldman-Bianco, 1991.

This film, based on the personal reminiscences of seven Portuguese women and men in New Bedford, Massachusetts (six of them immigrants from the Azores, Madeira and the mainland), reveals through their memories, songs, images from the past, and scenes of contemporary life, how they have recreated their homeland's past in their everyday lives in an American industrial city.

H.71. "The Shoemaker" (34 min). By Jerome Mintz, 1978.

This film follows the odyssey of an Andalusian shoemaker who, assuming that he would spend his last years among family and friends in his native village, ends up following his children when they leave to work in a tourist town, and struggles to adapt to the isolation of his new environment.

H.72. "The Spirit Possession of Alejandro Mamani" (27 min).

This portrait of an old Bolivian man near the end of his life, who believes that he is possessed by evil spirits, reveals his personal tragedy, and grapples with issues of the unknown, old age and death.

H.73. "Water From Another Time" (29 min). By Richard Kane and Dillon Bustin, 1982.

The filmmakers visit three older residents of Orange County, Indiana: Lotus Dickey, 70, a retired factory hand and fiddle player and singer, Elmer Boyd, 80, who has kept a daily journal since 1923, and artist and poet Lois Doane, 87, one of whose poems inspired the film's title.

Elders Share the Arts (ESTA)
57 Willoughby Street
Brooklyn, NY 11201
(718) 488-8565

Though their film list is short, it is worth special mention, for they are a community organization that has pioneered the use of oral history and the arts in Living History programs with elders and intergenerational groups (see also **G.122-G.124,** and **H.88**)).

H.74. "Arts and Minds: Bridging Brooklyn's Generation Gap" (16 min). By Wendy Cole.

This is a short documentary of an ESTA intergenerational workshop involving school children and older adults from a neighboring senior center in Brooklyn.

H.75. "Elder Voices" (26 min). By Eric Breitbart.

This portrait of sessions of an ESTA Living History Theater workshop at Amsterdam Nursing Home in Manhattan, serves as a training video for nursing home workers on developing living history projects with frail elderly.

H.76. "ESTA Profile" (16 min). By Hank Linhart.

This is a short documentary profiling all of the Elders Share the Arts programs, including their living history workshops, Pearls of Wisdom programs (featuring elder storytellers), and their annual Living History Theater Festivals.

Filmakers Library
124 East 40th Street
New York NY 10016
(212) 808-4980   Fax (212) 808-4983

Filmakers Library distributes films on a variety of social themes, including the subject of aging.

H.77. "Aging in the Soviet Union: A Toast to Sweet Old Age" (37 min). By Richard Breyer, 1987.

Documents the support for elders in Soviet Georgian culture, focusing on an elderly widow in an urban setting, an older couple on a small farm in the Caucasus, and the residents of a retirement home in Tbilisi.

H.78. "Alice and Lena" (38 min). By Mary Patierno, 1990.

This film focuses upon two sisters in their 70s, daughters of Italian immigrants who grew up in New England in a family of eight children, and who never married, never left home, and lived their entire lives together, defying tradition by remaining single, yet emblematic of a tradition of strong family ties sustaining people throughout their lives.

H.79. "A Family in France: A Story About the Passing of Time..." (40 min). By Andre Dryansky, 1993.

This is a portrait of a country family living in Cassaniouze, a small village in the Auvergne province with 700 people, most of whom are retired; featured in the film are Jean Panou, a retired stonemason, and his wife Angele, both born in the village over 80 years ago, and four of their eight children, none of whom remained.

H.80. "Giants of Time: The Wisdom of Age" (57 min). By Juniper Films, 1993.

This film records the personal experience narratives of several Australian women and men, all over 90, who recall memories of personal and historical events, including the events that compelled many of them to leave their native countries, and who speak of contemporary concerns with peace and the environment, and they share the perspectives they have gained through lifetimes of experience.

H.81. "The Grand Generation" (30 min). By Paul Wagner, Steven Zeitlin and Marjorie Hunt, 1994.

This portrait of six American elders–ballad singer Nimrod Workman, *albedos* singer Cleofes Vigil, embroiderer Ethel Mohamed, African-American former union organizer and civil rights activist, Rosina Tucker, baker Moishe Sacks, and Chesapeake bayman Alex Kellam–was inspired by the Smithsonian project, "The Grand Generation," which produced a landmark traveling exhibit and book (see **E.1**).

H.82. "Happy Birthday, Mrs. Craig" (55 min). By Richard Kaplan, 1990.

This film celebrates the life of Mrs. Lulu Sadler Craig, the daughter of slaves, whose family were homesteaders in the "Black Colony" of Nicodemus, Kansas and who moved, in 1915, to the prairies of Colorado, where she lives today, as it documents the reunion of Mrs. Craig's far-flung family, representing five generations of African-Americans, on her 102nd birthday.

H.83. "Mama Benz, An African Market Woman" (48 min). Produced by SFINX FILM/TV, 1994.

Focusing on one woman who presides over a cloth market in Lomé, Togo, this film looks at her role within the markets of Africa, often dominated by strong older women affectionately referred to as Mama Benz, for their trademark prized possession, a chauffeured Mercedes Benz, and who, despite their success, continue to take their accustomed place in the market stalls.

H.84. "River People: Behind the Case of David Sohappy" (50 min). By Michael Conford and Michele Zaccheo, 1991.

This film presents the story of Sohappy, an elder Native-American spiritual leader sentenced to prison for fishing salmon along Oregon's Columbia River out of season; he claims ancestral rights to fish the waters of *Che Wana* and has become a symbol of resistance for indigenous peoples in the Northwest U. S.

H.85. "Silent Pioneers: Gay and Lesbian Elders" (42 min). By Pat Snyder, Lucy Winer, Harvey Marks and Paula deKoenigsberg, in consultation with SAGE (Senior Action in a Gay Environment), 1985.

This film presents the diverse lives and cultural experiences of eight gay and lesbian elders, including a gay couple who have lived together for 55 years; a feminist author/political activist living in an intergenerational community in Florida; a former monk turned rancher who at age 80 has reconciled being gay and Catholic; an African-American great-grandmother who "came out" to her grandchildren; and an ex-waitress from Chicago.

H.86. "And Time Passes in a Flash of Lightning" (55 min). By Pasia Schonberg, 1984.

Four Canadians, ranging in age from 57 to 92, two of whom are mother and daughter, reflect on the life lessons they have learned over the years, their zeal for the challenges of life, and their growing appreciation for the importance of time.

H.87. "Turnabout–Gays in Their Nineties: A Theatrical Memoir" (58 min). Produced by Shire Films (Dan Bessie, Director, Helen Garvy, Editor), 1994.

This is a portrait of three men–Harry Burnett, a world-famous puppeteer, Forman Brown, a composer and lyricist, and Roddy Brandon, manager–who enjoyed a lifetime collaboration in the Turnabout Theater; the two surviving partners reminisce about the theater, and about their life together as gay men in an earlier era (they did not "come out" until their mid-80s).

H.88. "Women of Hodson" (30 min). By Josephine Hayes Dean, 1981.

This film depicts a group of women at the Hodson Senior Center in the South Bronx who create theater pieces from their own life experiences and share them with other elders, inspired by the direction of Susan Pearlstein, founder of Elders Share the Arts (see **G.122-G.124, H.74** and **H.76**).

First Run/Icarus Films
153 Waverly Place, Sixth Floor
New York, NY 10014
(212) 727-1711 (800) 876-1710   Fax (212) 989-7649

H.89. "Howard Finster: Man of Visions" (20 min). By Julie Desroberts, Randy Paskal, & Dave Carr, 1988.

This film explores the unique work of Reverend Finster, of rural Summerville, Georgia, who, after 45 years of preaching, received instruction from God in 1976 to paint spiritual messages; the film explores the psychology of this now-famous folk artist (see also **E.188, E.218**).

H.90. "The Learning Path" (59 min). By Loretta Todd, 1991.

Native Canadian director Todd, a Metis, introduces Edmonton elders Ann Anderson, Eva Cardinal, and Olive Dickason; using documentary footage and re-enactment, she weaves together the life stories of three women who have struggled to preserve and teach traditional culture and language in native schools.

H.91. "South: The Singing Sheikh" (11 min). By Heiny Srour, 1991.

This film presents the music of Sheikh Imam Mohammad Ahmad Eissa, born in 1918, renown for his folk songs indicting the ruling classes in his native Egypt; banned from state television and radio, he has been imprisoned many times for his outspoken lyrics.

H.92. "The Spirit Possession of Alejandro Mamani" (28 min). By Hubert Smith and Norman Miller, 1989.

"In a Bolivian village, one of the village elders discusses his belief that he is possessed by evil spirits that are driving him to his death...His anguish and that of the family point out a common problem with the aging."

H.93. "Uminchu: The Old Man & the East China Sea" (101 min). By John Junkerman, 1991.

This film is a portrait of 82-year-old Shigeru Itokazu, who fishes marlin with a hand-held fishing line and spear; "Itokazu and the residents of tiny Yonakuni island, a volcanic rock near Okinawa, tell stories of their battles with the sea and of their traditional way of life."

H.94. "Your Own True Self" (43 min). By Paul Athanas and Jay Rooney, 1992.

In 1979, David Greenberger an activities director at the Duplex, an all-male nursing home in Jamaica Plain, Massachusetts, started interviewing residents for an in-house magazine, *Duplex Planet* (see **D.127**); this film pushes the folklore envelope a bit as it captures the quirky wit of members of an aging subculture; while not an ethnographic account, or even an oral history, it is an unorthodox record of the expressive behavior of an aging male community.

Flower Films
10341 San Pablo Ave.
El Cerrito, CA 94530
(510) 525-0942   Fax (510) 525-1204

Flower Films is esssentially the production/distribution company for filmmaker Les Blank, who, with Chris Strachwitz of Arhoolie Records, and others, has been documenting the traditional music and culture of the southern U. S. and many other communities.

H.95. "Always for Pleasure" (58 min). 1978.

This film documents neighborhood celebrations of Mardi Gras and other holidays, focusing on African-American parades that pay homage to the Louisiana Indians who harbored escaped slaves; these parades are viewed as rituals of celebration that bind community members, old and young, together.

H.96. "Chulas Fronteras" (58 min). 1976.

This film documents the musical culture of the Texas-Mexican border, and includes such veteran Norteña musicians as Flaco Jimenez, Lydia Mendoza, Narciso Martinez and others old and young who represent the Chicano border culture and experience.

H.97. "Dry Wood" (37 min). 1973.

This film provides a glimpse of black Creole life in French Louisiana, through the music of elder musicians Bois-Sec Ardoin and Canray Fontenot.

H.98. "Hot Pepper" (54 min). 1973.

This is a portrait of Clifton Chenier, the "King of Zydeco," a music combining Cajun and African-American elements, as practiced by Chenier in the dance halls of South Louisiana.

H.99. "In Heaven There Is No Beer?" (50 min). 1984.

The dance, food, music, and religion of Polish-American polka is explored in this look at the community of polka dancers across generations and cultural boundaries.

H.100. "J'ai Été Au Bal (I Went to the Dance)" (84 min). 1989.

The history of the music of Southwest French Louisiana is presented in this film, featuring performances and recollections of Cajun and Zydeco musicians, including Clifton Chenier, D. L. Menard, Canray Fontenot, Amede Ardoin and others.

H.101. "Julie: Old Time Tales of the Blue Ridge" (11 min). 1991.

80-year-old Julie Lyon, sister of old timey fiddler Tommy Jarrell (see **H.102, H.104**) tells tales of her Appalachian childhood in North Carolina and her first romance.

H.102. "My Old Fiddle: A Visit With Tommy Jarrell in the Blue Ridge" (17 min). 1995.

A sequel to "Sprout Wings and Fly" (**H.104**), this film features the folk wisdom and reminiscences of the Appalachian fiddler and raconteur.

H.103. "Puamana" (38 min). 1991.

This film focuses on the life and music of Auntie Irmgard Farden Aluli, one of Hawaii's best loved musicians and composers, shown performing with her nieces in the group Puamana, and telling stories of the musical Farden family.

H.104. "Sprout Wings and Fly" (30 min). 1985.

This is a portrait of Appalachian fiddler and ballad singer Tommy Jarrell, at home and in his community, with scenes of music-making, reminiscing, and storytelling.

H.105. "A Well-Spent Life" (44 min). 1971.

This is a portrait of Mance Lipscomb (1895-1976) the legendary African-American songster from Navasota, Texas, featuring both reminiscences and music from one of the great country blues guitarists (see also **E.39**).

H.106. "Ziveli! Medicine for the Heart" (51 min). 1987.

A portrait of several generations within the Serbian-American communities of Chicago and California, highlighting their history, music, dance and religion.

Light-Saraf Films
264 Arbor Street
San Francisco, CA 94112
(415) 469-0139

The filmmaking team of Allie Light and Irving Saraf deserve special mention for their "Visions of Paradise," a series of films about self-taught older folk artists whose work has been inspired by a variety of spiritual and cultural sources.

H.107. "The Angel That Stands by Me: Minnie Evans' Paintings" (28 min).

Evans, an 88-year-old African-American painter from Wilmington, North Carolina, has created a world of mythical animals, religious symbols, and scenes of nature, inspired by her mystical visions and by the setting of Arlie Garden, where she was a gate keeper for almost 30 years, and where she did most of her painting.

H.108. "Grandma's Bottle Village: The Art of Tressa Prisbrey" (28 min).

Prisbrey, 84, created a series of 15 houses out of glass bottles, the first one built to hold her collection of 17,000 pencils, and others filled with objects rescued from the county dump, arranged in various themes in a compound with mosaic sidewalks.

H.109. "Hundred and Two Mature: The Art of Harry Lieberman" (28 min).

Lieberman, age 102, shares his art and his philosophy of life; the retired businessman is seen meeting with other elders at the Golden Age Club in Great Neck, New York, where he began his career as an artist at age 80, and teaching young students as an "artist in residence" at Fairfax High School in Los Angeles.

H.110. "The Monument of Chief Rolling Mountain Thunder" (28 min).

Chief Thunder, age 71, lives with his young wife and children in the Monument, a concrete and stone house he built in the Nevada desert, inspired by a dream, and which he decorated with forms and arches; he also created sculpture, large and small, depicting Indian heroes, family members and friends

H.111. "Possum Trot: The Life and Work of Calvin Black" (28 min).

Born in Tennessee, Black panned gold in California, and the last 20 years of his life lived with his wife Ruby in an isolated shack in the Mojave desert, where he created over 80 wooden dolls, and built the Bird Cage Theater, where the dolls perform and sing in voices recorded by him.

The National Center for Jewish Film
Brandeis University
Waltham, MA 02254-9110
(617) 899-7044 Fax (617) 736-2070

The Center hosts an archive of films and photographs on Jewish subjects, a research center and a library serving educational institutions, community groups and the public.

H.112. "The Bene Israel: A Family Portrait" (33 min, Marathi with English subtitles). By Karen Nathanson and Jean-Francois Fernandez, 1994.

Documents the Bene Israel community—one of three groups of Jews presently living in India—through the lives of three generations of the Wakrukar family.

H.113. "East Endings" (52 min). By Mark Jay, 1994.

This film documents a commemorative dinner in which a group of old friends get together at Bloom's kosher restaurant in Whitechapel, England to celebrate the 82nd birthday of Harry Blacker, artist, author and satirist, and share memories of the Jewish community in London's East End in the 1930s.

H.114. "Forever Activists!: Stories From the Veterans of the Abraham Lincoln Brigade" (60 min). By Judith Montell, 1991.

At the time of a 1986 reunion of the Abraham Lincoln Brigade, which served in the Spanish Civil War of 1936, Montell filmed and interviewed former members, now in their 70s and 80s, as they retraced their steps on the old battlefields where they fought alongside the defenders of the democratically elected government of the Spanish Republic against Franco's Fascists; the journey is a symbol of their continued commitment to social justice.

H.115. "Free Voice of Labor: The Jewish Anarchists" (60 min). By Steven Fischler and Joel Sucher, 1980.

This films evokes the life of Jewish immigrants who took part in the anarchist movement in the U. S. at the turn of the century, combining archival footage and interviews with elders who recall their lives as members of the Jewish-anarchist subculture, and who describe the sense of dedication to a set of ideals that remains with them as they look back upon a lifetime of activism.

H.116. "The Last Jews of Radauti" (25 min). By Lawrence Saltzman, 1978.

This is a portrait of a small Jewish community in Romania by an American photographer who spent two years there, documenting the everyday activities of the old Jews who still live there.

H.117. "Meet Me in Miami Beach" (18 min). By Bonnie B. Cohen, 1994.

This short documentary is narrated by three elderly Jews in their 90s who have retired to Miami Beach, who share their memories, describe life in the Jewish community there, and the experience of growing old and losing friends; the film also constrasts the life of elderly Jews with the new youth culture in the beach community.

H.118. "Nana: Un Portrait" (23 min, French with English subtitles). By Jamil Simon.

This is a portrait of Louise Zilka, an 80-year-old Jewish woman who reminisces about a life of contrasts; in the midst of a life fleeing persecution in her native Bagdad for havens in Beirut, Cairo, and eventually New York, she also raised seven children, and embraced traditional roles of mother and wife.

H.119. "The Paper Bridge" (95 min, German with English subtitles). By Ruth Beckerman, 1987.

Combining rare footage and oral testimony, this films documents Beckerman's return to the Jewish communities that inspired childhood stories she heard from her parents, from the small towns around Theresienstadt to remnants of communities in Bucovnia, Romania and finally Vienna, where her parents met after the Holocaust; along the way she interviews surviving residents about Jewish life before the war.

New Day Films
22-D Hollywood Avenue
Hohokus, NJ 07423
(201) 652-6590   Fax (201) 652-1973

New Day Films is a cooperative of independent producers of films that, in their own words, have "challenged the status quo."

H.120. "Breaking Silence: The Story of the Sisters at Desales Heights" (58 min). By Susan Pointon and Tommie Dell Smith, 1994.

This film portrays the lives of twelve elderly nuns inside the cloistered walls of the 150-year-old monastery, as they prepare, for the first time in their adult lives, to face the world outside; it addresses the changing role of women and the fate of those whose roles are no longer valued.

H.121. "The Double Burden: Three Generations of Working Women" (56 min). By Marlene Booth, 1992.

Booth documents the lives of three families–Mexican-American, Polish-American and African-American–each with three generations of women who have worked outside of the home, while also raising families.

H.122. "Hopi: Songs of the Fourth World" (58 min). By Pat Ferrero, 1983.

Amidst images of the land and life of the Hopi Indians, several membes of the Hopi community–a farmer, religious elder, grandmother, painter, potter and weaver–speak about the preservation of of traditional ways.

H.123. "Kicking High...In the Golden Years" (58 min). By Grania Gurievitch, 1986.

Integrated with scenes of six older African-American women preparing for a performance at a senior center in Queens, New York, are the reflections of these elders on their families, work experience, and other activities past and present, homes, recorded at home and in their communities.

H.124. "Murray Avenue" (28 min). By Sheila Chamovitz, 1984.

This is a portrait of life along Murray Avenue, which runs through the heart of Squirrel Hill, an old Jewish neighborhood in Pittsburgh; the film focuses on the tradespeople, many of whom are older European-born Jews who arrived there after World War Two, and who are about to retire.

H.125. "Quilts in Women's Lives" (28 min). By Pat Ferrero, 1981.

Traditional quiltmakers, most of them older women, talk about their lives and share their art, among them a California Mennonite, an African-American in Mississippi, and a Bulgarian immigrant.

H.126. "Seeing Red" (100 min). By Jim Klein and Julia Reichert, 1983.

Several elders, former members of the American Communist Party, share memories of their personal and political lives in the 1930s through the '50s, not only talking about the positive and negative aspects of their life in the Party, but also revealing the ways in which they recall a community and a culture of commitment that continues to define their present outlook and identity.

H.127. "Small Happiness: Women of a Chinese Village" (58 min). By Carma Hinton and Richard Gordon, 1984.

This documentary looks at life in the village of Long Bow, where young and old women discuss their lives, and the changes that have occurred in the ways in which women are viewed and treated in rural Chinese society.

H.128. "Summer at the Loucheux" (27 min). By Graydon McCrea and Linda Rasmussen, 1983.

An intergenerational portrait, this film documents the yearly July visit of Alestine Andre, a young contemporary Loucheux woman, to her family's summer fishing camp in the Pacific Northwest, as Andre listens to the stories of her grandmother, contributing to her understanding of her culture and herself, and instructs her niece in the language of this Native American community.

H.129. "Union Maids"(45 min). By Julia Reichert, Jim Klein, and Miles Mogulescu, 1976.

Three women recall their lives as activists in the U. S. Labor Movement in the 1930s; on one level it is about sitdowns, scabs, goon squads, unemployment, hunger strikes, and the birth of the Congress of Industrial Organizations (CIO); on another level it is a study of how these elders continue to draw, through their memories, from the spirit and sense of community of the subculture of the labor movement.

H.130. "With Babies and Banners" (45 min). By Lorraine Gray, 1978.

Forty years after the historic sitdown strike at the General Motors plant in Flint, Michigan, in 1937, nine women recall the ways in which, as working women, wives, mothers and sisters, they became the backbone of the strike through their support efforts; again, as in "Union Maids" (**H.129**), the viewer witnesses living history, as well as the present sense of identification with the subculture of the labor movement through these elders' memories of community, network-building and solidarity.

H.131. "Yudie" (20 min). By Mirra Bank, 1974.

This is a portrait of the filmmaker's great aunt Yudie, Eastern European Jewish immigrant, and longtime resident of New York City's Lower East Side; she talks about the immigrant experience, her life in an old (now former) Jewish neighborhood, her sense of independence, and the process of aging.

Northeast Historic Film
P. O. Box 900
Bucksport, ME 04416
(800) 639-1636   Fax (207) 469-7875

Principally an archive with millions of feet of regional footage (Maine, New Hampshire and Vermont), it also publishes a catalogue of archival film collections, and distributes videotapes, ranging from features to documentaries and student works on New England subjects.

H.132. "Around Cape Horn" (37 min). Produced by the Mystic Seaport Museum, 1980 [1929].

Presents scenes Captain Irving Johnson photographed aboard the bark *Peking* in 1929, described by him in 1980.

H.133. "Ben's Mill" (60 min). By Michel Chalfour and John Karol, 1981.

A portrait of Ben Thresher, who runs a water-powered mill in Barnet, Vermont, and who puts a wide range of hand tools and recycled material to such purposes as fixing hoe handles, making a horse-drawn sled, and constructing a wooden tub for watering cattle.

H.134. "Dead River Rough Cut" (55 min). By Richard Searls and Stuart Silverstein, 1976.

Presents the lives and philoshophies of two elder Maine woodsmen-trappers.

H.135. "Hap Collins of South Blue Hill, Maine: Lobsterman, Craftsman, Painter, Fiddler, Poet" (56 min). By Jeff Todd Titon, 1989.

Titon' s oral history interview with Collins, multifaceted Maine elder, along with field footage.

H.136. "An Oral Historian's Work" (30 min). By Edward Ives, 1987 [A project of Northeast Archives of Folklore and Oral History].

Professor Ives, founder of the Maine Folklife Center, demonstrates, through a series of interviews with woodsmen and river drivers, the techniques he has refined in 30 years of work in the field (see also **A.25)**.

H.137. "Our Lives in Our Hands" (50 min). By Karen Carter, Harald Prins, Bunny McBride and Bruce Jehle, 1986.

A documentary on the life of the Micmac Indians in northern Maine, with a focus on the traditional craft of woodsplint basketry, featuring elder basketmakers (see **E.104**).

H.138. "Portrait of George Hardy, the Deer Isle Folk Artist" (30 min). By Gabriel Coakley, 1995.

Hardy, a retired mason who began carving lifelike birds and whimsical animals when he was 60, "talks about art, life Downeast, the loss of his wife, and loneliness."

H.139. "Woodsmen and River Drivers: 'Another Day, Another Era'" (30 min). By Edward Ives, 1989 [A project of Northeast Archives of Folklore and Oral History].

Individuals who worked for the Machias Lumber Company before 1930, share their memories of the lumber camps, log jams, and other aspects of the woodsman's life.

PBS Video
1320 Braddock Place
Alexandria, VA 22314-1698
(800) 344-3337

"American Patchwork: Stories and Songs About America" (60 min. each). Produced by Cultural Equity, 1991.

This series, hosted by Alan Lomax, explores the cultural diversity of the United States through song, dance, story and festival. Four of the five titles feature traditional artists young and old; one focuses exclusively on older musicians.

H.140. "Appalachian Journey": Looks at the regional traditions of the Smokey Mountains.

H.141. "Cajun Country: Don't Drop the Potato": Traces the history of the French-speaking Louisianans and looks at storytelling, Cajun and Zydeco music.

H.142. "Dreams and Songs of the Noble Old": Veteran folk music scholar and collector Alan Lomax revisits the Southern United States and talks with several older musicians who represent the traditions of the region in which he began his fieldwork in the 1930s and '40s.

H.143. "Jazz Parades: Feet Don't Fail Me Now": Explores New Orleans neighborhood dances and celebrations of Mardi Gras.

H.144. "The Land Where Blues Began": Explores the Mississippi Delta region and the social, cultural and emotional background of the blues.

H.145. "Ballad of a Mountain Man: The Story of Bascom Lamar Lunsford" (58 min). By Donn Rogosin, Sherry Abaldo, and Gary Steele, 1990 [1989].

Traces the background of one of the elder statespersons of Anglo-American folksong, who worked to preserve the music and dance of Appalachia, and staged one of the first folk music festivals.

"The Coming of Age" (30-60 min). Produced by Wisconsin Public Television, 1993.

While this series, which, attempts to confront and transcend the stereotypes of aging in the U. S., doesn't really address folklore and aging per se, three titles contain some relevant moments.

H.146. "Celebrating the American Family": Through photographs, diaries, letters and oral history, this program reviews the history of family life in the U. S.

H.147. "Creativity and Aging": This film explores creative learning experiences of elders, including Elderhostel programs [which include many courses and activities related to folklore and folklife] and recreational activities.

H.148. "Generations Together" (30 min): An exploration of the role older adults play as contributing members of a changing society; among those featured is Edward Barber, a Native American tribal judge still serving his community at age 75.

H.149. "Good Morning Blues" (59 min). Produced by Mississippi Authority for Educational Television 1988 [1978].

A survey of the development of Mississippi Delta blues, it features performances by several elder statespeople of the genre, including Son House, Bukka White, Big Joe Williams, and Furry Lewis.

H.150. "In the White Man's Image" (60 min). By Christine Lesiak and Matthew Jones, 1991.

Carlisle School for Indians, which operated from 1870 into the 1930s, tried to "civilize" Native Americans by suppressing all expression of Native traditions; this film features the recollections of Native elders who attended the School, which operated from 1870 into the 1930s.

H.151. "The Pueblo Peoples: First Contact" (30 min). Produced by KNME, Albuquerque, New Mexico and the Institute of American Indian Arts, 1990.

This program is an attempt to present the Pueblo people's views of the first encounters with Europeans, told exclusively through their voices; it features the views of religious elder Mecalita Wystalucy, member of the Zuni tribe.

H.152. "Seasons of A Navajo" (60 min). Produced by KAET, 1985.

Documents the lives of Chauncey and Dorothy Neboyia, who subsist in Arizona's Monument Valley with farming, weaving and tending sheep, and live in a traditional hogan without water or electricity, while their children live in tract homes, and their grandchildren attend modern public schools.

H.153. "Surviving Columbus" (120 min). Produced by KNME, Albuquerque, New Mexico and the Institute of American Indian Arts, 1992.

This film uses stories of Pueblo elders, as well as interviews with Pueblo scholars, archival photographs and historical accounts to chart the struggle of New Mexico Pueblo Indians to survive the legacy of "discovery" and control their own lives.

Terra Nova Films
9848 S. Winchester Ave.
Chicago, IL 60655
(312) 881-8491 (800) 779-8491   Fax (312) 881-3368

Terra Nova distributes a select list of films on a variety of social issues, with a special focus on aging.

H.154.. "Aging in Rural America." Produced by the Ohio University Telecommunications Center, 1985.

Presents the views of seven older adults who have grown up in farming communities, and who are seen in their homes, shops, and gardens, and on their farms; they talk about lifestyles, community, neighbors and the experience of aging.

H.155. "Cottonman" (30 min). By Ralph Braseth, 1992.

A portrait of Floyd Holman, 78, an African-American farmer who raises cotton in Abbeville, Mississippi, one of the few who still pick cotton by hand; he discusses his philosophy of life, and his views on marriage, children, hard work and neighbors.

"Harvest of Age." Produced by Spindlekin/Patische Productions, 1995.

A series of three films exploring the life and role of elders in Native American, Italian and Doukhabor communities in British Columbia.

H.156. "My Memories Are Here—Italian Elders" (27 min): Italian elders in Trail, B. C., recall weddings, music and pastimes and discuss what it is like to grow old.

H.157. "Pulling Together—Community Doukhabor Elders" (29 min): Community Doukhabor elders from British Columbia's Kootenay Valley talk about their lives within the context of the sect's continual search for peace and harmony.

H.158. "Something Left to Do—Elders of Sto:Lo Nation" (24 min): "Three Native American Sto:Lo elders reflect on life and death and demonstrate through dance, prayer and preserving ancient sites how they fulfill their obligations as Indian elders to preserve the culture and link the generations."

H.159. "Legacy: America's Indian Elders" (29 min). Produced by Philomath Films for the National Indian Council on the Aging, 1994.

Elders from several tribes, including Navajo, Sioux and Tohono O'odham speak about the federal government's string of broken promises and the devastating effects on traditional Native American communities, particularly upon the native elderly.

H.160. "Luther Metke at 94" (27 min). By Jorge Pareloran and Steven Raymen. 1979.

This study of the psychology of aging is a portrait of Metke, a resident of Oregon's Cascade Mountains since 1907, veteran of the Spanish American war, and an early labor organizer, who began building log houses in his 70s and writing poetry in his 80s, and continues to live an independent life in a rural setting.

H.161. "The Queen of Falcon" (18 min). By Ralph Braseth, 1991.

This film explores the town of Falcon, Mississippi, and its popular elder resident, Mabel Ross, 88, a local teacher, and newspaper columnist for many years who in her "retirement" runs the local post office.

H.162. "A Source of Strength: Jewish Identity in Later Life" (30 min). By Jack Saul and Phil Lee [produced by Mirror Productions], 1985.

This film focuses on the role that ethnic heritage plays in reinforcing identity among Jewish elders.

University of California Extension
Center for Media and Independent Learning
2000 Center Street, Fourth Floor
Berkeley, CA 94704
(510) 642-0460 Fax (510) 643-9271

The Center both sells and rents films and videos of independent filmmakers on a variety of subjects, with strong representation in North American ethnic studies and world cultures.

H.163. "American Chinatown" (30 min). By Todd Carrel, 1982.

Documents the plight of the mostly elderly residents of the small northern California town of Locke, site of the last rural Chinese community (see **D.278**).

H.164. "The Ballad and the Source" (16 min). By John Cohen, 1983.

This is a musical portrait of English folk singer Walter Pardon, who carries on an old tradition in Great Britain of unaccompanied ballad singing.

H.165. "Boneshop of the Heart: Folk Offerings from the American South" (53 min). By Scott Crocker and Toshiaki Ozawa, 1991.

Features interviews with several southern folk artists, including elders Vollis Simpson, Thornton Dial, Sr., and Bessie Harvey.

H.166. "Clementine Hunter, American Folk Artist" (28 min). By Katina Simmons and Christine Patoski, 1993.

Filmed in conjunction with a retrospective exhibition organized by the Museum of African-American Life and Culture, this is a portrait of Hunter (1887-1988), of Natchitoches, Louisiana, who began, in her 50s, to paint scenes from her memories of life on the Melrose Plantation at the turn of the century (see **E.220**).

H.167. "The End of an Old Song" (27 min). By John Cohen, 1972.

Filmed in the mountains of North Carolina, this film revisits the region where English folklorist Cecil Sharpe collected British ballads in the early 1900s; features an interview with balladeer Dillard Chandler.

H.168. "Gypsies Sing Long Ballads" (29 min). By John Cohen, 1982.

This film celebrates the song tradition of Scotland's "Traveling People," and feautures older Gypsies singing unaccompanied British ballads.

H.169. "Haa Shagoon" (29 min). By Joe Kawaky, 1983.

Documents a day of Tlingit Indian ceremony in Alaska, higlighted by a sacred peace ritual performed by elders and others as a cultural event and an appeal for justice in their struggle against the exploitation of their lands and water.

H.170. "High Lonesome Sound" (30 min). By John Cohen, 1963.

Portrays the music of religious worshippers, miners and farmers as an integral part of life for mountain people in eastern Kentucky; includes such elder musicians as banjo player and singer Roscoe Holcomb.

H.171. "Ki Ho'alu: That's Slack Key Guitar" (57 min). By Susan Friedman, 1994.

A portrait of the famed slack key master, Raymond Kane; the film interweaves musical segments with stories told by numerous artists who describe the beauty of the music and the wider problems of cultural transformation.

H.172. "Medicine Fiddle" (81 min). By Michael Loukinen, 1992.

Depicts the Native and Mètis fiddling and dancing traditons on both sides of the U. S. and Canadian border, and features Ojibwa, Menominee, Mètis, and Ottawa fiddlers and dancers, including several elders.

"Pomo Basketweavers: A Tribute to Three Elders" (29 min each). By David Ludwig, 1994.

This is a series of documentaries on the baskets of the Pomo Indians of northern California, each one dedicated to an elder craftsperson.

H.173. "The People, the Baskets": An overview of Pomo culture, featuring the work of basketweaver Laura Somersal (1892-1990).

H.174. "A History of Change, a Continuing Tradition": A history of the Pomo, exploring changes in the art of Pomo basketweaving, featuring a biographical tribute to Elsie Allen (1899-1990), one of the most revered Pomo basketmakers (see **E.97**).

H.175. "The People, the Plants, and the Rules": Explores the close relationship of the Pomo to their environment, and the spiritual responsibilities to the natural world, and features a tribute to Mabel McKay, a dream weaver, healer, and basketmaker (see **D.386**).

H.176. "Sucking Doctor" (45 min). By William Heick, 1964.

Documents a curing ceremony among the Kahia group of Southwestern Pomo Indians, led by Essie Parrish, a shaman and spiritual leader.

H.177. "This World is not Our Home" (13 min). By Kim Johnson, 1994.

Introduction to the history, culture and traditions of the northern California Pomo Indians, seen through the eyes of tribal elder Elvina Brown.

H.178. "When I Was Fourteen: A Survivor Remembers" (57 min). By Marlene Booth and James Goldner, 1995.

Gloria Hollander Lyon, a Czech Jew now living in San Francisco, recalls being sent to Auschwitz with her family at age 14, surviving six other camps, rescued by the Swedish Red Cross and "restored to life" by a Swedish family before emigrating in 1947; she reunites with her Swedish "family" and celebrates life and her survival.

Vermont Folklife Center
P. O. Box 442
Middlebury, VT 05753
(802) 388-4964

The Vermont Folklife Center "documents and interprets the cultural traditions and living history of Vermont and the surrounding region"; they also distribute a selected list of publications and films.

H.179. "Educated Hands: Newt Washburn, A Life With Baskets" (12 min).

Washburn, a National Heritage Award recipient, practices an art that began in his family with his German immigrant grandfather, who married an Abenaki basket maker in Canada; he describes the process of making baskets and introduces his granddaughter Leah, who is carrying on the family tradition.

H.180. "On My Own: The Traditions of Daisy Turner" (28 min). By Jane Beck. Montpelier: Vermont Folklife Center and the University of Vermont, 1986.

Turner, a 102-year-old African-American woman, shares her personal reminiscences and the oral traditions of a family whose rural life in Vermont, and living memory of slavery, is recounted in stories, some of which she heard in her youth.

H.181. "Things That Move" (9 min).

Homer Miller of North Wolcott, Vermont, creator of windmills, birdhouses, swings and other works from recycled material, describes his creative process within the context of a long life spent on a Vermont farm.

H.182. "Vermont Folk Artists" (21 min)

Six Vermont folk artists provide personal insights about their work: a basketmaker, three folk painters, a quilter and a woodcarver.

OTHER FILMS (LISTED BY SUBJECT)

Folklife—General

H.183. "The Bear Stands Up" (29 min). By Ward Serrill, 1994. [distributed by director (PO Box 9318, Ketchikau, AK 99901)].

Portrait of Alaska Native Esther Shea, an elder of the Tongass Bear Clan.

H.183.a. "Bless Me With a Good Life" (29 min). By Hank Rogerson and Jilann Spitzmiller. Los Angeles: Philomath Films, 1994.

Portrait of American Indian elders and their struggle with poverty.

H.184. "Celebrate" (10 min). Madison, Wisconsin: Bi-Folkal Productions, 1982.

"A look at how birthdays are celebrated around the world and at our own birthday traditions," this is part of a "Bi-Folkal Kit" called "Remembering Birthdays," one of several multisensory packages produced by Bi-Folkal Productions (1-800-568-5357) to encourage reminiscence among elders (see also **H.203**).

H.184.a. "Crow Dog's Paradise" (28 min, 16mm). By James Hoagland and Mark Elliott. Boulder, Colorado: Centre Productions, 1979.

This film is a portrait of medicine man Henry Crow Dog, born in 1899, and living on the Rosebud Sioux Reservation in South Dakota, who describes the centrality of ritual and performs several, including one for the release of his son, Leonard Crow Dog, a member of the American Indian Movement (AIM) who was arrested during the occupation of Wounded Knee in 1973.

H.185. "The Face of Wisdom: Stories of Elder Women" (8 videocassettes, 28 min each). New York: Phoenix Films, 1994. [v.1] Aurora Pacheco [v.2] Betty Kozasa [v.3] Barbara Mettler [v.4] Francis O'Brien [v.5] Glenora Sayers [v.6] Leontine Kelly [v.7] Nellie Red Owl [v.8] Rose Lucey.

These films present stories from the lives of eight culturally diverse women, each in their 70s or 80s, who are resources for wisdom and understanding in grappling with the challenges of contemporary society.

H.185.a. "Finnish American Lives" (45 min, 16mm). By Michael Loukinen, Tom Davenport, Kathleen Laughlin, and Deborah Dickson. Up North Films, 1982.

Documents three generations of a Finnish-American farm family in the Upper Peninsula of Michigan, headed by 92-year-old patriarch Erikki Vourenmaa, born in Finland in 1888, and who emigrated at age 22.

H.186. "Going Home, a Grandmother's Story" (26 min). By Joan Weibel-Orlando and Thomas Fleming. Los Angeles: University of Southern California, Department of Anthropology, 1986.

This film documents the process by which an Oglala Sioux grandmother reenters her ancestral community after 26 years in Los Angeles; it addresses adaptation, cultural continuity and creative role management in old age.

H.186.a. "Her Mother Before Her" (22 min). Jocelyn Riley. Madison, Wisconsin: Jocelyn Riley Productions, 1992.

> Six Winnebago women, Ruth Cloud, Rebecca Greendeer, Karen Martin, Naomi Russell, Arvina Lowe Thayer, and Irene Thundercloud, tell stories of their mothers and grandmothers.

H.187. "Irene Goodnight: A Film" (24 min, 16 mm). By John Echeverria and Benjamin Miller, 1975. [N. p.] Filmtech.

> "A documentary which follows an aging Iowa farmer through a cold January day as he does his daily round of chores and struggles to get enough wood to keep the furnace going; he watches the farm he has built slowly collapsing and finds the past within his movements in the present."

H.187.a. "Joe Albert's Fox Hunt...and Other Stories from the Pine Barrens of New Jersey" (58 min). By Julie Gustafson and John Reilly, with Karen Mooney. New York: Global Village, 1980.

> This is both a portrait of 81-year-old Albert, who tells stories about his participation in working-class fox hunts in the Pines, and who is seen playing gut-bucket base in in an old-timey band called the Pineconers, and a documentary about traditional land use (see **D.213**).

H.188. "Ka Leo o na Kupuna, Inc." (27 min). Honolulu: Alu Like Oahu Island Productions, 1986.

> Kupuna Lilia Hale, Helen Ching, Ahnes Wright, Albert Like, Cecilia and Abel Kaiahua, Harry Kuukahi, Mae Kaleo and Thelma Field discuss their outlook and work as members of Ka Leo o na Kupuna, a group of Hawaiian elders dedicated to the preservation of the Hawaiian language.

H.188.a. "The Krugers, Texas Immigrants" (28 min). By Sandra Mintz, Larry Cormier, and John Boutin. San Antonio: University of Texas Institute of Texan Cultures, 1980.

> In a series of interviews, Bert Kruge Smith, born in 1915, tells of the immigration and lives of her Russian Jewish parents who moved to Wichita Falls, Texas, illustrating the impact of ethnicity on her life and those of other Texans.

H.189. "Last Stand Farmer" (25 min). By Richard Brick. Silo Cinema, 1975.

> This documentary records, through four seasons, the life and philosophy of a 67-year-old Vermont hill farmer and his wife as they struggle to keep their farm going, using only nonmechanized 19th century farming techniques.

H.189.a. "Louie" (28 min). By Donald Schwartz, Jennifer Woolcock, Nancy Schreiber, and Barry Harfenes. Washington, D. C.: Public Television Library, 1979.

> "A portrait of 80-year-old shopkeeper Louis Gzinterman, a strong-willed, independent individual with a desire to help others; shows how his age has not limited him or his vision of life."

H.190. "Luisa Torres" (43 min, 16mm). By Jack Parsons and Michael Earney. Boulder, Colorado: Centre Productions 1981.

> Documentary about an elderly Hispanic woman living in northern New Mexico "whose simple life has kept her in touch with the earth and the traditions of her

ancestors and has brought her contentment, dignity and wisdom." [sponsored by the Anthropology Film Center Foundation, with funds from the New Mexico Arts Division and the National Endowment for the Arts].

H 191. "Miles of Smiles, Years of Struggle: The Untold Story of the Black Pullman Porter" (59 min). By Jack Santino and Paul Wagner. Briarcliff Manor, New York: Benchmark Films, 1982.

Retired African-American Pullman porters look back at the occupational culture of Black porters, relations with white passengers, and the formation of their own union, the Brotherhood of Pullman Porters (see D.179).

H.192. "The Miracle of Intervale Avenue" (65 min). Teaneck, New Jersey: Ergo Media, 1987.

This film documents the lives of a small community of elderly Jews who continue to live and work in a once predominantly Jewish neighborhood in the South Bronx that is now inhabited by poor African-American and Hispanic people (see D.305).

H.193. "Miss Nora's Store" (28 min). Baltimore: University of Maryland at Baltimore, 1989.

This film presents life experiences of individuals 65 to 97 who demonstrate the strength of character, desire for independence and deep-rooted memories of rural elders; it also discusses geographical, psychosocial and cultural barriers to health and social services for the rural aging.

H.194. "Native American Culture: Respecting Our Elders" (30 min). By Jan Kraepelian. Arcata, California: Humbolt State University, 1991.

Native American community members and an HSU professor discuss the role of elders in Native American culture; features interviews with Native Americans and a Japanese-American who offers a cross-cultural perspective.

H.195. "Number Our Days" (29 min). By Lynne Littman and Barbara Myerhoff. Los Angeles: Direct Cinema, 1983 [1977].

Anthropologist Myerhoff documents the lives of elderly Jews whose social lives revolve around the activities of the Israel Levin Senior Adult Center in Venice, California; her comments are interspersed with interviews with elders and scenes of activities at the Center (see D.307).

H.196. "Off My Rocker" (29 min). By Daniel Boyd. Williamson, West Virginia: Opequon Productions, 1981.

This film features 78-year-old Clara Cassify of Harper's Ferry, West Virginia, who shares her outlook on life and aging.

H.197. "Pueblo of Laguna: Elders of the Tribe" (14 min). Washington, D. C.: Department of Health and Human Services, 1981.

Documents a culturally sensitive model project for the delivery of comprehensive services to Native American elders at Laguna, New Mexico, including transportation, housing, nutrition, health, recreation and community involvement (see also G.18).

H.198. "Rocking Horse Cowboy" (24 min, 16mm). By Carl Jones. Chicago: Encyclopedia Britannica Educational Corp., 1976.

"The true story of a modern day cowboy facing the problems of old age."

H.199. "Steady as She Goes" (27 min, 16 mm). National Film Board of Canada, 1982.

This film documents the work of George Fulfit, who in his retirement has perfected the art of building model ships in bottles.

H.200. "Tradition Bearers" (47 min, 16 mm). By Michael Loukinen, Kathleen Laughlin and Mirek Janek. Marquette: Northern Michagn University, 1983.

Blending oral accounts with historical photos, this film presents the lives and works of four Finnish-American traditional artists, including a 97-year-old immigrant woodworker, a 90-year-old immigrant storyteller, another storyteller born in the U. S., and a lumberjack/musician.

H.201. "Undermining the Depression" (25 min). By Jim Likowski and Bonnie Thompson. Eugene, Oregon: Rainlight Films, n.d.

Older residents of Jacksonville, a hamlet in the Bear Creek Valley in southern Oregon, where gold was discovered in 1851, recall how backyard gold mining helped them to survive the Great Depression; their stories are presented along with historical photographs and diagrams.

H.202. "Valley of the Old Ones" (26 min). Paramus, New Jersey: Time-Life Films, 1975.

Looks at the history, present conditions an prospects of the people of Vilcabamba, Ecuador, many of whom are over 100 years of age.

H.203. "Voices From the Depression" (29 min). Madison, Wisconsin: Bi-Folkal Productions, 1978.

Folksongs and stories describe the experience of the Depression, from the dust-bowl farms to union struggles; part of a multisensory kit produced by Bi-Folkal Productions to encourage reminiscence among elders (see **H.175**).

Traditional Music

African-American

H.204. "Alberta Hunter: Blues at the Cookery" (45 min, 16mm). New York: Teleculture, 1982.

At age 87, Hunter still performed at the Cookery in New York City; she reminisces between sets about her life as a blues singer with such musicians as Louis Armstrong, Fats Waller and Sidney Bechet; later working as a hospital nurse for 20 years before returning to her singing career at 82.

H.205. "Banjo Man" (26 min, 16mm). Narrated by Taj Mahal. Texture Films, 1978.

"Presents the life and music of 80-year-old John 'Uncle' Homer Walker, a native of Summers County, West Virginia, who has been playing the banjo for 60 years."

H.206. "Deep Blues" (90 min). By Robert Mugge, Eileen Gregory, John Stewart, Robert Palmer and Erich Roland. San Rafael, California: Tara Releasing Film, 1992.

A tribute to the Mississippi blues and various blues artists, with performances by elder blues performers Booker T. Loury, R. L. Burnside, Jack Owens and others.

H.207. "Ella Jenkins for the Family" (28 min). Produced by Smithsonian/Folkways, 1992 [1990]. (Distributed by Rounder Records, Cambridge, MA).

A concert by Jenkins, singer of African-American spirituals and children's songs from the sea island community of St. Simon, South Carolina, recorded in Chicago in 1990.

H.208. "The Facts of Life" (28 min). Evanston, Illinois: Beacon Films, 1982.

Features the life and work of blues musician Willie Dixon, born in 1915, who wrote over 700 blues songs; he is shown at home, in his recording studio and in performance.

H.209. "John Jackson: An American Songster" (29 min). By Andrianna and Robert Duerr, Ambrogio and Tito Tonelli, Kate Edwards and Susan Brady. N.p.: Rhapsody Films, 1986.

This film is a portrait of Jackson, an African-American singer and guitarist from Virginia, born in 1924; and whose repertoire includes blues and Anglo-American folksongs.

H.210. "Libba Cotten: An Interview and Presentation Ceremony" (48 min). Produced by the Schomberg Center for Research in Black Culture, New York Public Library, 1985.

Taped at the Schomberg Center, Cotten talks about her life, her career as a singer/songwriter, and performs two of her songs, including her signature "Freight Train."

H.211. "Maxwell Street Blues" (56 min). By Linda Williams, Raul Zaritsky, and Sandra Lieb. Chicago: Facets Multimedia, 1987 [1983].

This film presents a portrait of the fabled Chicago neighborhood where blues has long been, and continues to be, performed on the street corners; features historical background and present-day stories of some of the veterans of Maxwell Street.

H.212. "Sam Chatmon: Sitting on Top of the World" (29 min). Jacksonville: Mississippi Educational Television, 1983.

This film pays tribute to Chatmon, one of the elder statespeople of Mississippi Delta blues and former member of the Mississippi Sheiks; he is shown at his home in Hollandale, Mississippi, and performing in Washington, D. C.

H.213. "Sippie Wallace, Blues Singer and Song Writer" (23 min). By Roberta Grossman and Michelle Paymer. New York: Rhapsody Films, 1986.

A film portrait of Beulah "Sippie" Wallace, 83-year-old blues singer and song writer, featuring conversations with Wallace, concert footage, and historic recordings and photographs.

H.214. "Step it Up and Go: Blues in the Carolinas" (59 min). By Bob Royster, Michael Oniffrey, Jeff Anderson and Glenn Hinson. Chapel Hill: University of North Carolina Center for Public Television, 1989.

Traces the development of blues in the Carolinas through interviews with veteran blues musicians and still photographs.

H.215. "Willa Mae Buckner, Snake Lady/Black Gyspy" (25 min). By Gaile Welker. Greensboro, North Carolina: Lookin' for the Blues Productions, 1994.

A portrait of Buckner, born in Augusta, Georgia, in 1922, who left home at 14, joined a minstrel show, and went on to a career as belly dancer, gospel and calypso singer, and tap dancer, and in 1964 created her own snake dance show and accompanied a number of circuses in the U. S.

H.216. "Yank Rachel, Tennessee Tornado" (28 min). By Jay Zoxhowski and Michael Atwood. Indianapolis: WFYI-TV, 1989.

This film discusses the life and music of blues musician James "Yank" Rachel, and features him and friends talking and performing.

H.217. "Yonder Come Day" (26 min). By Milton Fruchtman and Werner Bundschuh. Carlsbad, California: CRM Films, 1993 [1975.]

Bessie Jones, born in Dawson, Georgia 1902, and founding member of the Georgia Sea Island Singers, talks, at age 72, about the legacy of African-American slave songs, music and games, and her efforts to pass along her heritage to new generations, including students at Yale, who go into a local neighborhood to share with young schoolchildren what they have just learned from Jones (see **E.45**, **E.46**).

Anglo- and Other European-American

H.218. "Adirondack Minstrel" (19 min). By Jack Ofield and Richard Francis. Bowling Green Films, 1976.

Lawrence Older, a traditional singer, guitarist and fiddler from Upstate New York, performs and talks about his music, relating it to his logging experience.

H.219. "Alfred Bailey, Fleming County" (120 min). Morehead, Kentucky: Appalachian Development Center, Morehead State University, 1985.

An interview with, and performance by, old-time fiddler Bailey, born in 1918 (part of the series "Vintage Fiddlers of Eastern Kentucky" [see **H.221**, **H.223**])

H.220. "Almeda Riddle: 'Now Let's Talk About Singing'" (29 min). By George West, Cary Pollock, Willie Allen, Dave Parker and Paul Wagner. Little Rock, Arkansas: Talking Traditions, 1986.

This is a portrait of the traditional Ozark folk singer and her repertoire of Anglo-American ballads (see **E.54**).

H.221. "Clyde Davenport, Wayne County" (120 min). Morehead, Kentucky: Appalachian Development Center, Morehead State University, 1985.

An interview with, and performance by, old-time fiddler Davenport, born in 1921 (part of the series "Vintage Fiddlers of Eastern Kentucky" [see **H.219**, **H.223**])

H.222. "Frank Warner" (53 min). New York: Clearwater Publishing, 1985 [1965].

Warner sings songs of the Adirondack Mountains. [This is part of a series of public television programs, "The Rainbow Quest," hosted by Pete Seeger in the 1960s.]

H.223. "Hiram Stamper, Knott County" (120 min). Morehead, Kentucky: Appalachian Development Center, Morehead State University, 1985.

An interview with, and performance by, old-time fiddler Stamper, born in 1892 (part of the series "Vintage Fiddlers of Eastern Kentucky" [see **H.219, H.221**])

H.224. "A Kingdom of Fiddlers: The Story of Old Time Music Traditions in the Rural Community" (18 min). By Phil Martin and Lewis Koch, 1991 [1983].

Presents folk music and dance in Wisconsin and the upper Midwest, relating it to community life, and discusses the role of elder musicians as tradition bearers.

H.225. "A Life of Song: A Portrait of Ruth Rubin, Yiddish Folksinger and Folklorist" (38 min). By Cindy Marshall. Somerville, Massachusetts: Cindy Marshall Productions, 1987.

This film shows the collector, performer and Yiddish folklorist Rubin in performance and working to revive the Yiddish language and the culture of which it was a part.

H.226. "Music in the Old Time Way: An Exploration of Traditional Music from the Southern Appalachian Mountains" (60 min). By Philip S. Morgan. Seattle: Moving Image Productions, 1986.

Filmed in Virginia and North Carolina in 1985, this is a survey of traditional Appalachian Old Time dance music, tracing its history, and presenting performances by some of its tradition bearers.

H.227. "The Old Time Music Maker, Melvin Wine" (27 min). By Robert Boles. Glen Arbor, Michigan: Communicraft Productions, 1993.

This film examines the life and music of Wine, master fiddler, teacher and National Heritage Award winner from West Virginia.

H.228. "A Singer of Tales" (10 min). By Richard March and Richard Viduti. Bloomington: Indiana University Archives of Traditional Music, 1980.

A retired steel worker sings Yugoslavian epic songs in his home, accompanying himself on the guslar, while a couple of neighbors listen; he is interviewed about how he learned to sing, the content of the songs, and about his instrument.

H.229. "Texas Style" (28 min). By Bruce Lane. Santa Fe, New Mexico: Onewest Media, 1986.

Features three generations of champion fiddlers from the Westmoreland family, and traces the ancestry of Texas-style fiddling from its Appalachian roots to the present.

H.230. "The Weavers: Wasn't That a Time" (78 min). By Jim Brown, Daniel Ducovny, Tom Hurvitz, and Paul Barnes. New York: MGM/UA Home Video, 1983.

Documents the 1980 reunion of the Weavers (Pete Seeger, Lee Hays, Ronnie Gilbert and Fred Hellerman) for a concert in Carnegie Hall, and includes reminiscences of these elder statespeople of the folk revival and left movement in the U. S.

Asian-American

H.231. "Singing to Remember" (17 min). By Robert Lee, Tony Heriza and Jean Tsien. New York: Asian American Arts Centre, 1992.

> Portrait of Ng Sheung-Chi, a storytelling folksinger born in 1910 in a small Chinese village in Taishan County, now living in New York City, who performs the Taishan narrative song form of *muk-yu*; he often sings with other Chinese-American elders in the park, at a local senior citizens center, and on the streets of Chinatown.

Hispanic

H.231.a. *"La Musica de los Viejos*—The Music of the Old Ones." By Jack Parsons and Jim Sagel. Derry, New Hampshire: Chip Taylor Communications, 1983.

> This film is a "musical roadtrip," visiting elder Hispanic musicians who live in small mountain villages from Santa Fe to La Mesa in northern New Mexico (see **E.66**).

Traditional Arts

H.232. "Agueda Martinez: Our People, Our Country" (18 min). By Esperanza Vasquez, Joe Bencomo and Mark Rassmussen, with Moctezuma Esparza Productions. Minneapolis: Educational Media Corp., 1977.

> Martinez, a 77-year-old woman of Navajo-Mexican descent, tells of her life, describes her work as a rancher in Medanales, New Mexico, and as a master weaver, and explains her values of self-sufficiency, family solidarity, religious commitment and living in harmony with the land and nature.

H.233. "Alex Stewart, Cooper" (20 min). Knoxville: Tennessee Department of Conservation, n.d.

> Stewart, a master cooper from Hancock County, Tennessee, demonstrates his skills as a woodworker (see **E.168**).

H.234. "The Art of Theora Hamblett" (22 min, 16 mm). By Robert Oesterling. University: University of Mississippi, 1966.

> Mississippi folk artist Hamblett (1895-1977), interviewed in her home, talks about her life and paintings, inspired by visions, dreams, and early memories.

H.235. "Brother Harrison Mayes, Middlesborough, Kentucky" (58 min). By Eleanor Dickinson. San Francisco: Eleanor Dickinson, 1980.

> Mayes, 84, a former coal miner turned folk artist and religious sign maker, is interviewed and seen at work erecting large cross-shaped signs on southern highways.

H.236. "The Cloth Speaks to Me" (16 min). By Esperanza G. Martinez. New York: The Quilting Partnership, 1995.

> Older African-American women display their quilts and describe how they serve as artistic chronicles of their individual lives and experiences.

H.237. "Elijah Pierce, Woodcarver" (20 min, 16mm). By Carolyn Jones. Columbus: Ohio State University, 1974.

Pierce (1982-1984), son of an ex-slave born in Baldwyn, Mississippi, discusses his life and the sources of inspiration for his carvings (see **E.213**).

H.238. "Fanny Lou Spelce, Folk Artist" (36 min). By Brian Owen, Sandra Mintz and Larry Cormier. San Antonio: Institute of Texan Cultures, 1980.

Spelce, born in 1908, is interviewed at home and at work talking about her painting, and about life in Texas at the turn of the century, memories of which provide subject matter for many of her pictures.

H.239. "Foxfire" (21 min, 16mm). By Emil Willimetz, Andrew B. Nemes and Yanna Brandt. McGraw-Hill, 1976.

Describes the work of Eliot Wigginton, a high school English teacher in Rabun Gap, Georgia, who had his students interview elders in the local Appalachian hill community about traditional crafts and ways of life (see **B.13**).

H.240. "Grandma Moses" (22 min, 16mm). By Jerome Hill. Ann Arbor: University of Michigan (distributed by Film Images, Oak Park, Illinois), 1960.

The famous "primitive" painter at age 90, is shown in scenes on her upstate New York farm, her photograph album, her painting technique, and a number of her paintings (see **E.198, E.208**).

H.241. "In the Barnegat Bay Tradition" (39 min). Trenton: New Jersey Network, 1982.

Sam Hunt demonstrates the building of a sneakbox, and the carving of wooden decoys for duck hunting along New Jersey's Barnegat Bay, and comments about this popular aspect of New Jersey folklife.

H.242. "It's One Family–Knock On Wood" (24 min). Brooklyn, New York: Tony DeNonno Pix, Inc., 1982.

This is a film portrait of Sicilian-American marionette maker Michael "Papa" Manteo, 72, of Brooklyn, New York, and his family, guardians of a legacy of five generations preserving a form of traditional Sicilian marionette theater.

H.243. "Juan Felix Sanchez" (30 min, 16mm). By Dennis Schmeichler and Calogero Salvo. Berkeley, California: EMC, 1983.

Portrait of Sanchez, an 82-year-old Venzuelan folk artist, who talks about his life and works, which include weaving, sculpture and architecture.

H.244. "Learned It in Back Days and Kept it: A Portrait of Lucreaty" (29 min). By Dan Kossof and Peggy Bulger, with WJCT-TV, Jacksonville, Florida. White Springs: Florida Folklife Program, 1981.

Lucreaty Clark, born in 1904, who learned to make white-oak baskets for use in the cotton fields, is seen making baskets, sharing her outlook on family, religion, customs and foodways, and reviewing the history of North Florida's rural African-American community for her granddaughter who has returned to live with and learn from her.

H.245. "Manuel Jiménez: Woodcarver" (22 min). Produced by Judith Bronowski and Robert Grant. Santa Monica, California: The Works, 1989 [1977].

Interview with Jiménez, born in 1919 in the small village of Arrazola, a farming community in the valley of Oaxaca, where he continues to make hand-carved wooden figures with a machete and kitchen knife (see also **E.266, H.251,** and **H.254**).

H.246. "Mario Sanchez: Painter of Memories" (17 min, 16mm). Produced by Jack Ofield. Hudson, New York: Bowling Green Films, 1978.

A portrait of the life and work of Sanchez, born in 1908 in Key West, a Cuban-American wood painter, who comments on the technique and subject matter of his works, and reminisces about his family and old neighborhood.

H.247. "The Meaders Family: North Georgia Potters" (31 min, 16mm). By Robert Glatzer, Ralph Rinzler and Robert Sayers. University Park: Pennsylvania State University Audio Visual Services, 1981.

Depicts several generations of the Meaders family as they work at the site of the family kiln in Cleveland, Georgia, where family members have produced traditional pottery since 1893 (see **E.124**).

H.248. "Missing Pieces: Contemporary Georgia Folk Art" (30 min). By Steve Heiser Portland, Oregon: Odyssey Productions, 1976.

Features 19th-century pictorial quilts of ex-slave Harriet Powers, and the work of contemporary folk artists, including potter Lanier Meaders, painter Mattie Lou O'Kelley, carver Ulysses Davis, painter Ed Martin, and the visionary environmental art of Reverend Howard Finster. [funded by Georgia Council for the Arts and Humanities, the National Endowment for the Arts, and Georgia E-TV Network].

H.249. "Mohawk Basketmaking: A Cultural Profile" (28 min, 16mm). By Frank Semmons. University Park: Pennsylvania State University Audio Visual Services, n.d.

This film focuses primarily on the life and work of Mary Adams; along with other elders interviewed for this film, she expresses her concern for the survival of the craft, and her pleasure in the fact that two of her children have taken it up.

H.250. "Nellie Mae Rowe–Folk Artist" (14 min). Charleston: South Carolina: Charleston Communication Center, 1975.

Depicts a visit to the Vinings, Virginia, home of African-American folk artist Rowe (1900-1982), who talks about her life and shows some of her drawings in pencil and crayon, hand-made dolls and gum sculptures.

H.251. "Pedro Linares, Folk Artist" (23 min). Produced by Judith Bronowski and Robert Grant. Santa Monica, California: The Works, 1989 [1974].

An interview with Linares, 72, a papier-mâché artist who works with his sons and grandsons on the roof of their small house near Mexico City's Central Market (see also **E.266, H.245,** and **H.254**).

H.252. "Queena Stovall: Life's Narrow Space" (19 min). By Jack Ofield. San Diego, California: Bowling Green Films, 1980.

Portrays the life and work of Stovall, a 90-year-old artist living in Virginia, who paints country life as she remembers it, including farm animals, barns, auctions, butchering, ice cream making, and other aspects of rural living.

H.253. "Reverend Howard Finster: Man of Visions" (23 min). By John F. Turner. Berkeley, California: John F. Turner, 1981.

A portrait of Finster, a 65-year-old Baptist minister from Georgia, who talks about his art, including narrative paintings and his "Paradise Garden," an environmental folk sculpture (see also **E.188, E.218**).

H.254. "Sabina Sánchez and the Art of Embroidery" (22 min). Produced by Judith Bronowski and Robert Grant. Santa Monica, California: The Works, 1989 [1976].

An interview with Sánchez, 65, whose embroidered blouses reflect the imagery of Mexico's rural San Antonio Castillo Velasco, where she lives, a flower-growing village in the Oaxaca valley (see also **E.266, H.246, H.251**).

H.255. "Santeros: Saint Makers" (38 min). By Louise Cox, Ray Telles, Herb Ferrette, and Mark Adler. Teresita Productions/KCET Latino Consortium [funded by the National Endowment for the Arts, Folk Arts Division and New Mexico Arts Division] 1986.

Several santeros, carvers of wooden religious figures, describe their work and how they took up this traditional Mexican-American craft.

H.256. "Stitching Memories: The Art of Ethel Mohamed" (22 min). By Charles E. Martin. Clinton: Mississippi College, Learning Resources Center, 1982.

Mrs. Mohamed discusses the beginnings of her embroidered "memory pictures," and interprets different scenes from her stitchery (see also **H.81**).

H.257. "The Stone Carvers" (29 min). By Marjorie Hunt and Paul Wagner. Los Angeles: Direct Cinema, 1984.

Documents the work and memories of two generations of Italian-American artisans, ornamental stone carvers who have spent their lives working on the Washington Cathedral.

Health and Healing

H.258. "Chief Two Tree, Cherokee Medicine Man" (27 min). By John Goforth and Wayne William. Greenville, North Carolina: Center for Medical Communications, East Carolina University, 1986.

Presents the indigenous healing practices of Two Tree, elder and Chief of the North Carolina Cherokees.

H.259. "Curanderas: Traditional Healers" (42 min). By Marta Solomayer. Tucson, Arizona: Division of Social Perspectives, College of Medicine and the Southwest Institute for Research on Women, Women's Studies Dept., University of Arizona, 1985.

A portrait of women folk healers in Mexican-American culture, and the historical influences on the development of the healing system known as *curanderismo*.

H.260. "Elder as Healer" (105 min). New York: Panacea Productions, 1992.

Documents a workshop conducted by anthropologist Joan Halifax at an Omega

Institute conference on "Conscious Aging: A Creative and Spiritual Journey," held in New York City in May, 1992; Halifax presents a cross-cultural perspective on the ways in which elders may perform a healing role.

H.261. "Granny Woman" (30 min). Johnson City, Tenne. ee: Broadside TV and Videomaker, 1988.

Presents the life story of Sarah Maddux, a midwife from the rural hills of East Tennessee, who describes her experiences delivering babies in the absence of doctors or clinics.

H.262. "The Hawaiian Art of Healing" (34 min). Honolulu, Hawaii: Na Maka o ka Aina, 1991.

Henry Auwae discusses his lifelong experience with traditional healing practices and demonstrates the preparation and use of Hawaiian medicinal plants.

H.263. "In the Way of Our Grandmothers" (27 min). Tallahassee: Florida State University, 1982.

Elder African-American midwives describe their years of experience delivering babies at home (see also **F.108**).

H.264. "Little Medicine Thing: Emma Dupree, Herbalist." By Walter Shepard and James Young. Greenville, North Carolina: Office of Health Services Research and Development, East Carolina University School of Medicine, 1980.

In an interview with Dupree, born in 1897, she shows her garden, describes how she uses various herbs, and talks about the "signs" in her life that have pointed to her vocation as a healer (see also **F.28**, **F.34**, and **F.40**).

H.265. "Medicine People: Healing and Teaching" (17 min). By Barbara J. Major and Jennie R. Roe. Tucson, Arizona: Native American Research and Training Center, University of Arizona, 1988.

Describes the continuing role of traditional healers among the Navajo and depicts an alcohol abuse rehabilitation center for Native people in Long Beach, California.

H.266. "Mrs. Sadie Nickpeay" (29 min). By Ronald A. Shecut, Jiff Huff and Martin Alexander. Columbia: University of South Carolina, Instructional Services Center, 1980.

Nickpeay, a former midwife and trainer of midwives, describes the historical role of midwifery and its importance in South Carolina.

H.267. "Traditional Birthing: Maude Bryant" (19 min). By Tim Carey. Carrboro, North Carolina: Health Sciences Consortium, University of North Carolina at Chapel Hill, 1984.

Maude Lee Bryant (1898-1983), a midwife, shares her experiences of 100 births in rural North Carolina.

Author Index

Subject Index

[NOTE: The range of genres and other topics listed below is fairly well cross-referenced; for listings by area or location, the reader is advised to search under countries and regions, as well as specific provinces, states, counties and cities; ethnic groups whose borders may cross political boundaries are listed along with the region or country of origin (in parentheses) that is named in the text cited; where occupations are listed, the subjects may be active or retired; all (auto)biographies not entirely self-composed are listed under "oral history/life history," since most life histories cited feature interview excerpts; finally, only subjects specifically named in the titles/annotations in this book are listed below, so there may may be additional sources of topical information in a given work (especially surveys of several topics or groups).]

Aaron, Jesse, E.179
Abaluyia (Kenya), C.89
abandoned elders, tales of, D.42, D.402
Abkhaz Republic, C.56
Aboriginal, D.46, D.47, D.49, D.51, D.52
Abraham Lincoln Brigade, veterans of, H.114. *See also* Spanish Civil War
Acoma Pueblo. *See* Pueblo Indian
activists, D.55, H.36, H.85, H.114, H.115, H.230. *See also* anarchists; civil rights activists; communists, socialists; suffragists; trade union activists
Adams, Logan, H.20
Adams, Mary, H.249
Adirondack, D.191, D.192, D.226, E.68, E.100, H.218, H.222
adult day care centers/programs, G.16, G.128. *See also* senior citizen centers
Afgan refugee. *See* refugees
Africa, B.35, C.19. *See also under names of specific countries and groups*
Africa, Central, C.24
African-American, A.8.1, A.50, B.56, B.57, C.80, C.124, C.125, C.129, D.119, D.123,
D.139, D.146, D.161-D.184, E.16, E.25, E.32, E.33, E.81, E.99, E.106, E.142, E.148-E.150, E.153, E.158, E.166, E.174, E.179, E.181, E.182, E.186, E.191, E.196, E.200, E.206, E.209, E.213, E.216, E.219, E.220, E.222-E.224, E.228, E.237, E.238, E.239, E.251, E.259, E.267, E.269, E.271, E.273, E.274, E.282, F.28-F.32, F.34-F.50, F.103, F.105, F.108, G.66, G.84, G.92, G.112, G.121, G.124, G.125, G.128, H.10, H.22-H.24, H.26-H.31, H.34, H.35, H.81, H.95, H.97, H.98, H.100, H.121, H.123, H.125, H.143, H.144, H.1156, H.166, H.171, H.191, H.204, H.206-H.217, H.236, H.244, H.250
Afro-American. *See* African-American
Ahousat (British Columbia), D.403. *See also* Native American Indian
Alabama, D.159, D.181, E.57, E.153. E.171, E.190, E.196, E.200, E.206, E.221, E.271, F.53, F.64, F.103, F.105, H.21
Alaska, D.149, D.309-D.317, D.326, D.332, D.340-D.342, D.347, D.348, D.362, D.366, D.370, D.373, D.374, D.389, D.406, E.21, E.271, F.106, F.107, H.54-H.57

About the Author

DAVID P. SHULDINER holds appointments as Humanities Program Co-ordinator with the State of Connecticut, Department of Social Services, Elderly Services Division, as Adjunct Faculty in the School of Family Studies, University of Connecticut, and in the Gerontology Program at Saint Joseph College, and has taught folklore at Trinity College. He is the editor of the journal, *Folklore in Use*, published in England and the author of *Aging Political Activists: Personal Narratives from the Old Left* (Praeger, 1995).